Thomas Bernhard

Thomas Bernhard

The Making of an Austrian

Gitta Honegger

Yale University Press   New Haven and London

Designed by Sonia L. Shannon.
Set in Bulmer type by Tseng Information Systems, Inc.,
Durham, NC.
Printed in the United States of America.
Library of Congress Cataloging-in-Publication Data
Honegger, Gitta
Thomas Bernhard : the making of an Austrian /
Gitta Honegger.
p. cm.
Includes bibliographical references and index.
ISBN 0-300-08999-6 (cloth : alk. paper)
1. Bernhard, Thomas.   2. Authors, Austrian—
20th century—Biography.   I. Title.
PT2662.E7 z6848   2001
838'.91409—dc21
[B]   2001017971
A catalogue record for this book is available from
the British Library.

10 9 8 7 6 5 4 3 2 1

For Manfred

I hate books and articles that begin with a date of birth. Altogether I hate books and articles that adopt a biographical and chronological approach; that strikes me as the most tasteless and at the same time the most unintellectual procedure.
—Thomas Bernhard

Contents

Preface

THOMAS BERNHARD CAME OF AGE WHILE Austria was digging its way out of the devastation of World War II and burying itself in silence about the Holocaust. His career spanned the second half of the twentieth century. His writing and the way he constructed his biography map Austria's struggle for self-definition after the collapse of the Habsburg monarchy and in the aftermath of the Holocaust. He became the first writer of his generation to unrelentingly expose Austria's pathology of denial. The national uproar caused by his works and public statements illuminate Austrians' convoluted ways of *Vergangenheitsbewältigung*, the coming to terms with their Nazi past—or rather their defiant avoidance of doing so.

This book shows that Bernhard was as much a product of his native culture as he was its scourge. Someone suggested that its title should be "The Unmaking of an Austrian." Wasn't Bernhard, recognized abroad for his literary vision, reviled and ostracized in his own country, treated the way Austrians have traditionally treated their native geniuses, from Mozart to Mahler to Freud (and from Herzl to Hitler, as the Hungarian-born émigré playwright George Tabori would add with his survivor's black humor)? Historically, the best of them had to gain recognition abroad and die before they were reclaimed and mythologized as national treasures. That is only part of Bernhard's story, however, and the easy—and easily misleading—part. It suggests some sort of redemptive reversal where there is none. Being Austrian always implies, in Bernhard's words, "everything that comes with it," meaning the legacy of guilt and liabilities as well as a proud tradition of cultural achievement. Bernhard set out to take on both the challenge of genius and the ghosts of history. As energetically as he dramatized himself as the unwanted outsider, he constructed himself as the penultimate insider. In a sequence of transformations from peasant outcast to cosmopolitan country squire, the illegitimate lowborn child made himself the legitimate heir to a native intellectual ancestry of his own choosing. The renegade son laid claim to a cultural nobility Austria had forfeited. Such a feat required a brilliant performer. As that performer, Bernhard is the unmistakable product of his culture. Austria's performative culture is the legacy of the intertwined theatrics of the Habsburg monarchy and the hegemonic Catholic Church. With the monarchy gone, the

Church and the theater kept alive its dramaturgy of high culture. The rituals of faith and genius come to an annual climax in the Salzburg Festival. Bernhard attacked its lavish celebrations of "high art" and their pretentious audiences, both mimicking the gestures of a dead culture, yet they propelled his ambitions, set his standards, and honed his performative skills. Before Bernhard trained as an actor he studied to become an opera singer. This book examines how Bernhard's theatrical background informed not only his plays but also his prose, in which he staged himself in the act of writing. It was Samuel Beckett — with whom Bernhard is often compared — who supplied the paradoxical existential mechanism for the pratfalls in his post-Habsburg *Welttheater*, his thoroughly theatricalized universe. If Bernhard's fictional stand-ins keep slipping on Middle European weltschmerz and angst, they pull themselves up by the tattered bootstraps of Beckett's clowns: "I can't go on, I'll go on." As every performer knows, the show must go on.

The mechanism of the theater provided Bernhard with a model for his vision of the world as a repetition of gestures that simulate and thus perpetuate a life long gone. The performative force of repetition in his *theatrum mundi* extends beyond the theater and produces an essentially dead society animated by the strings of tradition. As an existential tool, the theater helped Bernhard prevail in the face of an ongoing, life-threatening illness. Schopenhauer's will to survive, a dark, ubiquitous force of nature made conscious, manifests itself in his compulsive self-performance. "For decades," Bernhard writes in *Wittgenstein's Nephew*, ". . . I cherished and exploited both my lung disease and my madness, which together may be said to constitute my art."[1] In Bernhard's etiology of culture, his "madness" is a symptom of his Austrianness, which he cultivated even as he denounced its corruption and perversion.

Bernhard's life and work are inextricably intertwined with Austria's convulsive history in the twentieth century. Born in 1931, he was old enough to be fully aware of the Nazi rule and the war as he experienced them but too young to be actively involved in the politics of Austro-fascism and anti-Semitism. His immediate postwar perspective, as reflected in his early works and recalled in his memoirs, was shaped by his childhood in rural poverty on the fringe of Salzburg, a small city that prided itself on its elite culture and pedigreed wealth. His defining childhood experience of World War II was the Allied bombings, not the deportation and extinction of Austrian Jews. It was only when his attention shifted from the countryside to Vienna that he touched on the "Jewish question." Quite tentatively at first, he began to introduce Jewish characters. More often than not he did so in passing, in almost buried references that reveal the Austrians' awkwardness in talking about Jews while adding little to the thrust of the narrative. His transformation from rural iconoclast to cosmopolitan eccentric brought him closer to Vienna's Jewish heritage, from the cultivated lifestyle of its upper class, the *Grossbürgertum* to the revived tradition of the Jewish cabaret. Both are reflected in his last play, *Heldenplatz*, which focuses on a Jewish family, returned émigrés in contemporary Vienna. But the suicide of its patriarch, the devastating neuroses of his wife, and the bitterness of his brother and daughters allow for no sentimental sympathy. Their response to the racial humiliations they suffer along with a thoroughly corrupt political system and the moral bankruptcy of the Catholic Church makes them as vitriolic, paranoid, and xenophobic as the rest of Bernhard's Austrians and as tyrannical, elitist, and pigheaded as his earlier madmen and malcontents. So everyone was scandalized. By the time of his death one year later, Bernhard had become an icon for the histrionic excesses of the tortured Austrian psyche. The performative force of his myth eclipsed all reasoned assessment of his literary achievements. His growing esteem abroad as one of the major figures of contemporary literature caused further embarrassment back home. The artist who most advanced Austria's cultural standing in the world also soiled its political image. He died maligned as a notorious *Nestbeschmutzer.* (Literally the term means "someone who soils his own nest." An Austrian joke puts it more succinctly: Someone defecates in the middle of the room. Another person comes in and says, "It stinks." The latter is called a *Nestbeschmutzer.*)

Bernhard's will, revised two days before his discretely staged death, prohibited all further publications and productions of his works in Austria until the expiration of the copyright. Under the circumstances, the provision appeared shocking, a painful, bitter, final act of revenge. It might also turn out to be his most effective play script, the plotting of his afterlife. As he must have calculated, his prohibitions triggered a nationwide drama of legal evasions and ethical speculations that threatens never to end. More than anything else, the drama of his will has defined his fame in Austria.

His works have been translated into more than twenty languages, including Korean and Chinese. His plays are produced around the world. In the time-honored tradition Bernhard loved to satirize, Austria has officially reclaimed its nasty problem child as a national treasure alongside that other ungrateful son of Salzburg, Wolfgang Amadeus Mozart.

Bernhard was not a political writer, nor was he a "political animal." In the ideological conflicts of the postwar era he represented no ideology. An autodidact under the early defining influence of his maternal grandfather, Bernhard absorbed what suited his interests and ambitions. No vision of utopia sprang from his experience of the world, ravaged as he found it (and himself) by disease, eclipsed by the madness of recent history, in the permanent shadow of death. By their "nature" humans are a part of the destructive force of nature as well as its victims — that is to say, we are our own victims. While such a concept may suggest that he was rationalizing Nazi atrocities, his early writing combed the Austrian landscape for their pestilent residues. Though he insisted that nature did not interest him at all and that he never wrote about nature, his writing was all about nature, albeit not as the Alpine haven Austria struggled to project in its longing to sanitize its image after World War II. Bernhard's Austrian countryside offers no respite from the ravages of nature and history. If the castles and patrician estates overlooking neatly groomed fields and villages reflect centuries of cultivation, their expertly forested hunting grounds hold the remains of hunters and hunted in as many centuries of killings, war crimes, and local violence. Devastating floods, forest pests, and human diseases assert the brutal force of nature against the pathetically anachronistic effigies of culture.

Bernhard's high visibility in Vienna during his final years was his last stand against nature, including his own rapidly weakening body, a defiantly final embrace of the city as the epitome of spectacularly staged effigies. His late prose works center on his cosmopolitan stand-ins, cultural émigrés on the run from their rural roots, the moribund heirs of Habsburg nobility staging their testaments as virtuoso writing acts — all rehearsals of Bernhard's final will, which yielded the dramaturgy of his afterlife.

The charismatic product of his culture, he in turn indelibly inscribed himself in it. He forged a unique language of hyperbole and contradiction that seeped into the vernacular and transformed the ways its speakers respond to the world at large. Ironically, his performative grammar and incendiary vocabulary have been appropriated by politicians of all persuasions, exploited by the media, and imitated by lesser writers. His outrageous invectives became idiomatic, his name a fetish that stands for an alternative Austrianness that — *naturgemäss,* or "in the nature of things," to use the most widely appropriated term Bernhard reactivated — turned into yet another cliché. Journalists, even scholars so thoroughly internalized his language that they write about him in an (untranslatable) Bernhard-speak that reinforces the cliché. He is the *Übertreibungskünstler* (master of exaggeration), a *Verrammlungs-fanatiker* (one who fanatically locks things away), the *konservative Anarchist* (conservative anarchist), the *Charismatiker* ("charismatic"), the *Mittagesser* (lunch eater), even an *österreichisches Weltexperiment* (literally, an Austrian world experiment), the *Bernhardiner* (a St. Bernard dog) — *wild son of a bitch* who staged the *österreichische Weltkomödie* (literally the "Austrian world comedy"), to cite just a few titles of books and articles about him.

For the reasons I have indicated, this book is by necessity a cultural biography. It is as much about Austria as about Bernhard. The interactive influences in the co-evolution of the recovering nation and one of its most prominent sons cannot be traced in a linear biography. The fragments salvaged from the ruins of World War II yielded a synchronicity of cross-influences from which Bernhard derived his self-perception. The process of his self-invention reveals more about him and the world he lived in (and staged so masterfully) than a chronological account of his life and work could do.

Bernhard's five volumes of autobiographical narratives provide the connecting thread in the drama between the *Dichtung und Wahrheit,* the fiction and fact, that constitutes the life and times of Thomas Bernhard. Written at the apex of his career, his memoirs ostensibly cover his childhood and youth. From the vantage point of the middle-aged man, they include the shifting perspectives of self-perception and self-construction within a culture that was also struggling to reinvent itself. I use his memoirs as a tool to analyze the subtext and performative strategies of his narratives, all of them self-constituting speech acts. The tension between the facts of his life and their fictionalization on the stage of contemporary Austria against the larger canvas of postwar Europe yields the drama of cultural and moral survival between two fins de siècle.

In retrospect, his autobiographical project marks the turning point both in his life and in his work. As more or less straightforward narratives they mark the end of his experimentation with literary influences and intertextuality and set the stage for his subsequent monological prose. His lifelong illness had reached its terminal stage. In the face of extinction he immortalized his physical presence in the performance acts of his writing.

The memoirs are often considered Bernhard's literary masterwork, particularly in the English-speaking world, where they are published in one volume under the title *Gathering Evidence*. Relentlessly facing the "truth" about himself, his family, and his culture, he produced his greatest work of fiction.

Bernhard constructed both himself and his work from the relics of traditions that had lost their moorings in the Habsburg monarchy. The entire culture was on artificial life support in Bernhard's vision, shaped as it was by the trauma of World War II and his own frail health. His preoccupation with artifice was also a radical reaction against his rural environment, which had been exalted by Nazi poets for its "natural" beauty and healthfulness. His training in opera and classical theater reinforced his idea of artificiality. A passing flirtation with the Austrian avant-garde of the 1950s, particularly the concrete poetry of the Vienna Group, gave him enough of a taste of self-conscious artificiality to return to "nature" as he experienced it—as the scene of physical decay and hidden shame inscribed with the memories of history and, above all, a nightmarish hell of provincialism. The fear of provincialism was the legacy of World War I, which left the Habsburg Empire shrunken to a tiny *Alpenrepublik,* soon teeming with Nazi impersonations of the proud *Volk* in dirndls and lederhosen. As Bernhard soon enough discovered and decried, some of the same artists and administrators who guided Nazi culture where also empowered to define Austria's post–World War II cultural identity as leading officials in the state funding of the arts. Ironically, the way out of Austrian artistic provincialism led once again to Germany. Although ambivalent about their relationship with their recent nemesis and apprehensive about being subsumed under "German culture," Austrian artists and intellectuals sought the larger audiences and financial resources that the land of the economic miracle had to offer.

Bernhard's breakthrough came in Germany in 1963, when Suhrkamp/Insel Verlag published his first full-length novel, *Frost.* Suhrkamp published all his subsequent novels up to his autobiographical project, which was published by the Austrian Residenz Verlag. It seems fitting enough that he should come home, as it were, to a Salzburg-based publisher for his memoirs. They represent also another homecoming: the coming to terms with his family. By the time he finished the last volume, his illness had reached another critical stage. Aware that this was the final phase, he arranged to be near his brother, a physician, whom he helped to establish a practice in Gmunden, near his farmhouse in Upper Austria.

Suhrkamp took on his late works again and also published all his plays. His first full-length play, *A Party for Boris,* premiered in 1970 at Hamburg's renowned Schauspielhaus, one of Germany's leading theaters. The much acclaimed production inaugurated the lifelong collaboration of Bernhard and Claus Peymann, his producer and director, whose unfailing commitment to the playwright's difficult theatrical vision made Bernhard one of the most prominent, if not necessarily popular, forces of the German theater. Having established himself as a German writer of growing international reputation, he retreated to his isolated farm in Upper Austria, whence he manipulated Austria's political theater at large with an occasional incensed editorial or vitriolic open letter to a politician, a few select television appearances, and some provocative speeches when he accepted awards. Sought out by neighboring descendants of Austria's aristocracy, whose friendship he cultivated, ruthlessly exploited, and routinely broke off, he fashioned himself into a native iconoclast with impeccable taste and an unpredictable temper. His travels throughout Europe, accompanied (and often financed) by one or another of his elegant doting friends rounded out his mature image of the pedigreed cosmopolitan.

It was the German Claus Peymann that staged Bernhard's spectacular if fateful homecoming at the last stronghold of imperial glory, the Vienna Burgtheater. When he became its artistic director in 1986, Peymann, the old lefty and erstwhile terrorist sympathizer, inducted Bernhard as poet laureate of the emperor's very own theater. The return at long last to the old empire's venerable shrine made him a bona fide aristocrat and a martyr. The monarchy's ambivalent legacies of patronage and Catholicism, which he so fiercely attacked throughout his life, caught up with him in the end.

Although this study is loosely organized along the time line of Bernhard's life and work, its primary focus is thematic. I am most interested in the various stages of his self-construction in response to his place in history as an Austrian and as a major literary figure. He was acutely aware of both his predicament and his calling, and he merged them in a virtuoso performance that dramatizes the fatal obsessions of his culture and satirizes his codependent relationship with it. His biography emerges in fictionalized self-performances that produce the drama of his reception, which iterates the world he is writing about and sets the stage for yet another act in the coproduction of self and public. Repetition becomes the self-generating principle in this process and Bernhard's primary obsession. His works reflect one another, pick up on earlier pieces, revisit the same landscapes. In a country as small as Austria, claustrophobia reinforces the sense of a synchronicity that defies linear description and lends itself to a theatrical sense of merging times.

I come to this project as a theater scholar and practitioner and as an Austrian (in all the senses of the term I have indicated) whose efforts to reconstruct herself as an American were strongly supported by Bernhard, many of whose plays I translated. Especially useful for this work was my experience as a dramaturg—a function recently imported from the German theater, still an unpronounceable mystification to most Americans. Unlike the activity of the play doctor, with which it is so often associated in the United States, the task of the dramaturg is to explore the various influences that come to bear on a performance text and bring it to life. All of Bernhard's writings are performance texts. The uniquely performative force of his texts within Austrian culture yield the drama of its self-definition after World War II.

I obtained the biographical information for this work from Dr. Peter Fabjan and Susanne Kuhn, Bernhard's brother and sister, and in countless conversations with his friends and colleagues, as well as from published sources. At the time of this writing, his papers are still in the process of being catalogued under the (tight) control of a few Austrian scholars of German literature. Mrs. Kuhn is in charge of his correspondence, which is not accessible at all. It includes the entire correspondence between Bernhard and his long-time companion, Hedwig Stavianicek, a woman more than thirty years his senior whom he met when he was nineteen. According to Mrs. Kuhn, their letters are a moving chronicle of their relationship, charting its emotional ups and downs as well as the important influence Frau Hede had on his thinking and writing. Bernhard's will prohibited the publication of any of his letters or notes. Some correspondents have found ways to circumvent the stipulation. In the meantime, the testamentary ban on productions of his plays in Austria has been lifted. The reinterpretation of his will is still in process, and the public outrage and debate it has fueled keeps alive the public drama of Thomas Bernhard.

I knew Thomas Bernhard during the last ten years of his life. We first met during his week-long stay in New York in October 1979, his only visit to the United States. He traveled with his brother and his close friends Victor and Grete Hufnagl. As I had translated his plays, he wanted to meet me. He told me that Suhrkamp's evaluators were impressed by my most recent translation,

The Hunting Party. Then he asked me whether I could help him find a store in New York that sold Arrow shirts. I did. The remainder of our afternoon was spent choosing shirts. In the ensuing years I saw him regularly during my annual visits to Austria, at his farmhouse in Obernathal or in one of Vienna's coffeehouses. I came to know him as a gracious if a bit awkward gentleman of the old school, as they say, with a quirky sense of humor, a genuine openness toward my work and life "in translation," as it were, as a "naturalized" American citizen, and a special interest in the ritualized encounters between my widowed mother, a diehard Viennese, and her only child, who made her home abroad.

During Bernhard's lifetime I met a few of his friends, among them Frau Stavianicek. In the course of my research I met many more: Christa and Franz Joseph Altenburg, Ingrid Bülau, Jeannie Ebner, Ulrike and Gabriel O'Donnell, Karl Ignaz Hennetmair, Victor Hufnagl; Gerhard Lampersberg, Wieland and Erika Schmied, Klaus Gmeiner and Sybille Dahms (his colleagues at the Mozarteum), and Theodor (Teddy) Podgorsky, a good friend of Paul Wittgenstein. I am grateful for the information they shared with me.

My special thanks go to Hermann Beil for many long conversations over many years; Claus Peymann for his early encouragement; Thomas Nowotny, Austrian consul general in New York, for his early support of my Bernhard translations; Ministerialrat Wolfgang Unger; Hans Nadolny, Deutsches Theater Berlin; Michaela Giesing, Hamburger Theaterarchiv; Gisela Prossnitz, Archiv der Salzburger Festspiele; Günther G. Bauer, former rector of the Mozarteum; and Manfred Laubichler, Sr. Friederike Zeitlhofer, the librarian at New York's Austrian Institute, was there for me from the beginning. Hans Jürgen Syberberg offered a stimulating perspective on postwar German theater and generously shared his thoughts on Thomas Bernhard and Oskar Werner.

I am grateful to my editors, Barbara H. Salazar, who cleared her way through the Austrian psyche, and Margaret Otzel at Yale University Press. Jonathan Brent believed in this project from the start and always offered encouragement.

This book owes most of all to Manfred Laubichler, Jr. As a biologist and historian he sharpened my field of vision and tools of inquiry. His intellectual generosity is boundless. So is his patience. As an Austrian at Princeton he made *Heimat* possible again.

This project was supported by research grants from the Austrian Min-

istry of Culture and Education, the Catholic University of America, and the
Haslauer Stiftung, Salzburg.

The first chapter is based on an article that appeared in *Performing Arts Journal* 9, no. 3 (1997), Johns Hopkins University Press, publisher. Parts of Chapter 6 appeared in *Theater Magazine* 30, no. 1 (2000): 49–55; parts of Chapter 11 appeared in *Partisan Review* 3 (1996): 528–31. I thank the editors for permission to use the material in revised form.

Unless I indicate otherwise, the translations are my own.

Thomas Bernhard

CHAPTER ONE

Fool on the Hill

Thomas Bernhard's Mise-en-Scène

*When we look down from this undoubtedly most beautiful spot
in the Alpine foothills . . . from an elevation such as this onto a
landscape such as this you see, we instantly think of everything
that is happening in this landscape, that ever happened and will
happen there . . . all that is past and present and the future . . . it
is not possible to look on this landscape in any other way.*

—Thomas Bernhard, *"Ungenach"*

IN HIS QUASI-AUTOBIOGRAPHICAL WORK *The Cellar* Thomas Bernhard describes what he calls the most decisive period of his life: instead of
continuing his high school education, which had been interrupted by World
War II, the fifteen-year-old became a grocer's apprentice in the blue-collar
district of Salzburg. During that two-year period, at his grandfather's instiga-
tion, he also began his musical training as an opera singer. His teacher was
Maria Keldorfer, who sang the part of Sophie in Richard Strauss and Hugo
von Hofmannsthal's *Der Rosenkavalier* at its world premiere in Dresden. During the festival weeks he loved to climb up on Mönchsberg and sit under a tree
just above the Festival Theater to listen to the opera rehearsals.

> I had a favorite spot above the Riding School from which I could listen
> to the operas which were being performed there. One was *The Magic
> Flute,* the first opera I ever saw performed and one in which at one time
> or another I played no fewer than three parts: Sarastro, the Speaker, and
> Papageno. In this opera, which throughout my life I have made a point
> of hearing and seeing as often as possible, all my musical desires were
> realized to perfection. I sat there under the tree, listening to the music,

and there was nothing in the whole world that I would have taken in exchange for what I felt as I sat there listening. . . . For years I went up onto
the Mönchsberg in order to listen to rehearsals of operas that were to be
performed in the Riding School.[1]

The musical scores would echo in the syntax of his writing; the operatic archetypes would appear in a dense web of signifying chains sliding across the
topography of his work; the operatic dramaturgy would provide the underpinning of his philosophical metatheater.

From his favorite spot below Fortress Hohensalzburg, the landmark castle
on Mönchsberg (Monk's Mountain, which happens to face Nonnberg, Nun's
Mountain, with the fortress tucked between them), he must have had a dramatic view of the city below. The heavy bombings toward the end of World
War II tore an apocalyptic intaglio into the architectural orgy of its large Italian-
style plazas, surrounded by baroque churches, palaces, and arches leading
through webs of medieval alleys and courtyards. Mozart's baroque wunder-
kind hell nestled in a soft bend of the Salzach River: the dazzling architectural
composition of monastic asceticism exploding into sensuous dramatizations
of the seductive physicality of death now frozen in a surreal inferno of gaping
domes, cathedrals split in half, convents torn open, spilling their once carefully cloistered entrails; Hitler's dream of a mega-Acropolis on Kapuzinerberg
(Capuchin Mountain), immortalized in Alfred Speer's architectural plans,
hovering above the still pastoral scenery of his theater of war like an unfulfilled
curse. Capuchin Mountain is named after the Capuchin monastery, a fortress-
like structure bracing the mountain on the eastern bank of the Salzach River,
right across from Mönchsberg, open to the young Thomas Bernhard's view.

Buried in the ruins of World War II was the city's shameful Nazi past.
Together with its original splendor, its original sins would eventually also reemerge and blend into the splendidly restored scene. Bernhard would be the
first to excoriate the hypocrisy, expediency, and greed of its inhabitants and
the fascist underside of its powerful Catholic legacy. For centuries Salzburg
had been the capital of an independent state ruled by the Church, presided
over by prince archbishops.

By the time Bernhard wrote *The Cellar,* the city had been restored to its
unblemished beauty. Max Reinhardt's opera stage, the old Felsenreitschule —
the archbishops' "Riding School in the Rock," which had been blasted right
out of the rock on which the town was built — had been redesigned and en-

larged as the festival's majestic open-air stage. The many cathedrals, cloisters, and castles crowning the mountains that weave through and around Salzburg had risen from the ashes in all their awe-inspiring grandeur as daunting reminders of the ever-watchful eyes of godly authority. Every fifteen minutes a symphony of bells resounding from myriads of whitewashed steeples, then as now, reminded the inhabitants that there was no escape from the piercing scrutiny of the Church; that the whole city was a stage where sinners were watched, wherever they might be. Spellbound by the sonorous scene, one can't help being awed by the genius of Max Reinhardt, Austria's Ziegfeld of German classical theater, who transformed a Catholic nightmare in all its perverse splendor into his version of a theatrical *Gesamtkunstwerk,* a synthesis of the arts. Reinhardt, who founded the Salzburg Festival in 1920, continued to stage his spectacular megaproductions right up to 1937, the summer before the Anschluss and his emigration to the United States.

Originally Reinhardt had envisioned the entire city as the setting for his mise-en-scène, which would restore to the theater the festive uniqueness of ceremony it had for the Greeks. Instead, Salzburg turned into a theme park, nourished by Mozart and the conspicuous triumvirate of Reinhardt, the German composer Richard Strauss (who would continue his career under the admiring patronage of the Nazis), and the aristocratic playwright-librettist Hugo von Hofmannsthal (the quintessential fin-de-siècle Austrian, who died in 1929, many years before his children were forced to flee from the Nazis). The conductor Herbert von Karajan, Salzburg's postwar favorite son despite his highly problematic Nazi past, ruled over the city for many decades. To this day he exercises posthumous power — his more progressive detractors would call it his artistic stranglehold — over the festival. He was Bernhard's earliest and most lasting musical influence: "Ever since my childhood I have seen Karajan's genius develop and come closer and closer to perfection; I have attended almost all his rehearsals of concerts and operas in Salzburg and Vienna. The very first concerts and operas I heard were conducted by Karajan," he wrote in *Wittgenstein's Nephew.*[2]

But it finally was up to Hollywood to give Salzburg its quintessential mythical family and recast it as the object of global desire, cloistered in kitsch and saturated with the sound of music. Never mind that the mountains Julie Andrews climbs from her supposedly downtown convent (actually located twenty miles east) are miles across the border in Bavaria; that the front of the Trapp residence is Fronburg Castle, to the south of the city; and that its backside is Leopoldskron Castle, at the other end of town. They all come together in the evenings, over mugs of beer and bottles of wine, at open-mike *Sound of Music* singing contests for hordes of eager tourists, predominantly American and Japanese, joined in multi-accented harmonies of "Edelweiss." It's all part of the annual summer spectacle of an entire city performing itself, selling itself shamelessly to fit all high- and lowbrow expectations: the lederhosen and the dirndls, the Alps and the *Schlag* and the *Knödls,* Mozart on chocolate balls and in concert halls, the wannabe literati in the outdoor cafés along the Salzach River; Everyman in front of the cathedral called upon by Death across the Domplatz with the setting sun casting long shadows of the magnificent baroque facades over the audience in the square and the chilly evening breeze blowing in from the mountains. Therein lie the archaeological, anthropological, and political roots of Bernhard's theatricalized ontology and etiology of Austria's cultural pathology. Eventually Bernhard himself became an integral, if enthusiastically hated, staple of the festival. Several of his plays that premiered at the festival consciously deconstructed its glamour.

Twenty-some years after his adolescent excursions to his hillside opera watch, Bernhard would find himself on another hill, overlooking the other city that became fateful to his life and work. He had just completed his third major novel, *Verstörung (Gargoyles).*[3] After the removal of a tumor from his chronically ailing lungs, he was hospitalized at Baumgartnerhöhe on Wilhelminenberg, on the outskirts of Vienna. The sanitarium is adjacent to Steinhof, Vienna's historic mental institution, with its unique fin-de-siècle church crowning Wilhelminen Mountain. Steinhof would serve as a point of reference for Austria's state of mind in many Bernhard texts. As Bernhard tells it in his quasi memoir *Wittgenstein's Nephew,* while he was staying at Baumgartnerhöhe, his good friend Paul Wittgenstein (actually Ludwig Wittgenstein's grandnephew) was in Steinhof, committed there once again by his family. The two men sneaked out to meet on a bench halfway between the Hermann and Ludwig pavilions, Bernhard's and Wittgenstein's respective places of confinement. Fourteen years later Bernhard would write: "This meeting on the bench, with each of us wearing the appropriate uniform—I that of a lung patient, he that of a Steinhof lunatic—had the most shattering effect on me."[4] All Paul could say was "Grotesque, grotesque," before he was shaken by sobs and Bernhard led him back to his pavilion. Not included in the freeze-framed image of their encounter on a bench at the arbitrary border between mental and physical decay was the panoramic view that extends from their hill beyond Vienna all the way to Hungary, beyond fairly recent borders into the former empire. The narrator doesn't need to describe the geography at large. It is embedded in the history and mythology of Steinhof, a favorite Bernhard scenario.

The institution opened in 1908 in the presence of the ill-fated archduke Franz Ferdinand, the kaiser's difficult nephew, whose assassination in Sarajevo triggered World War I. The "white city," as it was called by one of the leading art historians, was the world's largest, most advanced institution of its kind.[5] Nestled in the hills of the Vienna Woods, with rows of pavilions in the style of patrician mansions arranged around Otto Wagner's famous fin-de-siècle church, Steinhof still looks like a miniature imperial village. Some still call it a microcosm of the capital at its feet. The hierarchy of class was preserved in the location, architecture, and interior design of the individual buildings. An exclusive block of Italianate villas was reserved for the aristocracy and upper bourgeoisie. There were libraries, winter gardens, a jewel of a theater, elegant reception and banquet halls, and drawing and smoking rooms with storybook views of rolling hills cradling the monarchy's metropolis. Bars were discretely set into the windowpanes to give the impression of wrought-iron ornamental grillework. Everything was arranged to simulate the continuation of exclusive sophisticated leisure. The pavilions for the lower classes were more stripped down and situated near the institution's workplaces for the inmates. With its stables and pigpens, its butcher shop, bakery, laundry, smokehouse, and mortuary, its "workhouse" with locksmith, blacksmith, bookbinding, and print shops and many other workshops, Steinhof represents an odd replica, cynics might consider it a fitting continuation, of the feudal structure of the old Habsburg country estate.

Gargoyles deals with the inevitable demise of a large aristocratic estate and the rural economy sustained by it. It is a theme Bernhard will thread as a leitmotiv through nearly all of his works. In retrospect they add up to one single-minded composition, its themes and variations orchestrating the collapse of the Habsburg Empire. *Gargoyles* features an eccentric aristocrat and mad philosopher, Prince Saurau, the next-to-last male descendant of a powerful dynasty who may well owe some of his enlightened insanity to Paul Wittgenstein. With an extensive monologue that explodes the boundaries of a prose narrative, the prince emerges as a dazzling madcap stage character against the grotesquely tragic backdrop of a dying culture.

Appropriately enough for Bernhard's perception of the world, Steinhof flourished for a while as a hideaway for uncomfortable members of wealthy families. Later exploited by the Nazis to facilitate the deportation and murder of Jews and other "undesirables," whose names and numbers have not yet been adequately established, it never regained its original distinction after World War II. Nevertheless, it continues to play a major role in the popular imagination. The beautiful facades, now somewhat in disrepair, overshadowed by tall pine trees whose rustling underscores the all-pervasive silence, exude an eerily melancholy serenity. But the stillness is occasionally disrupted by a scream, a moan, a spectral figure dressed in nothing but pajama pants turning the corner; an old woman sitting on a bench, rocking a bed that has been wheeled outdoors, staring at the open-mouthed face of the sleeping old man hooked up to tubes, swaddled like a baby in a heavy blanket; a middle-aged woman with ruddy features and disheveled hair eagerly sucking on a cigarette—the scenic clichés of despair turned shamelessly real, putting the metaphor-chasing tourist-turned-voyeur to shame. Such contrasts animate the dramaturgy of Bernhard's literary endgames.

Otto Wagner's church at Steinhof stands as the only fin-de-siècle church, an ambitious synthesis of ecclesiastical architecture, religious artwork, and ritual objects site-specifically designed to accord with the most advanced standards of psychiatric care. The battles surrounding the construction and particularly the interior design of the church could not be outdone even by Bernhard's most outrageous histrionics. Artistic designers were at odds with financially prudent clerical consultants; a conservative Catholic hierarchy aghast at Kolo Moser's original modernist designs for mosaic representations of Bible stories warred against an imperial bureaucracy caught between its traditional cultural megalomania and its historical alliance with the clergy. The political intrigues and verbal assaults contributed to a frustratingly comic scenario that is conceivable only in Robert Musil's Kakania, in the city of Bernhard's literary ancestors, Ferdinand Raimund, Johann Nestroy, and Karl Kraus.

The church's cupola, once sparkling gold, now oxidized green, balanced on the white, cross-shaped crypt, is widely visible above the wooded hills, like an oddly displaced emblem of the imperial crown. During the tumultuous planning stages one incensed state representative warned, "The golden dome will shine all the way to Hungary so that the Hungarians can say, 'That's where the idiots live who pay 70 percent of our bills.'"[6]

While this sort of mentality with its hideously amusing menace is at the core of Bernhard's relentless variations on *Homo austriacus,* the archaeology of the institution holds the locus of a personal conflicted desire that is the driving force of nearly all his works: it is the longing to locate himself within the Habsburg tradition in full awareness that the very idea is madness. As an illegitimate child born into a scattered, impoverished family, he sought to construct himself within a continuum of culture that preserved the grace, elegance, and sophistication associated with nobility at the same time that he documented its inevitable deterioration. Paul Wittgenstein provided a connection not only to the philosopher but also to a family that represented the *Grossbürgertum,* the bourgeois elite, which rivaled the old aristocracy in influence, power, savoir vivre, and exquisite taste. Throughout his life Bernhard accepted the patronage of descendants of the Habsburg nobility and their cosmopolitan satellites only to sever the connection abruptly. In an effort to become a part of Austria's bona fide elite, he played the part of its most relentless critic. In public he took the part of the Fool, traditionally an intrinsic part of the court.

Ultimately there is no contradiction between Bernhard's literary wrath and his private desire. His infatuation with a defunct aristocracy is part of his obsession with death. Bernhard's starting point is a dead society. Traditions provide merely the stage directions for the enactors of a memorized culture. His mise-en-scène reenacts again and again its final dying process. It reflects his own confrontations with death, first as a young boy during the bombardment of Salzburg in World War II. In his unsparing coming-of-age memoir, *An Indication of the Cause,* he documents the cinematic hyperreality that the spectacle of war presents to the awestruck boy. After the first bombing of Salzburg he was swept along by throngs of people as they emerged from their shelters and converged toward the cathedral, which had been hit by a

> so-called aerial mine, and the dome had crashed into the nave. We had reached the Residenzplatz at just the right moment: an enormous cloud of dust hung over the ruined cathedral, and where the dome had been there was a great gaping hole the size of the dome itself. From the corner by Slama's we had a direct view of the great paintings that had adorned the walls of the dome and were now for the most part savagely destroyed, what remains of them standing out against the clear blue sky in the light of the

afternoon sun. It was as though the gigantic building, which dominated the lower part of the city, had had its back ripped open and were bleeding from a terrible wound. The whole square below the cathedral was strewn with fragments of masonry, and the people who had come running like us from all quarters gazed in amazement at this unparalleled and unquestionably fascinating picture, which to me seemed monstrously *beautiful* and not in the least frightening. Suddenly confronted with the absolute savagery of war, yet at the same time *fascinated* by the monstrous sight before my eyes, I stood for several minutes silently contemplating the scene of destruction presented by the square with its brutally mutilated cathedral—a scene created only a short while before, which had still not quite come to rest and was so overwhelming that I was unable to take it in.[7]

On his way to look at other scenes of destruction, he stepped on "something soft," which he took to be the hand of a doll, but "in fact it was the severed hand of a child. It was the sight of the child's hand that quite suddenly transformed the first attack on the city by American bombers from the *sensation* it had been up to then—a sensation which produced a state of feverish excitement in the boy I was at the time—into an *atrocity,* an enormity" (90–91). There is a totemic quality to the child's severed hand as a ghostly plaything. It will inform the fragile anatomy and shell-shocked aesthetics of Bernhard's *Homo ludens.*

Three and a half years after the war, not quite eighteen, he found himself in the "death ward," hospitalized with pneumonia. It was the beginning of a lifelong battle with life-threatening pulmonary illnesses. In *Breath: A Decision,* the sequel to *The Cellar,* he recalls the adolescent's first encounter with a scenario that would become paradigmatic for his theater of death:

All the patients were on drips of some sort, and from the distance the tubes looked like strings. I had the constant impression that the patients lying in their beds were marionettes on strings—though left lying in their beds and only rarely, if ever, manipulated. But in most cases, these strings to which they were attached were their only remaining link to life. I often reflected that if somebody were to come along and cut the strings, the people attached to them would be dead in no time. The whole scenario was much more theatrical than I was ready to admit. The ward was indeed a theater, however conducive to pity and fear, a marionette theater in which the strings were worked by the doctors and sisters—on the one hand according to a highly sophisticated system yet on the other, it seemed, quite arbitrarily. . . . The marionettes I saw in the death ward were of course old, for the most part exceedingly old, quite outmoded and of no possible value; moreover, they were so impossibly worn out that they were only ever manipulated with reluctance, after which they were very soon thrown on the rubbish heap to be buried or burnt. It was perfectly natural for me to think of them as marionettes and not as human beings — to think that sooner or later everybody must become a marionette, to be thrown on the rubbish heap and buried and burnt, no matter where they had once performed, no matter when or for how long, in this marionette theater we call the world. (233–34)

Schopenhauer's world of objects interlocked in intricately connected chains of causality and rattled by the all-pervasive will provided the philosophical underpinning for Bernhard's anthropology of marionettes. He was introduced to Schopenhauer by his maternal grandfather, the novelist Johannes Freumbichler, who had a great impact on his life (and who died in another wing of the hospital where his grandson lay in the death ward). During his extended hospital stays over the next two years Bernhard would have ample time to think and read.

His damaged lungs cut short his dreams of becoming an opera singer. A few years later he turned to acting. The only education Bernhard formally completed was as an actor and director at the Mozarteum, Salzburg's well-known Academy for Music and the Performing Arts, which he attended from 1955 to 1957. By that time he was already a published poet and had been working for three years as a court reporter and theater critic for Salzburg's socialist paper, the *Demokratisches Volksblatt.* A fellow student remembers Bernhard's coy explanation that having written so much about the theater, he had gone there just to find out for himself what it was all about. One long-time director of the Mozarteum suggests that this was his way of rationalizing his failure to get roles in many productions, and that all his later works can actually be read as the performance pieces of a frustrated actor.[8] They are driven by one speaking voice, which enacts rather than describes the subject's state of mind, more often than not in extreme agitation. Syntax scores identity. The self is constituted in speech. The dramaturgy of Bernhard's language in performance owes more to Schopenhauer's *World as Will and Representation* than to Sigmund Freud and Jacques Lacan. Bernhard squarely stages *Vorstellung,* which in German connotes performance as well as representation and imagination, inside the skull. The brain, since Kant the locus of time and space, becomes the promptbook for reality in the mise-en-scène of Schopenhauer's will, which casts itself as self and others and projects itself into the world. Bernhard's *Kopftheater,* his theater of and in the head, is a *Vorstellung* as representation of self through the will performing itself in language. Speech objectifies *Vorstellung* (imagination) as *Vorstellung* (performance). In Bernhard's ferocious mise-en-scène of Schopenhauer's philosophy there is no world outside *Vorstellung* as performance and representation in the theatrical sense. Bernhard's idea of *Homo ludens* also takes care of the Schopenhauerian dilemma of the subject as self and other. The former can be validated only in the perception of the latter. In Bernhard's self-performances, the speaker becomes his own spectator. One of his recurring images is a person sticking out his tongue in front of a mirror. According to his good friend Paul Wittgenstein, Bernhard told him that he masturbated naked in front of a mirror.[9] Perhaps it was his farcical homage to the Schopenhauerian battle between pure will and physicality, or the representation of himself caught in his texts between the stage as mirror and the Freudian mirror stage.

In *Gargoyles* Schopenhauer is dealt an unusual oedipal blow that turns the ingestion of the *Über*-father into a savage slapstick routine. The elder Saurau, the prince's father, spent the last weeks of his life locked up in his room, eating nothing but the "crucial" pages torn out of *The World as Will and Representation.* "Schopenhauer has always been the best nourishment for me," he wrote on a scrap of paper a few hours before his suicide. At first, the prince says, his father wanted to hang himself, "but at the last moment shooting seemed to him better. And so the last communication from him, written on a blank page torn from the front of *The World as Will and Idea,* consisted of the two words 'shooting better.'"[10]

During the last two weeks of his life the elder Saurau had used a bucket for a toilet and emptied it out the window. Thus his (and Bernhard's) revered intellectual progenitor ends up as aristocratic waste in a post-Habsburg courtyard. Saurau's scatological ritual is derived from the time-honored medieval institution of the *Plumpsklo,* one of those endearingly graphic inventions of Austrian dialect, meaning something like "drop john." In Salzburg its indelible imprint can be seen from afar on the city's most famous and widely visible sight, the historic fortress of Hohensalzburg, on top of Mönchsberg. The ruling bishops who barricaded themselves inside the fortress when they were threatened

by their insubordinate subjects used a second-story windowsill facing the city
as a toilet seat. Whatever it says about the holy men's attitude toward their rebellious flock below, their droppings etched a dark wide track into the stone.
It towered above the young Bernhard on his hillside post as he listened to
opera rehearsals and performances in the Festspielhaus, the princely bishops'
former riding school in the rock.

If the theatrical apparatus seems an annoyingly overused existential paradigm, it aptly reflects the excessively co-active relationship between theater
and Austrian culture. Not unlike the famous textbook example of the orchid
that has compensated for its lack of nectar by developing petals that resemble
a female bumblebee to attract the male pollinator, Austrian theater and society
perfected their own brand of co-evolution in a constantly refined process of
sublime simulation and blatant gratuitousness. Leave it to Bernhard's shifting angles of ire to assign the roles of majestic flower and bumbling bee in
the spectacle of politics and the politics of a spectacular culture. The empire's
symbiotic dramaturgy of Catholic and Habsburg ceremonials, the enormous
cast of its centuries-old intricate bureaucracy with its minutely defined, painstakingly differentiated roles, the role-playing in the assimilation of Vienna's
multiethnic transplants from all regions of the dual monarchy, the histrionic
excesses of representation in competition with other empires left a problematic legacy, a wildly anachronistic poetics of politics that continues to animate
the affairs of the drastically shrunken state.

Vienna's formidable satirist Karl Kraus exposed the Habsburg dramaturgy of its own and the world's collapse as early as World War I, a time
"when operetta figures acted out the tragedy of mankind." [11] In hindsight,
Robert Musil needed to invent a name that would cover the entire realm of
the *kaiserlich-königlich Reich,* the imperial royal empire at the brink of collapse, with its realpolitik enacted in a cloud-cuckoo-land of possibilities. "If
there is a sense of reality, there must also be a sense of possibility" is the title of
Chapter 4 of *The Man Without Qualities.* But the childlike charm of the name
Kakania for k.-k. (short for *kaiserlich-königlich,* pronounced *ka-ka*) quickly
dumps the dreamer back into reality: *kaka* is the Austrian child's socially approved expression for shit.

Childish scatology has a long tradition in the history of Austrian genius.
Mozart's excremental references in his love letters to Constanze are the best-
known example. They are part of what the Austrians have perfected as *blödeln*

(acting silly, fooling around), referring not just to behavior but to conscious performance with an emphasis on verbal agility. Bernhard was a master of *blödeln.* His closest friend for ten years, Karl Ignaz Hennetmair, liked to shock scholars who wanted to preserve their revered image of the serious *Dichter* of Doom with glimpses of Bernhard's *Blödeleien,* many of which he taped with the full knowledge of his friend.

The German language facilitates the merging of madman and fool as a theatrical archetype. Popular idiom does not distinguish between a "crazy" and a fool; *Narr* covers both. It embraces both Bernhard and Paul Wittgenstein, the writer and the philosopher's (grand)nephew, two fools on the hill, both consummate performers of their respective illnesses: "For decades Paul *lived* the part of the madman; similarly I *lived* the part of the victim of lung disease. Just as for decades Paul *played* the madman, so I *played* the victim of lung disease; and just as he *exploited* his role for his purposes, so I *exploited* my role for mine."[12]

Both inhabit their illnesses as acutely conscious representations of their lives. Fools as they are in the city of Freud, they even derive considerable pleasure from their madness. Illness becomes the text of survival. The *Über-lebenskünstler* is Bernhard's central archetype: the survival artist as a virtuoso performance artist. In a world without monarchs the theater provides the model and mechanism for the continuation of ritualized courtly tradition. The Vienna Burgtheater, Austria's national theater, proudly kept the imperial name that designates not only its former symbiotic relationship with the court but its present function as a substitute for imperial power and ceremony, a truly palatial showcase of historic simulation. Bernhard never tired of attacking the Burgtheater as a relic and refuge of untalented, conniving dilettantes, all the more vigorously when he himself became its controversial playwright in residence of sorts during the last years of his life.

In a cabaret-like sketch of that period he puts his sentiments in the mouth of Claus Peymann, the Burgtheater's real-life artistic director. The setting of the short piece "Claus Peymann and Hermann Beil on Sulzwiese" is a popular meadow on another hill with a picture-postcard view of Vienna. There another pair of fools, the charismatic artistic director, famous for his definitive productions of Bernhard's plays as well as for the controversies they aroused, and his dramaturg, Hermann Beil, sit under a linden tree, chewing on their Wiener schnitzel and on their traumatizing experiences in the Burgtheater as the hot Young Turks from Germany. In Bernhard's monomaniacal style, Peymann

fantasizes to his speechless dramaturg about presenting all of Shakespeare's
plays and all the sonnets in one "evening," while

> Thomas Bernhard thinks that the Burgtheater
> should be *starved out*
> in the most charming Austrian manner
> but he didn't say what he meant exactly
> The Burgtheater could also be wrapped up
> and sent to Mongolia federal express
> with no return address of course
> He also said he could well imagine himself
> singlehandedly without another helping hand
> armed only with a twelve point pickaxe
> hacking it into the ground
> so that all that's left is a stinking pile of rubble
> with all its actors sitting on top of it
> naked and exposed
> reciting Shakespeare and Nestroy
> with such unbelievable dilettantism
> that eventually they would become such a public nuisance
> that all the psychiatrists in Vienna would issue an order
> to have them committed to a speech class for beginners
> where they'd be stuck for the rest of their lives
> because of their incompetence
> He could also imagine
> that in an instant the Burgtheater could become
> a national mental institution
> for those who have proved themselves incurable
> so that over night Vienna would have
> its only mental institution on Ringstrasse
> right across from City Hall
> and the director of this institution
> where no one can be cured
> would be Vienna's mayor Mister Zilk
> who as we all know
> resides right across the Burgtheater
> Vienna's mayor will simply be appointed director

of the only government approved mental institution for the
performing arts
it's really very simple
The Burgtheater could also be left as is and turned into
a theater museum and instead of the actors
there could be wax figures on stage
and wax figures in the audience
and every two hours the curtain would rise
and the wax figures on stage would bow
and the wax figures in the audience would applaud
and then the curtain would fall again
that would be Bernhard's ideal theater[13]

Bernhard was only half kidding about his "ideal theater." The characters
in his plays have something of wax figures about them, variations of just a few
archetypes from the same mold, animated not by individual passions but by
the mechanism of passed-down rhetoric and gestures. The passions and plea-
sures lie in the act of acting both on stage and off. The art of it is the key to
continuity, as long as the machinery doesn't break loose from the actor and
start running on its own. Then the actor drops dead in an instant; his character, however, keeps going. In Bernhard's postimperial universe, this process
has been going on for centuries. It may explain the almost mythical importance the Burgtheater holds for Austrians as their temple of a bizarre kind of
survival. It may even shed some light on Bernhard's renegade will, which prohibited productions of his plays at the Burgtheater after his death until the
expiration of the copyright. Perhaps it was his attempt to short-circuit the process, to escape the machinery that would inevitably turn him into a ghostly
stock puppet. And it did.

An elaborate Bernhard industry began to flourish shortly after his death
in 1989. In the true Austrian tradition that Bernhard so often attacked, the
adulation is but the flip side of the official outrage against him during his lifetime. Perhaps even his posthumous transformation into a treasured cultural
icon was part of his shrewdly calculated mise-en-scène: the last laugh is the
Fool's as he makes fools of everyone else. Bernhard set up his kind of theater
even beyond the grave: a theater not of repeat performances but of an ongoing
comedy that is the tragedy, or vice versa, of Austria as he saw it.

Bernhard's chronic lung ailments had become so exacerbated by a heart condition that he could anticipate his death with some certainty, particularly under the candid care of his half brother, Dr. Peter Fabjan, a physician. Like some of his fictional characters, he used that knowledge to strategize his death and afterlife.

The full consequences of his will are still in the process of unfolding. The ban on the productions of his plays was lifted just in time to generate more opportunities to commemorate the tenth anniversary of his death. The provision prohibiting the publication of his notes and letters is still under discussion and has been circumvented occasionally. The first brazen violator was Karl Ignaz Hennetmair, Bernhard's closest friend and confidant between 1965 and 1975, before they parted abruptly, never to be reconciled. A World War II veteran and consummate entrepreneur as a shoe salesman, contractor, pig farmer, and dealer in real estate, among other things, Hennetmair brokered all of Bernhard's real estate purchases, stood by his side in his early negotiations with producers and publishers, counseled him in his battle against a pig farm to be built across from his farmhouse (which eventually found its way into the play *Der Theatermacher),* and made his nearby home and extended family available for meals, holiday celebrations, and general refuge from the isolation of Bernhard's own rural residence. Shortly after Bernhard's death, he was among the first to come out with an intimate view of the reclusive writer. During one year of their friendship Hennetmair kept a journal that chronicled their joint daily routines. An abbreviated version was published in 1992 as the "sealed diary."[14] Surprisingly, Hennetmair also published his correspondence with Bernhard, claiming the letters are his legal property and he can use them as he pleases. Although neither publication revealed any coveted secrets, they showed a much more down-to-earth and vulnerable Bernhard than he let his public see. Hennetmair's business savvy, peasant wit, and common sense made for a potent antidote against culture-conscious neighbors chasing the increasingly famous *Dichter* in their midst.

After Bernhard's death Hennetmair emerged as the worthy executor of his unwritten testament — his legacy of foolery. In the process, he asserted himself as a formidable public fool in his own right, in the style of a cunning court jester. A self-appointed sleuth, Herr Hennetmair pieced together his scenario of Bernhard's will and death. According to Dr. Fabjan, Bernhard, like the narrator of *Concrete,* had suffered many years from sarcoidosis, an incurable disease of the immune system that affected his lungs. During the last twelve years of his life he also developed a heart ailment that he knew was terminal. Expecting his death at any moment, he delayed it through sheer willpower, his "unbelievable will to live." [15] In the final stage of his illness his lungs were so flooded with fluid that he had to sleep sitting upright. The doctor promised that he would make sure his brother could die comfortably in his sleep rather than choke to death. Bernhard died on February 12, one day after the anniversary of his grandfather's death, which was also the day after his birthday. According to Hennetmair, Bernhard had always wanted to die on the same day as his grandfather. Matters didn't work out quite according to plan: he had such a good time the evening before that he forgot to take his medication on time, and the delay postponed his scheduled death till the following morning. He passed away peacefully in the presence of his brother.

What piqued Hennetmair's curiosity was the change in Bernhard's testament that made his brother his sole heir. This move, he speculated, might have been the final twist in Bernhard's ultimate revenge play. For wouldn't the revelation of the date and revisions of the will, signed in the presence of his brother, make the doctor an immediate suspect in his sudden death, thus subverting the sentimental subtext of an assisted suicide? [16] In post-Habsburg Kakania, it's a moot point whether Hennetmair, once Bernhard's substitute brother, concocted his own melodrama of spurned love and jealousy or whether he had touched upon the truth. He did touch upon the truth. He had come closer than was comfortable to the possibilities in Bernhard's imagination.

His strategies continue to be a major irritant to the tightly controlled Bernhard industry. In true Bernhard spirit, Herr Hennetmair thrives on being a nuisance to official agents of the postmortem Bernhard enterprise and its satellites of obliging scholars. They look down on Hennetmair's intimate grassroots take on the man whom he obviously reveres and still loves. He has assembled his own Bernhard archives, which in tandem with his personal recollections serve as an invaluable source of information, particularly since the Bernhard estate is still restricted until its administrators have figured out how to get around the law and still remain faithful to Bernhard's spirit.

CHAPTER TWO

In Search of Family

Vater bist Du's?
Drohest du mir
aus dem Dunkel her?
Hier siehe dein Kind!

Father, is it you
threatening me
from the dark?
Here, see your child!
—Hugo von Hofmannsthal, *Die Frau ohne Schatten*

Was my family, including my grandfather, right or wrong to
eliminate my father from my life?

—Thomas Bernard, *In the Cold*

The likeness between us was amazing. It was not just that my face
was similar to my father's; it was the same face.

—Thomas Bernhard, *A Child*

DURING WORLD WAR II, BERNHARD'S GUARDIAN, Emil Fabjan, a soldier on the Russian front, came to visit his family in the Bavarian village of
Traunstein. Thomas, about ten years old, eagerly awaited his arrival. As soon
as he saw his new father approach, the boy ran toward him excitedly with outstretched arms. But the man paid no attention to him. He walked straight past
him, his eyes fixed on his biological son, Peter, a toddler then, too young to
recognize the strange man in uniform.

Fabjan never adopted Bernhard as his son. Bernhard would never refer to him as his stepfather, only as his guardian. His half sister, Susanne Kuhn, who was an infant then, vividly recalls Bernhard's bitter memory of the incident. She also shows her visitor a framed picture of her father pacing with the six-year-old Thomas near the hospital where Thomas's mother was about to give birth to his brother, the first child of the man next to him. There is a touching gentleness between them. Both have their eyes cast down. The little boy's face is set in deep concentration as he tries to synchronize his steps with those of the man. His thoughtful expression seems to indicate his attempt to enter his adult companion's inner state of concerned anticipation.

Bernhard never got to know his biological father, who never acknowledged his paternity. His mother's pregnancy is said to have been the result of rape, possibly a date rape. In the course of his life Bernhard would gleefully point out tables in several inns in Salzburg as the site where he was "made."[1] In his memoir he states cryptically: "It is not without significance that it was my mother herself who revealed to me exactly where I had been conceived."[2] The repeated reference to the table suggests a crude joke on the altar where his mother's virginity was sacrificed. In his writing Bernhard frequently uses the awkward term "making children." It has a deliberately ugly ring to it.

"They made children together, but were basically quite unsuited to having children and never really wanted children, my father only wanted heirs, not children, not descendants, just heirs," writes the suicide-bound architect of *Correction*.[3]

If Bernhard's father wanted neither a descendant nor an heir, his maternal grandfather provided him with another kind of patriarchal ancestry. An anarchist dreamer and novelist, Johannes Freumbichler introduced his grandson to the great minds, the intellectual nobility of Western civilization. Against all odds, he set out to groom his grandson as their heir. Otherwise, Freumbichler, a complicated, difficult man, did little, if anything, to contribute to the financial support of his family or to provide any sense of stability. His wife and daughter, both utterly devoted to him, worked as servants in other people's homes so that he could continue to write in the cities he found suitable for the pursuit of his obsession.

Bernhard's grandmother Anna Bernhard was no less nonconformist. She was married and the mother of two children when she ran off with Freumbichler. They lived together for thirty-four years before they finally married. It was a life of hardship and deprivation, stable only in its focus on Freumbichler's literary ambition. Freumbichler, who transferred his obsession with genius to his grandson, didn't live to see the fulfillment of his dreams. Bernhard's grand-mother died in 1965. Her husband would become the predominant archetype in Bernhard's recurring cast of obsessive characters; her presence is harder to trace. She merged into the composite of that rare woman in Bernhard's life and work who is noticed through her silence or absence. Whether as listener in lieu of an audience and a frequent target of verbal abuse or as a dead person remembered by the narrator, she generates his language; that is, his work and life. The narrator is always male, always in a performative mode, and arguably the stand-in for Bernhard himself.

Freumbichler was born in 1881 in Henndorf, on Lake Wallersee, fifteen miles north of Salzburg, his family's ancestral village. Their descendants still live there. At the age of fourteen he left home to attend *Realschule*, or high school, in Salzburg instead of going to work in his family's business, a general store that his father had expanded into a thriving wholesale trade in butter and lard.[4]

In high school Freumbichler joined a fraternity, Der eiserne Ring (The Iron Ring), whose members were intensely romantic, steamily idealistic ado-lescents who adopted names from German (Cheruskian) mythology, such as Rüdiger, Sieghart, Tuisko, and Gieselher. They strove to emulate the virtues, nobility, and idealism they associated with their ancient heroes in a spirit of horny rebellion against the repressions, hypocrisy, and provincialism of Salzburg. Freumbichler's closest fraternity brother was Rudolph Kasparek, a.k.a. Gieselher. They were roommates and clandestine lovers, and remained intimate friends until Kasparek's death of tuberculosis at thirty-four. It was through Kasparek and another fraternity brother, known as Tuisco, that Freumbichler met the woman who would become his lifelong companion.

Tuisco roomed in the Salzburg home of Anna Bernhard, the wife of a tailor and mother of two children. Forced into an unhappy marriage by her parents at age seventeen, the twenty-four-year-old Anna fell in love with both Kasparek and Tuisco. In 1902 Freumbichler moved on to Saxony to attend engineering school. The following year he changed to another school in Thü-ringen, where Kasparek joined him after he was expelled from the *Realschule* in Salzburg. Their separation brought out Kasparek's physical attraction to his friend. Their intensely homoerotic relationship notwithstanding, Kasparek initiated the heated correspondence between Freumbichler and Anna Bern-hard, who had turned all her attention to Tuisco after Kasparek left. In her letters to Freumbichler she pours out her misery with her husband and her intensifying passion for Tuisco. He describes his happy life with his Rudl and offers words of comfort and strength. "A great movement has been formed, the emancipation or liberation of women with the goal of giving back to women their freedom and welfare. . . . Dear Mrs. Bernhard! The sun of a new era is shining. We are on the threshold of a new world which will sweep away all pain and sorrow!"[5]

Not quite a year into their correspondence, in December 1903, they met in Salzburg, and in January Anna left her husband and children. Pregnant with Freumbichler's child, she moved with him to Basel, where he continued his engineering studies. In April 1904, still married to Karl Bernhard, she gave birth to a daughter, Herta, who was to be Thomas Bernhard's mother. As far as the law was concerned, Herta's father was Karl Bernhard.

For the next nine years the family's moves between Switzerland, southern Tyrol, Germany, and Salzburg were driven by Freumbichler's determination to be close to Kasparek, his need intensified by their shared passion for writing and their hopes for literary careers. Anna was an ardent supporter of both men's aspirations. She even wanted to write a biography of Kasparek. Destitute after his parents lost all their money to a swindler, Kasparek tried to work his way to Freumbichler in Basel, but he got only as far as Zürich. Eventually he reached Meran, and Freumbichler joined him there in the fall of 1905 while Anna Bernhard, pregnant again, returned with Herta to Salzburg. Their first son, Farald, was born in Salzburg and died there three months later, in March 1906. Anna and Herta rejoined Freumbichler, who now had a job as an office clerk in Meran.

That October Kasparek moved to Munich to establish contacts to advance both his and his friend's literary careers. Four months later Freumbichler again left his family, this time for three months, to be close to his friend and follow up on professional contacts. In 1908 he quit his job in Meran and moved his family to Munich, where he set to work on a "major" novel. In 1910 their son Rudolf Harald was born. Everybody called him Farald, the name that Kasparek had suggested for their firstborn son. Freumbichler's mother, Rosa, helped out with food. She, too, believed her son was a genius, and so was bound to have to struggle with deprivation. "Every poet has to struggle, and this is true also for you," she wrote to him.[6] Her support did not extend to acceptance of Anna Bernhard, however. If that woman who had left her husband and children came to Henndorf, people would gossip. Nevertheless, she offered to take care of the grandchildren so that Anna could work to support the family. Now Freumbichler divided his time between Henndorf and Munich.

At the beginning of 1912 the family moved to Salzburg. They spent the spring of 1913 in Bozen, where Freumbichler hoped to cure his tuberculosis. There he met Clarita Thomsen, a wealthy patron of the arts. She admired Freumbichler's writing, though she was enough of a realist to know that it was too longwinded for popular consumption. Still, she provided financial support for the family until her death in 1926. Through the years Anna Bernhard wrote repeatedly to "Frau Doktor," begging her yet again for money to support her companion, who still hadn't found a publisher for his ambitious writing projects but was too restless to hold a job.[7] Clarita Thomsen scolded Freumbichler for putting all the financial burden on Anna, but she sent money.

Anna completed training as a midwife in 1913 but she never practiced her profession. In 1916, at Thomsen's suggestion, they moved to Vienna in the hope that its cosmopolitan atmosphere would be more conducive to Freumbichler's writing efforts. During their years in Vienna they moved from apartment to apartment and were often separated when Anna found work as a sleep-in domestic servant. Their correspondence is a moving testament to Freumbichler's often desperate mood swings and Anna's unfailing commitment to the genius she saw in him.

As World War I progressed, money and food grew scarce. Herta and her brother were sent to their grandmother in Henndorf. Some of Freumbichler's earlier works were published in newspapers and magazines. In 1919, at age thirteen, Herta moved to Zürich to work as a maid. Two years later Freumbichler called her back to Vienna. He was lonely, desperate in his isolated struggle to prevail, unwilling and unable to hold on to boring clerical jobs. With his wife working as a live-in maid to support him, he wanted his daughter home to take care of him. Unquestioning, Herta handed over the money she had saved from her earnings in Zürich. In return, he announced ambitious plans to get her out of domestic work: he would have her trained as a ballet dancer. His obsessive dream of rising above the ordinary and finding redemption in art enveloped his children, too. (In Bernhard's play *Force of Habit* the circus director Caribaldi, whose daughter fell to her death from a trapeze, takes his granddaughter through puppet-like dancing drills.) Eventually Herta had to work in other households again and share her income with her father. In the meantime his old friend Kasparek had had to abandon his own failed dream.

Unable to find a publisher, struggling with his lifelong heart and lung disease, he was stranded in Innsbruck, where he worked as an unskilled laborer. He died there in 1920.

The economic crisis of the 1920s brought more hardship and emotional setbacks for Freumbichler. Despondent and ever more isolated, he found it increasingly difficult to muster the energy to write. But he kept going, always encouraged by his unwavering companion. "Schreib für die Ungeborenen" (Write for those not yet born), Anna Bernhard wrote to him.[8] Her letters also express her remarkably open sensuality: "[In the past] the majority of women could never show their true selves to their husbands, for to show sensuality was strictly forbidden. Women have never felt differently from today's women, they were just never allowed to express it: this is how we are. Today one may be, besides wife and mother, also the man's lover."[9] Yet she was quick to comply when Freumbichler suggested it might be better to live as "comrades," so that he could focus solely on his work. His grandson seems to have fully internalized this view. In the course of his career Bernhard attracted quite a few dedicated "comrades," only to sacrifice them to the higher purpose of his writing. Unlike his grandfather, Bernhard always maintained a sense of ruthless irony even in regard to himself. He was better equipped to do so at the height of success than his grandfather had been in the abyss of continuous failure. Herta shared her mother's devotion to Freumbichler. She continued to work in various households until 1929 while Anna Bernhard worked at home for a while as a seamstress.

In June 1930, more than eight months before Bernhard's birth, Herta Bernhard, then twenty-six years old, went to Holland to look for work with the help of a friend from Henndorf, Aloisia Ferstl. From Arnhem she wrote home that she had found a job as cook for a "baroness." It was the household of the president of the court. When she discovered that she was pregnant, she fell into a deep depression.[10]

"I was always told that she didn't want me and tried to avoid having me. But she *had* to have me, the source of her unhappiness, as she called me to my face on every possible occasion, on countless occasions," Murau, the narrator of *Extinction,* obsesses about his mother.[11]

Herta tried—unsuccessfully—to find a job in Holland for the father of her child. At that time Alois Zuckerstätter lived in Tyrol and worked as a carpenter, but he soon found himself out of work again and returned closer to home, in the vicinity of Henndorf. In the meantime, Herta's good friend Aloisia was able to enlist the help of an Austrian couple both knew, Josef and Caroline Weiss, in the nearby village of Veenendal. Herta stayed with them for six weeks, until she was accepted in a clinic and school for unwed mothers in Herleen. The young women were trained as midwives and could stay until their babies were weaned. After the birth of Nicolaas Thomas Bernhard on February 9, 1931, Herta was eager to get out and find work, not only to support herself and her son but also to provide financial assistance to her parents in Vienna.

For the next two years Herta Bernhard and her son stayed in Holland, mostly in Rotterdam, where her friend Aloisia lived. While she scrambled for work in households and factories, the baby was cared for by foster families and for a time in a home for "illegitimate children." One of the families that took in the six-month-old child owned a trawler moored in Rotterdam harbor. Although he was their only foster child, in his memoir Bernhard dramatized his infancy as one of "seven or eight newborn babies [who] hung in hammocks from the wooden ceiling" below the deck.[12]

In the meantime, Herta and her mother tried to force Alois Zuckerstätter to assume some responsibility for his son. He was back in the Salzburg area, a drifter and occasional petty criminal. In 1932 he managed to leave Austria for Germany, presumably to escape a paternity suit. In a last-minute decision, Herta Bernhard declined to sign her seven-month-old son over to a wealthy Dutch couple who were ready to adopt him.[13]

In 1933 she returned with her son to Vienna and once again moved from household to household as live-in cook and domestic help while Thomas stayed with his grandparents. In 1934, when Freumbichler and Anna moved back to the Salzburg area, they took Thomas with them. In Seekirchen, on Lake Wallersee, Freumbichler hoped once again to find conditions that would enable him to devote all his time to his literary pursuits. His grandson, impulsive, pigheaded, and given to temper tantrums, must have provided some interruptions. Even so, Freumbichler was eager to nurture the boy's lively intelligence. He took him along on his visits to Carl Zuckmayer, the famous German novelist and playwright who lived at the other end of the lake, in Henndorf. Anna had sent Freumbichler's manuscripts to Zuckmayer, and in time he was to be instrumental in finding a publisher for Freumbichler's novel *Philomena Ellenhub*. With his grandfather, young Bernhard got to meet Zuckmayer's illustrious circle of friends, among them the established and upcoming writers, performers, and artists of the 1930s and their industrialist patrons.[14]

In 1936 Herta Bernhard married Emil Fabjan, a hairdresser's apprentice, and moved with him to Traunstein, a Bavarian village just across the border from Salzburg. In that Depression year it was the only place near Herta's family where Fabjan could find a job in a beauty parlor. In January 1937 Thomas joined them, heavyhearted at leaving his grandfather. He was in the middle of his second year at school. About two years later Freumbichler and Anna rented a place near Traunstein, in the village of Ettendorf.

This is where the memoirs that cover Bernhard's life until the age of nineteen begin. That is, *A Child* describes the life of the six-year-old boy, but in fact it was the last of the volumes to be written. His reflections about his *Herkunft*, his ancestry, reach back much farther. His inventions, whether intentional or not, are as integral a part of the truth about himself as the facts, whether told to him or withheld from him and later unearthed by others. In this light, the order of the writing is not unimportant. Each of the original works is published individually. The American edition contains all five works. True to Anglo-Saxon positivism, it begins at the "obvious" beginning, with *A Child*. The placement is highly problematic, particularly in this kind of unrelentingly self-exploratory project. The sequence of remembering is as much part of the autobiographical work as the narrated memories; the chronology of the writing is as revealing as its content.

In what adds up to a classic oedipal scenario, Bernhard could tackle his earliest childhood only after he had concluded his account with the nineteen-year-old leaving the Grafenhof sanitarium. At the end of the fourth volume, *In the Cold*, the young man reenters the world completely on his own. His mother and grandfather have died. In the book he also kills his father. He learned, he writes, that his father had been either shot or beaten to death in unknown circumstances in 1943. Bernhard never knew that in fact his father had committed suicide. Alois Zuckerstätter was found dead from gas inhalation in his Berlin apartment on February 11, 1940.[15] Whether Bernhard freely invented his version of his father's death or repeated what he had been told, he killed his father, once and for all. Bernhard was in his late forties when he wrote *In the Cold*. Unlike his dramatic and psychoanalytical precursors, this middle-aged Oedipus heeded Tiresias' warning. He resolved not to question further. The woman who could have told him more was killed in a car accident before she was to meet Bernhard:

Eight years ago I traced a woman who had been a friend of [my father's] at school. She had been a class-mate of my mother's and it transpired that she had known my father as well. I went so far as to arrange a time for us to meet, and she for her part agreed to tell me about my father. However, on the day before we were due to meet I came across a horrific picture in the newspaper—a picture of two decapitated bodies on the Salzburg exit from the Autobahn. My mother's school friend, the only person who could have told me anything about my father, had been killed in an accident. This horror picture made one thing clear to me: I must not ask any more questions about my father.[16]

The fatal accident happened in August 1973. The decapitation is Bernhard's dramatization.[17] The image would return in his final novel, *Extinction,* but there it is the narrator's mother who is decapitated in a car accident that also kills his father. Instead of asking any more questions about his father, Bernhard killed him and his mother over and over again in his works.

During his last stay in Grafenhof, Bernhard made the decision to live. As his ensuing life shows, it was a decision to give birth to himself. He could do so only after his parents and his grandfather—his "true" father—were dead. *In the Cold* does not mention the event of that period that was most decisive for his future life: his meeting with the woman who would become his *Lebensmensch,* his companion for life, Hedwig Stavianicek. More than thirty-seven years his senior, Frau Hede had been a patient at Grafenhof and frequently returned to the picturesque mountain resort of St. Veit, where the sanitarium was located. She first noticed Bernhard in the choir of the village church. He had made it a habit to sneak away from the sanitarium for singing lessons, and the lessons led to a solo at Sunday mass. Although Bernhard talks about his secret escapes, he makes no mention of the crucial encounter. He can't. Frau Hede is his future, not his past. Mother figure and beloved, she helped him to a new life. The child that is born in the act of writing is not identical to the child that is being written. In the chronology of Bernhard's evolution as a writer *A Child* is the appropriate closure of his memoirs. The encounter with his early childhood marks a new beginning. But first he had to go through his victory over death.

In the sanitarium of Grafenhof, the eighteen-year-old patient revisits his early adolescence and opens a Pandora's box of questions about his ancestors, most urgently his phantom father. But it isn't the young man who still struggles with unresolved questions, it is the middle-aged writer at the apex of his career. He does it in the way he knows best. He stages himself in various settings at Grafenhof and watches what happens—not just to the youth he once was but to the man who keeps writing and watching. He places the youth "on a tree-stump between two beeches," as on a stage. Once again Bernhard finds himself on a hill that affords an auditorium-like view of the proceedings: "I sat on the tree-stump between two beeches and watched the men taking their walks below." [18]

Two Bernhards are watching: the writer in the process of writing and the young man being written. The view of the patients circling in pairs on their daily walk in the looming shadow of the 6,000-foot Mount Heukareck leads to another scenario: "I sat on the tree stump and watched beyond the scene I was watching the time I had spent in Salzburg between Grossgmain and Grafenhof." [19]

The time he refers to is the brief interval between his extensive hospital-izations and, before that, the period of his apprenticeship to a grocer. That period is covered in detail in *Der Keller* (*The Cellar*).[20] As he restages mo-ments from that time, among them repeated visits to his grandfather's grave, he introduces again and again the site of the observations and the main actor—that is, himself at eighteen—suspended in the act of observing: the four-page passage contains six references to his sitting on the tree stump. In the theater of Bernhard's mind the sanitarium grounds are transformed into a theatrical setting that yields multiple stages within stages. One of the German terms for stage, *Schauplatz*, generally refers to the place of action, the setting, but its literal meaning is a place to look, to see. The young man's tree stump is the *Schauplatz* from which he observes the *Schauplatz* below. Behind the tableau vivant of the circling men staged by the middle-aged Bernhard through the eyes of his younger self is another scenario, which opens into yet another, and so on: stages within stages, boxes within boxes, layers of actions and their perceptions bleeding into one another in ever-receding frames of time. Every-thing is repeatedly brought back on track with a reference to the performative site and action: sitting on the tree stump. The last time the site is introduced, narrator and observer are catapulted toward the central question:

Sitting on the tree-stump, I pondered my origins, asking myself whether I really ought to be interested in knowing where I came from, whether or not I should risk unearthing the facts, whether or not I had the courage to submit myself to a full investigation. It was something I had never done before: it had always been forbidden, and I had always recoiled from it myself, from removing one layer after another and *getting to the bottom.* . . . Was I now in the mood to surrender myself, with only myself as a witness? To do what I never dared to do under the eyes of my family, let alone my mother: to reconstruct my mother's origin at last?[21]

Who is asking and who is witness to whom — the middle-aged narrator or his eighteen-year-old subject? The text yields no answer; the writing is yet another inconclusive transgression. The punishment is inscribed in the site: the stump of a tree flanked by two beeches. The beeches frame the mutilation of the third tree and foreground its absence like a phantom limb. Sitting on the stump, the adolescent experiments with voyeuristic speculations about his origin and phantom father. The adult writer compulsively revisits himself at this scene of castration and kills his father on the spot: "He died in 1943, but the way he died is not known to me. Some say he was beaten to death, others that he was shot — by whom or by which side I do not know. I have meanwhile grown accustomed to living with this uncertainty, never having had the courage to penetrate the human and political fog surrounding his death" (306).

The adolescent's oedipal trauma continues to plague him into middle age. Along the way Bernhard compulsively staged and restaged the presumed murder of his father. As he dwells on his father, the scene segues imperceptibly from the tree stump to the dormitory, from daylight into the dead of sleepless nights: "I would lie in my bed by the door of the dormitory with the covers pulled up to my chin while the others slept and see myself trying to clear the undergrowth from around my origins, but my unremitting efforts were of no avail, since the further I penetrated into the thicket, the deeper the darkness became and the more impenetrable the undergrowth" (309).

The darkness outside converges with the darkness, the "undergrowth," of his mind as the appropriate setting for his hidden, obscene pursuits: "Was I really interested in these guardians of secrets who had taken refuge in death, vanishing from the scene at the end of their lives, vanishing into thin air, but leaving their secrets behind for me to speculate on, secrets with which I had nightly intercourse as I lay in bed?" (310).

His failed attempts to penetrate the past constitute a bizarre ritual of incestuous necromancy. Literally translated, Bernhard describes himself as "fornicating with the riddles of the bearers of all secrets." The bearers of the secrets are all the dead members of his family. The punishment is built into the act: it invariably renders the perpetrator exposed in his impotence. "But these people in my story refused to become involved in my game. They saw through my motives for embarking on my expedition and showed their contempt, wherever they encountered me, by immediately withdrawing" (311).

The scenario evokes a familiar childhood experience: the little boy peeking into his parents' bedroom at night. In the darkness of the dormitory, on the brink of death, the proto-oedipal patient has "nightly intercourse" with fantasized moments of his ancestors, participating in his own conception, as it were. But he runs up against the unsolved riddles of the Freudian Sphinx who lurks in the thicket of his mind. "Where did my grandfather in fact come from? And my grandmother? On both my father's side and my mother's? Where did they all come from, these people who had me on their consciences and from whom I demanded enlightenment? When I called to them they vanished like spectres" (309).

The middle-aged writer asking these questions over and over again is still "fornicating with the riddles" in the theater of his head instead of going straight to the public records or the Red Cross, which traces lost relatives.

A retired French professor of literature did just that. Louis Huguet, self-appointed Bernhard genealogist, had devoted many years to painstaking research into Bernhard's ancestry. His single-mindedness would qualify him as a bona fide Bernhard character. The result of Huguet's labor had all the ingredients of a Bernhardesque joke. On the day of Bernhard's funeral his half brother, Dr. Fabjan, received the first telegraphed communication from Alois Zuckerstätter's daughter, Hilda, who lived in Frankfurt an der Oder. Contrary to the information Bernhard reportedly received during his only visit with his paternal grandfather in 1945, his father had not "fathered five children" during his marriage in Germany, but only one (307–8). And the Red Cross had traced that one, Hilda, at Huguet's request. The professor rushed to the telephone to inform Hilda Zuckerstätter of the death of the half brother she had not known she had. According to Huguet, she was "deeply shaken by this unexpected information." Whatever her emotional state, one week later she inquired at the court of Gmunden about her claim to inheritance as next of kin. It was rejected on the grounds that her father had never acknowledged paternity of his son.[22]

Alois Zuckerstätter didn't change his ways much after he left Austria. Working at odd jobs, he eventually landed in Berlin. There he met the woman he married after she found herself pregnant by him. Unable to cope with his alcoholism, his new wife left him and moved with their baby daughter, Hilda, to her native Frankfurt an der Oder. This was about the same time the court finally caught up with Zuckerstätter on behalf of Herta Bernhard. Throughout the years she had fought in vain for child support. He had to undergo a blood test, which confirmed his fatherhood. His son had to submit to the same humiliating procedure: "I can see myself at the age of seven or eight going to the town hall of Traunstein, holding my mother's hand, to have a blood sample taken to establish the paternity of Alois Zuckerstätter. The blood sample confirmed paternity, but my father could not be traced, and so he paid no allowance for me."[23] This is one of the scenarios Bernhard restages on the grounds of Grafenhof, from his lookout on the tree stump.

The timing of his autobiographical project is remarkable. Bernhard's lifelong illness had broken out once again in full force. He was in a condition similar to the one he had been in during the teen years covered in his memoirs. Only this time there was no question that his illness was terminal. He knew that he had few years left.[24] He put himself in the care of his half brother, Dr. Peter Fabjan, a resident doctor of internal medicine at the hospital of Wels, a dreary provincial town in Upper Austria. Bernhard helped him finance a practice in the town of Gmunden, about five miles from his farm, and eventually bought an adjacent apartment when his progressively deteriorating condition called for his brother's close attention. Dr. Fabjan points out that he was able to extend his brother's writing career by ten years.[25]

It was at this point in his life that Bernhard began to reconstruct his biography. The act of remembering became yet another act of self-generation. And it was at this point that he reconnected with his biological family, his stepfather and his half brother and half sister, Susanne Kuhn. He had deliberately distanced himself from them after his mother's death. That was the time of his meeting with Frau Stavianicek. Freed from his biological family, he could construct his cultural clan with the new mother figure, who would become his most intimate partner for life.

At long last he had originated himself. His birth coincided with his mother's death. Her dying had loomed over his first stay in Grafenhof. Fittingly enough, he stayed there for nine months. When he returned home, his "mother's death struggle was nearing its climax." It coincided with a dramatic turning point in Bernhard's fight for life. "Two days after being discharged from Grafenhof with a clean bill of health, I had open tuberculosis." [26] While his mother was dying from cancer of the uterus, he had to undergo a pneumoperitoneum, a procedure that involves surgical entry into the abdomen: "Now I was going to have an abdominal puncture, two fingers' width above the navel, to inject as much air as possible into the abdomen so as to compress the lungs and seal off the cavity in the lower right lung. I cannot say that I was properly prepared for this, and suddenly I was scared of having a pneumoperitoneum."

The head physician explained to him that "it was as simple as inflating a bicycle tire" (320). Back in Grafenhof, Bernhard had to deal with an assistant who had never performed the procedure before. It turned into a bloody mess. Horrifying as it must have been, Bernhard staged the procedure as a Grand Guignol scenario of an impotent rape and botched delivery.

> I had no option but to tell him what to do. He prepared the apparatus under my instructions and pushed it towards me. I waited, but nothing happened. He lacked the nerve. I now had to take the initiative. I literally ordered him to place the needle against my abdomen, then push it on with all its might and puncture the abdominal wall. I told him he must not hesitate for a moment; otherwise the pain would be excruciating and the whole business would become very bloody. . . . I told him that he must screw up all his courage and throw himself on my abdomen with the whole weight of his body. . . . As was to be expected, the first attempt failed. I doubled with pain, and blood spurted from my useless wound. But it was essential for more air to be injected, and so he made a second attempt, which was so amateurish that I screamed with pain and people gathered outside in the corridor. The amateur succeeded only gradually in piercing my abdominal wall, working by fits and starts and causing me quite unnecessary torment. Then, as if he had scored a triumph, he stood there and noted with satisfaction that the air was flowing into my abdomen and distributing itself, the mechanism was functioning. . . . There was an audible flow of air, and I saw the arrogant expression, which had been temporarily absent, return to his face. No one was more surprised than he was at the success of the enterprise. I remained lying there for a while, after which I was taken back to the loggia. I had never lost so much blood after an injection, and I had pains in the abdominal wall for days. (330–31).

The procedure grotesquely mirrors an awkwardly violent act of conception under the instruction of the victim, who is also the baby not yet born. The scenario even includes the proud father in the guise of the inept assistant who takes all the credit.

In the process of repeated pneumoperitoneum treatments Bernhard slowly regained his strength until he was able to make secret excursions to the village of St. Veit. This is where he met the woman who was to become his *Lebensmensch*. At this time, too, he learned of his mother's death through a brief obituary in the local paper. It seemed as if his mother died a long death in childbirth. Her death led her son back into life. After a period of utter dejection following her funeral, he gradually regained a foothold in life: "I now entertained the supreme ambition to return to full health." This ambition could be realized only by a determined act of transgression. "I decided to transgress the regulations and secretly go to the village every day" (334). He began to take singing lessons. He even organized a sled for himself, on which he rode to town every night. In hindsight, the young man's midnight excursions read like a young lover's clandestine courtship. He kept it a secret even in his autobiographical narrative, perhaps because he couldn't know then that he had indeed found the love — and mother — of his life.

Breaking loose from the deadly protective womb of the sanitarium, he finally succeeded in delivering himself. "I had to take my life into my own hands and, above all, into my own head" (334). Inside his head he would stage and restage his life. His theater of the mind became a phallic womb of sorts to which he retreated to deliver himself over and over again.

In the six years during which Bernhard published his memoirs, between 1975 and 1981, he also wrote and published seven new full-length plays and a collection of short satirical sketches. No wonder Henning Rischbieter, one of the most influential critics of the postwar German theater, suspects that Bernhard wrote his plays every time he finished a prose text and needed to recover.

Of greatest interest in conjunction with his autobiographical project are *Am Ziel* and *Über allen Gipfeln ist Ruh,* which coincide roughly with *In the Cold.*[27] Both plays introduce a writer. *Am Ziel*'s is a nameless character called simply The Writer, a young, highly successful playwright; *Über allen Gipfeln ist Ruh*'s is an old renowned writer with the resonant name of Meister, which translates into Master. Both are playfully self-conscious parodies of Bernhard at the height of his career. While he is in the excruciating process of coming to terms with his origins in his prose, he flirts with his fans and detractors from the stage in the figure of the writer.

He doesn't leave it at that, of course. *Am Ziel* tears once again into the wounds ripped open in his memoirs. In the play's first few minutes the character of the Mother tells her daughter about the birth and death of her infant son. The passage is shocking, both for its outrageous hyperbole and for its unresolved pain. I quote it at length to show the buildup of Bernhard's obsessive self-torture, which is also an act of exorcism.

> I didn't want that man
> The foundry and the house at the shore
> and then a child on top of it
> your brother poor thing
> two and a half years and gone
> [drinks cognac]
> He had a face like an old man
> I didn't want him he was too ugly
> can you imagine
> he looked ancient
> that happens once in three million
> everything about him crippled
> That's the punishment I thought
> now you're punished
> I kept thinking of nothing but
> how to get rid of him
> once I had the idea
> to burn him in the oven
> but then I swaddled him again
> and sang him a song
> I got sentimental
> and that was even more hideous
> I tried to reason with myself
> but secretly I wished for the death of my child
> all the time
> I didn't dare to show my child

everybody wanted to see it
but I didn't show it
I always said the time will come
I was wrong my dear . . .
Then I went to the sea and thought it would get better there
but that's when it was worst
I wanted to pull the blanket over its head
and suffocate it
but I didn't dare
I thought that this would ruin me too
why do this to myself
because of a human being that's not really human
a shriveled little animal
I hated Richard
Your father was the unhappiest man
one could imagine
he always came out here from town and asked
how's our child
I hated it when he asked me that
I thought you made the child you bastard
and now you're still asking
how that cripple is doing
I had to imagine what it'll be like
when that cripple is fifteen or twenty
or twenty five
But that was not to happen
I wished for his death so intensely
that he died
as usual I hated
to pull back the little curtain
he was still in the wicker carriage
but there he was dead all of a sudden
suddenly his face was beautiful
ancient but beautiful
because I thought about his death so intensely
Richard you understand

> your father the Wagner fan
> just when I was about to show my child
> it was dead [28]

The revoltingly graphic details of the mother's feelings for her infant son—written around the same time as Bernhard's autobiographical explorations of his birth—echo his anguished self-perception. But a few lines later Bernhard identifies himself with the Mother as she talks about her mother's response to her own birth. It is yet another variation on the circumstances of Bernhard's birth:

> She deposited me somewhere in Holland
> in an inn
> she went into an inn
> to the bathroom
> and cut me off
> then she went out again
> to a girl friend who took her in for a week
> then she went to work again (22–23)

Merging the narrative of his birth with the stage character's, Bernhard eerily inscribes himself in both the Mother and her dead infant son. He also wrote himself into the play in a much more obvious manner in the character of the Writer, a playwright whose new play has just opened to a standing ovation. According to the title, he was *am Ziel,* he had reached his goal. The stage playwright, like Bernhard himself, had arrived. *Am Ziel* opened at the Salzburg Festival. Bernhard had become the festival's most celebrated and controversial playwright. His new plays were eagerly awaited and reviewed by Europe's leading critics and scholars. He was ready to be shown off by a proud mother, as it were. But it was too late. His mother didn't live to see his success. And as Bernhard knew by then, his illness was terminal. His mother's wish, like that of the play's Mother, would finally be fulfilled: she would be rid of him at last.

Bernhard's play opens the morning after opening night. Although the Mother barely knew the Writer, she was so carried away by his triumph that she spontaneously invited him to accompany her and her daughter to their seaside summer home the next day. He accepted as spontaneously. His visit provides Bernhard with ample opportunity to satirize himself. The play's the-

atrical and social setting, though purportedly in Holland, is a typically Bernhardian Salzburg Festival scenario. The entire play unfolds as a play within a
play, the latter being the larger spectacle of the Salzburg Festival itself, with
Thomas Bernhard as its leading actor.

The play's Writer exhibits many Bernhard characteristics. For one thing,
he lets himself be wooed by wealthy admirers and takes advantage of their
eagerness to snag a trophy guest:

MOTHER
. . . By the way he said
he'd love to be our guest
he'd love it that's what he said
that means that we have to pay
for his travel expenses

DAUGHTER
Yes that's what it means

MOTHER
Isn't it unusual
to pay someone's travel expenses all the way to Katwijk
someone we barely know

DAUGHTER
But he is well known
he is a celebrity

MOTHER
He may be a celebrity
but that doesn't mean I should pay for his travel
all the way to Katwijk

DAUGHTER
Of course we pay for his travel expenses mother

MOTHER
That's not my intention
on the other hand
how would it make me look
if I wouldn't pay for his travel
after all it was me who invited him to Katwijk. (72–73)

Many older women became Bernhard's traveling companions and paid
for his expenses.

According to the Mother, the Writer's plays always feature

> These horrible silent roles
> those perpetually quiet characters
> they do exist in reality
> One talks the other doesn't
> he might have a lot to say
> but he isn't allowed to
> he has to sustain the strain
> We burden the silent one with everything

Her daughter is such a silent character. The Writer replies, simply and
knowingly, "everything." (108–9)

The astonishing success of the play within the play, despite the insults it
hurls at the audience, mirrors the frenetic audience reactions to Bernhard:

> I can't understand
> why they applauded
> we are talking about a play
> that exposes every one of them
> and in the meanest way
> admittedly with humor
> but nasty humor
> if not with malice
> true malice
> And all of a sudden they applaud (38)

What the Mother says about the Writer's method and the audience's response
could be said of every one of Bernhard's plays that had been produced so far.
Bernhard's own voice is unmistakable in the Mother's response to audience
reactions:

> . . . people don't understand a thing
> and applaud till they drop
> because they happen to be in the mood to applaud
> but they also applaud the greatest nonsense
> They applaud their own funeral

> they applaud every time
> they get punched in the face (39)

Here too Bernhard stages himself as his maternal double. He is both Mother (as stage character) and son (as real-life author). The son speaking through his maternal stand-in is thus authorized to insult his real-life audiences.

Bernhard's next play, *Über allen Gipfeln ist Ruh,* premiered a year after *Am Ziel.*[29] This play's writer, Moritz Meister, has just finished a much anticipated tetralogy about a famous professor. Meister is a cross between Thomas Mann and Goethe, who supplied the play's title. "Meister," of course, calls to mind Goethe's Wilhelm Meister novels. He too exhibits many Bernhardian traces, which by now have become part of his myth. The writer and his wife live in a villa in the foothills of the Alps. They are visited by a young woman who is working on her dissertation, a leading journalist, and the writer's publisher, modeled on the well-known publisher Siegfried Unseld, the head of Suhrkamp Verlag.

Like Bernhard, Meister wanted to be an opera singer. His dream was cut short by a cold. Meister's wife, of Habsburg lineage, his ardent admirer, protector, and spokesperson for his genius, stands in for Bernhard's devoted companion, Frau Hede. Bernhard's mother makes a brief appearance as Frau Herta, the couple's invaluable live-in cook and housekeeper, who serves the meal to the famous writer and his guests. One of Bernhard's closest lifelong female friends, Ingrid Bülau, a pianist with whom he studied at the Mozarteum, is introduced and gleefully killed off:

> I had a girl friend in my early youth
> who wanted to become a pianist
> . . .
> a highly musical person
> who opened up music to me like a jewelry case
> the things I owe this person
> suddenly she died no one knew what from [30]

Bernhard's real-life friend didn't die; it was rather her career that ended. Bülau had to stop playing because of the crippling stress on her hands.

Freumbichler's writing habits are eulogized in Meister's discipline:

> He gets up at three in the morning and wraps himself in his horse blanket
> which he brought from Sicily twenty years ago

and he sits down at his desk and writes until nine
like Professor Stieglitz in his tetralogy [31]

The horse blanket is also highlighted in *Am Ziel* as the Mother's only possession, passed on to her by her father, that she brought to her marriage. It is
remembered in his memoir *The Cellar:*

> Every morning at three o'clock my grandfather made a fresh start on *The
> Valley of the Seven Courts,* which he planned as a book of five hundred
> manuscript pages. For years now the need to press on with the task had
> got him up at three o'clock to resume the struggle with death. Debilitated
> all his life by a serious lung condition, he had made it his custom to start
> the day at three in the morning by addressing himself to the terrible task
> that faces the fanatical writer and philosopher, wrapping himself in the
> horse blanket and fastening it round his body with an old leather belt.[32]

Meister writes prose that is "exploding with drama," according to his
publisher, who marvels that

> there are so many plays in your prose
> some chapters of your Germania novel
> are like plays
> strange

Meister replies, "A few others have said so too." Clueing his critics and scholars, Bernhard has the publisher make his point one more time: "Your work
is bursting with drama."[33] And so it is. His early novels feature long monological passages that jump off the page like performance acts. The works that
follow the memoirs consist of one uninterrupted, often breathless speech act,
performed rather than calmly observed and narrated, by a writing subject in
the process of writing. Whether this speaker/writer is Bernhard himself or a
stand-in character, he watches and stages himself in the act of writing. Though
he wrote only five more full-length plays during the eight years after he completed his memoirs, his later prose texts are scripted as self-performance acts.

Bernhard's memoirs mark a divide in his life and work. He had survived
not only the devastating experiences of his youth but also the unsparing exploration of them on which he had embarked as a mature writer who had entered
the final phase of his battle with lung disease. At that point, with death delayed

at ever shorter intervals, the comedic self-performance on the scene of tragedy creates a theatricalized *Lebensraum,* an alternate space of life. The—albeit illusory—immediacy of the speech act defies the physical deterioration that underlies the urgency of the narrative. Bernhard wrote his later novels at the point of dying. Like Bernhard in his autobiographical fictions, *Wittgenstein's Nephew* and *Woodcutters,* the fictional authors of *Concrete* and *Extinction* examine their personal and cultural biographies in the few months they have left to live. In *Extinction,* Bernhard inserts himself into the acts of writing that are the characters'—and his—final performance acts. If he is not in control of his body, he is in perfect control of his nonstop speech act, which often goes on for pages without a break.

If his later works spotlight the writer as bravura monologist, his earlier works, before the memoirs, dramatize the acquisition of speech. The narrators are young. In *Frost* a young medical student is assigned to observe a mad painter. In his notes he acquires the language of his subject, who becomes a substitute father. As the narrator of *Amras,* a student of science, tries to negotiate the task of chronicling his family's suicide pact, his fractured syntax scores the deterioration of his mind. In *Gargoyles* a student accompanies his father, a country doctor, on his visits to patients in remote rural areas. In the process of writing down his observations and particularly the mad prince's hundred-odd pages of monologue, he becomes a writer. The prince emerges as a cultural *Über*-father. Each of the three works is a bildungsroman of sorts. Each features a young man in the process of distancing himself from his parents, whether through tragedy or in a more predictable maturation process that is suddenly thrown off course by the intrusion of a pathologically charismatic father figure.

Correction was the last novel Bernhard published before the memoirs. Arguably his masterpiece, it is the culmination of the techniques and concerns of his earlier works and prepares the ground for his later self-performance texts. Here the narrator and his task of mapping his friend Roithamer's road to suicide are carefully introduced in the novel's first half. In the second part the narrator presents the result of his research—a compilation of notes and personal thoughts Roithamer jotted down on bits and sheets of paper. As the presenter of the material, the narrator becomes the dead man's impersonator.

Roithamer, somewhere around forty, is the first of Bernhard's central figures on the verge of middle age who are resolved to be the last of their line. That they also suffer from a terminal illness is less the cause of their decision than its reinforcement. Roithamer's father forced the continuation of the line. He left his beautiful, cultured first wife after their first child was born dead. In due aristocratic tradition, he married his second wife, "the butcher's daughter," for the sole purpose of producing heirs. Like Natasha, the unrefined sister-in-law of Chekhov's *Three Sisters,* she is an outsider, a birthing machine, and thus "by nature" — *naturgemäss,* one of Bernhard's signature terms — with no understanding of Altensam, the family estate, and its cultural legacy.

The historic ambiance of Altensam, located on a hill, is set off against the untamed dark countryside along the gorge down below, where Hoeller the taxidermist, Roithamer's classmate in elementary school, has his house and workshop. It is in Hoeller's garret, with a view of his friend stuffing dead animals, that Roithamer writes his life-consuming study. Its successive corrections lead to its annihilation and his death.

It has been frequently pointed out that the character that emerges from Roithamer's notes on shreds and reams of paper is derived in part from Ludwig Wittgenstein. The descendants of the Wittgenstein clan, whose country estates were near Bernhard's farm, provided him with concrete insights into post-Habsburg patrician settings. Roithamer's parental inferno, his ancestral burden, and the incestuous obsession with his sister that destroyed both, laid the primal scene for the existential hell of Bernhard's later patrician stand-ins. Aristocrats of the spirit, they are all male, all victimized by familial psycho-terror, unmarried, engaged in homoerotic bondings and/or quasi-incestuous love-hate relationships with their sisters, each the last descendant of a family line he is determined to bring to an end with his own imminent death.

The oppressive peasant milieu of Bernhard's early works has gradually given way to the cultured, if doomed, traditions of the aristocracy. The shift from rural brutishness to landed nobility is paralleled by Bernhard's changing self-presentation from peasant misfit to cosmopolitan country squire.

Paradoxically, once Bernhard constructed himself along the lines of his literary aristocracy, he obsessively staged its extinction over and over again. Moreover, he emphasized the radical cutting off of the family line as a moral imperative. In his fictional stand-ins he could merge his personal biography, overshadowed by his terminal illness and solitary lifestyle, with historical necessity: the ambivalent legacy of Austria's imperial history passed on and reflected in the moral corrosion of contemporary Austrian society could be stopped only by the fierce determination not to procreate. Outbursts against

the absurd sentimentality of producing children triggered by horrifying scenarios of parental psycho-terror abound in Bernhard's work. "Men like my
father do not want a child, they want an heir, and they marry late in life, for
this one compulsive purpose," notes the narrator of *Extinction* in the book
he finishes during the last year of his life, echoing the sentiments Roithamer
expresses about his family.

> In their desire for an heir they rush into marriage with a virtual stranger,
> about whom they know hardly anything. By the time an heir is born, they
> are fairly debilitated and can already be described as old. The mother
> promises to give her husband an heir and then proceeds to rob him of
> more or less everything. The new father, for his part, feels that he has
> done his duty to himself. Once the heir is born, he loses interest in the
> wife. Most of the time he punishes her by ignoring her, or, if the mood
> takes him and she gives him cause, he reproaches her for having grossly
> exploited his generosity and married him only to get her hands on his
> fortune. In due course they reproach each other with everything, and life
> becomes hell.[34]

In an interview Bernhard claimed that "people are mistaken to think they bring
children into the world. . . . They're getting adults, not babies. They give birth
to a sweaty disgusting beer-bellied innkeeper or mass murderer, that's whom
they're pregnant with, not children. People say they're expecting an itty-bitty
baby, but in reality they get an eighty-year-old who's drooling and wetting
himself all over, who stinks and is blind and limps and can't move from gout,
that's whom they bring into the world."[35]

"Parents have a child, and in doing so they bring into the world a monster that kills everything it comes in contact with, it seems to me," writes the
childless narrator of *Concrete,* whose terminal illness will bring the procreative
cycle to a halt.[36]

Like Bernhard himself, his literary doubles are unmarried, childless, and,
if not suicidal, terminally ill. The heir who eliminates himself as the designated
progenitor is Bernhard's ultimate parricide.

CHAPTER THREE

The Construction of Origin

Had I not been through everything that makes up my present existence, I would probably have invented it all for myself and ended up with the same result.

— Thomas Bernhard, *The Cellar*

ON JANUARY 11, 1951, BERNHARD LEFT Grafenhof without permission and refused to return. For a while he looked for job opportunities in the local business community. But, as he put it in *In the Cold,* "I was no longer capable of starting work with a firm. . . . I was revolted by any work, any job. I was disgusted by the stolidity of the working population, those in employment. I could see how repulsive they were, how utterly futile and lacking in purpose. I was appalled and horrified by the thought of working, of being employed by someone, just to be able to survive."[1]

About a year later, he landed a job as a reporter for the Socialist Salzburg paper *Demokratisches Volksblatt.*[2] Most of his articles appeared between 1952 and 1954. His contributions taper off in 1955. By that time he had made his first forays into Vienna's literary scene. In the fall of 1955 he auditioned and was accepted as an acting student at the Salzburg Mozarteum.[3]

In later interviews and biographical sketches, Bernhard emphasized his early stint as a court reporter; he never mentioned the numerous other topics he covered in Salzburg in the early 1950s. The courtroom stories were unsigned. Whatever his contributions were, they don't stand out among the court reports that appeared nearly every day. In retrospect, they offer a carnivalesque panorama of crimes and misdemeanors among the local residents as they negotiated their way between the hardships of the old farming way of life and the opportunities to profit from the U.S. occupation force.[4] Sly peasants, teenage prostitutes, petty thieves, black marketers, currency smugglers, in-

toxicated wife beaters, enraged wives, disfranchised relatives, spurned lovers
turned killers made up the cast of characters in these terse accounts. Ranging
from the banal to the grotesque, they made popular reading. Apparently Bernhard did his share to add suspense and sharpen the drama by adjusting facts
to suit his imagination.[5] Sometimes, rather than attend the sessions at court,
he leafed through the protocols and made up his own versions of the proceedings. "But since the [newspaper] writing came about pretty much by chance,
well, I remember, I made thirty schillings per contribution, whether it was
three lines or a whole page, it didn't matter. . . . So I tried to make sure to
get three articles a day, even something like 'The pregnant widow.' I went to
the district judge and asked: 'What's up today?' There were files and I copied
them quickly. That's how I made quite good money, up to ninety schillings a
day, that was a lot in those days."[6]

Quite obviously much that Bernhard read in those court files informed
his later fiction, and the experience turned him into a lifelong newspaper ad-
dict, regardless of the publication's quality. It became an obsession he often
refers to in his writings.

Notably missing from Bernhard's biographical summaries and reminiscences were his other articles. Unlike the anonymous courtroom reports, these
pieces bore his initials. They appeared almost daily, occasionally more than
one, as he struggled to meet his living expenses. They covered everything from
the conditions in occupied Salzburg to affectionate descriptions of seasonal
customs, daily routines, and historic landmarks in the surrounding villages;
from the dismal housing of refugees to vignettes of the summer festival. (The
twenty-one-year-old rookie journalist did not get to cover the actual productions; he still watched and described them from the outside, from his old
lookout on Mönchsberg.)[7]

It was in the so-called Reading Studio, sponsored by the Salzburg Volks-
hochschule, that Bernhard got to know American and English drama — Arthur Miller's *Death of a Salesman,* Clifford Odets's *Country Girl,* Christopher
Fry's *Phoenix Too Frequent.* He was particularly impressed by a reading of
Eugene O'Neill's *Ah, Wilderness!* at Salzburg's America House.[8] He also reviewed public readings from works by Ernest Hemingway, William Saroyan,
and James Thurber, as well as by German writers, including a spirited defense
of Bertolt Brecht. His pun-filled polemic was a satirical counterattack on the
Viennese critic Friedrich Torberg, whose dismissal of Brecht represented the
common Austrian attitude. Film reviews, reports on exhibitions, new books,

libraries, and student productions at the Mozarteum rounded out Bernhard's cultural journalism. It offered him an important learning experience in lieu of the high school and college education he had missed.

He also contributed to other publications, such as Vienna's Catholic weekly *Die Furche* and Munich's literary *Merkur*. The *Merkur* was the first to publish one of his poems, "Mein Weltenstück" (My Piece of the World), on April 22, 1952. The *Demokratisches Volksblatt* followed with a few short stories and poems.[9] Several poems appeared in *Die Furche* and for the first time in an anthology.[10] In 1952 he also gave his first poetry reading and received a favorable review from the editor in chief of the *Demokratisches Volksblatt,* Josef Kaut,[11] who later became the president of the Salzburg Festival.

In December 1955 *Die Furche* published Bernhard's scathing critique of Salzburg's resident theater, the Salzburg Landestheater, headed "Salzburg Waits for a Play." In an early outburst of the kind of enraged hyperbole that would become his trademark, he predicted the imminent demise of this "fairground of dilettantism," where "one operetta follows another, one tastelessness surpasses the other." He goes on to ask, "What then is theater? Does it consist exclusively of cheap, worn-out amusement? If yes, then it should be shut tomorrow." The article earned him his first libel suit, by the theater's artistic director. When the plaintiff lost his suit, he appealed, then withdrew his appeal. The legal proceedings dragged on for two years.

Two days after the article appeared, the cultural editor of another Salzburg paper, one of Bernhard's early supporters, wondered in his column: "What got into the kid?"[12] Bernhard's private response to a friend was: "The world got into me."[13]

Up to that point he was the good kid who overcame adversity and sickness, a young local writer of some promise whose poems and stories paid close and loving attention to the local milieu. It made him the natural heir to his grandfather Johannes Freumbichler, who had recently been honored posthumously as a treasured *Heimatdichter,* a poet of the homeland. Now all of a sudden this sheltered homegrown protégé had turned against the cozy provincialism of a popular local institution.

Thanks to the support of Frau Stavianicek, in whose apartment he stayed when he went to Vienna, he had been able to establish professional contacts there. His autobiographical short story "Grosser unbegreiflicher Hunger" (A Hunger Great and Unfathomable) and "Der Schweinehirt" (The Swineherd) were published in 1954 by the influential critic Hans Weigel in his prestigious literary magazine, *Stimmen der Gegenwart* (Voices of the Present), an important showcase for Austria's promising young writers. Frau Stavianicek, or "Auntie" (*die Tante*), as he teasingly referred to her in public, also introduced him to the world outside Austria. She took him to Yugoslavia, to Italy. It was the beginning of their many travels together.[14]

But first the promising young *Heimatdichter* had to come to terms with the concept of *Heimat*.

Heimat I. An Excursion

The evolution of both Bernhard's writing and his self-construction reflects the effort to shed the aura of provincialism without abandoning the landscape that was so crucial to his critical vision of contemporary Austria.

To Bernhard, as to other Austrian writers who came of age after World War II, *Heimat,* as the place that defined him culturally and politically, was and continues to be a difficult concept to come to terms with. It seemed irreparably contaminated by Nazi usage, particularly the exploitation of its ancient Gothic roots. (The Gothic *haims* and *haimopli,* referring to village and native field, served the Nazis' anti-urban ideology.)

Accordingly, the genre of the *Heimatroman,* the "homeland novel," became a serious liability for postwar writers such as Thomas Bernhard, who were rooted in regional traditions but developed a critical perspective on rural life as they knew it from personal experience. They had to overcome the image of the Nazi-friendly nativist genre writer and break through a vocabulary that passed on Nazi sentiments. If they exposed what lurked behind the persistent clichés of the purity of nature and rural innocence, they faced attacks by public officials for dirtying their country's image.

During the 1980s, the Austrians' troubled self-understanding had been fashionably labeled *Herkunftskomplex.* This "origin complex" reaches far back into the ethnic and social stratification of the Habsburg monarchy. Arguably one of the most characteristic aspects in the crisis of Austrian identity, it also is the source of the complex layers of tensions and contradictions in its cultural products. To understand Bernhard's public persona, literary output, and enormous posthumous impact on the culture, we need to examine him against the historical background in which he staged himself, his work, and even his afterlife.

The self-conscious agony over origin has a long history in the expansive geography of the Austro-Hungarian monarchy, its diversified cultures clearly distinguished by language, religion, and quasi-tribal interests but thrown together and reconfigured across ever-shifting borders and political alliances.

Heimat then came to mean a mixed bag of ethnic, regional, and political identification, an accidental place of birth determined by the vagaries of paternal careers in the service of imperial bureaucracy, and ultimately the increasingly uneasy allegiance to the all-embracing Über-family of the Habsburg dynasty. The titles of the emperor Franz Joseph, the dual monarchy's longest-reigning ruler, reads like Leporello's list of Don Giovanni's exploits. Both the Don and the dynasty pursued sexual politics to claim territory that was in the possession of others. "Alii bella gererent, tu felix Austria nube" became the Habsburgs' proverbial strategy of global expansion through marriage. It led to the maze of archduchies, dukedoms, counties, margravates, and principalities trailing the Kaiser's name:

> Emperor of Austria; King of Hungary, of Bohemia, of Dalmatia, Croatia, Slavonia, Galicia, Lodomeria, and Illyria; King of Jerusalem, etc.; Archduke of Austria; Grand Duke of Tuscany and Cracov; Duke of Loth[a]ringhia, of Salzburg, Styria, Carinthia, Carniola, and Bukovina; Grand Duke of Transylvania, Margrave of Moravia; Duke of Upper and Lower Silesia, of Modena, Parma, Piacenza, and Guastella, of Auschwitz and Sator, of Teschen, Friaul, Ragusa, and Zara; Princely Count of Habsburg and Tyrol, Kyburg, Görz, and Gradiska; Duke of Trient and Brizen; Margrave of Upper and Lower Lausitz and of Istria; Count of Hohenembs, Feldkirch, Bregenz, Sonnenberg, etc., Lord of Trieste, of Cattaro, and above the Windisch Mark; Great Voyvod of the Voyvodina, Servia, ...

Even this impressive list is somewhat abbreviated. And even though Austria nominally represented one half of the hyphenated dual monarchy, it actually was a tiny archduchy consisting of what today are Upper and Lower Austria.

"What's left is Austria," Georges Clemenceau said at St-Germain-en-Laye when the traumatic reconfiguration of Central and Eastern Europe was completed after World War I. What was left was a few German-speaking mountain regions encapsulating the collapsed empire's archducal heartland. This drastically shrunken Restösterreich, or left-over Austria, became the newly created First Republic of Austria. It was also the nucleus of what fin-de-siècle nationalists, including Social Democrats, envisioned as the hyphenated empire of Deutsch-Österreich. Only the peace treaty of St-Germain in 1919 prevented German-Austria from annexing itself to Germany.

To many intellectuals and artists of fledgling Austria, Berlin was the cultural capital, a cosmopolitan mecca of powerful publishers, producers, and art dealers. Connected to Germany by its native language, the First Republic perceived itself as an appendix of its giant neighbor. It lost some of its greatest talents to Berlin.

Ironically, the initial exodus of Austrian writers and artists to the Berlin of the Weimar Republic was a response to the parochial notion of *Heimat,* which became increasingly politicized in the years between the wars—the period leading up to Austro-fascism and finally the annexation to Germany. Officially reconceived as rural homeland, *Heimat* represented a sentimentalized Eden of bucolic purity as opposed to the urban decadence of Vienna under the corrupting influence of intellectuals, bohemians, and entrepreneurs, which is to say Jews and other Eastern Europeans.

In 1934, the first year of Austro-fascist rule, annual state prizes for literature, music, and the arts were introduced to support the forging of the new native Austrian of old Germanic peasant stock. The State Prize for Literature was to be awarded for "outstanding achievements . . . which in form and content must belong to the German-Austrian cultural territory and enrich the German-Austrian cultural heritage."[15]

By 1936 several versions of guidelines had been issued. They reflect the efforts of the appropriate ministerial councilors to articulate the concept and expectations of "native literature." In the final 1936 version such literature was "to stress native themes, so that one could hope to honor a work that can be defined as Austrian literature not just because of the writer's nationality but because of its subject matter." Content and meaning should come "from material concerning the Austrian *Heimat,*" defined as "the Austrian people and the Austrian soil"; another draft specified work based "on the landscape and the people of our *Heimat.*" The final version requested a work "that derives its content from . . . the Austrian *Heimat* and Austrian person."[16]

The new identity favored by the cultural politicians of the 1930s, to be forged with the help of regional writers, was a pure Austrian Germanness, purged of all the Slavic and Jewish blemishes of the Habsburg Empire, transcendentalized by Catholic hegemony, and embodied

in rural traditions and garb under the cleansing impact of Alpine innocence, and thus culturally superior to the Germanness even of the Germans. In this pathetic effort to resist the encroachments of the Nazi
empire the Austrians became all the more susceptible to the allure of
Aryan purity and the process backfired in the end.

Kulturpolitik, the politics of culture, or more precisely the national
policy of programmatically subsidized cultural representation, has a
long history in the Habsburgs' pursuit of cultural imperialism. Like
everything else that made the transition from the dual monarchy to
Restösterreich, it got hopelessly entangled in the messy leftovers of
imperial bureaucracy. Robert Musil, short-changed like the best of his
colleagues by the cultural administrators of the 1930s, wistfully titled
a diary entry of 1936 "Kulturpolitikskultur," culture of politics of culture,
which is to say a culture defined not by the excellence of its artistic
and humanist endeavors but by its politicization of mediocrity: "They
take everything mediocre, as long as it is politically correct, and try to
base the concept of a new Austria on it. They got it all wrong; instead of
simply accepting mediocrity and putting it to use, they define the entire
concept by mediocrity."[17]

The best-selling novels of that period led to the popularization of
a new literary genre, the *Heimatroman,* Austria's answer to the Wild
West epic (which, incidentally, also enjoyed great popularity, thanks to
Karl May, the nineteenth-century German elementary school teacher
and petty criminal who passed the time during his incarceration by writing novels about a mythologized, if not Germanized, American West,
which he had never seen). In its most extreme form the genre deteriorated into the *Blut- und Bodenroman* (novel of blood and soil), a blatant
glorification of a nativist ideology that celebrated the authentic and exorcised everything foreign.

The works of the most representative *Heimatdichter* of the 1930s,
many of them early admirers and propagandists of Hitler, retain their
great popularity to this day. Most prominent among them is Karl Heinrich Waggerl, the first winner of the State Prize for Literature in 1934, an
enthusiastic early supporter of Hitler and still one of Austria's most revered writers. His books continue to be required classroom reading. A
longtime resident of Wagrain, a picturesque mountain village fifty miles
south of Salzburg, he sentimentalized peasant life in his stories and
novels. His name has become synonymous with Salzburg and the surrounding countryside. This is Bernhard's *Lebensraum,* but its effects on
the two writers differed radically. From Waggerl's Wagrain one can see

the other side of Mount Heukareck, the mountain Bernhard contemplated from the sanitarium in Grafenhof. It is tempting to read a telling symmetry into the accidental semiotics of geography.

In 1938 Waggerl contributed to the so-called *Bekenntnisbuch österreichischer Dichter.* This "Book of Testimony of Austrian Poets" included the enthusiastic "testimonies" of seventy-one Austrian writers in support of Hitler and national socialism.[18] Invited to an "ethnic German" poets' week in Berlin, while the Nazi Party was still prohibited in Austria, Waggerl is said to have used the occasion to "present to the Führer in Berlin an homage signed by almost all inhabitants of his native village, which he had to smuggle across the border."[19] The story of his tryst with the Führer is told in a book titled *Heimkehr ins Reich: Grossdeutsche Dichtung aus Ostmark und Sudetenland, 1866–1938* (Return home to the Reich: Great German Literature from the Ostmark [the eastern borderland, Hitler's medieval term for Austria] and Sudetenland), also published in 1938. Its proud editor, Heinz Kindermann, would rise to prominence after World War II as the author of the ten-volume *Theatergeschichte Europas* (History of European Theater) and the venerated founder and head of the Institut für Theaterwissenschaft, the "science of theater," at the University of Vienna from 1942 to 1945 and again from 1953 to 1969. The dates speak for themselves.

After Hitler took over Austria, Waggerl served in the Nazi campaign, devising slogans for the subsequent plebiscite. Until his death he starred in the immensely popular annual Advent pageant at Salzburg's Festival Theater. Amidst living Christmas trees, a chorus of native shepherd boys, and a company of local amateurs enacting the journey of Mary and Joseph to Bethlehem, Waggerl would sit at a simple table reading from his own sentimental Nativity stories.

Bernhard's writer grandfather, Johannes Freumbichler, was rediscovered as a subversive *Heimatdichter* only in the 1970s. His novels and poems dealt with rural life amidst the corrosion of ancient social structures in the Salzburg area. One of the few to be published during his lifetime, *Philomena Ellenhub,* was awarded the State Prize in Literature in 1937.

At a time notorious for its officially supported literature in the service of the construction of *Heimat* and national identity, Freumbichler's novel stands out for its unconventional moral and political perspective. Within the stylistic conventions of the *Heimatroman* it is the coming-of-age story of a young peasant woman in the years between 1818 and

1848. *Heimat* is posited as an inner state and land as the expansion of self rather than dynastic property in the uniquely unsentimental portrayal of a strong woman. The daughter of wealthy farmers, Philomena is orphaned as a child and in charge of her siblings until the children are put in the service of various farmers in accordance with the medieval law (revived by the Nazis) that made the firstborn son the only heir of the father's estate. An unmarried mother, Philomena remains single and makes an impressively independent life for herself, her unwavering sense of self anchored in the continuity of communal bonds amid shifting familial and political configurations.

Freumbichler began *Philomena Ellenhub* in 1922 and finished the first draft in 1931, the year his grandson was born out of wedlock. An illegitimate child would not have been an issue for Freumbichler. The ostracizing of unwed mothers was part of the provincialism he despised. The erstwhile anarchist and unpublished writer remained an unrepentant outsider who made sure his dislike of provincialism was passed on to his first grandson. A neurotic tension between urban sophistication and provincialism pervades all of Bernhard's writings, fed by an ambivalent nostalgia for the lifestyle of Habsburg aristocrats in their elegant city residences and country estates. Bernhard's prime targets are social climbers from the provinces who come to Vienna to work their way up the heavily politicized professional ladders through shrewd maneuvers rather than genuine accomplishment. Once firmly ensconced in the post-Habsburg bureaucracy, which had changed little since Musil's assessment of its endemic mediocrity, they (not unlike himself) would acquire country estates or farms and set themselves up as landed gentry with aristocratic pretensions. In Bernhard's deconstructed *Heimat,* nature is never purifying, country life never wholesome.

Fear of provincialism, a legacy of the imperial class system, is an important part of the *Herkunftskomplex.* The Austrian's origin complex was further complicated after 1945 by shame not only over Austria's involvement in the Holocaust but over its politics of silence afterward. Günther Anders, Hannah Arendt's first husband, one of the few Jewish writers to return to Vienna shortly after the end of the war, describes in his journal the bizarrely histrionic atmosphere of uneasy silence:

> Vienna 1950
> Every moment one is in danger of forgetting and one mustn't forget for a single moment.

Yet, if one considers that the local population consists of yesterday's brutalizers and yesterday's brutalized, and that it isn't possible to tell who belongs to which group; that they sit next to each other in the trolley or even offer their seat to the other; that the former SA man, now a waiter, says "Thank you kindly, Herr Professor" to yesterday's camp inmate, now a customer; that the bullied one fills the coffers of the bully; and that in their daily interactions, as if by conspiracy, one never mentions the critical years to the other, because heaven knows what might turn up—it turns your stomach if you start thinking about it. But, as I said, one mustn't forget for a single moment; today's situation is a mockery of the bloody serious-ness of the past twelve years; it invalidates and degrades it to a spectacle; and this show closed because another one had been booked.

Yet no one should be blamed for this arrangement. The situation is unavoidable, it seems, if people are to go on living. Perhaps there would have been other possibilities immedi-ately after the catastrophe. But today it is too late.[20]

A rabid anticommunism as a result of the Soviet occupation of eastern Austria and part of Vienna until 1955 and the looming presence of Soviet military power in Czechoslovakia and Hungary overshadowed the need to come to terms with involvement in the Holocaust and deep-ened the bias against people of Eastern European descent. To compli-cate the situation, some of the returning Jewish refugees brought with them the conservative anticommunist stance of their host countries, particularly the United States. Others had become influential Commu-nists in response to the rise of the Nazis. Consequently, even after 1945 Jews could once again be identified as the dangerous other, on either side of the political divide. In the realm of *Kulturpolitikskultur,* the ap-propriate ministerial deputies were ambivalent if not embarrassed as to how to approach Austrian Jewish writers still in exile. "What are we supposed to do with all these Jews?" was one of the eerily resonant official responses in 1945 when Victor Matejka, Vienna's cultural coun-cilor, tried—unsuccessfully—to institute a program to repatriate Nazi refugees.[21]

Non-Jewish writers found themselves in a broken landscape of chasms that divided those who had come of age after the war, those who had successfully established themselves during the Nazi era, and those who chose a so-called inner emigration, a retreat from all political engagement as a means to cope.

When the State Prize for Literature, a stipend awarded to a promising writer—now known as the Great State Prize, to distinguish it from the so-called Little State Prize—was reinstated in 1950 after a twelve-year hiatus, it established a problematic bridge to the cultural establishment of the Austro-fascist period. Among the first winners were former members of the Nazi Party, Nazi sympathizers, and fellow travelers, among them Rudolf Henz (1953), Max Mell (1954), and Franz Karl Ginzkey (1956). Mell, whose poetry and plays exalted the mysticism of Austria's Catholic nationalism within the German Reich, continued to be one of Austria's most honored writers after World War II. His plays were produced at the Burgtheater and the Salzburg Festival and enjoyed great popularity. His cathartic Catholicism and mythical patriotism promised a redemption that was much in demand.

The novelist-playwright Friedrich Schreyvogl was one of the most problematic figures in Austrian cultural politics. A member since 1935 of the jury that selected the winners of the State Prize for Literature and himself the recipient of many prestigious awards, he was a member of Austria's (still) illegal Nazi Party, as well as of various official cultural associations in Nazi Germany, all the while solidifying his career as a popular Burgtheater playwright. His self-serving political maneuvering during the Nazi era aroused even the Nazis' suspicion, which he shrewdly used to exonerate himself after the war. In 1951 he once again was on the jury for the resurrected Great State Prize for Literature and held leading positions in influential cultural and political organizations: vice president of the Society of Authors, Composers, and Music Publishers; president of the Society of Literary Production (Literarische Verwertungsgesellschaft); vice president of the prestigious press club Concordia; and a member of the artistic council of the Salzburg Festival. He was also a member of West Berlin's Academy of the Arts and a board member of the West German Academy of the Performing Arts. In Austria he quickly regained his popularity as a playwright of optimism, who brought out the universal in the native spirit. Between 1954 and 1959 he was associate director of the Burgtheater and its head dramaturg.

Many others with political and artistic backgrounds similar to Schreyvogl's served as chairs and referees on peer panels for important fellowships and awards in both the 1930s and the early 1950s. Thus they contributed to the seamless transformation of the aesthetics, if not the ideology, of German-Austrian blood-and-soil authenticity into postwar nativism. Revealingly enough, in the early 1950s the prestigious Austrian literary prizes went to the same writers who were publicly supported during the Austro-fascist and Nazi years. No attempt was made to honor Austrian writers forced out by the Nazis or to offer them any other incentive to return from emigration.[22] As one of the pioneering scholars on that subject pointed out, conspicuously absent from the roster of award winners were Hermann Broch, Max Brod, Elias Canetti, Friedrich Torberg, and Alfred Polgar, to name just the most prominent among the many distinguished writers who were still alive in 1950.[23]

Regional art was quickly appropriated by a rapidly expanding tourist industry. Musil's *Kulturpolitikskultur* metastasized into a *Touristenkulturpolitikskultur,* a highly politicized culture that defines its Austrian identity by its appeal to tourists—that is, foreigners. In the 1930s, Austrian art had been extolled and subsidized to offset and insulate it against foreign influences; now, ironically enough, it was up to foreigners to validate the authenticity of Austrianness.

Bernhard was arguably the first to expose the shamelessness and hypocrisy of Austria's postwar politics. In any case, he was the most outspoken and he became a role model for the next generations of writers. The Austrian playwright and novelist Elfriede Jelinek, fifteen years younger than Bernhard, savagely satirizes the designation of tourists as desirable *Fremde* (foreigners), as in *Fremdenverkehr* ("dealing with foreigners" or tourist industry), as opposed to suspect *Ausländer* (also foreigners), impoverished invaders from Eastern Europe. Ironically, the majority of the Eastern Europeans, coming from former Habsburg territories, could be considered at least historical Austrians. To add to the confusion, the majority of desirable foreigners are Germans—ambiguous reflections of the utopian Austrian from the not too distant Nazi past.

Jelinek does not hesitate to dig in the fertile soil of Nazi sentiments for the roots of contemporary nativist rhetoric employed by rightist politicians, the tourist industry, and Green Party ecologists. Talk of the purity of the land easily translates into concerns about the (ethnic) purity of its population. The obsession with athletic superhumans continues in the young urban elite's devotion to health *über alles.*[24]

The regional writers Franz Innerhofer, Gert Jonke, Michael Scharang, and Norbert Gstrein subverted the *Heimatroman* with stark documentation of farming communities crumbling under an anachronistic feudal structure, perverted by the tourist industry, and disintegrating in a world of alcoholism, child abuse, wife battering, prostitution, and debased Catholicism. Gstrein documents in crisp, deadpan prose the tragic transformation of Tyrolians into impersonators of themselves for the delectation of Teutonic wannabe Tyrolians drooling over the nostalgic cliché of the yodeling yokel in lederhosen, heavy knit knee socks, and a hunter's hat sporting a *Gamsbart,* a tuft of chamois hair, climbing up or wedling down the Alps by day and at night climbing a ladder propped against a quaint cuckoo-clock chalet to the bedroom window of a blond-braided maiden.

When Bernhard first sought literary contacts in Vienna in the early 1950s, he was a tense, thin, acne-scarred young man with a few death-obsessed poems to his name: in the eyes of the capital's coffeehouse literati, an awkward stiff from the provinces. Intense and haughty, driven to attain an absolute standard of greatness drilled into him by his maternal grandfather and reinforced by his readings during his long illness, yet unsure of his calling, he had an acute critical eye that kept him at a distance from the trendily provocative intellectual scene. His public image in those years, somewhat mythologized decades later by himself as well as by former friends and colleagues, alternated between the raw peasant misfit who preferred driving a beer truck through the rough streets of Vienna to socializing with city aesthetes, on the one hand, and the impeccably dressed, painfully shy poet, inhibited precisely by his outsider status and lack of urban finesse, on the other.

Vienna in the early 1950s was just beginning to emerge from its wartime isolation. And if it still was cut up by the four occupying powers into strictly patrolled British, French, American, and Russian sectors, sealed off to some extent from the rest of the country and the world at large, it could at least ambivalently bask in the zither-drenched *Third Man* ambiance that made it an international movie hit as the hustler capital at the crossroads of East and West. Orson Welles had mingled with the star actors at Vienna's celebrated theaters, the Burgtheater and the Theater in der Josefstadt, among them Ernst Deutsch, a prominent Jewish actor who had spent the war years in London and Hollywood, and Paul Hörbiger, a member of Vienna's most celebrated actor clan, all of them declared Nazis. And Anton Karas, the composer of the melancholy *Third Man* theme, returned to and enlarged his *Heurigen,* one of Vienna's famed wine gardens in the vineyard-covered hills surrounding the city, where he continued to play the song on his zither to enthusiastic crowds until his death.

Vienna's young artists flaunted their outsider status. They gathered in groups that were loosely defined by their respective fields. Each group had its own café stronghold. Writers assembled at the Café Raimund around the powerful critic Hans Weigel, who had returned from Switzerland shortly after the war. Significant talents who would emerge as definitive figures of German-language literature in the second half of the century, such as Ilse Aichinger and Ingeborg Bachmann, were first nurtured by Weigel at the Café Raimund. His literary magazine, *Stimmen der Gegenwart* (Voices of the Present) introduced many new writers who would later gain prominence, among them Thomas Bernhard. Some of the more radical writers, later known as the Wiener Gruppe, the Vienna Group, split from the Raimund clique and moved to the Café Glory. Led by H. C. Artmann, a self-taught linguist and poet who was instrumental in introducing his contemporaries to James Joyce, Federico García Lorca, Pablo Neruda, and the French Surrealists, they would scandalize the city with their "concrete" poetry, Dada-inspired plays, and *fêtes macabres.* One such carnivalesque happening, a funeral procession through the inner city in 1953, featured participants in black garb and white makeup carrying wreaths and candelabra and reciting from Charles Baudelaire, Edgar Allan Poe, Gérard de Nerval, Georg Trakl, and Ramón Gómez in the original languages at historic sites. Fondly remembered as a watershed event that marked the much delayed emergence of an Austrian avant-garde, it seems in retrospect a rather belated juvenile homage to the French Surrealists.[25]

Writers, musicians, and visual artists mingled in the Strohkoffer (Wicker suitcase), a basement gallery and bar named for the cheap straw hangings that covered the walls. It was home to the Art Club, a short-lived but legendary loose-knit organization of experimental artists. They voraciously explored Surrealism, Futurism, and the possibilities of abstractions introduced to them by returning refugees from Italy and France. Among the members and marginal participants were the painters Arnulf Rainer, Friedrich Hundertwasser, and the future "Fantastic Realists," most prominent among them Ernst Fuchs, Wolfgang Hutter, Rudolf Hausner, and Anton Lehmden. Lehmden's nightmarish pastiches of inner and outer realities would diffuse into the topography of Bernhard's early novels.

Sealed off from the outside world by the Nazis and the horrors of the war, Austrians had had no contact for decades with international artistic developments, let alone the avant-garde. The young innovators eagerly sought entrée into the big world. Ironically enough, most of the poems, performance pieces, and prose texts of the Vienna Group were doomed from the start to be understood only in the German-language countries. Based on the programmatic deconstruction of syntax, spelling, and the specifically Austrian idiosyncrasies of the German language, they were virtually untranslatable. Some need translation even into standard German, particularly the works of H. C. Artmann. The group includes Gerhard Rühm, Oswald Wiener, and Konrad Bayer (who committed suicide in 1964 at the age of thirty-two), and marginally the concrete poets Ernst Jandl and Elfriede Mayröcker. Mayröcker was to make a thinly disguised appearance as Vienna's self-proclaimed Gertrude Stein in *Woodcutters,* Bernhard's savage response to his aging peers.

Artmann's seminal work of the late 1950s, *med oana schwoazzn dindn* (in black ink), rendered in the phonetic spelling of the dialect of Vienna's working-class districts, is a collection of satirical, raunchy poems in street language that expose the aggressions, hypocrisies, and appetites of the city's feisty archetypes. His playlets, poems, and stories mine the subversively hilarious truths in regional syntax and idiom. Artmann's disarming frankness, fierce loyalty to his proletarian roots, and down-to-earth bohemian mien made him the pivotal figure in Vienna's budding art scene. Tall and ruggedly goodlooking, a heavy drinker and unreformed womanizer, a familiar figure in the bars and cafés of the artistic and seedier underground, he kept an ambivalent distance from Bernhard, who by nature was a self-protective loner and only fleetingly attracted to the avant-garde scene.

Epater les bourgeois was one way for the younger generation to set themselves apart from the guilty. It would eventually be appropriated as a way of evading responsibility and critical self-examination in regard to the Hitler period, yet one more of the countless strategies in which Austrians became so infamously adept. The outsider bohemian creating an aesthetic alternative to the mainstream that passes on the legacy of guilt continued to be the bona fide paradigm for the first post–World War II generation of Austrian writers. The prominent German journalist Ulrich Greiner speaks of their *Karriereverweigerung,* their rejection of (traditional) careers after academic preparation for professions, supported by Austria's lavish social system. He points to Peter Handke, "who dropped out of law school the moment he found out that his manuscript 'Hornissen' [Hornets] had been accepted for publication. Gerhard Roth left medical school to become a writer. Gert Jonke kept changing his fields of study until he finally quit. This career rejection is the reason for the relatively large number of writers in Austria. A bohemian life is the alternative, writing and a literary existence become the medium for self-realization." [26]

Unlike their German colleagues, they rarely, if ever, engaged with politics in their writing. Quite the contrary, writing to them became an escape, their "inner emigration" a withdrawal into an alternative reality inside their heads. They could afford to lead the bohemian life of freelance writers thanks to the government's generous subsidies of exportable cultural products.

Bernhard repeatedly denounced the hypocritical pose of artistic autonomy made possible by government fellowships and awards. In view of the prizes and awards that he himself garnered and the continued financial support of various mentors and friends, his obsession with financial independence seems disingenuous. In a notorious television interview he insisted with characteristic hyperbole:

I always was a free person, I receive no stipend and I write my books in a completely natural way, according to my lifestyle, which is guaranteed different from all those people's. Only if you're really independent can you write really well. . . . Well, I always lived from my own initiative, never was subsidized, no one gave a damn about me, to this day. I am against all subsidies, all patronage, and artists, of all people, shouldn't be paid a penny. That would be ideal, then maybe they'd get somewhere. All doors through which artists want to pass should definitely be shut and locked. They shouldn't be given anything, they should be thrown out the door. That isn't done and this is why we have bad art here and bad literature. They crawl into some newspaper somewhere, into some minister's office, they start out a genius and end up in room 463 schlepping files, because they're taken care of until they die. That's not the way to write a good book. . . . No subsidy for artistic matters! Everything has to support itself! The same goes for big institutions, they shouldn't be subsidized. A business principle is needed here: Do or die. Everything cultural gets wrecked here, because everything gets supported. The stupidity someone produces can't be big enough, they'll stuff him with subsidies and ruin him. . . . It's all said in one sentence: Get rid of all subsidies and stipends. I wouldn't give ten schillings to a young artist. Let him get out and either he'll make it or he won't. Only Austria is a subsidy state, everything's subsidized here, every stupid brain gets swamped and bandaged with subsidies, and eyes and ears are stuffed with money by the state so that people don't see, don't hear, so they're nothing.[27]

The interview took place in 1984, in the wake of the scandal caused by his novel *Woodcutters,* in which he singled out a few of his close artist friends of the 1950s and ruthlessly took them to task for their later successful integration into Austria's pernicious *Kulturpolitik.* Ironically enough, the man who triggered the uproar by bringing a libel suit against Bernhard for his demeaning portrayal of himself and his wife was one of his earliest patrons, Gerhard Lampersberg. Despite his adamant denial, Bernhard had received several prestigious stipends and awards. In fact, he had described the bizarre histrionics of award ceremonies supposedly in his honor in *Wittgenstein's Nephew.* Bernhard was too crafty a strategist to just want to get away with a simple denial. It drives home, quite perversely, some of the points made in the novel. His assertion is so blatantly outrageous that it has to be intended to draw attention to itself, not simply to set himself apart but rather to include himself in a way as twisted as the culture to which he declares his allegiance, paradoxically and with a vengeance, precisely by his denial. His rage may well have been fueled by self-hatred.

When Bernhard made his initial contacts with Vienna's budding literary scene, he sought out the writer Jeannie Ebner at the Café Raimund. As the co-editor of *Stimmen der Gegenwart,* she was instrumental in getting his first short stories published. Thirty years later he would brutally ridicule her as Jeannie Billroth, the aging culture vulture of *Woodcutters,* posing as Vienna's Virginia Woolf.

In those early days of the Raimund clique they all were quite impoverished, struggling to keep their heads above water in the fragile postwar economy. The café provided a warm place to spend the whole day if necessary, with understanding waiters serving a *kleinen Braunen,* a demitasse of espresso with a touch of milk or whipped cream and a class of water he would refill periodically. Buttered rolls with chives were a popular low-budget lunch. There was plenty of time and good company ready to commiserate, argue, show off, and spin intrigues in endless discussions.

Bernhard may have actually been somewhat better off than most: he had the financial assistance of Frau Stavianicek. Auntie would remain his ubiquitous mentor, protector, and companion until her death in 1984. Married twice and long a widow when she met Bernhard, she provided him with his own room in her Vienna apartment, which he inherited after her death. By all accounts, she was an elegant, no-nonsense woman from an old officer's family, tall and stern and wealthy as the heiress of Hofbauer chocolate, the empire's leading brand of sweets, which continues to flourish as the trade-mark of tradition and excellence. Adding a bizarrely theatrical spin to their relationship, Auntie occasionally indulged in an archaic reenactment of Habs-burg etiquette, addressing Bernhard in the third person subjunctive.[28] If this conceit was for the benefit of their listeners, a ploy to delineate the hierar-chical distance between mentor and protégé or, conversely, between *Dichter* as Olympian and his mortal supporter, their correspondence over the years switched between the informal *Du* and the formal *Sie,* charting Bernhard's erratic responses to intimacy on any level. (Lifelong friends and colleagues such as the director Claus Peymann and his publisher, Siegfried Unseld, never breached the protectively formal *Sie.*)

While Frau Stavianicek remained Auntie to the world, in his books Bern-hard coined the term *Lebensmensch* for her importance in his life. A simple enough compound of "life" and "person," it conveys so much more than its idiomatic English equivalent, "companion," used and elaborated as "life sup-port" by the British translator of *Wittgenstein's Nephew.* The full meaning of the German word *Mensch,* as of the Yiddish *mensch,* is not only a member of the human species but one endowed with moral depth. In Bernhard's terse terminology, his *Lebensmensch* was the sustenance of his life.

> I use this expression [*Lebensmensch*] to describe the one person who has meant more to me than any other since the death of my grandfather, the woman who shares my life and to whom I have owed not just a great deal but, frankly, more or less everything, since the moment when she first appeared at my side over thirty years ago. Without her, I would not be alive at all, or at any rate I would certainly not be the person I am today, so mad and so unhappy, yet at the same time happy. The initiated will understand what I mean when I use this expression to describe the per-son from whom I draw all my strength—for I truly have no other form of strength—and to whom I have repeatedly owed my survival. From this woman, who is wise and sensible and in every way exemplary, who has never failed me in a moment of crisis, I have learned almost everything in

the past thirty years, or at least learned to understand it, and it is from her that I still learn everything important, or at least learn to understand it.[29]

Hede Stavianicek died in 1984, five years before Bernhard, who took care of her by himself during the last year of her illness. He never really got over her loss.

After a highly unstable childhood and a youth disrupted by World War II and forfeited altogether in his two-year struggle with tuberculosis, he found in Frau Stavianicek security, unqualified love, and the cosmopolitan sophistication of the Habsburg *Grossbürgertum,* Vienna's brahmins. She made him an enthusiastic traveler. She financed his training at the Mozarteum conservatory. Most important, Frau Hede led him toward the kind of focused discipline that enabled him to pursue his writing.

If it was Auntie who groomed him as a post-Habsburg gentleman, it was the composer Gerhard Lampersberg and his wife, Maja, an accomplished amateur opera singer — the Auersbergs of *Woodcutters* — who offered him the full experience of bohemian decadence under their quasi-aristocratic patronage. Their exquisite country residence, the Tonhof, became the summer retreat for the regulars of the Café Raimund, the members and hangers-on of the Wiener Gruppe and the Art Club. Jeannie Ebner introduced Bernhard to Lampersberg, who not only financed productions of his first one-act plays and librettos but largely supported him during his extensive stays at the Tonhof between 1957 and 1960.

Located in the picture-book village of Maria Saal, in the scenic lake county of Carinthia in southern Austria, the historic manor was originally a tower dating back to 1100. Remodeled several times over the centuries, it was in a romantically dilapidated condition when the Lampersbergs received it as a gift from Maja's parents and turned it into a summer refuge for aspiring artists whose provocative work was programmatically ignored by official *Kulturpolitik.* Restored and furnished with the ascetic elegance of landed nobility, the Tonhof eventually represented a jewel of proto-Habsburg rustic architecture. The hosts' neighbors and relatives, boasting genealogical connections throughout Europe's former aristocracy, joined belated Dadaists in artistic and erotic experimentation against the backdrop of gentle hills undulating toward the rugged Alpine border that cut into the old Habsburg kingdom of Illyria. The Lampersbergs' generous hospitality, their open marriage, his flamboyantly promiscuous homosexuality, in conjunction with their elevated position in the Catholic milieu as leading benefactors of the medieval village church and sanctuary—all this in an archetypal landscape of rural wholesomeness provided Austria's fledgling artists, literally starving and starved for both existential rebellion and its recognition, with a Surrealist renaissance of fin-de-siècle decadence and savoir vivre. Throughout the 1950s the summer camp of Vienna's neglected avant-garde, the Tonhof served as the bohemian playground for Austria's future, officially pampered artistic elite.

It was at the Tonhof that Bernhard first emerged as a playwright. Three short plays, *Die Erfundene* (The invented woman), *Rosa,* and *Frühling* (Spring), were put on in the Tonhof's barn in 1960. Bernhard wrote the libretto for one of Lampersberg's short operas, *Die Köpfe* (Heads), and Lampersberg in turn composed the twelve-tone music for his *Die Rosen der Einöde* (Roses of the Wasteland). The works are heavily influenced by Surrealist and Dadaist writings as reflected in the absurdist texts and concrete poetry of the Wiener Gruppe. Maja Lampersberg performed in the productions. She often joined Bernhard in recitals of arias and lieder at the barn and in the village church, whose pastor was an early supporter of the Tonhof scene.

Both Lampersbergs fell passionately in love with Bernhard. This situation, according to eyewitness accounts, led to bizarre scenes of melodramatically declared and denied passion, emotional breakdowns, and Gerhard Lampersberg's heartbroken descent into alcoholism and drug addiction, culminating in the abrupt breakup of the friendship in 1960.

Jeannie Ebner, not beyond suspicion herself of having conducted a bohemian affair with Bernhard, as suggested in *Woodcutters,* tells of a chilly day at the Tonhof when Bernhard was napping in his room. The door was open a crack, so Jeannie slipped into bed with him, her head at his feet, to warm up under the cover. It was all very chaste, according to the nature of their relationship, as good friends or brother and sister. She took the opportunity to urge him to stop toying with both Maja and Gerhard Lampersberg. He had once come downstairs with Gerhard to announce to Maja, "We love each other." Maja, in turn, had confessed to Ebner that Bernhard had "kissed her absolutely vulgarly." Years later she confessed to Ebner, "You know, I really loved Thomas. I was blind." Given to outbursts of jealousy, Frau Lampersberg called Auntie a "whore." According to Ebner, Bernhard was "more homo," as she put it, "than with women. But when they were older and could help him more, then he would do it with them too."[30] Longtime friends allude to Bernhard's homosexuality only indirectly, in mock discrete allusions or smug innuendoes. The subject is usually diverted by speculations about the degree of intimacy in his relationship with Auntie or his "problematic" ways with other women, as a rule much older than he, who worshiped and mothered him. Like Frau Stavianicek, they would serve as traveling companions and paid all expenses.

In a culture obsessed with tongue-in-cheek verbal plays, innuendoes and slips that suggest by veiling and deflect through seeming revelations, Auntie suggests the cliché of the older woman in a clandestine affair. But the German *Tante* is also the tongue-in-cheek code for the slang term *Tunte,* fairy or queer. With Bernhard's knack for punning, clowning, and teasing, it wouldn't be surprising if he enjoyed adding to Frau Stavianicek's stern public image as his intimate female protector that of a female impersonator. As a further indication of Bernhard's convoluted enactment of homosexual desire, one scholar also suggested that the deeply felt term that Bernhard applied to Auntie is masculine: *der Lebensmensch.*[31] In any case, there is a disturbing childishness in Bernhard's attitude toward sexuality, which seems to bring out childishness in everyone else as well.

In a much quoted interview Bernhard commented on the arrested development of his sexuality as a result of his illness. Typically he resorts to *blödeln,* a clownish coyness that reveals his inhibitions as it tries to dispel them:

> Sexuality was drastically restricted in my case, because the moment it began to stir, you see, and I noticed somehow, aha, these are pretty mysterious forces, which suddenly set you in motion and toward certain objects. [Laughs.] That's when I became mortally ill somehow. And that's why it was all quite bottled up and kept in check for years. Which is a pity, really, because just at the time when sexuality has its greatest appeal, that is when it awakens so to speak, when that little weenie starts to stir, to put it plainly, you see, that's when I was in the hospital. Everything was limp, more or less, and one lies there and is kept down, simple as that. When I finally got out, I was rather tired and a little weak. But, between twenty-two and thirty, everything was in place and normal, I believe, you see. With all the pleasure and all the ups and downs, literally and metaphorically — don't be embarrassed now.[32]

The age Bernhard refers to as his sexually most active coincides roughly with his initial involvement with Vienna's young bohemians, which he would bitterly reflect upon in *Woodcutters.* Here, as in all his literary and public performances staged as self-revelations, Bernhard flirtatiously drops plenty of clues like the breadcrumbs in the fairy tale that point the way out of the enchanted wood. In the fairy tale, birds pick up the crumbs and the clever little boy remains lost in the wood. In his tales from the Vienna Woods, Bernhard acts out both the boy and the bird, keeping himself hidden in the forest.

In a society that has turned malicious gossip into a sophisticated art, Bernhard's sexuality has remained a taboo subject. It has not been explored by scholars, never been addressed head on by friends and colleagues, and been ignored even by journalists. The issue seems to come under what might be the time-honored popular application, if not the mundane source, of Wittgenstein's famous logico-philosophical commandment "Whereof one cannot speak, thereof one must be silent." On the sociopolitical level the maneuver had been around for centuries and ferociously attacked by Karl Kraus — Wittgenstein's contemporary, to whom Bernhard is frequently compared — as the tactics of *totschweigen,* to kill with silence. This conspiracy of silence, one of the monarchy's most successful strategies, persists as one of its most problematic legacies.[33]

The training starts early in childhood, with the beginning of speech. "Darüber spricht man nicht" (one doesn't talk about that) is the well-bred child's first commandment regarding sexuality and politics. Perhaps not surprisingly, young Ludwig didn't talk until the age of four. Wittgenstein struggled throughout his life with the tension between his homosexuality and the most rigorous self-imposed standards of spiritual nobility in the empire's official tradition of Catholic-Spartan ascesis. Bernhard followed in the path of his role model in the construction of his public asexual, asocial persona.

The evolution of his public image from defiantly peasant outsider among city intellectuals to cosmopolitan aristocrat of the soul ennobled by a militant asceticism transcended any clues to his homosexuality that he planted, at times quite coyly, in his books. His will, prohibiting the publication of his letters, proves him an accomplished manipulator of the conspiracy of silence. It remains to be seen whether he succeeded in outmaneuvering the established tactics of *totschweigen* or actually played into them. Desexualized, he can be appropriated as a national icon and cultural export item by the very standards of Austria's duplicitous Catholic politics that he exposed so passionately throughout his life.

CHAPTER FOUR

The Staging of Kinship

The past of the Habsburg Empire is what forms us. In my case
it is perhaps more visible than in others. It manifests itself in a
kind of love-hate for Austria that's the key to everything I write.

—Thomas Bernhard, *interview, 1983*

IT IS HARD TO TELL HOW much Bernhard knew about his mother, the circumstances of his birth, and the whereabouts of his father, or, for that matter, how far he was willing to go to learn the truth. The authenticity of his autobiographical narratives lies in his power to reimagine himself within the context of a collapsed *Heimat* rather than in the accuracy of factual details.

The *totschweigen* that shrouds his father and other family matters was not unusual in Austria at that time. The reason for it was not always the most obvious—that is, an effort to erase all suspicion of a Nazi past. The Habsburg legacy left Austria a neurotically class-conscious society. Bernhard's attraction to the heirs of the monarchy's nobility and members of Vienna's old grand bourgeoisie was by no means uncommon. Manifest pedigree was a prerequisite for acceptance, recognition, and advancement. Its warrants were *Kinderstube* (literally children's room, figuratively manners that reflected proper upbringing), *Bildung* (education, seen as a rigorous humanist foundation for a self-generative process that shaped mind and character), and as a result of both *Kultur,* which informed the conduct of life and validated it as an ongoing work of art. Art was everything. It provided a counterreality that was ennobling and redemptive. *Kultur* could be acquired. But it wasn't good *Kinderstube* to introduce one's "uncultured" ancestors, until, of course, they too had become ennobled as and by art.

With Auntie's assistance, Bernhard perfected his cultural pedigree. During his visits to Vienna, Auntie functioned as the hidden guardian of Bernhard's contacts with the local literati. Wieland Schmied recalls the unknown young man who appeared at his home on the outskirts of Vienna to introduce himself to the then editor of *Die Furche.* While they went for a walk that lasted over two hours, Auntie waited in a nearby inn.[1] To Bernhard's fellow students at the Mozarteum, Auntie remained a nameless phantom figure no one ever met. In his new theatrical environment Bernhard turned her into a comedic stock character: the stingy aunt, a rich widow, who exercised considerable financial control over her pitifully starving young nephew.[2] According to Gerhard Lampersberg, understandably not given to fond memories, regulars at the Tonhof referred to her as the hooded crow who kept popping in to ask for "Thomas . . . where is he?" in a shrilly avian voice.[3] Be that as it may, Frau Stavianicek guided Bernhard through his personal and artistic explorations toward the kind of focused discipline that would enable him to prevail as a writer.

With Auntie providing an unshakably stable center, Bernhard branched out to try himself in a variety of quasi-familial configurations. Whether or not his relationship with Frau Stavianicek was at some point also sexual, it was exoticized by her early sense of his genius — a sense that no doubt was fueled by the pervasive passion and obsessive need for genius characteristic of the culture at large. It was the basis of some of his later relationships and quite possibly the reason for their sudden sobering breakups.

Bernhard's close professional and personal relationship with Wieland Schmied seems similarly eroticized by Schmied's admiration for his friend's superior talent. Born in Germany, Schmied started as a poet in postwar Vienna, in close contact with the emerging generation of artists and writers both in the city and at Lampersberg's Tonhof. He made his greatest contribution to the postwar culture of both Austria and Germany, however, as literary and art critic and as an editor with major publishing houses. Schmied's unfailing eye for genuine talent, his unassuming admiration for pathbreaking artists, and his ability to illuminate correspondences across ages and disciplines distinguish the informed enthusiasm of his writing as well as his personality. As editor of Insel Verlag, he eventually helped Bernhard's breakthrough when he championed the publication of *Frost.* Their friendship, erotically enhanced by Schmied's steadfast dedication and reverent loyalty, survived several hurdles. When Schmied married in 1966, he and his wife, Erika, a well-known photographer, and eventually their children provided Bernhard with a substitute family. The couple, both German-born, followed Bernhard to Upper Austria.

With the help of Bernhard's old buddy Karl Ignaz Hennetmair, the real estate agent, they bought a farmhouse in the same style as Bernhard's not far from Ohlsdorf. Bernhard, not one to share his friends and acquaintances generously, wasn't always happy with the arrangement. He became quite jealous when they hired his favorite handyman, who consequently had less time for him, and he occasionally grumbled that they copied even his furniture and antiques. Nonetheless, he took an active part in their expanding family. Erika Schmied's photographs over the decades iconize his rural, familial persona, equally at ease with their children and the local laborers at work at both homes. With her photographs of Bernhard's houses, taken several years after his death at his brother's suggestion, she in effect monopolized the architectural narrative of his biography. In tandem with her portraits of the writer as a young, aging, and dying man, they add yet another dimension to the posthumous construction of a national icon. Assembled in a popular traveling exhibit, they have also been published in a handsome book with a sensitive introduction by Wieland Schmied.[4] Erika Schmied's furtively composed interior views, such as rows of shoes and guns in the entrance hall, which caused much dismay among Bernhard's heirs, are less a violation of "how it really was" than staged fictions true to her model's spirit of dramatically condensed hyperbole.

At the Mozarteum, Bernhard met the music student Ingrid Bülau under circumstances that could be considered love at first sight. Bülau qualifies it as "sympathy at first sight." In any case, it kept them connected until his death. "I think, yes, it was love. But not infatuation," she muses, adding, "It came from him. The love came from him. The relationship was initiated by him."[5] It lasted over thirty years. They were frequent traveling companions.

A girlfriend had pointed him out her: "He's strange; he's for you." And he was. They met frequently, talked a lot, discovered their common interest in music and literature. To their delighted surprise, the favorite book of both was Thomas Wolfe's *Look Homeward, Angel,* which had just come out in German and captured the imagination of an entire generation. They enjoyed slipping into Salzburg's legendary and exorbitantly expensive Festival productions of Mozart's *Magic Flute* and other operas. They bought one ticket and shared the seat.

While most of the students kept their distance from the undernourished, acne-blemished, moody young man, Bülau often visited him in his small apartment on Freumbichlerweg, named after his grandfather, which he shared with another student. And she invited her starved friend to spend the summer in

Hamburg with her and her parents. "Let your aunt pay for the travel costs," she encouraged him. Apparently she did.

Bernhard instantly took to the accepting warmth of Bülau's parents. The pimples disappeared, his body filled out. He sang to her piano accompaniment, most of all Sarastro's arias from *The Magic Flute,* again and again. They sang Schubert and Haydn together. She taped him reciting the poems he worked on. He erased them, taped over, again and again. What he heard was never good enough. It was a good summer.

Bülau still lives in that house, which she inherited from her parents. Bernhard often visited her there, once with Gerhard Lampersberg, with whom he took off to cruise the Reeperbahn. He stayed there during rehearsals for the world premiere of his first full-length play, *A Party for Boris,* at the Hamburg Schauspielhaus. He left, however, before the opening. Bülau was one of the very few people to be invited for extended periods to his Ohlsdorf farm. When his illness took a turn for the worse during the last ten years of his life, she was at his side. "You could say yes, we lived together at times," she says, carefully choosing her words. There even was a time when they considered marriage.

Bülau never married. An accomplished concert pianist until a condition that affected the nerves of her hands stopped short her career, she now teaches piano. A perky diminutive woman with a puckish face that readily opens up in laughter, she has an infectious energy that instantly connects to her first-time visitor, as though they were longtime friends. Perhaps there is some truth to that conceit, based on their shared experiences of Bernhard. Bülau loves to talk about him. Her quick, straightforward sense of humor and unsentimental directness bring him to life as the third party in the conversation. To one surrounded by the sugary, slow-paced circumlocutions of the Austrian idiom, her frank northern wit and unaffected intelligence were a healing breath of fresh air.

In his effort to free himself from the restrictive milieu of his background, Bernhard moved through various roles in a sequence of familial setups. During the three years after his graduation from the Mozarteum he became a frequent visitor to the Tonhof and eventually a permanent guest. In this period three slim volumes of his poetry were published by major companies: *Auf der Erde und in der Hölle* (On Earth and in Hell), 1957, by Otto Müller Verlag, which also published *In Hora Mortis* (In the Hour of Death) the following year, and *Unter dem Eisen des Mondes* (Under the Steely Moon) by Kiepenheuer & Witsch in 1958. In the same year, Fischer Verlag published the libretto *Die Rosen der Einöde* (Roses of the Wasteland).[6] Lampersberg's musical version was presented at the Vienna Festival in 1959. Bernhard's relationship with Lampersberg became increasingly strained in the eccentric, often chaotic, if generous lifestyle at the Tonhof. Local lore has it that the lavish composer, in his passion for young men, decided one year to buy every local boy a moped for his sixteenth birthday. Lampersberg's entourage of artists, in urban bohemian getup, disrupted the picture-perfect serenity of this ancient mountain village as they sashayed around its historic shrine, an architectural gem. It was not unusual for a visitor to pass Lampersberg's wide-open bedroom door and see him in bed amidst a host of young men.[7] Blackmailed by some of his lovers, Lampersberg got involved in drug and alcohol abuse. His addiction led to violent outbursts and intrigues that set his guests against each other.

The Austrian writer Ingeborg Bachmann told a conflicted Bernhard: "You've got to get out of here or it's going to ruin you!" So he packed his bags and left, quite literally overnight.[8] Bernhard bragged that Bachmann was in love with him, but she was "too much for him." She would have worn him out.[9] Bachmann was Bernhard's first guest in Ohlsdorf and for a while toyed with the idea of settling down near him with the help of Hennetmair. In 1969, on the occasion of the publication of his short story "Watten" (a card game), she wrote an awed paean to Bernhard's pioneering achievement so far. In her view his recent prose far surpassed Beckett's in its compelling severity. The long-awaited, glorious new high point in German literature might well be in the making.[10]

After his dramatic breakup with the Lampersbergs in 1960, Bernhard spent the next few years traveling across Europe and to London, as well as in Austria. He visited and cultivated old and new friends, such as Count Alexander Üxküll and his wife, Countess Elisabeth (Lieselotte) Üxküll-Gyllenbrand Hammerstein-Equord. Bernhard met them early on in his journalist days in Salzburg, where Count Üxküll served as commissioner of refugees. Later the couple lived in Vienna, Bonn, and Brussels. Bernhard was a frequent visitor. He wrote *Gargoyles* in the Üxexternal residence. They introduced him to their blue-blooded relatives and friends, among them Countess Ludmilla Stolberg, who invited him to her family castle in Holland and traveled with him to his birthplace, Herleen, in the summer of 1961. He continued to travel with Auntie and frequently stayed with her in Vienna. A friendship that outlasted the Tonhof affair was with Annemarie Siller-Hammerstein, a distant relative of Maja Lampersberg. She was an aspiring set designer when she fell in love with him at the Tonhof. In 1963, on a government stipend in Poland, she invited him to join her, and they spent three weeks together in Warsaw, Kraków, and the Carpathian resort of Zakopane.[11]

In that period of extended travel and long visits with friends, Bernhard had no permanent residence. Nonetheless, 1960 to 1965 were crucially creative years, anchored, if anywhere, in Frau Stavianicek's home and company. He completed and published his first major prose works, *Frost* and *Amras. Frost,* in its first incarnation, was a cycle of poems. Bernhard took the prose version, purportedly written within seven weeks in 1962, to Wieland Schmied at Insel Verlag,[12] but he toyed with the idea of becoming a relief worker in Africa if the publication of *Frost* didn't work out.[13] It did work out. *Frost* was published in 1963 and put him on the map as a major talent who stood out for the force of his language and the darkness of his vision. It earned the novice novelist two awards, the Julius Campe Award in 1963 and the Bremen *Literaturpreis* of 10,000 marks in 1965. *Amras,* Bernhard's declared favorite of his prose works, had also been published by Insel Verlag in 1964 and solidified his standing as one of the most promising voices in contemporary literature. Critics compared him with Georg Büchner and Novalis.[14]

For the first time Bernhard found himself without financial problems. With the awards, income from his books, advances on new ones, and Auntie's money and encouragement, he could finance the purchase of a dilapidated fourteen-century farmhouse in Obernathal, at that time a tiny hamlet. After years of rootlessness, he wanted permanence, a place to return to.[15] Over the years he painstakingly restored his historic residence. Built in the traditional style of the area, the so-called *Vierkanthof,* a four-wing, rectangular enclosure, it afforded him the seclusion of a fortress. Deeply rooted in the history of the land and its people, it came to represent the reification of his reimagined self, his real lifework aimed at posterity, enshrining the tortured cultural ambivalences of his texts. By 1978 its interior had undergone several transformations that reflect the evolution of Bernhard's elective affinities, from local peasantry to Austro-Hungarian landed gentry. In its earliest phase, the rough, rustic furniture was appropriate to the original design and purpose of the place as a self-contained farm. It reflected Bernhard's delight that his official identity was now "farmer at Nathal." The designation was passed on to him with the title to the property, which still bore the medieval name of the village land. He proudly flaunted his bona fide occupation on the license plate of his duly acquired tractor and worked alongside his construction crew bare-chested and in lederhosen. He even designed some of the tables and chairs, heavy, angular pieces, their clean, unadorned surfaces reminiscent of Wittgenstein's architectural designs. Eventually he replaced them with much more delicate antiques in the empire's Josephine and Biedermeier styles, highlighted by a few period portraits, most prominent among them a painting of Joseph II, Empress Maria Theresa's reform-driven son, Mozart's ambivalent patron, the model of an enlightened ruler. These artifacts represented a fictitious ancestry, emblems of cultural nobility authenticated by Bernhard's literary accomplishments.[16] The ascetic elegance of the sparsely furnished rooms, each piece a carefully placed tribute to its historic legacy, is clearly influenced by the Lampersbergs' Tonhof. But while the architecture of the Tonhof—a manor in a compound of several buildings—calls for its sophisticated interior setting, the original organization of Bernhard's farm, with (former) stable and pig sty, barn, cider mill, and workshop attached to the living quarters to form a rectangle, seems to encase a world alien to its original purpose. It resembles a flight of gallery spaces, each an installation of Bernhard's imagined lifestyle. For imagined it always has been. Like the modernized, fully equipped, and ultraclean cowshed, many of the rooms were never used.

Initially he furnished one room at a time, each with a bed and a table as if for guests. But it was Bernhard himself who occupied them, moving from one room into another as soon as it was completed and living there for a while, as if it were the only one in the house. Over time he removed the beds and replaced them with other historic pieces, turning the interior into an exquisite multiple stage set, not for living but for his afterlife.[17] He rarely wrote when he was at home. In his correspondence and fiction he railed against an environment he found inhospitable, both in climate and in its people.[18] To the small rural community Bernhard remained an odd and at times belligerent outsider. According to local lore, mothers threatened their unruly children that they would send that weird recluse after them.[19]

Bernhard's steadfast friend for the next ten years was Karl Ignaz Hennetmair, the shrewd businessman and real estate agent who found Bernhard the farm near his own house in neighboring Ohlsdorf. The provincial homeliness of the Hennetmair household, which included a feisty grandmother, an obliging wife, and five children, provided domestic warmth that Bernhard could avail himself of or ignore according to his whim.

During their intense friendship from 1965 to 1975, Hennetmair served as Bernhard's business adviser, personal secretary, and property manager. A short, perky man with the devotion of Sancho Panza and Rumpelstiltskin's vengeful wit, Hennetmair helped strategize some of Bernhard's early confrontations with *Kulturpolitik* at large and the local politics of Ohlsdorf, maneuvering his Don Quixote past the windmills of his paranoia to victories on the professional and civic fronts. Like the Sancho Panza of the second part of Don Quixote, Hennetmair is eager to point out the mistakes of Bernhard scholars and the disparities between people, sites, and events and their fictional versions in Bernhard's texts. And he keeps pushing for legal procedures against Dr. Fabjan as his brother's murderer. The manic vengefulness of his crusade notwithstanding, his robust perception of Bernhard is rooted in the wicked imagination and humor the two of them obviously shared in their dealings with the world. It is a useful antidote to the all too somber hagiographies by those who never knew him.

In his short novel *Yes* Bernhard unmistakably introduces Hennetmair as the real estate broker Moritz: "Although a tough and shrewd businessman, one of the toughest and shrewdest I ever knew, he was also, and that very few people knew or indeed would have believed, a sensitive, delicately strung person, in whom the sensitive options were by no means crushed by his massive and, as it seemed to everyone who saw him, brutal or at least cold outward appearance."[20]

As Bernhard's real estate broker, Hennetmair exhibited considerable sensitivity to his client's erratic needs, and their friendship quickly blossomed. Eight months after Bernhard bought the farmhouse he wrote to Hennetmair from Yugoslavia that he had decided to sell it. Hennetmair maneuvered him out of his rash decision with remarkable skill. He sent him photographs of the property that he had taken "either to bring about a quick sale or to change your mind. But as you surely arrived at this decision after having given it sufficient consideration and achieved the necessary distance, and as you are aware of the magnitude of this resolution, I don't want to say anything at all that might get in the way of your decision."[21]

Letter and pictures had the intended effect. As soon as he received them, Bernhard had a friend wire back: "Don't take seriously sale of Bernhard house. He'll be in touch." In his follow-up letter Bernhard added a P.S.: "The pictures you took trigger a very melancholy state in me. . . . The property seems to be very beautiful!"[22]

There is no formal third-person address in their correspondence. Hennetmair wrote in the circumspect style of a Habsburg clerk. He elaborated his advice with a homespun homily from a "small booklet that promises to school the mind in such a way that it won't be burdened with worries anymore." He had found the text some fifteen years earlier when he was wrestling with considerable problems with the construction of his house. He had since lost the booklet, but he had memorized the passage he wanted to pass on to Bernhard. In tone and pedagogy reminiscent of Freumbichler's rural elders, it culminates in the autosuggestive exhortation: "I am the general and my thoughts are the troops in my command. At the right moment I must focus them on a certain point and assemble them there. Thus I am the competent strategist who cannot help but be victorious."[23]

Bernhard seems to have instantly seized upon these words. Like an incantation, they would plant themselves in the minds of his fictional stand-ins and drive them relentlessly toward some Nietzschean battle with the obstacles of existence. He acknowledged Hennetmair's folksy wisdom with unadulterated respect: "In recent years I haven't received such a reasonable [letter] but it is impossible for me to make a compliment, no matter in which direction, whoever the person, to whatever kind of mind."[24]

Their correspondence reveals a plainspoken vulnerability Bernhard never exposed himself in public without some sort of histrionic cover-up. On June 27, 1967, he wrote to Hennetmair from the sanitarium at Baumgartnerhöhe in Vienna: "I have a pretty big tumor and I'll be here for two months. All I can do is accept it, and I become strong in the process. I'll enjoy Nathal all the more. Maybe I won't have to have surgery and that thing will go away with medication. We'll see."[25] On July 9 he wrote:

I had surgery on Monday, I am doing well, but there's still a lot ahead of me, a return to Ohlsdorf is out of the question. Of course I would very much enjoy your visit, it's easier to talk, but it mustn't be a torture for you. . . . At least I don't have CANCER, as the doctor assumed, as he confessed to me now. I'd be the cheeriest person, believe me. Here everything is awful, but that's the way it has to be, I guess. Left and right they are dying, all gone — not I — no! — It must be beautiful up there [in Ohlsdorf]. And the grass keeps growing over my house and BIRD SHIT over my car! *It'll take months.* Maybe I'll be lucky. My aunt helps me a lot, she visits frequently — otherwise I reject all visits — except when you show up someday, that'll make me happy.[26]

Thirty years later, with the passion of a spurned lover, Hennetmair called Bernhard a monster, but still he spoke of him with the protective discretion of a steadfast friend. According to Hennetmair, Bernhard had done him a terrible wrong. The hurt of the unspeakable injustice could never be undone. But that is as much as the otherwise compulsively loquacious chronicler would reveal. The story goes that Hennetmair, who had the keys to all of Bernhard's houses, used his main residence for amorous encounters. When Bernhard returned from one of his frequent trips, he found overflowing ashtrays, empty bottles, and other telltale signs around the living room sofa.[27] After their blowup, says Hennetmair, Bernhard had tried a couple of conciliatory gestures, such as greeting him at the post office. But he underestimated the pigheaded pride of his offended buddy. The two would never speak again.

Heimat II. An Excursion

Karl Ignaz Hennetmair

The first-time visitor to Hennetmair's rural home is invited to the spacious country kitchen, fed a hearty meal by his quiet wife, and tested, as it were, for cultural affinities and shared linguistic codes that communicate subtext and ground laughter in the chasm of a common history. The conversation is driven by Hennetmair's obsessive energy, which he shares with some of Bernhard's monologuizing characters. His wife listens attentively, sometimes nodding in agreement or shaking her head as though still bemused by one episode or another, such as Bernhard playing dead with old *Omi,* Hennetmair's mother.[28] As the sun goes down behind the snow-covered fields in front of the kitchen windows, Frau Hennetmair disappears into the pantry and her husband ushers his visitor into his office, which is cluttered with his scrapbooks of World War II. He is in the process of sorting them for an exhibit. They chronicle his wartime experiences, from the French campaign to the Russian front. Picture postcards with familiar scenes alternate with increasingly disturbing snapshots of fellow soldiers, columns of prisoners of war, and Jews being brutalized by the German army during the Russian campaign. As Hennetmair turns the pages from Freiburg to Shitomir with stops along the way accompanied by descriptive comments and wistful ruminations, it becomes uncannily apparent how shrewdly Bernhard appropriated the ritual in the last act of his play *Eve of Retirement.*

In the play, Rudolf, a former camp commander, now a respected

judge on the eve of his retirement, celebrates Heinrich Himmler's birthday with his sisters. As they do every year, they conclude the occasion
with a nostalgic journey through the family album, which takes them
from childhood to World War II and culminates in scenes of Auschwitz.
The coziness of family remembrances segues smoothly into eerily sentimental reflections on atrocities, as if those photographs were just a
few treasured mementos among many:

> VERA (*turns a page*)
> Awful
> those faces
> utter neglect
>
> RUDOLF
> That's a snapshot of the Jews
> they sent us from Hungary
>
> VERA
> And they were put into the labor camp
>
> RUDOLF
> Yes and no
> only those who were fit of course
> not the others
> The Jews of Hungary were a tricky case
> we couldn't really use them
>
> VERA (*turns a page*)
> Bruges right
>
> RUDOLF
> That's when we made a trip to the Ardennes
> and went to Bruges
> and to Brussels
> you see that's where we lived
> I marked it with an arrow
> That was some hotel
> Deluxe. . . .[29]

Among Hennetmair's snapshots is one very similar to a well-known
photograph that shows German soldiers cutting the beard of a Jewish
prisoner. It places the host, intense and eager to share the agony of
his past, in a disturbingly ambiguous light. What distinguishes the wit-

ness from the accomplice, the chronicler from the executioner? Unlike Bernhard's Rudolf, who became assistant camp commander in Auschwitz, Hennetmair saw action in the Russian campaign. He claims that those who didn't want to work in the camps were sent to their almost certain deaths on the eastern front. He points out the dwindling number of soldiers in his photographs. The most important thing, he says again and again, was to remain in that group. Often he can't sleep at night, he adds.

Bernhard's stage characters echo Hennetmair's language. Its distinctive idiom and wistful pitch are the distillations of countless reiterations of wartime experiences at dinner tables all over Austria for the purpose of mental and emotional self-preservation in the compulsive repetitions of an excruciatingly painful text.

Yes, published three years after their breakup, is Bernhard's public acknowledgment of his indebtedness to Hennetmair. The narrator's desperate visit with his friend Moritz, "whom, as I have to admit, I have always sought out as a doctor and therefore like a life saver, like a mind and body saver," frames the compassionate if disturbingly self-absorbed account of the narrator's brief intense friendship with "the Persian woman." [30] Based, like most of Bernhard's work, on autobiographical precedent, the story offers some revealing clues not only to his perception of women but also to his pretty relentless use of his female companions for his own needs. At Moritz's home office the author's stand-in meets a Swiss engineer and his "Persian woman friend," who are building their retirement home on a desolate plot purchased from the shrewd but principled real estate agent. Instantly attracted to the woman, whose state of deep depression mirrors his own, the narrator accompanies her on long walks through a "larch-wood" and talks with her about music and philosophy. After three months of total isolation during which he has agonized over his scientific study, he suddenly finds himself in the company of a perfect soulmate, his match in sensibility and sickness.

But he quickly recoils from her "shameless" revelations of her doomed relationship with "the Swiss," desperate attempts though they are, quite like his own, to hold on to life. When she met her companion as a student in Paris, she instantly made up her mind to invest everything she was in his career as a world-famous engineer. "And as long as she had been able to develop the *talent* of the Swiss . . . all had gone well, her system had only broken down at the moment when the talent or genius of the Swiss was no longer capable

of further development. That was now two decades ago. From that moment onwards everything had become even more horrible for her." (120)

In the end she throws herself "under a lorry loaded with several tons of cement" (133). "Yes," the final word of the story, following her laughter, was her answer to the narrator's question whether she would kill herself someday. His own survival, inspired by her presence and credited to Moritz's unconditional openness to his "emotional and mental sickness" (1), is due mainly to his withdrawal from the woman's pain. The novel's ambiguously affirmative title may well be haunted by the narrator's disturbingly frank assertion of his own ruthless embrace of life.

What makes Bernhard's surrogate recoil from the woman right from the start is his own panicked preconceptions. He delivers his clichés with the histrionic authority of a defiantly misogynous comedy routine:

> ... such women as the woman friend of the Swiss come together with men like the Swiss and turn them into celebrities, they perceive what, using all possible efforts and contrivances, may be made of such a man and they achieve their goal when by their endeavours they make such a man, a basically and naturally quite unambitious, indeed in his disposition lethargic, man, into a celebrity, not and never over a period of years but by quite simply, from the very moment of their coming upon one another and coming together, by forcing him into a hard and cold career. (87)

By his own admission, Bernhard himself was quite adept at exploiting his female friends with similar drives. His lifelong companion first noticed the nineteen-year-old lung patient singing in the village church and was bent on turning him into a world-famous opera singer.[31] When his weak lungs put a halt to his early dreams of that career, Frau Stavianicek was quick to recognize his literary talent and drive him to realize it to its fullest potential. Ingrid Bülau was charmed by the exuberant gaiety of her impoverished *Dichter* colleague and helped him overcome his darkly brooding silences in her family's Hamburg home.

From his early days as a writer and performer it was clear to his colleagues and friends that he aspired to some absolute standard of achievement. "The only thing that interests me is my stone monument," the fledgling playwright told Annemarie Siller as he flirted with her.[32] Her cousin Maja Lampersberg has this to say about the Tonhof tête-à-tête: "A cousin was quite in love with him; he kissed her once, or she him. In any case, he came down to us right away, 'Pepo [her husband's nickname], I need to talk to you. What shall I do? Do I have to marry her now?' That's how naive he was and terrified. But my cousin was very sweet, she laughed and it was all over. We know from others that he was always very shy. But what he aroused in many people was fascination." [33] The sophomoric tone is typical of the kind of sexual gossip circulated about Bernhard after his death.

After Hennetmair's ignoble fall, Bernhard firmly planted himself in the marriage of Christa Altenburg, another relative of Maja Lampersberg, whom he first met at the Tonhof when she was fourteen. Her husband, Franz Josef, a ceramicist with a winningly self-deprecating humor, is a direct if not quite legitimate descendant of Emperor Franz Joseph. Children who resulted from a Habsburg's extramarital affair were traditionally awarded a surname that discretely established their aristocratic status. Christa Altenburg, a warm, no-nonsense woman, is also of noble though not so exalted lineage. Both have the comfortable self-assurance of those whose breeding is self-evident. Their home, which also serves as his studio, in a gently unrolling, mountain-hemmed valley not far from Bernhard's farmhouse, was once a mill. The visitor is received in the spacious, invitingly lived-in courtyard, but not by both together. Their perceptions of Bernhard differ, and they want to give each other the opportunity to tell their own story. His is tinged with irony, hers protectively idealized. Bernhard was close to her. He demanded complete attention, and Christa freely gave it to him. On long walks they talked for hours on end. Later she realized that it was Bernhard that did most of the talking and that his monologues were bits and pieces of his works in process. He showed up almost every day, just in time for the midday meal, which many Austrians still savor as the high point of the day. The ability to prepare and appreciate a good meal is an essential qualification for acceptance on all levels of society. Christa Altenburg is known as an excellent cook. While he showed little interest in Franz Josef's ceramic sculptures, he did appreciate the nobleman's knack for *blödeln*, and that's how they passed their time together when he wasn't asking practical questions about the maintenance of their house and grounds. Over the years Bernhard was quite fascinated by her pregnancies, the apparently mechanical regularity of conceptions and births. And to a point, he participated in the children's lives, as he did as a regular member of the Schmied and Hennetmair households, arriving with gifts and advice. In all the families, though, some of the children, notably the older ones, felt somewhat left out by his need for the total attention of one or both of their parents.

Both Altenburgs acknowledge that he did come between them and that his closeness to Christa not only tested their marriage but was a strain on their family life. He enjoyed doing that to quite a few couples. Not all of them were as secure in their relationship as the Altenburgs, who felt that ultimately their marriage was strengthened by the experience.

Another couple, Victor and Grete Hufnagl, divorced on account of her obsessive infatuation with Bernhard. They remarried after Bernhard showed no interest in an intimate relationship with Frau Hufnagl. Grete Hufnagl-Feige, a former singer, was familiar to Bernhard from her recitals at the time he was considering a career in opera. Her husband, a Viennese architect, also owned a historic mill in Bernhard's vicinity. Both thrived on the company of the *Dichter*. Both were ready at any time to serve his every whim, and he took full advantage of their devotion. They took him to lunch. They took him to dinner. They drove to any restaurant he suggested, Victor saying how much he looked forward to the house specialties, Greta agreeing enthusiastically. Suddenly Bernhard would change his mind and suggest another restaurant in a totally different direction. Grete Hufnagl immediately ordered her husband to change course. She did all kinds of chores for him, and when he had had enough of her, she let him chase her away. She was ready to do anything for him. When they went together to the local café, he asked her to wait for him at another table: he saw someone else he preferred to talk to. Obligingly she sat alone. Worse yet, when she and a friend joined Bernhard for lunch, Bernhard paid for the friend and left Frau Hufnagl to look after herself. Yet she put up with everything and jealously staked her claim to him. When she was introduced to Ingrid Bülau in Gmunden, she tersely informed her: "You are aware of my relationship with Thomas." Coolly asserting her priority status, Bülau countered that it didn't interest her in the least.

Ten years after Bernhard's death Victor Hufnagl bears neither his wife nor Bernhard a grudge. "It isn't as if I was a model husband," he concedes cheerfully. He enjoyed Bernhard's sense of humor. They laughed a lot together. They even traveled to New York together. After Bernhard's death, Greta lost all interest in life. She didn't talk to anyone. Her husband forbade her to speak in public about Bernhard. According to friends, her mind deteriorated until she had to be put in a home.[34]

Like the Altenburgs' chivalric ménage à trois, most of Bernhard's elective kinship arrangements were erotically charged with layers of possibilities. Played out as they were against the speculations of the community at large, they fostered a deliciously conspiratorial intimacy among participants and on-lookers alike. Did they or didn't they? Even if they didn't, it was enough of a thrill to be so closely associated with genius. And he apparently played the comedy for all it was worth. In theatrical terms, he was mugging and shame-lessly milking the jokes. The spectators took great pleasure in seeing a rival's send-up in one of his books—until the pie landed in their faces.

Not that it was all fun and games. Underlying the manipulations and the-atrics was a fairly steady pattern of attachments within the context of familial archetypes. Since these people also served as substitute kin, in a sense all of his attachments were quasi-incestuous. They suggest the foundation for the in-cest motif that runs through nearly all of Bernhard's works. There is Auntie as mother and beloved; Ingrid Bülau as sister and beloved; the Lampersbergs as artistic parents. The Lampersbergs' open marriage lets Bernhard in as son and spouse. Hennetmair, from a social milieu akin to Bernhard's, was an antidote to bohemian, upper-class excess: a solid brother, in his cunningly worshiping way also a lover. Grete Hufnagl was the abused wife who keeps coming back, no matter how brutal the punishment. Christa Altenburg, the cultured wife and mother on a pedestal, corresponds to Bernhard's idolized genius husband and father to her children. Thus removed from corporeality, he becomes su-perior to the real husband whose Habsburg connection is a constant source of Bernhard's envy and social unease.

His literary reputation together with his mystique as a secluded icono-clast made him a coveted status symbol. Among his preferred hosts were the descendants of European aristocracy. In their company, Bernhard could avail himself of the aura of pedigreed lineage. Paradoxically enough, while his writ-ing mercilessly dragged the skeletons of history out of the most respected Aus-trians' closets, he let their dust settle on the construct of his persona like the patina of cultural authenticity.

For the nouveaux riches and socialites, the friendship of an artist of Bern-hard's caliber vouchsafed the nobility of the spirit that in Austrian culture ranks higher than wealth. Gerda Maleta, the wife of an influential conserva-tive politician, was one of the privileged women who devoted much time and energy to his needs and whims during the last seventeen years of his life. She and her late husband served as models for the president and his wife in his play *The President*, as well as for the general and his wife in the play *The Hunt-ing Party*. Their lifestyle, with their farm close to Bernhard's, their apartment in Vienna's imperial administration compound, and elegant travels in select company, served Bernhard's taste and provided some incidental details of his later work. After Bernhard's death, Frau Maleta, a bubbly, chubby woman, perpetually blonde and rosy-cheeked, the operetta cliché of girlish sweetness turned to motherly merry widowhood, rushed to claim her territory in Bernhardian quasi-erotica.

"It's impossible to write next to you," he once told her (with the proper formality of the third-person address), she reports proudly of their sojourn in Sicily, "you've got two ounces of brains and seven pounds of sex."[35] She happily accepted his assessment as a compliment to her femininity, unaware that in fact he intended to insult her. In her postmortem epistolary memoir *Seteais* Maleta sadly reminds Bernhard of their compromising encounter during a joint visit to Berlin. He unexpectedly popped into her hotel room. Finding her partially disrobed, he wrongly interpreted her exposure as a deliberate invitation:

> Your wrong assumption about me was very embarrassing and almost hurt-ful; you never believed what really happened. It was during our stay in Berlin. As I already mentioned, I had been in India before our trip to Berlin and that is where I lost eighteen pounds. Proud as I was to have acquired an almost girlish figure, I packed a youthful outfit for our trip. Just as I was getting into this suit in my hotel room, you came in to dis-cuss our next endeavors. Thrilled by your visit, I jumped up from my chair and the wrap skirt, because of my vivacious move and the missing pounds, opened by itself, fell to the floor, and I stood there in my under-wear. But you took this to be a come-on and part of my seductive strategies and you left the room grumbling. . . . Even later you stuck to your con-viction that I consciously staged this . . . farcical moment with the wrap skirt. At that time I still was a sensitive apprentice in regard to our inter-action and friendship and I suffered when you didn't acknowledge my honesty and love of truth. Later, experience and reason prevailed over misunderstandings.[36]

In his works Bernhard took brutal revenge on those who had done noth-ing but play into his infantile needs and cunningly exploitative manipulations. His relentless depictions of the archetypal woman as an intrinsically stupid, mercilessly destructive fortune- and status-hunting birthing machine suggests the self-hatred of the accomplice. It may account for his sudden unexplained withdrawals from short-lived intense friendships.

No doubt, for some of his doting female companions the arrested sexuality that stemmed from his long life-threatening illness in adolescence added to his mystique of unavailability, which was absurdly enhanced by his literary images of a crippled sexuality and pathetic couplings for procreative purposes. His memoirs graphically describe the experience of his sick body after a pneumoperitoneum: "When I explored [my body] with my hands I could feel the air under my skin: I was nothing but an air-cushion. As a result of all the medication I had had to take for such a long time, a reddish-gray rash formed all over my body." At an age when he would naturally be preoccupied with his body as a site of pleasure, he was obsessed with its medically induced changes, "a medical curiosity to doctors and patients alike, bloated and utterly unsightly." [37]

In *Gargoyles,* Bernhard transfers his early observations in the pulmonary ward to the country doctor's student son and condenses them in disturbingly compelling images of physical repulsiveness. A young man, the narrator's age but "looking twice as old," had "much too narrow a cranium. His eyes seemed to be starting out of his head. When his sister drew the blanket away from his body I saw that he had one long and one short leg. . . . If he stood up and started to walk, I thought, his motion would be like a huge insect." The stomach of this Kafkaesque youth with the Oedipus limp "was like an asthmatic sphere that his arms anxiously cradled for long moments. His head was relatively small; you saw that most plainly when he held it toward his protuberant belly in order to hear better the noises inside his stomach." [38]

The disturbingly ugly vision of the human body throughout his work is in striking contrast to Bernhard's personal appearance, which was impeccably elegant, with the sort of casual flair that distinguishes the born aristocrat from the stilted perfection of acquired status. Even his early identification with blue-collar workers and rugged peasants can be reconciled with the true aristocrat's affinity to the "real" people as opposed to the snobbishness of social parasites.

The landscape of his body provided the model for his *teatrum mundi:* the World as death and performance; a rotting stage, dressed from the prop room of history in the anachronistic splendor of the emperor's old clothes.

CHAPTER FIVE

Fatherland/Mother's Body

Land of mountains, land by the river,
Land of fields, land of spires . . .
Homeland are you to great sons.

— National anthem of the Second Austrian Republic

Doctor, did you ever see your mother laughing? No, you never saw
her laughing. And has your son seen his mother laughing? No, he
never saw her laughing.

— Thomas Bernhard, *Gargoyles*

MOST OF BERNHARD'S SELF-SELECTED KIN live in the vicinity of his
farm in the state of Upper Austria. It is the quintessential Austrian landscape,
with perfectly tended wheat fields and pastures, neatly fitted between the
slopes that yield to rough majestic mountain ranges. Chestnut-lined roads lead
to the castles on the peaks and the farmhouses below. The topography still
reflects the old feudal hierarchy in the ancient heartland of Austria, midway between Vienna and Salzburg. It is saturated with history. In 996 Upper Austria
and what is now the state of Lower Austria became the medieval Babenberg
margravate of Ostarrîci, which became the Habsburg archduchy of Österreich, which constituted the core of the Habsburg lands, which expanded into
the Austro-Hungarian Empire.

With the acquisition of his farmhouse in Upper Austria as a center of
permanence, Bernhard planted himself as close to "origin" as he could get.
Whether as rough "farmer at Nathal" or refined recluse, he went on to stage
himself in the landscape, while in his writing he reconstructed the myths of
its history. Many of Bernhard's selective family stand-ins are the descendants
of those up on the hill, the Sauraus, the O'Donnells, the heirs of Wolfsegg

castle, the Wittgensteins. Their names also enter his books. There they become strangely disembodied signs that evoke not faces and characters but the
unspoken dramas of their history inscribed in the land. The landscapes are
not visualized in images but staked out in names: Ungenach, Aurach, Södingbach, Stillwoll, Knobelberg, Gratwein, Puschachsee, Puschachtal. . . . They
are the names of real villages, mountains, and forests, drained of all sentimental notions of *Heimat*. What's in a name? Darkly threatening vowels drowned
out in guttural consonants, a topography etched deep in the collective unconscious, whence they emerge as the ghosts of history.

In popular lore these are enchanted landscapes: mountains peopled by
medieval princes, castles sunk into lakes, forests haunted by witches and gob-
lins. For the three-year-old Bernhard, Lake Wallersee, where he lived with his
grandparents, was a "completely unsolved mystery and lay at the centre of numerous fairy tale stories which my grandfather made up specially for me just
before bedtime."[1] To the child growing up after World War II it was also a
landscape riddled with unexploded grenades, lacerated by bomb craters, and
haunted by overheard stories of wartime hiding places, women and children
on the run, escaping soldiers, rape and mutilations.

In Bernhard's archaeology of madness, the traces of imperial masters
and subjects become the stuff of disenchanted fairy tales. The lost princes and
ephemeral princesses, the sorcerers and old hags, wicked stepmothers and
abandoned children embedded in the geography inscribe their archetypal features in the pathology of the local people. In Bernhard's post-Freudian reading of the land, its names, like ciphers in a code, hold the key to archetypal
family constellations, acted out again and again under the spell of *Herkunft*.

Amras, Thomas Bernhard's second major prose work, published in 1964,
takes its inspiration from the Habsburg castle of Ambras, the historic landmark of the village of Amras, on the outskirts of Innsbruck, the Tyrolian capital.[2] Bernhard's Amras is also a suburb of Innsbruck, but the castle is reduced
to a tower. It serves as a last refuge and a temporary quarantine for two brothers,
aged twenty and twenty-one, one an epileptic, the other mentally disturbed.
Their maternal uncle, the owner of the tower, put them up there after the
death of their parents by overdose of sleeping pills in what was to have been
a family suicide. The troubled survivors of their parents' suicide plot are the
postimperial variants of the old folk song's *zwei Königskinder,* two royal children, doomed by their secret passion. The family suicide was intended to end
once and for all the long family history of epilepsy, passed on from the mother

to the younger son, who eventually jumps to his death from the tower. His older brother, as narrator and last survivor, chronicles the story in a mental institution. His disjointed presentation reveals a brilliant mind holding on to moments of inspired lucidity as he heads into darkness and finally extinction.

Ostensibly the contemporary tale of two brothers, the tragic survivors of attempted suicide, it is also Bernhard's first foray into Habsburg mythology. Although the castle and imperial grounds from which the story takes its title seem excised together with the *b* from "Ambras," the geography and history are all the more accurately encapsulated in the amputated letter. They are the phantom presences that permeate the story of the gradual decline and abrupt extinction of a distinguished patrician family. The Habsburgs' acquisition of the castle and their indebtedness to its successive lienholders resonate in Bernhard's account of the gradual loss of the family estate that once surrounded the tower of Amras. The land had to be sold to cover the expenses of the mother's illness and her physician husband's antiquated aristocratic lifestyle and to compensate for his financial incompetence.

Heimat III. An Excursion

1. The Castle

The original fortress that preceded the castle of Ambras dates back to the eleventh century. In the course of its long history, it was destroyed in a war between German dukes, rebuilt, remodeled, and expanded according to the tastes of its owners. The Habsburgs moved in when they acquired the Tyrol in the fourteenth century. Emperor Maximilian I, "the last knight," made it his hunting residence. In the sixteenth century it was redesigned as a jewel of Renaissance architecture. During the eighteenth century it served as barracks and field hospital and was ransacked, set afire, and eventually occupied by French-Bavarian forces during the Napoleonic Wars. In the nineteenth century it was reconstructed in the then-fashionable neo-Gothic style. Archduke Franz Ferdinand had begun to restore its sixteenth-century look when his assassination in Sarajevo aborted his plans and set off World War I. After World War II the castle was restored to its Renaissance design.

It was during the Renaissance that Ambras achieved its architectural distinction and romantic gloss, thanks to Archduke Ferdinand II (1529–95). The second-born son of Emperor Ferdinand became archduke of Tyrol after his father's death. He made Ambras and the grounds a gift to his morganatic wife, Philippine Welser, and their two sons. As a commoner she was not recognized as a member of the imperial household and her children were not in the line of succession to the crown. After Philippine's death Duke Ferdinand married his cousin and thus continued the time-honored Habsburg tradition of incestuous procreation. As their only child was a daughter, his branch of the Habsburg dynasty died out. The motif of the extinction of a distinguished family line, so deeply embedded in the history of Ambras, was not lost on Bernhard.

Philippine's recipes and descriptions of medicinal herbs are exhibited in the castle along with her cutlery. Bernhard appropriated "the knife of Philippine Welser" as a Freudian prop in his tale of extinction. Duke Ferdinand became famous for his *Kunst- und Wunderkammer,* his chamber of artistic and natural curiosities—stones, fossils, amber, artifacts carved from coral and ebony, artworks that depict the grotesque in humans and nature. It is tempting to envision the young Thomas Bernhard in these galleries. The collection suggests the grotesque visions in the tortured minds of many of his characters, if not some of their physical deformities.

One painting, *The Court Cripple,* shows a bearded man lying on his stomach, face turned to the observer, his thin hands parallel to his body, his emaciated arms and legs twisted outward at elbows and knees. Next to *The Court Cripple* are *The Hairy Man Petrus Gonsalvus from Teneriffa* and several smaller paintings of his children. Posing formally in darkly exquisite court costumes, they have the quietly menacing, fuzzy features of mythical forest creatures. The court giant and court dwarf stand next to each other on another large canvas. Above the portrait of Count Vlad, better known as Dracula, hangs the gruesome portrait of a knight, Gregor Baci, a heavy pole piercing his partly shaved skull from the right eye through the back of his neck. The mesmerizing horror of the archduke's Renaissance freak show resurfaces in Bernhard's scenarios of physical and mental decay. Across the hall from the portrait gallery, a small statuette called *Little Death* poses seductively in a graceful dance step. The delicate skeleton is covered by a tattered Harlequin-like suit, one arm curved above the head with several bows in his hand, his body angled slightly toward his lowered arm, which holds the bow. Death as Cupid and clown: Freudian perception draws from a long tradition. The dancing skeleton is emblematic of the brothers' macabre dance of death in Bernhard's tower of Amras.

A large hall is lined with the armor not only of knights but of giants, dwarfs, and children, like iron husks of the people transformed into oil on canvas in the portrait gallery.

The archduke's collection is displayed in its original layout in the so-called Lower Castle. More recent portrait galleries in the Upper Castle feature members of the Habsburg dynasty from its earliest days: emperors, kings and queens, archdukes flanked by hunting dogs, duchesses and cardinals, nuns and children line the whitewashed walls of adjoining rooms strung along a perfectly centered row of carved doors, open to permit an unimpeded flow of light. Portrait after portrait depicts an unsmiling narrow face flattened in the two-dimensionality of royal authority, the subjects' kinship marked through centuries by what has become known as the "Habsburg lip"—the lower lip thrust forward by a protruding jaw. The line-up of so many Habsburg faces that are instantly recognizable by their mouths eerily reinforces Bernhard's obsession with hereditary traits. In his Austria, they can always be traced back to the legacy of the imperial family.[3] The narrator of *Amras* studied cell biology and genetics. His younger brother, Walter, inherited his mother's epilepsy.

Within the walled grounds of Ambras the model for Bernhard's tower is surprisingly small, about 10 meters (30 feet) high. Rather than the imagined residential or dungeon-like structure, it is a covered staircase to the top of the wall. Approached from the city, it can be seen precariously perched on the edge of a steep cliff that drops sharply into a gorge far below. From that side of the tower one has a splendid view of Innsbruck, squeezed between the mountains and ravines far down on the valley floor. Echoes of rapids and of water plunging over granite rocks are carried on the damp, dark waves of windswept evergreens. The thickly forested slopes encircling the cultivated castle park and gardens were once a game preserve for royal hunts. In these surroundings the tower appears as delicate as its fictitious inmate's health, the perfect metaphor for his suicide as well as its actual site.

2. The Tower

The tower as a fortress housing the mentally ill occupies a central position in the Austrians' collective imagination as the so-called Narrenturm, in popular idiom "tower of nuts." It is one of Vienna's controversial historical sights. The Narrenturm was the brainchild of Joseph II, whose portrait hangs in Bernhard's house. The emperor personally participated in the design of Austria's first modern, consolidated hospital complex, the Allgemeine Krankenhaus (General Hospital), and paid for its construction from his private funds. Opened in 1784, the Narrenturm, a six-story, perfectly cylindrical structure, was one of the innovative elements of the complex, conceived to "remove . . . from society and out of sight of its human members" those of Joseph's subjects who caused "damage or disgust"—that is, the "insane and those afflicted with cancers and similar damages"—to a "distant hospital."[4] The Viennese soon dubbed it the *Gugelhupf,* after one of their traditional pastries, a kind of pound cake with a similar shape and also "filled with nuts." The name survives in the expression "getting oneself into the *Gugelhupf*"—going nuts. The Narrenturm was closed in 1861 after a visit by Kaiser Franz Joseph, who was so scandalized that he instigated the development of a new mental institution, which would eventually lead to the establishment of Steinhof.

Since 1971 the Narrenturm has been a controversial museum housing the pathological collection of the University of Vienna's school of medicine. Its circular galleries display the skulls of criminals, fetuses, hydrocephalic infants, and other sensations, among them the skeleton of a midget with an oversized skull dubbed "the little princess." It is said that items are regularly stolen. To some observers the Narrenturm is the most telling monument to an imperial legacy that encompasses the bizarre as well as the majestic.

Also thanks to the Habsburg legacy, Vienna is home to one of the most poignant representations of the insanity of human ambition expressed in the construction of a tower: Pieter Bruegel the Elder's painting *The Tower of Babel.* Flanders was part of the Habsburg Empire's Spanish Netherlands in the sixteenth century. The Bruegel family ran a flourishing artistic enterprise and sold many paintings to the Imperial court. The focal point of the Kunsthistorisches Museum's Bruegel hall, *The Tower of Babel* has become part of the city's geography, a site to be visited and revisited to contemplate human genius and megalomania and the ensuing confusion of languages. It is the perfect backdrop if not source of inspiration for the linguistic obsessions of Austrian philosophers, most prominently Ludwig Wittgenstein and the writers he influenced, among them Thomas Bernhard.

The idea of the tower as defense, refuge, and megalomaniacal delusion returns in Bernhard's 1976 novel *Correction.* There it informs the concept of the cone-shaped edifice that Rothaimer, the Wittgenstein-inspired architect and thinker, builds as a home for his beloved sister in the center of one of Austria's thickest, darkest forests. Ironically, the construction of the cone that had been conceived as the representation of perfection turns out to be the perfect representation of mental disintegration.

When Bernhard underwent surgery for a lung tumor at the Baumgartner-höhe sanitarium in the Steinhof compound in the summer of 1967, the site and the timing couldn't have been more Bernhardesque. If it hadn't happened that way, he would have had to invent it. He had just finished his novel *Gargoyles*. Steinhof, Vienna's legendary institution, was the perfect setting to round out the staging of Prince Saurau, the novel's mad prince, whose obsessive monologues dominate its second half (115 pages in German), making him the show-stopping forerunner of the monomaniacal speakers in Bernhard's later plays.

Gargoyles was the first novel Bernhard wrote after he bought his farmhouse. As narrated by a twenty-one-year-old mining student who accompanies his father, a rural doctor in the hinterlands of Styria, on his round of house calls, it has all the stuff of a fairy tale. The journey of father and son takes them deep into the woods, through remote villages and past isolated dwellings, along gorges and ravines to their final climb to the castle of Hochgobernitz. The names of the places along their route evoke its nightmarish atmosphere: Södingbach, Stiwoll, Knobelberg, Gleinalpe, Gratwein, Holzöster, Übelbach, Ligist, Unzmarkt, Oberwölz, Krimml, Krottendorf, Römaskogel, Bundscheck, Hauenstein, Hüllberg, Puschachtal, Wölkerkogel, Rachau. These are strange-sounding compounds of familiar and archaic nouns and names. They lead the reader with childhood roots in Austria into a disquieting world on the edge between legend and history, between myth and memory. They are the remembered road signs passed on family trips across the country, signs that led to hidden places with unspoken secrets. They also recall hikes and play among the ruins of medieval forts and renovated castles atop ridges and mountains said to enshrine hexed princes, legions of dwarfs, evil rulers and their noble victims, the true emperors, dukes, counts, and maidens from the many-branched family trees of Austria's oldest ruling dynasties.

The geography of *Gargoyles* is a composite of various Austrian landscapes. It is peopled by menacing peasants, devious sons, rebel sons, dying sons, and mothers long dead, brought to a climax in an encounter with a doomed prince in his cursed castle high up on a mountaintop. Geological and cultural landmarks are redistributed and endowed with the shattered myths of decaying archetypes born of the experience of war and annihilation in the rubble of a morally and physically collapsed culture.

The doctor's earliest calls that day, while his son was still sleeping, were at 2 A.M. The first involved a twenty-six-year-old former teacher who was dying in his parents' house. His incestuous childhood trauma has the trappings of a classic fairy tale:

> Once when he was a boy, his grandmother had taken him along into the deep woods to pick blackberries. They lost their way completely, wandered for hours, and could not find the way out of the woods. Darkness fell, and still they had not found the path. They kept going in the wrong direction all the time. Finally, grandmother and grandson curled up in a hollow, and lying pressed close together, survived the night. They were lost all the next day and spent another night in another refuge. Not until the afternoon of the second day did they suddenly emerge from the woods, only to find they had all along gone in a direction opposite from that of their home. Totally exhausted, they had struggled on to the nearest farmhouse.
>
> This ordeal had quickly brought about the grandmother's death. And her grandson, not yet six, had had his entire future ruined by it, my father said.[5]

There is no "happily ever after" to the story this father tells his son:

> . . . in the Obdach grammar school there had been a scandal over the teacher's relations with a nervous boy, and the poor fellow had to leave his post. He sought refuge in the Tyrol, then in Italy, and finally in Slovenia. For two full years, the man had lived like an outlaw, moving among people of foreign speech and subsisting mostly on small thefts. Then he had suddenly come back across the frontier, totally deranged, and had given himself up to justice. He was quickly brought to trial, and the court in Brock sentenced him to two years in jail and two additional years in a milder house of correction. He served his sentence in Garsten.[6] Released, . . . the teacher returned to his parents, who owned a small farm in Salla and who had nursed him lovingly. "Of course you could say that the teacher died of heart disease, of a so-called cardiac rupture—you could make it that simple," my father said. "But it wasn't that."

In the dying teacher's face my father had clearly seen, he said, a man's accusation against a world that refused to understand him. (54)

The teacher's unsettling early death doesn't violate the world of German fairy tales. They never promise that their young heroes (and readers) will live "happily ever after." Rather, they conclude with the laconic mantra: "and if they didn't die, they are still alive today." It is intriguing to speculate that the difference between Anglo-Saxon optimism and Teutonic gloom might thereby hang on the closing line of a fairy tale.

As in a fairy tale, there is a touch of magic: a chestnut tree blooms in September. The doctor wanted to show it to his visiting son first thing in the morning, but their day together begins with the fatal bludgeoning of the local innkeeper's wife by one of the patrons, a drunken mineworker.

On their baroquely Kafkaesque journey to the castle, father and son stop at the home of Bloch, a Jewish real estate broker and patient of the doctor, to return some books by Kant and Marx and exchange them for some works by Diderot and Nietzsche. Bloch, whose father was "murdered by the Germans," is the only Jew in town. There is a resident physician in the town, "but Bloch had relieved this doctor of the lasting shame of having to treat a Jew, which Bloch was, by consulting my father," reports the son. A friendship developed that had, according to the father, "something philosophical about it." The two of them "conducted 'autopsies on the body of nature' as well as 'on the body of the world and its history.'"

Bloch, the victim of anti-Semitism, the pragmatic sage at the edge of the forest, is also a shrewd businessman whose dealings may sooner or later jeopardize the forest. After two years of negotiations, he has just purchased extensive farmland, which he intends to divide into more than a hundred lots for development. "*Naturally* I'm not liked," he concludes his story (20–22). Like the riddle in the fairy tale, the comment in its cryptic brevity is brimming with ambiguities. Cutting up farmland for commercial purposes is distasteful to the community for ecological and cultural reasons. These objections feed into the anti-Semitism that still pollutes the environment. The author himself doesn't seem to be immune to it. The perception of the Jew as insular Shylock figure persists. But Bloch's unsentimental business acumen also invites comparison with the doctor's task of cutting and draining the focus of infection: the ancient fertile lands that carry the historic disease. Perhaps it is their ability to cut to the bone, so to speak, that adds "something philosophical" to their friendship.

The doctor's route takes father and son deeper into the forest, to the hunting lodge of an industrialist, who lives there in the most radical isolation, in an incestuous relationship with his half sister, who appears and disappears in ghostlike silence after she has let them in. In his obsessively stripped-down lifestyle this mad thinker in his emptied space is the forerunner of many Bernhard characters inspired by Wittgenstein. "The house certainly gave the impression of being inhabited solely by the industrialist and his half sister. It felt as if no other soul had entered it for decades. It was not, as such hunting lodges usually are, filled with hunting gear, but was almost empty. . . . No pictures on the wall, not a picture in the whole house. The industrialist said he hated pictures. He wanted everything as empty as possible, as bare as possible" (44). Such descriptions fueled the rumors that soon began to circulate through Vienna's coffeehouses and theater bars about Bernhard's reclusive lifestyle in the backwoods and added to his reputation as a weird, hostile loner. To guard himself against any distraction the industrialist planted "everywhere, hidden in the woods . . . unemployed millers, miners, and retired woodsmen as guards whose task was to keep people from disturbing him." Finally, "in order to have nothing around that might interfere with his work, . . . he had ordered destroyed 'the last real distraction I have had in Hauenstein.' He had ordered all the game that still remained in the forests to be shot, collected, and distributed preferably to 'the poorest people' in the whole vicinity" (50–51).

To reach Bernhard's hard-to-find house from the picturesque town of Gmunden, one had to drive or walk through patches of forest and be prepared to be locked out. Sometimes the wide gates would be open and Bernhard's green Mercedes visible in the converted garage wing. A single first-story window would also be left open a crack for mail and messages. Otherwise, the all-pervasive silence would be interrupted at best by the grunt of a pig in the neighboring farmer's barn. All the same, the hopeful visitor/voyeur's already aroused imagination couldn't help the sensation that someone was watching from inside.

According to the doctor, the industrialist's sister began to show signs of insanity, "a madness rooted deep in clericalism," as soon as they moved into their secluded house. The father notices in her "the withdrawn look characteristic of women in insane asylums." Subject to her brother's control, "in her extreme loneliness she was always close to the point of taking her own life" (47).

Bernhard's half sister suffered from what were then termed nervous breakdowns. She talks about her growing years, when she was completely ignored by the men in the family, her father, brother, stepbrother, and grandfather Freumbichler, as they sat around the kitchen table absorbed in conversation. "I didn't count," she says matter-of-factly.[7]

Silent women and/or women silenced by death haunt the countryside of *Gargoyles,* as in future Bernhard works. As in the fairy tale, the real mother is dead. Both the doctor's and the prince's son have lost their mothers when they were young. While the bizarre scenarios of the patients' living conditions in remote corners of Austria's countryside dominate the narrative, only a few cues to the cause of the sudden death of the doctor's wife less than three years earlier are scattered, ever so fleetingly, throughout the journey of father and son. One has to read very attentively to pick up the thread of her story.

Although it is never articulated, the mother presumably killed herself. According to the father, his daughter takes after her mother: "As for my sister, he'd been noticing things in her that were just like my mother, psychological and physical things. From day to day these elements grew stronger, her character more and more resembling our mother's. . . . Her moods changed rapidly; she was constantly in danger, completely subject to her nervous system. She had been isolating herself from us more and more, withdrawing into herself. . . . It is not improbable, my father said, that her psychic illness is more and more affecting her organic state. 'I am always frightened for her'" (36–37).

The doctor medicalizes his daughter's path to suicide the way he analyzed his wife's. The problems of the women in his family become a professional rather than a personal issue that defers the nagging question of accountability. In a letter the narrator wrote to his father a few days before his visit, he asked "who was to blame for my sister's most recent attempt at suicide, or for my mother's early death" (19). His father never mentions the letter. The narrator had planned to spend the day with his sister. He joined his father instead.

Later on their journey he recalls the bandage that still circles his sister's wrist. His father remarks that "a weekend was too short a time for me to be home from Leoben. . . . We never got around to having a real talk. He himself, he said, could not have a good influence on my sister, but possibly I could." It occurs to the narrator that "quite independently from one another, both of us had been thinking about my sister" (57–58).

They both started to think about her while they were driving through a narrow gorge that led to their next stop, a mill in the depth of its forbidding darkness. The absent bodies of the women reenter the narrative in the sexualized topography of the landscape.

At the mill, father and son come upon the scene of a bizarre castration ritual. "At first I saw nothing in the outbuilding," the doctor's son recalls.

But then, when I had become adjusted to the darkness and the curious smell, the smell of flesh, I saw lying on a long board across a pair of saw horses a heap of dead birds. They were from the aviary, I saw at once, the finest exotic birds. The beautiful color nauseated me. These slaughtered birds were in fact the most beautiful specimens from the cage, and I turned around to the miller's son with a questioning look.

All three of them, he said, he himself, his brother, and the new young Turk who had been working in the mill only for a few days, had gone to the cage first thing in the morning, even before sunrise (But a sunrise in this gorge is impossible! I thought). They'd taken half of the birds, the finest first, and killed them with as little damage as possible to their precious plumage. How? They had wound the birds' necks rapidly around their index fingers several times and squeezed the heads. I counted forty-two birds all together. After they were through with the day's work, they were going to finish off the rest, the miller's son said. His uncle, he said, had started raising birds about twenty years ago and lived only for those birds. He had died three weeks ago, and the birds had begun raising a terrible racket. It was driving them half crazy. . . . So yesterday their father had told them they could finish off the birds, to shut them up. They had done a lot of thinking about the mode of execution, and finally hit on the idea of not chopping off their heads like chickens, but doing it so there would be no sign of outward damage. That way they wouldn't have to part with the birds. . . . They intended to stuff the birds themselves and fill a whole room, their dead uncle's room, with them. (62–63)

Traditionally the mill is a storybook emblem for rural serenity. Bernhard comes closer to the European imagination in the Middle Ages. Millers, who by necessity lived outside the village community, were considered seducers, murderers, and sorcerers. In any case, they played an important role in the landed gentry's economy. This mill, too, had once been owned by the Sauraus. In addition, Schubert's song cycle *Die schöne Müllerin* resonates in the collective memory. Given Bernhard's passion for music and infantile jokes, it is not unlikely that the beautiful miller's daughter played her part in the inspiration for this garish scenario, together with Mozart's bird catcher Papageno in

Bernhard's favorite opera, *The Magic Flute*. Lost in English is the association between the German *Vögel*, bird, and the vernacular *vögeln*, to fuck.

After they left this Grand Guignol of castration panic, father and son "drove deep into the gorge. At its end, where it was darkest, my father said, we would have to leave the car and walk up to the castle" (65). On the way, the son remembers the scene they left. When the miller's sons started to kill the birds, "because it hadn't entered their minds how brutal it was, they had laid the first corpses right in front of the birdcage, where the other birds could see them, and these first they had killed simply by squeezing their throats, which caused blood to spurt out. But then one of them thought to wind the birds' necks around the finger and break the spine; and for that they went behind the cage. . . . You could hear the backbone breaking under the head" (70).

Still in the car, the narrator tries in vain to strike up a conversation with his inattentive father about his mining studies in Leoben. Then, fleetingly, his sister enters his mind again. "My silence is the opposite of my sister's. . . . For a moment I thought: You intended to spend the day with your sister" (72).

Shortly thereafter, they park their car beside a waterfall. In order to reach the castle, father and son have to climb out of the gorge on a hazardous footpath up a steep rock. They meet the prince at the inner wall of the castle, where he resides with his two sisters and two daughters. His son studies in Cambridge. Outer and inner walls protect the—predominantly female—inhabitants like monumental medieval chastity belts. The intruders who have left the womb of the gorge ascend along an appropriately phallic cliff to the last of the imperial *Über*-fathers.

In the prince's long monologues, his female relatives are silent, spectral presences. They do not physically enter the encounter with the doctor and his son. Like ghosts they appear and disappear in the prince's narrative: they cook, they organize the yearly theater presentation at the castle, and sit with their guests late into the night. The older sister accompanies her brother on his walks through the forest. Sometimes the prince reads to them—not, as planned, from demanding literature such as Goethe's *Elective Affinities* but from an old London *Times*. Later he reads Goethe by himself, "defeminized" (154).[8] They have no language of their own and the prince invests no thoughts in them aside from fleeting remarks about their daily routines. Irritating as they may be in their traditional functions, he depends on them, most of all as the audience for his narcissistic self-performances.

Like the doctor's wife, the prince's wife must have died young. He can still hear her speak, although he cannot see her. Female physicality is transferred to the landscape: both the prince and the doctor recall the recent flooding of the valley below the castle. The father describes the scene in images that evoke a catastrophic stillbirth: "The whole region was afflicted by a mild but 'insidious' smell of decaying cadavers — on both banks of the Ache a great many drowned cattle had been wedged against houses and trees, torn open, bloated, some 'dismembered by the power of the water' (my father), and many head of livestock from the Saurau barns in the valley had not yet been cleared away" (104).

When the flood receded, workers on both riverbanks were busy "dragging wood and corpses out of the water" (105). The German term for "flood" are *Flut* (flood) and *Hochwasser* (high water). The words that stand out are "flood" and "water." By association, the sound of *Flutwasser* (floodwater) evokes *Fruchtwasser* (amniotic fluid). The maternal body, associated with nature, is the site of death and destruction. Decay in nature is reflected in human disease. It is the maternal body that carries and passes on the disease.

Here Bernhard continues an antiquated medical notion that was conspicuously exploited by the Nazis and stubbornly persists in the cultural stereotypes of his time. In *Amras*, the mother's epilepsy was passed on to one of her sons. The family suicide pact was a radical attempt to discontinue the maternal hereditary material. In both works, the pathologized, absent female body is inscribed in the landscape. In the prince's worst nightmare, his anarchist son is out to destroy the family estate. He wants to "let the harvest rot . . . to let Hochgobernitz decay, to liquidate Hochgobernitz" (134). By letting the harvest rot he would let his "paternal inheritance run down and be destroyed." The paternal inheritance is the diseased female body that's inscribed in the farmland. The extinction of the rotting crops on the ancestral estate would accomplish the extinction of all hereditary diseases embedded in the landscape. The German *Erbgut*, inheritance, applies to both genetic inheritance and property. The prince's sisters and daughters are unmarried. The extinction of the line is covered on all fronts.

Saurau dreams that his extinction as a suicide is scripted by his renegade student son on a sheet of paper "moving slowly from far below to high up, paper on which my own son had written the following." The paper becomes the phallic instrument of patricide committed through the act of writing and staged as a suicide: "I see every word that my son is writing on that sheet of paper," the prince said. "It is my son's handwriting it. My son writes: . . . Eight months after my father's suicide—note that, Doctor, after his father's suicide, after my suicide; my son writes about my suicide!—eight months after my father's suicide everything is already ruined, and I can say that I have ruined it. I can say that I have ruined Hochgobernitz" (125).

The ferociously Freudian send-up of symbols is characteristic of Bernhard's blend of shtick with angst as a way to exorcise demons. But they keep returning with the repetitiousness of a comedy routine and the inevitability of tragedy.

Suicide continues to loom large in the immediate future of the narrator's sister, who takes after her mother. Her brother "had never even thought of taking [his] life." He is saved for a while by the power of his writing, the Lacanian symbolic order shared by the men in his story.

The journey of father and son begins with the real murder of a woman. Its unspoken subtext is the symbolic murder of a young girl: The sister's voice is excluded from her brother's writing, her (self-)mutilated body inscribed in the land. While driving through it with their father, the son finds his voice in the speech of the fathers.

Before the maternal body can be buried in the land it has to be destroyed for good, with all its products. The future must be extirpated, together with the past, with *Herkunft*. This was the project of *Amras*.

The project fails. Suicide as the ultimate delivery from the maternal body is aborted. The surviving sons are confined by their maternal uncle to the tower of Amras, the town's historic landmark. Located in the apple orchards that once belonged to the family, it is deeply embedded in their childhood memories as the site of seasonal family celebrations and the secret sanctuary for the boys' panicked encounter with their sexuality, "seeking refuge and finding refuge from nature's fury sodomizing us." [9]

A phallic symbol on the outside, the tower offers its interior as a substitute womb for the young men prematurely delivered from death. Locked up inside, they lose command of language. They revert to what Julia Kristeva calls the semiotic stage, the child's prelingual state, preceding the separation from the maternal body. The narrator's breathy writing is marked by elliptic sentence fragments. "Our way of talking was suddenly . . . choked, trampled into submission, panicked in fragmentary parts" (24).

Both lose interest in their intellectual pursuits: "In those weeks it seemed to us as if my natural sciences died on us along with the parents, as if they had committed suicide together with the parents . . . as if Walter's music had also been dead since then" (20).

The tower's interior evokes Plato's cave in Luce Irigaray's subversive scenario, where it is the excluded woman's womb, the site of men's captivity, the stage of their (symbolic) delusions and foreclosed desires.[10]

> Through the floors and walls we were closely connected to all of nature, that is to say through a double mental connection, not just through the air, to all of nature . . . we listened for hours at the shores . . . we heard a mixture of all kinds of languages, the miscellany of sounds filled our heads that were, at times, devoid of all flesh, of all blood . . . this is when we saw ourselves as two doubled mirror images of the universe . . . often we really were so high up in our contemplation of the stars that we shivered with cold, we *ourselves* the water, the rock.
>
> . . . Our temples pressed to the floors and walls we watched the rotation of millions of light-years, far away . . . conical tops, globular celestial bodies, the precise pliancy of mathematics. . . . (29–30) (T.B.'s ellipses)

With the disintegration of the symbolic order (*Sätzezerbröckelungen,* the crumbling of sentences), the younger brother's epilepsy breaks out again along with an even more pronounced and daily intensifying resemblance to his mother "physiognomically, also in his taciturnity, complexion, tone of voice, psychic reactions, bodily functions" (14).

Inside the phallic womb the younger brother begins to embody the absent mother. The intrusion of the maternal body, the origin of all sickness, cannot go unpunished.

> Often, when we knew that our souls, and even our brains had become numb to pain, we lacerated our bodies, with great agitation, here and there, chest, back, thighs and knee joints, also the palms of our hands and the backs of our heads, not each other's, but each on his own, in brotherly fashion, abandoned to the speed of our actions bursting from the first spring in our own nature . . . contrapuntally we banged our heads, ever more rhythmically, against all four walls . . . in the darkness, wantonly, with imploring laughter, guided by odors that is to say by our sores, holding on to nothing but air, that damned oxygenous stuff, we delighted in tearing apart our trousers and shirts . . . each on his own we were the de-

structive center of destruction . . . pathological in our differences . . . soon
we exhausted ourselves in our exaltations. (22–23)

Fraternal incest is enacted on the maternal body, which is destroyed in the
eroticized self-mutilation. The transgression is exorcised / exercised in effigy.
Their uncle provided them with straw mattresses to sleep on. "Recently we
always turned our straw mattresses inside out, aroused by the foul odor of their
bowels . . . we thoroughly took revenge on our diseased bodies and minds"
(23). The womb turned inside out is the sons' vengeance on their mother, the
origin of everything sick in (their) nature.

Even the tower's structure approximates Plato's cave: The young men's
living quarters are on the middle floor. With the shutters closed most of the
time, it is dark inside the tower. The only access to their cave is below them,
behind their backs. The tower is enclosed in yet another cave, the towering
sheets of Alpine rocks.

> Only rarely did we dare to go to the windows and push back the shutters:
> we looked, it seemed to us in the howling storm, at randomly crippled
> apple trees, into an oddly clamorous landscape deafened by its own dark-
> ness and natural riddles and mental collapse, populated—not really it
> seemed but only appearing to be—way down below, by human beings,
> down at the far border of the apple orchard where the circus had been, a
> defiant high alpine landscape unscathed by its strangeness, except maybe
> on some of its black and brown and occasionally white surfaces, a land-
> scape consisting solely of provincial, punishable actions, constantly stir-
> ring up trouble. (14–15)

What the brothers can make out in the shadowy gloom, far in the distance, is
a circus—a childhood world of magic performativity.

If the Alps close in the tower as a cave within a cave, the brothers are
trapped in yet another cave, inside their own heads, their *Kopfhöhlen*, skull
caves. The Latin *cava*, cave, is also a term for the Roman amphitheater. The site
of their enactment of primal obsessions and desires is elusive: a stage within a
stage within a stage in the all-encompassing theater of the womb that turns out
to be all of Austria. Bernhard appropriates his scenario from the Habsburgs'
hunting residence. The only tower there is surprisingly small. All that's left
in Bernhard's leftover Austria is a pathetically small structure, the metonym
for the castrated empire that serves as metaphor for the maternal body: the

Alpine womb enclosing the phallic cave enclosing Bernhard's *Kopftheater,* or theater, the *cava* of the head, the womb in the head. The historic question of origin merges with the trauma of birth, iterated again and again as self-birth through performance.

With *Amras,* as text and historic site, Bernhard set the Platonic stage for his panicked encounters with the feminine and its silencing, which generates his writing and performance.

With characteristic exaggeration of the obvious, Bernhard inserts a potent prop into his phallic cave: "the knife of Philippine Welser," a family heirloom that frightens the epileptic brother while the narrator uses it to cut the smoked meat that hung in the kitchen. The meat triggered in the brothers "a phantastic picture of killed military stuff, of dead asses and heels and heads and arms and legs dangling down from the darkness of the kitchen ceiling . . . a fiction, produced by our inborn amplifiers of horror, of corpses, of male corpses falling towards each other forever, rhythmically" (33–34).

Philippine Welser, the untitled wife of the emperor's son, played her part in the extinction of one branch of the Habsburg dynasty. Her two sons were cut off from the Habsburg line of succession. Her legacy is played out in the family suicide project of Bernhard's *Amras.* In his theater of the womb history is restaged as a castration nightmare with the graphic props of a post-Freudian farce.

Farcical elements keep asserting themselves against the Strindbergian marriage hell depicted in Bernhard's third novel, *The Lime Works.* It begins like a murder mystery. A crippled woman has been killed. All evidence points to her husband as the murderer. The ensuing narrative leads into an isolated world of sickness, gloom, psycho-terror, and codependence between an aging couple. By contrast, the details of the discovery of the woman's body and the murder suspect have all the ingredients of a *Bauernschwank,* a peasant farce — a genre that has a long tradition and enjoys great popularity in Vienna as well as in the hinterlands. For two days after the murder, Konrad, the suspect, had been hiding in a manure pit, where the police finally found him. He smelled so bad that they first took him home to change his clothes. He seized the opportunity to offer his captors several bottles of schnapps, which they gladly accepted. Because they were in a hurry, they had to take five or "maybe even six bottles" with them and polish them off on their way to jail, and the usual half-hour drive stretched into two and a half hours.

And when they finally got there, Konrad tumbled out of the wagon head first; with his handcuffs on he couldn't hold on to anything and maybe one of the officers pushed him a little, and him without any shoes on, all he had on his feet was a pair of felt socks, they say, because the police were in too big a hurry to give him a chance to put on a clean pair of shoes; as for the shoes he had on when they dragged him from the manure pit were so bloated with liquid manure that he couldn't possibly have gotten into them again, and they wouldn't give him time to get a fresh pair from his own room; it was, Wieser said, inhuman.[11]

Wieser is one of several names dropped by the narrator. They suggest the sources of his story, which is pieced together from rumors picked up in local taverns. In the ever-shifting perspectives the reader could easily overlook the fact that the narrator is an insurance salesman with a knack for engaging prospective customers in gossip, who recently sold Konrad a life insurance policy. Only a couple of hints are buried in the overall thrust of the narrative.

The handling of the dead woman's body creates complications for both the murder suspect and the police:

. . . at Laska's they say that Konrad had tried at first to drag the corpse out the upstairs vestibule, which has a window overlooking the water; like every man who has just killed someone, Konrad thought, says Wieser, that he could get rid of the victim, and the first thing that naturally occurred to him was to drag the body to that window and then, after weighing it with some good-sized object of iron or stone, as Fro thinks, simply drop it out the window. . . . Konrad soon realized that he could not drag the body to the window overlooking the water, because he simply did not have the strength, besides which it may have dawned on him that it would not make sense to throw the body into the water that way, because even a medium-bright flatfoot would soon have seen through so clumsy a way to dispose of the victim, as Wieser says; malefactors always began by thinking up the craziest ways to cover their tracks, and what could have been crazier in this case than to toss the Konrad woman out the window. So when Konrad had dragged her about midway he gave up the idea, possibly he decided at that point not to get rid of the body at all is Fro's guess, but in any case he dragged it right back, the blood pouring from it harder all the time, dragged it all the way back to her room and somehow he mustered the strength to prop her up in her chair again, as the police reconstructed what happened; they say Konrad admitted that his dead wife kept sliding through his arms to the wooden floor as he tried to get her back into the chair, it took him over an hour to get the heavy, lifeless woman's body that kept slipping down on him back into that chair. (8–9)

However garish the reality of the transaction, in the way it is related, through several stages of hearsay, it plays out as a slapstick routine. The lifeless heavy body recalls an old children's game, *Müller Müller Sackl* (miller's sack), preferably played at the edge of a lake or pool. One child plays dead, making herself as heavy as she can, and two others lift her by her arms and legs, swing her back and forth, and finally throw her sideways into the water.

The police officer has his problems with the sacklike body. "Reservist Moritz, incidentally, is said to have acted quite against regulations when he pulled the Konrad woman's body upright in the chair where it lay slumped forward, with her head ripped to pieces from the shot or shots from that carbine. . . . The reason Moritz straightened it out was that he was afraid its own shifting weight would send it suddenly slipping from the chair to the floor" (7–8).

Playing dead was one of Bernhard's favorite games. In his childhood he did it to scare and punish his mother. As an adult, about the time he wrote *The Lime Works,* he persuaded the Hennetmair "Omi" to act out entire funerary scenarios with him, with flowers, candles, the works. Given Hennetmair's business acumen and knack for gathering information on the road potentially useful for closing a deal, Bernhard's infamous real estate broker is not an unlikely inspiration for the insurance salesman–narrator. The limeworks actually did exist once, not far from Bernhard's farmhouse. There are no traces of it left. Hennetmair takes visiting Bernhard pilgrims to the site to show them "the limeworks that aren't there anymore."

Bernhard's limeworks, once a thriving business operated by Konrad's family, are abandoned save for the main building, where the murder took place. Konrad had to buy the property back from his conniving nephew, under the protest of his ailing wife, who hated the place. He remodeled it into a "dungeon"-like home to seal himself off from the world in order to complete his lifelong study on the sense of hearing, with his nearly paralyzed wife serving as the primary object for his experiments. This is where he hopes to commit to paper his life's work, which he has finished in his head.

The building is surrounded on three sides by rocks and water, which serve as acoustic screens for Konrad's auditory experiments. Only a "single stony path" leads to the entrance through thick shrubbery specially purchased in Switzerland to completely shield the fortress from sight. The site once again recalls Irigaray's savagely parodic restaging of Plato's cave. The dungeon-like home, a cave within a larger natural cavelike enclosure of rocks and water, is approachable by only one (vaginal) path.

> Whoever sees the place will turn around and take to his heels, whoever enters or visits will leave it and take to his heels. How often Konrad had observed a man come out from behind the thicket, look alarmed and turn back, it was always the same reaction, Konrad was supposed to have said; people step out of the thicket and instantly turn back, or else they step inside the limeworks and immediately come running out again. They always have a feeling of being watched, approaching a structure like the limeworks one always has a feeling of being watched. (8–9)

If the womb-cave attracts men who are not deterred by its forbidding exterior, they will be horrified by its interior. If they feel watched, it's not by a visible guard or Konrad, whom they presumably came to see, but by an invisible other inscribed in the (womblike) structure itself.

Rocks and water provide a natural echo chamber for this aged Narcissus. His auditory experiments on his ailing Echo consist of reciting sentences in her ear, a hundred times slowly, then a hundred times as fast as possible, choppily. The focus is not on the articulation of meaning but on the clarity of vowels. Nonsense sentences such as "In the Inn district it is still dim," for the drill of a given vowel, are familiar to every actor. Apparently those torturous speech exercises had a lasting effect on Bernhard, the former acting student. His aging Narcissus pours his sounds into yet another cave, his wife's head, through the ear's narrow passage, yet another representation of the birth canal, Konrad's lifelong obsession. When he is finished, he demands an immediate description of the effect his spoken sentences had on her ear and her brain: "He would alternate, for instance, between reciting the sentence . . . into her left ear, then into her right ear, then moving from one ear to the other and back again" (77–78). This could go on for hours on end. He learned to ignore her complaints about the length of the exercises and continued until she collapsed.

No wonder that the murdered woman's brains, spilled on the floor, reminded the attending magistrate "in texture and color of Emmenthaler cheese, says Wieser. Hoeller confirms this statement" (10).

Whether the comparison of the woman's brain to cheese highlights the gore of the scene or the prevailing attitude about the contents of a woman's head as it is passed on and confirmed by various male informants is up to the reader to decide, or rather to reveal about himself. In Bernhard's Platonic Grand Guignol the woman's brains had literally been hollowed out by her man's drills. They resulted in yet more replications of the cave that's come to resemble the holes in Swiss cheese.

The sounds reproduced by his wife were never to Konrad's satisfaction. Following Plato's dramaturgy, Konrad's aural inseminations resulted, predictably enough, in poor representations. The truth, Konrad's grand study, remained locked inside his own head.

The novel's final image is of one unable to give birth to himself: ". . . he had lacked what was perhaps the most important quality of all: fearlessness in the face of realization, of concretization, fearlessness simply, when it came to turning his head over, suddenly, from one moment to the next, ruthlessly flipping it over to drop everything inside his head onto the paper, all in one motion" (241).

The failed head birth that concludes the narrative reconnects to its opening, when Konrad, having murdered his wife, returns to a womb of sorts by hiding in the manure pit. Tasteless as it is, this panicked representation of the birth of a (male) mind through manure is an apt representation of the (male) imagination at work here and the place it belongs. In any event, the reported beer-hall gossip, the initial introduction of the female corpse as an unwieldy, blood-smeared dummy, foregrounds the disintegrating body of a woman in juxtaposition to the deteriorating mind of a man. His is the madness of a man caught up in the delusions inside Plato's feminized cave.

The way Konrad sets himself up in the remodeled limeworks allows no intrusion from the outside world. The surrounding landscape, unlike that of Bernhard's earlier works, never enters the narrative; the focus is exclusively on the interior, the cave, Konrad's birthplace, both real and reimagined as the site of his self-birth. In ironic contrast, all the information about the Konrads' domestic inferno is based on hearsay, constructed on the outside.

Horrifying as this living hell is, Bernhard delights in slipping in a few parodies of himself and his own experiences in remodeling his farmhouse, which also represented an ancient family property passed on through many generations. The first thing Konrad did after he acquired the place was to have all the doors bolted and all the windows barred: "I ripped out the ornamental ironwork and installed functional iron bars, he has been quoted as saying, those thick walls and the iron bars sunk into them instantly show that this is a prison" (15).

Although Bernhard did not rip out the ornamental ironwork from his windows and his house was clearly visible from the road, it was hard to find during his lifetime. (After his death directional signs went up.) Very few people outside his most intimate circle of friends had access to it. Often even the invited visitor found the forbidding black doors to the courtyard shut. A row of tightly closed shutters above the latticed first-story windows reinforced the aura of armored impenetrability. Journalists, admirers, and voyeurs would camp out in the vain hope of encountering the (in)famous genius. Accordingly, wild rumors about his lifestyle spread rapidly. All the rooms were said to be painted black and barely furnished. In *The Lime Works*, one of the informants is reported to have told about "a dream of Konrad's: in a sudden, not readily classifiable fit of insanity (catatonia) Konrad had taken to painting the whole interior black, from all the way under the roof to all the way downward, gradually, to the ground, using a mat black varnish" (212).

The gossipy structure of the novel has a performative function that works beyond the text: it is in the nature of rumors to spread and be transformed in the process. The dramaturgy of gossip continues outside the work and affects the construction of the writer himself.

The author of *The Lime Works* was perceived as a mean, enraged misanthrope, barricaded in his farmhouse, where he locked himself up in one room at a time, sexless, friendless, joyless, a shoe fetishist at best, with his documented minimum of fifty pairs of shoes, indulging in childish masturbatory performances such as those reported by his friend Paul Wittgenstein. From the beginning of his career, his prose had fed such visions.

Paul's claim to fame—a book of a thousand and some pages he said he had worked out in his head (which he never committed to paper but quoted at length)—must have contributed to Konrad's obsession.

Smaller details of Bernhard's own remodeling projects, from his preference for larch wood for the floors to a pigpen converted into a cider press, bespeak Bernhard's preoccupations as a self-styled gentleman farmer.

Other than his writing project, Konrad has good reason to barricade himself. He had been convicted several times for libelous comments about Austria and his fellow citizens. His isolation might prevent him from getting into
further trouble.

> ... he daily committed the error of expressing himself, of expressing opin-
> ions, of telling facts that always fitted the definition of a so-called libel
> of somebody; no matter what he said, he always turned out to have said
> something libelous, but strictly speaking, you might say that everything
> he could say about this weird country, with its extremes of inhumanity
> and irresponsibility all on the increase as they were, could be considered
> a so-called libel, entailing the highest probability of his being haled, in
> consequence, before an invariably prejudiced, biased court ... he was in
> perpetual danger of being denounced, slandered, charged and convicted,
> no matter what he might say or come out with. . . . (106)

Bernhard knew what he was talking about. By the time *The Lime Works*
was published he had scandalized Austria with similar actions. In 1968 he was
awarded the *Förderungspreis für Literatur,* the so-called Little State Prize for
promising writers, as opposed to the Great State Prize. which he never received. His acceptance speech caused an uproar. On paper, it reads more like
a dirge than an offensive provocation:

> One goes through life, impressed, unimpressed, through the scenery,
> everything is exchangeable, trained somewhat better or worse in this state
> of [stage] props: wrong! One understands: an oblivious nation, a beauti-
> ful country — these are dead or conscientiously unconscionable fathers,
> people with the simplicity or the baseness, the paucity of their needs. . . .
> It's all an acutely philosophical and unbearable prehistory. The epochs
> are dimwitted, the demonic in us is an ongoing patriotic dungeon, in
> which the elements of stupidity and ruthlessness have become our daily
> call of nature. The state is a product continuously doomed to fail, its
> people condemned to incessant infamy and feeblemindedness. . . .
>   . . . We are Austrians, we are apathetic; we are life as crass disinterest
> in life; in the process of nature we are megalomania, delusion of future.
> . . . Means toward the end, creatures of agony, we can explain everything
> and understand nothing. We populate a trauma, we are afraid, we have a

right to be afraid, we can see, if only dimly, way in the back: the giants of fear.[12]

Austria's minister of education and culture, Herr Dr. Theodor Piffl-Percevic, who was in charge of the ceremony, responded with a defiant exclamation: "Wir sind trotzdem stolze Österreicher!" (We're still proud Austrians!).[13] Adding an ironic twist to the minister's outraged patriotism was his recent contribution to the education of Austrian youth: it was he that caused a four-volume edition of the collected works of Max Mell, the early Hitler enthusiast, to be distributed as required reading for Austrian high school students.

In 1969 Bernhard was awarded the Anton Wildgans Prize by the Austrian Association of Industrialists. When it became known that for his acceptance speech Bernhard planned to deliver an extended version of his controversial acknowledgment of the Little State Prize, the award ceremony was canceled without explanation. Anton Wildgans was a minor figure (1881–1932) in German-language literature. The unpretentious Austrianness of his small world of ordinary people was honored (much to Robert Musil's ennui) by the cultural politicians of Austro-fascism and continues to be a source of traditionalist comfort. Nonetheless, in 1918, this beloved, quintessentially Austrian writer wrote to the publisher Karl Wolff:

> . . . you don't know what it means to want to live as an intellectual in Vienna and Austria, to want to be heard there. It makes you think you are locked up in a padded cell. You can scream all you want in there, you can turn somersaults. No sound comes through, not the slightest shadow of your movements reaches the outside. This city drowns in the banality of its popular songs, this city compromises all seriousness in the eyes of the world. There is no intellectual community in this city, only philistinism to promote what's half done, inferior, frivolous. . . . Talents shoot up like mushrooms, but only to be exported, if they don't want to perish at home. That's how it is in this country that's still loved more than anything else![14]

His letter may well serve as proof of Wildgans's Austrianness. Its sentiments put him in the company of some of the greatest local artists. The award of a literary prize in his name to Bernhard seems an inspired choice, perhaps more so than the jury realized.

CHAPTER SIX

Native Son

Is It a Comedy? Is It a Tragedy?

*It is extremely interesting to me not to know for once what's being
played. Is it a comedy? Is it a tragedy?*

— Thomas Bernhard, *"Is It a Comedy? Is It a Tragedy?"*

BERNHARD WAS ALREADY A WELL-ESTABLISHED writer before he
gained attention as a playwright. His first full-length play, *A Party for Boris,*
written in 1967, was produced and published in 1970. One story goes that in
1967 Bernhard had already shown the play to his old mentor from the *Demokratisches Volksblatt,* Josef Kaut, who was then the president of the Salzburg
Festival, in the hope that he would produce it there. He didn't. Then Bernhard offered it to the Burgtheater, which also rejected it. According to this
account, it was important to him that an Austrian theater—a major Austrian
theater, that is—produce the first full-length play of a major Austrian writer.[1]
The two rejections may explain why he finally wanted no Austrian to have
anything to do with it. Hermann Beil, later Bernhard's most trusted dramaturg, tried to get the play for his Austrian-born, enfant-terrible artistic director,
Hans Hollmann, who had just taken over the highly acclaimed Theater Basel
and was eager to mount the production. They were unaware that a young
up-and-coming German director, Claus Peymann, soon to become Beil's col-
laborator, had secured the rights from Bernhard's almighty publisher, Suhrkamp Verlag, for a world premiere in Hamburg a year later than Basel wanted
to do it. In the late 1960s Peymann had made his name premiering the first
plays of another Austrian, Peter Handke—*Offending the Audience; My Foot,
My Tutor;* and, most notably, *Kaspar*—as associate director of the innovative
Frankfurt Theater am Turm (TAT for short).[2] As Bernhard tells it, Peymann
found *A Party for Boris* in a pile of neglected plays in the dramaturgy office

at the Schauspielhaus Hamburg. His much praised production inaugurated a theatrical partnership that would have a profound impact not only on their individual careers but, arguably, on the profile of German-language theater in the following two decades.

Bernhard's work as a critic for the *Demokratisches Volksblatt* had provided him with on-the-job training in contemporary plays, and his court reporting had introduced him to dramas that unfolded outside the theater. The cultural events he covered outside the Festival season were fairly provincial in scope by the admittedly elitist if not utopian standards of cosmopolitan culture that prevailed then as they do now in Austria.

His legal bout with the artistic director of the Salzburg Landestheater in 1955 apparently ended his career in journalism and launched him into theater studies at the Mozarteum, which he finished in 1957 with a diploma in directing. Bernhard liked to say that he wrote his thesis on Antonin Artaud and Bertolt Brecht, and the information was passed on in early biographies. But in fact no thesis was required for directors at that time and no paper on the subject was preserved, although Bernhard may well have been assigned to write an essay for class.[3] Be that as it may, throughout his career Bernhard dropped names to suggest intellectual pedigrees for himself and his characters. In this case he projected himself as heir to the polarity of approaches that defined the theater in the first half of the century. On a less calculating note, the fib highlights areas of interest and influence that can be traced as they emerge and are then rejected in the development of both his fiction and his dramatic work.

Bernhard was not an outstanding student at the Mozarteum. He fared best in his elective singing classes. In his first year he was given few opportunities to appear onstage. He was too shy to ask for parts but protested vehemently when he didn't get them. In his second year he gained attention as an old sorcerer in a Christmas play for children written by one of Bernhard's few friends among his fellow students, Klaus Gmeiner, who went on to become a director and head of the literary program of Radio Salzburg. Today Gmeiner remembers his classmate as a consummate performer. Yet a member of his play's cast, Hedda Parson, has no recollection of Thomas Bernhard in the production. According to Sybille Dahms, who often worked on scenes with him, the roles he landed most frequently where scurrilous old men.[4] His contemporaries agree that his outstanding strengths were his sonorous speaking voice and rhetorical skills, which he applied most successfully in the role of

Thomas Bernhard with his mother

Thomas Bernhard and his stepfather waiting for his brother to be born

Thomas Bernhard and his grandfather Johannes Freumbichler

Thomas Bernhard and his grandmother Anna Bernhard.
(bottom) Salzburg Cathedral after the Allied bombing of October 16, 1944

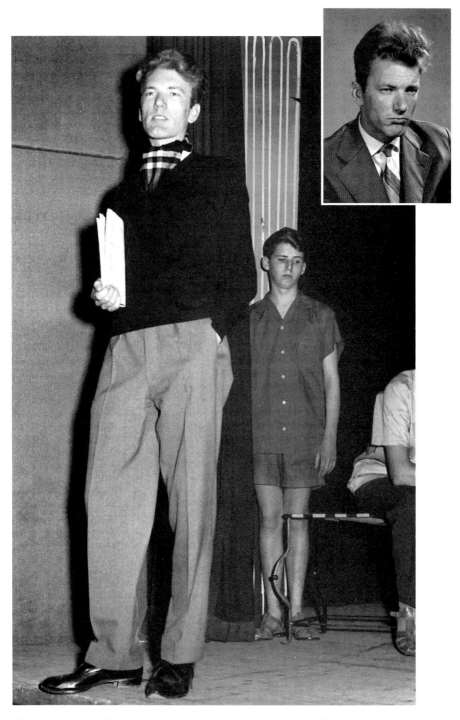

Thomas Bernhard in the Mozarteum production of Jean Anouilh's *Antigone*, 1957.
(inset) Thomas Bernhard in 1957

Thomas Bernhard as sorcerer/magician in the Mozarteum production of Klaus
Gmeiner's *Enchanted Forest*, 1956

Mount Heukareck: view from the Grafenhof sanitarium

Contemporary view of the Festspielhaus and Salzburg Cathedral from the Mönchsberg
(at the time Bernhard described it in his memoirs, the festival stage was not roofed)

Bernhard's farmhouse in Obernathal

(top) *A Party for Boris,* Hamburg Schauspielhaus, 1970: Angela Schmid as Johanna and Judith Holzmeister as the Good Woman

(bottom) *The Ignoramus and the Madman,* Salzburg Festival, 1972: (*left to right*) Bruno Ganz as Doctor, Angela Schmid as Queen of the Night, Maria Singer as Frau Vargo, and Ulrich Wildgruber as Father

Force of Habit, Salzburg Festival, 1974: Bernhard Minetti as Caribaldi and Anita Lochner as Granddaughter

The Hunting Party, Vienna Burgtheater, 1975: Klaus Höring

Bernhard Minetti in *Minetti,* Staatstheater Stuttgart, 1976

Immanuel Kant, Staatstheater Stuttgart, 1978: Peter Sattmann (*left*) as Kant and
Traugott Buhre as Ernst Ludwig

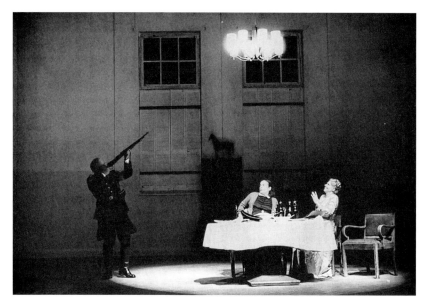

Eve of Retirement, Staatstheater Stuttgart: (*left to right*) Traugott Buhre as Rudolf, Kirsten Dene as Clara, and Eleonore Zetzsche as Vera

Bernhard Minetti in *Der Weltverbesserer,* Bochum, 1980

Thomas Bernhard in Ohlsdorf, 1981

Thomas Bernhard and Hedwig Stavianicek in Ohlsdorf

Thomas Bernhard and Hedwig Stavianicek in Ohlsdorf, 1967

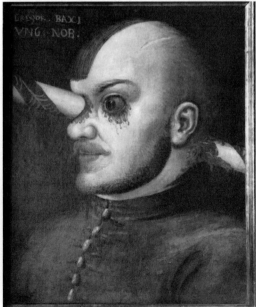

(top) *The Court Cripple*
(German, second half
of 16th century),
Ambras Castle

(bottom) *Gregor Baci*
(German, 16th century),
Ambras Castle

the Speaker in Jean Anouilh's popular World War II version of *Antigone*. His performance garnered enthusiastic praise in an otherwise unfavorable review from his former employer in the *Demokratisches Volksblatt*.

Gmeiner, who thinks that Bernhard would have become an accomplished actor, recalls him as a rather mean-spirited, scheming fellow, highly critical of his peers and given to making nasty comments about them behind their backs. Not surprisingly, he made few friends. Gmeiner enjoyed his friendship to a certain point, but didn't let it get too close. Yet Sybille Dahms, who became a distinguished actress at the Düsseldorf Schauspielhaus and later the head of Salzburg University's Dance Research Institute, appreciated him as a considerate colleague and diligent, astute observer at rehearsals and in class, witty if at times sarcastic in his comments. By his own admission terrified of forgetting his lines, as he frequently did, he was always ready to prompt his peers. Some say his difficulty in remembering his lines was one of the reasons he didn't become an actor. One might even suspect that the interminable monologues without punctuation that would become a trademark of his plays were born in part of *Schadenfreude,* the malicious joy of passing on the terror to actors who had made it in the profession.

Whether or not he actually intended to pursue a career as actor, director, or singer, Bernhard once more committed himself to the specific cultural ambiance of Salzburg. Its year-round aura of small-town provincialism also earned the conservatory's acting department its second-rate status among German-language theater schools. The annual rites of homage to genius during the summer festival were less the exceptions than proof of the self-conscious provincialism of a city that yearned for cultural transcendence. Like all worship, Salzburg's midsummer culture cult was staunchly conservative. There was to be no deviation from traditional ceremony. The gods and goddesses of the international music world came to be worshiped at the stone altars of tradition. Appropriately enough, the opera house and concert hall were carved directly into the rocks that had shielded the city against foreign invasion since the days of the Celts. In contrast to the music scene, whose international artists of necessity introduced some cultural variations into rigid conventions, the theater, bound by language, was restricted to native German-speaking actors. Conventions, in the gemütlichkeit of familiarity, slipped into all too easy routine and eventually settled into mediocrity.

The sloppy conventionality of the Mozarteum's theater training program, in telling contrast to its world-renowned music school, was perfectly adapted to Salzburg's cultural ecology, precariously balanced as it was between the lure of genius and the (reassuring) force of habit. Bernhard, torn between the two, was a perfect product of his environment. Gauged by reputation and the career tracks of its alumni, the Mozarteum's theater division lagged far behind Vienna's Max Reinhardt Seminar. Producers, directors, and agents searched for new talent in Vienna, not Salzburg. The Mozarteum's graduates had to struggle for footholds in the profession. Bernhard had no intention of doing that, according to Gmeiner. From the beginning he had aimed for greatness of some sort. Ambitious, inhibited, and with an as yet not fully identified talent, he was as susceptible to Salzburg's self-aggrandizement as he was contemptuous of the provincialism that drove it. "He seemed so much more sophisticated than the rest of us," says Gmeiner. "I came from a small town in Carinthia. I was excited by all the theater in Salzburg. Bernhard called most of it dreck. He just knew better." Somehow he created the impression that he would be something great—just what that would be, no one could tell, including himself.

By the time Bernhard wrote *A Party for Boris,* ten years or so later, he had learned both to exploit and to subvert Salzburg's ritualized obsession with performance and *Kultur.* Some of the festival's most conspicuous scenarios are woven as leitmotifs through his dramatic work.

The traditional focal point of the festival's repertory of plays was, as now, Hugo von Hofmannsthal's adaptation of *Everyman* in front of the cathedral, presented in accordance with Max Reinhardt's original production of 1929. During a sumptuous banquet hosted by Everyman, he is summoned by death just as the sun disappears behind the medieval fortress on Mönchsberg, which serves as the natural backdrop to the scene. Death's calls for Everyman reach the audience from all sides as their echo bounces off the mountains and over the courtyards.

As critics have frequently pointed out, there is hardly a play in Bernhard's dramatic canon that doesn't exploit the melodramatic or farcical possibilities of drawn-out dining rituals and their deadly aftermath. More often than not they climax in the death of one of the central characters.[5] In Catholic Austria, particularly in the archbishopric of Salzburg, the associations with the Last Supper were as obvious (or *naturgemäss)* for Hofmannsthal as for Bernhard.

A Party for Boris leads up to the birthday celebration for Boris, the legless husband of "The Good One," the legless benefactress of the asylum where she organizes the party for him and the thirteen other legless inmates. Boris's final collapse while beating the toy drums he has received as a gift is an ironic variation of Everyman's final banquet.

Peymann's production of *A Party for Boris* opened in Hamburg on June 26, 1970. The fifteen legless characters struck a chord at a time when Germans were struggling to come to terms with their crippled self-image as "good Germans" and trying to reconcile their collective guilt with the "economic miracle" of the 1960s. In theatrical terms both writer and director impressed critics with their ability to fill the big stage of the 1,300-seat Deutsches Schauspielhaus. Bernhard's compulsive speech arias and the minimalist grandeur of Peymann's staging echoed and subverted the grand tradition of German dramaturgy. In the wake of the radical theater movement that unfolded in alternative workshop spaces in the 1960s, here was a playwright who promised to revitalize the German Hof- und Staatstheater (Court and State Theater) by infusing it with elements of the theater of the absurd and his own bizarrely tragic vision. Other productions in big European theaters soon followed, in Zürich, Vienna, Munich, Warsaw, and Berlin, among others.

In October 1970 the Deutsche Akademie für Sprache und Dichtung awarded Bernhard the prestigious Büchner Prize for *A Party for Boris* and *The Lime Works.* Named after the rebellious playwright-scientist Georg Büchner, who died in 1837 at the age of twenty-three and whose work was not produced until a century after his death, the award is generally associated with the pathbreaking dramatic vision that made Büchner a forerunner of modern drama. Accordingly, the honor put Bernhard on the map as a playwright. German commentators, much more punctilious and less malicious than their Austrian colleagues, agonized over whether the celebration of a writer with such a relentlessly critical vision of his times signaled utter contempt for the whole process or plain incomprehension of what Bernhard was about. Weren't the jurors in fact suggesting that "he didn't really mean what he said"? And what about Bernhard himself, who in his acceptance speech restated his dismal opinion of the world but took its kudos in stride? Ten years later he indignantly resigned as corresponding member of the academy in protest against the induction of Walter Scheel, the former president of West Germany, as an honorary member. "I ask myself what such a mediocre and obscure politician has to do with an academy for language and poetry. I have to assume that more mediocre and obscure politicians will become elected members," and he listed Franz Josef Strauss, Helmut Schmidt, and Karl Carstens as likely suspects.[6] A bit later, in

Wittgenstein's Nephew, Bernhard offered an explanation for his acceptance of awards until the age of forty:

> If one disregards the money that goes with them, there is nothing in the world more intolerable than award ceremonies. I had already discovered this in Germany. They do nothing to enhance one's own standing, as I had believed before I received my first prize, but actually lower it, in the most embarrassing fashion. Only the thought of the money enabled me to endure these ceremonies; this was my sole motive for visiting various ancient city halls and tasteless assembly rooms — until the age of forty. I let them piss on me in all these city halls and assembly rooms, for to award someone a prize is no different from pissing on him. And to receive a prize is no different from allowing oneself to be pissed on, because one is being paid for it. I have always felt that being awarded a prize was not an honor but the greatest indignity imaginable. For a prize is always awarded by incompetents who want to piss on the recipient. And they have a *perfect right* to do so, because he is base and despicable enough to receive it. Only in extremities, when one's life and existence are threatened — and only until the age of forty — is one justified in receiving any prize or distinction, with or without an accompanying sum of money. When I received prizes I did not have the excuse that I was suffering extreme hardship or that my life and existence were threatened; hence by receiving them I made myself not only low and contemptible but positively vile, in the truest sense of the word. On the way to the Grillparzer Prize, however, I believed that this time it was different. The prize carried no emolument. The Academy of Sciences meant something, I told myself, and its prize meant something.[7]

Bernhard received the Grillparzer Prize, too, for *A Party for Boris.* Named in honor of Austria's foremost classic playwright, Franz Grillparzer, it is awarded exclusively to dramatic works. The award ceremony was held on January 21, 1972, the hundredth anniversary of Grillparzer's birth. The proceedings were not nearly as tidy as the Büchner ceremony, which, according to one newspaper account, resembled a commencement exercise, with the recipients "neatly lined up in front of an autumnal floral arrangement like so many well-behaved high school seniors."[8]

The histrionics of the Grillparzer event topped even the Little State Prize fiasco. In 1980 Bernhard wrote to the Austrian Congress of Writers: "There

was considerable delay in the Academy of Sciences before they could hand
me the award, because none of the people who wanted to honor me knew me,
so they first had to find me in the tenth row of the auditorium."[9] The ensuing spectacle, in part a game expertly staged by Bernhard in retaliation for
the organizers' failure to recognize him and welcome him properly, is vividly
brought to life in *Wittgenstein's Nephew*. When no one was there to greet him
upon his arrival, rather than identify himself he defiantly took a seat in the
middle of the tenth row. Only after protracted haggling did he let himself be
dragged to the first row, next to the minister.

Bernhard's dramatic exposure of the pretenses of the celebrants of High
Native Culture was small comfort to his own bruised ego, which wasn't quite
so immune to provincial snobbery as his contemptuous stance suggested. By
now he was a famous writer, after all; he had a right to expect to be treated accordingly. His humiliation was caused not only by a breach of etiquette but by
the unforgivable failure to instantly recognize the *Dichter*. It would have been
below his dignity to introduce himself. The hierarchic structures of Habsburg
culture remain deeply embedded in the aspirations of its fiercest detractor.

Bernhard was well on his way along a trail of notorious national controversies. In Peymann he found a congenial director not only of his plays but
of the cultural drama that surrounded many of them. In the summer of 1972
Peymann directed his second full-length play, *Der Ignorant und der Wahnsinnige* (The Ignoramus and the Madman). It had been commissioned by none
other than Josef Kaut for the Salzburg Festival. After the success of *A Party for
Boris,* Bernhard's former boss, now the festival's president, rushed to offer the
city's native son all the lavish resources the theater had to offer — and Peymann
exploited them to the full.

The play is Bernhard's response to the festival's many productions of *The
Magic Flute* and the dehumanization of the artist into a hypersensitive performing mechanism. Bruno Ganz, the rising star of Peter Stein's legendary
Berlin theater, the Schaubühne am Halle'schen Ufer, played a young doctor
who waits out a performance of *The Magic Flute* in the dressing room of the
celebrated coloratura soprano, where he lectures her blind alcoholic father
on the dissection of a corpse. His minute descriptions are punctuated by the
neurotic singer's late arrival and her whirlwind incursions to change costumes
between her breakneck arias. After the performance, father, daughter, and
physician dine at an elegant restaurant. At the end of the meal, all the lights
in the house go out. While the darkness draws the audience into the blind

father's "vision," it also is the fitting finale to the doctor's preoccupation with a corpse. It is both the appropriately melodramatic apotheosis of the Queen of the Night and a reflection of the singer's state of mind. Night, her character's domain, also dissolves the performer, who collapses at the table. After so much preoccupation with the body, as scientific object and as a mechanized instrument, the actors end up disembodied. They disappear in the darkness; only their voices are heard. In the end, the darkness swallowed even the production itself: it closed after one performance. The total darkness called for by the text was in irreconcilable conflict with the city's fire laws. It ignited the first of several theater scandals inspired by Bernhard and set in motion by Claus Peymann.

The young German director, a product of the rebellious student movement of the 1960s, took care to uphold his nonconformist image in his Austrian debut. When he agreed to work at the Salzburg Festival, the mecca of Capitalist Masterpiece Culture, some German commentators fretted that he was selling out to the mainstream. So Peymann opened his culture war, calling Salzburg "chic shit" and a "gigantic *Nockerl* flambé." The *Salzburger Nockerl*, a local specialty, is made of egg white and sugar beaten and baked into an enormous mass of cloudlike fluff. His efforts to calm the countercultural purists did nothing to facilitate his communication with the local technical team. The director's frustration with the leisurely work habits of the stage crew unleashed a more traditional culture clash between Teutonic rigor and Alpine gemütlichkeit. According to contemporary reports, Peymann insisted on rehearsing the second act's elaborate meal with the expensive dishes and wines prescribed by the text. "But the Salzburg Landestheater isn't located on the Halle'sche Ufer; here they are used to more casual manners, more modest demands," commented the bemused critic of *Theater Heute*. The backstage drama reflected the historic ambivalence of Austrians toward the mighty "Prussians," or "Piefke," as they were called in derision in the local dialect:

> Peymann's rigorous working methods together with the serving of real Pommery for rehearsals of the scene, of real steak tartare ordered from the kitchen of the Österreichischer Hof [Salzburg's foremost luxury hotel], prepared and then not even eaten, made for bad feelings among the backstage crew. Linguistic difficulties arose every time expletives were hurled in Berlin and Salzburg slang and misunderstood. Various chicaneries followed: the fire marshals were called because the first-act set obstructed

the fire curtain. And finally Peymann was prohibited from turning off the exit lights for the play's final moment.[10]

The war over the exit lights has become legendary in the annals of the Salzburg Festival. Peymann withdrew the (exorbitantly expensive) production after its opening night, July 27, 1974. Following a venerable Salzburg tradition, tickets to the dress rehearsal had been distributed among Salzburg residents. At the last minute Peymann banned an audience. In the chaotic rehearsal that followed emergency exit lights were by no means the primary issue. Peymann requested new props; when the property master could not produce them, he threw a tantrum. The crew walked out. The director apologized. The rehearsal proceeded. The festival administration reasoned that without an audience there was no concrete need for emergency exit lights in the auditorium. Peymann was granted his wish, in the odd hope that he would realize he didn't need them after all. Peymann, however, was all the more convinced that the lights had to be off. In any case, they went back on for opening night, which was a huge success, particularly in the influential German press. Some local responses were less elated. Bernhard telegraphed the festival's president: "I hope to find you all the way on the side of the highest standards of seriousness and art, rather than on the side of local stupidity, meanness, and depravity, and I congratulate you on an outstanding production." The next day Bernhard wired, "A society that can't deal with two minutes of darkness can do without my play." The day before the scheduled second performance, Peymann declared that the production would go on only if the exit lights were turned off. The administration declined and the performance was canceled, too late to inform all ticket holders. A crowd assembled in the theater lobby. Peymann appeared with a sign: "Two minutes of darkness and we'll perform." Bernhard showed up and declared he would cut the final scene so that the play could be performed. The festival management declined. Ticket holders got their money back. All further performances were canceled. In an about-face, Bernhard protested in a long telegram to Josef Kaut. Although the festival administration had guaranteed that opening night could be performed under the same conditions as the dress rehearsal, Kaut broke their agreement at the last possible moment. "You yourself admitted to me after the opening that you tricked Peymann in order to secure the opening."[11] Bernhard's old buddy Hennetmair proudly claims co-authorship of the message. He kept the original draft in Bernhard's hurried handwriting as proof of their joint effort.

Hennetmair also took his friend, who was too upset to drive, to the post office and helped him wire his ire.

The cancellation of performances enraged the local citizens, who saw their taxes being wasted on a project that was too expensive for ordinary Salzburgers to attend to begin with. The critic of *Theater Heute* surmised that in Austria, where, "as everyone knows, everything is permitted that's prohibited," the fire regulations could have been "quietly circumvented." [12]

As far as the critics were concerned, the production was an unqualified success. *Theater Heute*'s reviewer saw Bernhard as a product of Salzburg's operatic splendor and its baroque infatuation with the sensuality of death who was driven to turn these festival trademarks into their opposites. He took the comforting warmth out of *The Magic Flute* and made it "the occasion for a theatrical deep freeze." The doctor's precise descriptions of his craft are pitted against his attacks on the mechanization of all artistic endeavors, while the celebrated singer in her anguish is reduced to a marionette. In preparation for his part, Bruno Ganz spent six months at Berlin's Institute of Anatomy and brilliantly appropriated the bearing of the seasoned pathologist. Germany's most discerning critics, not usually known for outbursts of unbridled enthusiasm, raved about Ganz's brilliant performance of Bernhard's monomaniacal speech acts. Their force was transmitted with such economy and precision that "the play's uneventfulness never became a problem." [13]

The set designer was Karl-Ernst Herrmann, who had created the set for *A Party for Boris* and would design all of Peymann's Bernhard premieres except *Immanuel Kant.* With the soprano's "cold, white, aseptic" [14] dressing room, dominated by a huge mirror, Herrmann introduced the kind of minimalist interior that would become his trademark. Herrmann's ascetic spaces highlighting one or two defining pieces of furniture, lit through high windows and sharply animated by a door's opening and deliberate closing to the world outside, reflect the central character's perception. So compelling were his designs for Peymann's Bernhard productions that to several generations of theatergoers, critics, and scholars they came to define Bernhard's dramaturgy of a minimum of themes and their obsessive variations. Reinforced by Bernhard's loyalty to the director and his team, this quasi-sacred exclusivity was further supported by the self-assured authority of Germany's power critics, who saw themselves (as they still do) as the arbiters of culture and categorically rejected subsequent productions of his plays that opted for a humbler realism. In hindsight, this kind of monopoly, inspired as it was, may have prevented the exploration of other perspectives and made for the limited exposure that Bernhard's plays had during his lifetime.

Six weeks after the Salzburg debacle, *The Ignoramus and the Madman* opened at West Berlin's Schlosspark Theater, staged by Dieter Dorn.[15] It fed the debate about the nature of Bernhard's realism. The question was whether the detailed rendering of the environment and the actors' matching psychological approach made Bernhard's world too normal or gave his characters an appealingly accessible humanity. Although Bernhard found Dorn's approach wrong, apparently he respected it. The director acknowledged his mistakes in a conversation with Bernhard.[16] His confession must have earned him the author's approval, for he directed Bernhard's next two plays, *The Hunting Party* at Berlin's Schiller Theater and *Force of Habit* for the Salzburg Festival. A disastrous production of *The Ignoramus and the Madman* in Munich led Bernhard to impose stringent restrictions on all productions of his plays.

The debate about Bernhard's brand of realism sharply polarized critics in their responses to two productions of Bernhard's next play, *The Hunting Party,* his declared favorite. The Vienna Burgtheater, not to be outdone by Salzburg or dwarfed by the Germans' ferocious appetite for renegade Austrian artists, had commissioned the play and signed Peymann to direct. Only eleven days after the Vienna premiere, Dieter Dorn's production opened at the Schiller Theater on May 15, 1974. At a time when the German theater was strongly influenced by Brecht's politicized aesthetics, critics on both the left and the right questioned Bernhard's relation to contemporary realities. Ostensibly Bernhard transferred to the stage the milieu of his fiction: a hunting lodge, presumably in (though not specified as) the familiar landscape around Salzburg. The owner of the estate is an ailing World War II general who lost an arm in the Battle of Stalingrad. His forests and hunting grounds are also dying, infested by bark beetles. Nearly blind from glaucoma, he can't see the devastation. The general is out hunting in the company of high-ranking ministers, a young prince, employed as the gamekeeper, and his princess. The general's wife plays cards with a young writer. The writer agonizes about nature, human and otherwise. His musings about artificiality in art and life as enacted by humans, about the levels of reality lived, remembered, observed, and dramatized, beg the question: dramatized by whom—the "real" people acting out their lives or the author observing, exploiting, and manipulating them? Furthermore, who are the "real" people onstage, anyway?

The cast of characters led some post-Brechtian dialectical materialist critics to expect a more "realistic"—that is, more overtly political—confrontation with postwar reality. Viennese audiences, for their part, seemed rather bored—cynics might say precisely because the avoidance of reality was their reality anyway, and they were more imaginative at it than the characters they saw onstage. Be that as it may, a story Bernhard loved to tell about opening night sums up the local response. Ten minutes into the performance he couldn't take it any longer and walked out. As he retrieved his coat, the checkroom attendant, a kind old lady, said understandingly: "You don't like it either, do you?"[17]

The production was problematic from the start. Bernhard originally wanted Bruno Ganz to play the writer. He had dedicated the play to him. Furthermore, he had written the part of the General's Wife for Paula Wessely, a much beloved Viennese actress, whose near-mythical status in the German-language theater made her comparable to Helen Hayes in the United States or Dame Edith Evans in England. The Burgtheater's resident ensemble, a mighty company of more than 140 actors who could not be fired after ten years of employment, objected to the casting of a guest star. And Wessely, sixty-six years old at that time, declined. According to Bernhard, she was no longer up to memorizing pages of monologue without punctuation.[18]

There was more to Bernhard's casting wishes than meets the eye. It was the beginning of a strategy that would become a crucial aspect of his dramaturgy. It is deeply rooted in the tradition of a rotating repertory company, where the same actors can be seen in several roles in a single week. The characters an actor plays within a short period of time and repeats over years reflect upon each other in his presence onstage—if not in his performance, then in the audience's memory. The dissecting technique of Bruno Ganz's razor-sharp pathologist in Bernhard's previous play would bear on the writer cutting down his hosts' pretenses and historic guilt. Even more to the point, Paula Wessely not only was a brilliant actress, beloved for the depth of feeling she brought to her characters, but also was a woman with a well-known past: she and her actor husband, Attila Hörbiger, were enthusiastic supporters of Hitler. Her political past, known to everyone and shared by many of her admirers, carried its own unspoken performative force. Thus her artistic and personal biography would have brought a chilling tension between real, perceived, and performed realities to her presence onstage as the General's Wife. If Bernhard's theater lacks a clearly drawn political perspective, it shrewdly incorporates the workings of Austrian politics in the interplay of innuendoes, the silence of collective memory, and verbal excess. The realism of his play is interactive with his culture to the point where he himself is caught inside its drama. His dramaturgy, so intimately connected to the dynamics of the society he denounces, includes him as its product and producer. To outside observers, particularly the so-called Sixty-eighters—the antiestablishment rebels of the 1960s—this made him suspect as a reactionary.

The directorial approaches to *The Hunting Party* in Vienna and Berlin once again were at opposite ends of the dramatic spectrum. As usual, Peymann and his set designer, Karl Ernst Herrmann, opted for their brand of hyperrealism: the hunting lodge featured a wall covered with 625 antlers. Subsequent theater lore insisted that they were real antlers. Given Austria's obsession with hunting and the plenitude of the real stuff adorning even the humblest homes, real antlers would have been cheaper than the rubber replicas made for the production,[19] as Austrian taxpayers often pointed out to stress the cost of Peymann's megalomania. Peymann unleashed another fracas with his request for a real, full-sized ham. A new one would have to be purchased for every performance at a cost of $200. The Federal Administration of State Theaters, which controls the Burgtheater's budget, said no. A benefactress contributed the real thing just for opening night. It didn't save the show.

As far as the actors' performances were concerned, the terse realism Peymann demanded from his performers collided with the Burgtheater's tradition of impassioned grandiloquence informed by the baroque hyperbole of local manners. Oddly enough, what might have seemed a perfect match between Bernhard's "Austrianness" and the native or long assimilated sensibilities of his actors turned out to be a fiasco. While Bernhard extrapolated a sparse musical score from the convoluted indulgences of native speech to highlight its deadly mechanism, the actors' emotional delivery undid the process. All that was left was false pathos. Thereafter Bernhard relied on the company of actors that Peymann developed as artistic director of the Stuttgart Theater and took with him to his subsequent posts in Bochum and the Vienna Burgtheater. Their post-Brechtian realistic acting style and controlled northern speech rhythms served as counterpoint to the lilt of local idiom and heightened its dissonances, the breaks in the mechanism.

Dorn in his Berlin production stressed the characters' artificiality in both speech and movement, but failed to sustain it throughout. The actors' efforts to humanize their function as stylized speech machines demonstrated once again that an aesthetic for Bernhard's dramaturgy had not yet been found.

Only one actor instinctively grasped Bernhard's world: Bernhard Minetti, well known as a Beckett actor, in the role of the General. This was the first of Minetti's many definitive creations of Bernhard characters. Not only was he their ideal interpreter, his persona and theatrical instincts contributed to Bernhard's understanding of the characters he was to write, both for Minetti and in his fiction.[20] Henning Rischbieter, editor in chief of *Theater Heute,* a Brechtian realist with little taste for post-Habsburg self-absorption, praised Minetti's performance in *The Hunting Party:* "At times Bernhard Minetti's General was almost a caricature of a military brain, a hollow comedy brimming with cheap derision that would suddenly switch to cutting anger, a mean, threatening mood, and finally to a tired, cynical self-destructiveness. . . . I've rarely seen a more radical (and therefore critical) portrait of an authoritarian personality."[21]

Siegfried Melchinger, who panned Bernhard's first two plays, now raved:

Amidst all the experiments, the irritations, obscurities, etc. . . . finally a play! One could say that this author, who had some success with two plays, rather shared the general preoccupation with eccentricity, the bizarre and way-out—which used to be called "the absurd." . . . It seems to me that the most decisive step he took beyond his earlier theater with *The Hunting Party* was his distancing himself from the bizarre. He turned to the center and almost gave up the eccentric. Let me add here a quote from Hanna Arendt, who calls "the experience of dying, the inner realization of one's own mortality, the experience most hostile to politics." It states the reason why the theater of Thomas Bernhard is in no way out to change the world. It diagnoses the world and in this sense it is in tune with the great works of world theater, with Sophocles, with Shakespeare, with Büchner, with Chekhov.[22]

In the sociopolitical upheavals of the 1960s and early 1970s the conservative Melchinger was in sharp contrast to the old and young leftists among the critics who saw the theater as a powerful political force and expected innovative aesthetics to reflect or anticipate social change. The critics' disagreements revealed as much about their political attitudes as about their dramaturgical preferences.

Benjamin Henrichs, a rising critic for *Die Zeit* who was to become one of Bernhard's most devoted admirers, called *The Hunting Party* "a touchingly antiquated, sentimentally metaphysical play," in contrast to Chekhov's *Cherry Orchard*, which it echoes in its final scene.[23]

Bernhard's next play, *Force of Habit*, which premiered that summer in Salzburg, leaned more toward the bizarre, though modified by an accessible sense of humor, as Bernhard returned to the world of performers to explore the absurd mechanism of existence. Featuring an old circus director who keeps rehearsing Schubert's *Trout* Quintet with his company members between their routines but never manages to play it to the end, it was praised by some critics as the long overdue new German comedy. The production was directed by Dieter Dorn, who brought Minetti with him from Berlin for the role of Caribaldi. In *Theater Heute*'s annual survey of critics, *Force of Habit* garnered the most votes for best play and Bernhard Minetti those for best actor. Benjamin Henrichs in *Die Zeit* called it "the first German comedy since time immemorial."[24] Some found it boring. Henning Rischbieter called it "enervating" in its grinding repetitiousness.[25] Rischbieter went further, condemning the play as "bankruptcy on the highest level. Thomas Bernhard is an authoritarian writer. This is why intellectuals succumb to him who don't admit to themselves that they are tired of the anti-intellectual fashion; Thomas Bernhard is a reactionary writer."[26] Rischbieter's reaction is indicative of the ongoing division among German critics as to the theater's political responsibilities in general and Bernhard's stance in particular.

Across the border Caribaldi's recurring line "Augsburg tomorrow" in anticipation of the circus's next stop in yet another dismal provincial town aroused Augsburgers to threats of legal action. (The fact that Brecht had been born there and had left as soon as he could supported Bernhard's view.) Bernhard responded in an open letter from Lisbon to the *Frankfurter Allgemeine Zeitung:* "From Lisbon I perceive Augsburg as even more awful, through and through, than in my new play. My pity for Augsburgers and all those in Europe who see themselves as Augsburgers is boundless and absolute."[27] For those who wonder why he singled out Augsburg, of all places, as the metonym for pan-European provincialism, the choice was in all likelihood inspired by a popular Austrian sausage called Augsburger, similar to a knockwurst, usually served fried in halves on top of mashed potatoes.

Despite the outrage in Augsburg, the production established Bernhard's international reputation as a playwright, and translations and productions soon followed in London, Paris, Rotterdam, and Madrid. One of Bernhard's best known and most frequently produced plays, it holds an important place in the evolution of his writing. With the constantly interrupted rehearsal of Schubert's quintet in a dingy trailer under the guidance of a foolishly inspired tyrant (his name suggests Garibaldi, the celebrated fighter for Italian unification in the nineteenth century) Bernhard constructed a perfect theatrical model for his literary universe. Nothing distracts from the central action, which has been polished to machine-like precision by years of repetition. The constant disruptions create the need to go on once again. An impossible dreamer, Bernhard's Caribaldi is neither a mythical war hero nor Broadway's gentle Don Quixote fighting windmills in pursuit of his impossible dream. He is a tyrant who mercilessly tortures his company with his drills, performing the last rites of European culture in a trailer of the provincial circus it had become. With *Force of Habit* Bernhard created his most compelling theatrical metaphor for the single-minded pursuits of the central characters of his fiction—and their cost.

As one critic put it, the play's Salzburg premiere inaugurated what was to be Bernhard's *Machtergreifung,* his take-over of power in the German-language theater during the following season.[28] The tongue-in-cheek appropriation of Nazi terminology suggested that yet another Austrian had managed to take over the much bigger country, this time in the cultural rather than the political sphere.

Unbenownst to the public, Austria's cultural politicians tempted Bernhard with a much more concrete *Machtergreifung:* with all the histrionic secrecy of a Habsburg cabal, they asked whether he would be interested in becoming the artistic director of the Burgtheater, starting in September 1976. According to Robert Jungbluth, then chief of Austria's federally run theaters, it was a sort of game, because everyone was sure he would reject the offer out of hand. To everybody's surprise, he accepted. So Herr Jungbluth traveled to Gmunden and talked to Bernhard for four hours in his customary meeting place, the local café. Bernhard had already thought about directors, dramaturgs, and artistic staff. Even the wily general secretary must have had a tough time undoing the mess he had started.[29]

Bernhard commented in 1978 that at first he treated the whole thing as a joke, but then he thought, "Why not? I can do that for a couple of years. With full commitment, the way one writes." But he would have made a clean sweep of the Burg, sending most of the company into retirement and bringing in the critic, translator, and writer Hilde Spiel as the dramaturg. "Most probably they would have fired me after six months." He publicly denied the story only after some papers had created the impression that he himself, "that pitiful poet," had "feeblemindedly" applied for the job, without having been invited to do so.[30] Perhaps his public embarrassment was one of the reasons Bernhard would have none of his plays produced at the Burgtheater until Claus Peymann became its chief eleven years later.

In the meantime, Peymann, in his first season as artistic director of the Württembergisches Staatstheater Stuttgart, staged *The President*, Bernhard's fifth play. The opening on May 21, 1975, followed five days after its premiere at the Vienna Burgtheater, under the direction of Ernst Wendt, who had been dramaturg for Peymann's Hamburg production of *A Party for Boris*. The close race for the world premiere was a clear indication not only of Bernhard's growing importance but also of the fierce cultural competition between Austria and Germany. The leading Austrian theater found itself in a difficult position. Although repeatedly vilified by Bernhard, it couldn't risk confirming his criticism by letting the Germans prevail once again.

The play was Bernhard's response to the political assassinations that plagued Europe at that time. It focuses on the president of an unnamed country and his wife as they prepare for the funeral of one of his ministers, who, like the first lady's dog, has gotten in the way of bullets intended for the president. Their anarchist son is a prime suspect in the assassination attempt, which is followed by another that kills the president.

With its absurd operetta scenario—the president's wife is more upset by the loss of her pet than by the death of the minister and the president entertains a starlet while on a political mission in Portugal—it hardly seemed to be the political message play some people expected. Peymann made sure the message wasn't lost: it was scheduled to open on the first day of the Baader-Meinhof trial in Stuttgart. Named for the founders of the radical Red Army Faction, the Baader-Meinhof group (or gang, depending on one's political persuasion) was responsible for the assassination of German business leaders and politicians, and took other lives in the process. The group's antiestablishment politics, directed as it was against the Nazi past and the continued authoritarianism of their parents' generation and its leaders, had the sympathies of many of their left-wing contemporaries. The police's brutal methods during the seven-year hunt for various members of the group, their treatment in jail, and Ulrike Meinhof's suicide in Stuttgart's Stammheim prison in May 1976 recalled Nazi tactics at a time when Germans were struggling to come to terms with their past. The trial's bizarre procedures and the criminal department's unlawful surveillance of the inmates and their lawyers intensified the arguments about civil rights and the limits of state authority.

The production of *The President* triggered more heated debates about Bernhard's political relevance, while audiences in both Vienna and Stuttgart left in droves during the intermission. Peter Iden attacked Bernhard in the *Frankfurter Rundschau* for his "pessimistic denial of reality," his "crassly reactionary worldview." Calling him "socially irrelevant," he accused him of "elitist arrogance; glorification of mercilessness; delicious rejection of democracy, justice, humanity." Altogether the play presented "reactionary, dangerous, vulgar material."[31]

Rolf Michaelis argued in *Theater Heute:* "Isn't Bernhard's critique of the times much stronger . . . for his refusal to put a fascist dictator on the stage in a 'normal' play with dialogues and exchanges of arguments—because in that kind of regime there is no opposing argument? Isn't the author consistent in his exposure of the total isolation and alienation of those in power by having them monologuize?" He found that *The President* continued in the comic vein of *Force of Habit.* If it is "a dark Dance of Death," it is rooted in the unmistakably "Alpine Austrian" tradition that funerals must be fun ("Lustig soll die Leich sein"). Referring to Bernhard's solipsistic monologues, the critic continues: "Comparisons of directorial approaches in Vienna and Stuttgart were overwhelmingly in Peymann's favor."[32] Peymann's staging, in Herrmann's elegant setting, exploited the characters' operetta features with relish, thus highlighting a critical perspective inspired by Karl Kraus's acerbic vision of World War I as "those bloody years preserved only in dreams, when operetta figures performed the tragedy of mankind."[33] In revealing contrast, the director Ernst Wendt, a North German in Vienna, categorically did away with the fluff to clear the Burgtheater's venerable stage for an earnest exploration of the play's themes of death, terrorism, murder, and decay.

The critics' and audiences' unease with Bernhard's plays would continue throughout his career. During his lifetime his plays always drew limited audiences. The mixed responses to *The President* did not diminish Bernhard's dominant position in the German-language theater. Both the Salzburg Festival and Claus Peymann commissioned a play. The results were *Die Berühmten* (The Famous) and *Minetti,* respectively.

Minetti opened the Stuttgart season of 1975–76 under Peymann's direction on September 1. *The Famous* led to another Salzburg imbroglio. As a crude satire of the pretenses and pressures of the festival scene, it was rejected

by Josef Kaut for reasons of "subject matter and execution."[34] Bernhard retaliated with an open letter in the prestigious German weekly *Die Zeit.* The
Burgtheater valiantly stepped into the breach—and produced a dismal flop,
due partly to weak direction.

Both *Minetti* and *The Famous* are about the theater. Back to back, as they
were written, they reflect Bernhard's response to his stage experiences as well
as his new status as a celebrity. Both explore "what's in a name" and the performative force of fame. What is it that validates someone as an artist—public
recognition, as in *The Famous,* or the conduct of one's life? For thirty years
Minetti (the stage character) has been rehearsing passages from *King Lear,*
alternately in English and in German, in front of a mirror in his sister's attic in
Dinkelsbühl (the name of the town is equivalent to hinterland). The points of
contact and difference between the title character and his famous performer
generate the drama of identity: What constitutes an actor—the performance
act or its recognition? the performer himself or his roles? In the hotel lobby
where Minetti waits (in vain) for the artistic director of the Flensburg theater
he tells his story, first to an older woman who is just trying to get through the
night, then to a young girl who is waiting for her boyfriend. He introduces
himself as an actor. But the only person who has seen him act in thirty years is
himself, when he has watched himself in the mirror. The stage character is enacted by another real actor. But the real actor wouldn't be the actor he is at that
moment without the part he is playing. Whom does the audience perceive,
the real Minetti or the performed Minetti, and who is who in the moment
of performance? What constitutes the "real" Minetti, the actor everyone has
seen in so many unforgettable roles? His career constitutes a major part of his
biography, including his flourishing years in Berlin throughout the Nazi era.
It is immaterial whether Bernhard intentionally plays with or buries such details. Minetti's name in the title reinforces and undermines his biography. The
ambiguity highlights its problematic as part of his identity.

Bernhard's "famous" include the living, who remain nameless on stage,
and the dead, whose names have become legend. The former join one of
their own, a celebrated bass-baritone, in his palatial Salzburg summer residence, which suggests Leopoldskron, Max Reinhardt's castle. Identified only
by their professions as conductor, director, actress, publisher, pianist, and
soprano, the guests are easily recognizable, at least to a select in-group: the
conductor is Herbert von Karajan, the publisher Siegfried Unseld. Status
casts character. Recognition validates the insider. But there's a catch: Bern-

hard's unnamed celebrities have predecessors, whose names have achieved immortality. Life-size puppets seated at the dinner table with their living heirs represent the group's legendary role models. Their fame, having outlived their deaths, entitles them to their names; among them are the bass-baritone Richard Mayr, the tenor Richard Tauber, the soprano Lotte Lehmann, the actor Alexander Moissi, the actress Helene Thimig, the director Max Reinhardt, the conductor Arturo Toscanini, the pianist Elly Ney, and the legendary German publisher Samuel Fischer. Never mind that their fame is also limited to the memory of an elite group of cognescenti. Elitism is just another form of provincialism.

The meal ends with the absurd killing—in effigy, as it were—of the puppets, the artistic ancestors, by their respective heirs. But the idols don't go away. Their portraits grace the castle's walls as their nameless successors sit beneath them in animal masks, engaged in art-talk, pseudo-philosophizing, and insider gossip. Finally their culture-babble is drowned out by animal noises, topped by the rooster/conductor's triple cockadoodle-doo.

It is interesting to compare Bernhard's *Minetti* and *The Famous* with Peter Handke's *Ride Across Lake Constance,* directed five years later by Claus Peymann at Berlin's Schaubühne. Handke also explores the relationship between an actor and performance. His characters have the names of famous German stage and film stars. But the actors do not play the stars, they simply play games; the names have nothing to do with the characters. If they have a function, it is to highlight their identities as actors and the household names that make them instantly identifiable under the rubric "actors." They also need names for purposes of identification on stage. Their games involve simple gestures, movements, and tasks carried out at the order of other members of the group. Handke's play stands out as a sophisticated theatrical model of Wittgenstein's explorations of language games (how is the order to lift a brick and carry it to a designated place understood and carried out?) as quasi-Althusserian appellations: the order produces an action that makes the performer of the task identifiable, at least during the time he performs the task.[35]

Bernhard's nameless and iconic famous perform a *Kasperltheater* of Cruelty, a crude Punch and Judy send-up of Freud's *Totem and Taboo.* His aging sons and daughters of Salzburg's Olympians act out their anxieties of influence in a massacre of vanities. The appropriation of status produces identity. In the world of cultural royalty that replaced the Habsburgs, wars of succession are fought beyond death.

Although ignored by producers, *The Famous* occupies an interesting place in Bernhard's dramatic work as well as in his biography. If he established himself as a brazenly nonconformist playwright, with his third festival commission he was well on his way to become a Salzburg icon, a mainstream star. Ironically enough, his own cultural conditioning threatened to catch up with him. The play's display of its author's intimate knowledge of the musical and literary scenes implicates him in his own satire as a sentimental fan, boastful insider, and brazen climber. "I don't need the festival," Bernhard concluded his open letter to Josef Kaut, which was published in *Die Zeit* on August 29, 1975.[36] Widely publicized, it served as a timely disclaimer of complicity. As it turned out, Bernhard was right. He didn't need Kaut or the festival. In the subsequent years Claus Peymann took over as his primary director. Together with the dramaturg Hermann Beil, the set designer Karl-Ernst Herrmann, and the brilliant young players he gathered at his Stuttgart Theater (whom he would also take along to Bochum and Vienna), Peymann would develop what was generally perceived as the definitive approach to Bernhard's plays. In the end, Peymann reinstated Bernhard in Salzburg and finally in Vienna. During his inspired if stormy tenure at the Burgtheater he transformed the stronghold of imperial traditionalism into one of Europe's most progressive institutional theaters and made Bernhard's plays the pivot of his repertory. Bernhard himself turned into an icon, glorified, reviled, defamed, and mythologized, at long last the imperial city's native son.

CHAPTER SEVEN

Playing Against

An Austrian Maverick in the German Theater of Guilt

*I write for one person only, the actor . . . and I know a thing or
two about actors.*

— Thomas Bernhard, *interview, 1998*

CLAUS PEYMANN DIRECTED ELEVEN OF BERNHARD'S seventeen full-
length plays. As artistic director of three leading theaters, he also commissioned most of the works and produced three of the plays he did not direct, in addition to staging several of the short satirical sketches Bernhard
called "dramalettes." At first sight, the brash director from northern Germany
couldn't have been more different from the Alpine recluse. Peymann, a loud-
mouthed, savvy self-promoter, represented Germany's politicized theatrical
vanguard. Bernhard, an awe-inspiring novelist rather contemptuous of contemporary theater, kept dramatizing Karl Kraus's vision of operetta heroes
"acting out the tragedy of mankind." Their association over many years pro-
foundly influenced each other's aesthetics, *Weltanschauung,* and career and
left its mark on the culture at large. Ultimately Bernhard owed his emergence
as an internationally respected playwright to Peymann's unshakable commitment; without Peymann he might have been known as a remarkable novelist
who occasionally indulged in histrionics.

Producing his plays was always a risk. None of them was a popular success. Opinions remained deeply divided. If they were not crowd pleasers,
Peymann's productions nonetheless gained much attention, thanks to his exquisite directorial imagination and his knack for producing the cultural drama
around the theatrical event. Bernhard certainly was aware of Peymann's multiple talents. He virtually granted him a monopoly on directing his plays.

From its earliest days, Peymann's theater throve on opposition. *Theater*

Heute described him and his closest longtime collaborators (the dramaturgs Hermann Beil, Uwe Jens Jenssen, and Vera Sturm and the director Alfred Kirchner) as a "group of theater people who understood art as opposition and made it [their] mission from the beginning," taking their cues "from all kinds of phenomena in the political or municipal sphere or in cultural politics, and there were always colliding planes."[1]

Born in Bremen in 1937, Peymann grew up in the era of Konrad Adenauer, which was marked by its silence about the Holocaust in the frantic preoccupation with economic recovery and the Cold War. It fueled his generation's frequent clashes with their elders' politics as they turned to the left. The theater Peymann found in the 1950s was, in his words, "firmly in the hands of the generation that not only survived fascism but in part tolerated or supported it, a generation that included Gustaf Gründgens, Heinz Hilpert, Hans Schalla, Karl Heinz Stroux, and Boleslav Barlog, but also Hans Schweikart and Harry Buckwitz."[2] These were the star directors, doubling as *Intendanten,* or artistic directors, who built the reputations of their theaters amidst the reconstruction of such bombed-out cities as Düsseldorf, Göttingen, Bochum, Berlin, Munich, and Frankfurt. The growing fame of their *Stadttheater* rescued even the smaller cities from the dreaded aura of provincialism and established them as centers of urban sophistication and culture attractive to business leaders. Peymann came to the theater more or less by chance as a student at the University of Hamburg. Student theaters were thriving on rebellion against the established theaters, with their backward political leanings, their preoccupation with the box office and the revival of the classic German theater tradition. The student theater festival in Erlangen, the annual high point of the student theater movement, attracted leading journalists and theater artists from across Europe, such as the French director Patrice Chereau, who is best known for his stunning productions of Richard Wagner's Ring cycle at the Bayreuth Festival from 1976 to 1980. Peymann gained attention with two Brecht productions: *The Day of the Great Scholar Wu,* the 1955 satire on East Germany's chief of state, Walter Ulbricht, in 1962 and the *Antigone-Modell 1948* in 1963, for which he reconstructed Brecht's staging and Caspar Neher's original set. The teacher was Brecht. Coming to terms with Brecht, his politicized dramaturgy versus his political biography, shaped the work of young directors in both Germanys. After the Berlin Wall went up in 1961, West Germany's state theaters boycotted Brecht, but student theaters continued to stage his plays. Their leftism, according to Peymann, prepared for the protest movement of

the late 1960s.[3] At that point the political impetus of the student theater movement was no longer needed, and it merged with the student protest movement.
Peymann went to Frankfurt, where he introduced himself with Peter Handke's
Offending the Audience. Although no love was lost between Handke and Bernhard, Handke's title could serve as the leitmotif of Bernhard's dramaturgy, on
stage and off.

Peymann, then, was already a master at staging productions within the
larger political context so that plays and external events would interact. *Kaspar,* Peter Handke's seminal play about the construction of a person through
media-speak, opened in 1969 amidst the uproar against the passage of emergency laws to expand the government's authority and restrict the rights of citizens in national crises. Eighteen years later Peymann still recalled the opening:

> On the day of the opening of *Kaspar* there was a huge demonstration
> against the emergency laws in Bonn. In the morning, all of us, the actors
> and I, were in Bonn. There were vehement confrontations with the police,
> and in the evening hundreds of demonstrators returning from Bonn tried
> to block our performance. They demanded the cancellation of such an
> elitist artistic event for being unpolitical. . . . We performed *Kaspar* never-
> theless and the demonstrators understood that the play tells about exactly
> the kind of manipulative processes that the emergency laws tried to make
> possible. They understood that it is, in fact, a political play.[4]

The following year he joined Peter Stein in the reorganization of the
Schaubühne am Halle'schen Ufer, which was to become West Germany's
leading theater of the 1970s and 1980s. Its productions would be matched only
by Peymann's work in Stuttgart and Bochum. Peymann did not stay beyond
the first season. He directed Handke's *Ride across Lake Constance* but left the
production before its opening in January 1971, frustrated by the company's
resistance to what they found an elitist, precious text.[5] His relationship with
the Schaubühne ensemble had already been strained by his absence in 1970,
while he directed Bernhard's *Party for Boris* in Hamburg.

When Peymann became artistic director of the Stuttgart theater, he relied on a small company of young actors, many of them members of the resident company. They were to work with him over the next twenty-five years
and develop a distinctive acting style derived from Brecht, transformed by the
alternative theatrical impulses of the 1960s, and animated by a playful sense of
humor—a rarity in the German theater. It softened the self-righteous political

earnestness that was de rigueur among the rising artistic and intellectual elite of grown-up student rebels.

At the same time that Peymann's state theater programmatically provoked the cultural politicians, he depended on their financial support. His dramaturgy, in its framing and feeding of the larger conflicts in the public arena, depended on political antagonists. The public dramas he created served to authenticate the moral integrity of the plays he directed.

Upon his arrival in Stuttgart in the fall of 1974, the city provided him with a fertile environment for his brand of confrontational theater, possibly more than he had bargained for. With the leaders of the terrorist Red Army Faction, better known as the Baader-Meinhof group, held in Stuttgart's high-security Stammheim prison, the city was the center of international attention.

The Federal Republic had gone through its first postwar recession after its phenomenal economic recovery in the 1950s and early 1960s. In 1966 the conservative Christian Democratic Union and the Socialist Party had formed a coalition government under the conservative chancellor Kurt Georg Kiesinger. (It lasted until 1970, when the Socialists merged with the Liberal Democratic Party under the Socialist chancellor Willy Brandt.) The apparent merger of interests seemed to leave no room for opposition amid growing frustration over an antiquated university system, the controversy over the so-called emergency laws, which gave the government unprecedented power to limit individual rights, and the escalating war in Vietnam, which was being financed largely by West Germany's payments for U.S. military protection and economic investments. This situation led to the formation of opposition movements outside institutional channels, the so-called APO, or extraparliamentary opposition. The theater saw its function as providing support for the APO movement. The APO demonstrations intensified the anxieties of a population already nervous about Brandt's more relaxed *Ostpolitik,* his effort to reestablish channels of communication with East Germany closed after the Berlin Wall went up in 1961.

Hans Filbinger, who had been elected governor of Baden-Württemberg, of which Stuttgart is the capital, by a landslide in 1966 on a harsh law-and-order platform, was a rabid foe of *Ostpolitik,* deeply suspicious of the intellectual left, and a leading proponent of the federal government's program of censorship and surveillance in its effort to combat terrorism. He went so far as to blame the universities and above all Theodor Adorno and the Frankfurt School, who had great influence on the student movement, for the wave of terrorist assassinations. Ironically, the government's measures against the extremist outgrowth of a movement that had begun in protest against the continued silence about the Holocaust were reminiscent of Nazi tactics. So were some of the terrorists' strategies. As the terrorist attacks escalated to force the freeing of the Baader-Meinhof group, so did the repressive measures taken by the government. The legacy of Germany's past broke through a mutually reflective mirror of terror and repression.

One of the most disputed decrees was the so-called *Radikalenerlass* (Radicals Decree) of 1972. Intended to exclude from federal employment anyone who had been involved in anticonstitutional activities, it led to an elaborate mechanism of investigations. Between 1972 and 1976, when the decree was suspended, about half a million applicants were examined as to their "loyalty to the constitution"; 430 candidates were rejected in the process. The measure particularly enraged students and recent graduates, who were the most likely candidates for public service in schools, universities, and the government. Although many of them had had at least a fleeting association with the antiwar and campus reform movements of the 1960s, they clearly dissociated themselves from the extremism of the few small splinter groups that survived into the 1970s. The investigations, conducted by the individual states with various degrees of punctiliousness, blurred the line between subversive activities and passing or suspected affiliation with suspicious groups or individuals. The government's perceived persecution of Germany's youth clashed with the increasing revelations about the Nazi pasts of high-ranking government officials, who were still in office or receiving generous pensions.[6] Hans Filbinger was one of them.

In Bernhard's most frequently produced play, *Eve of Retirement,* inspired by the revelations, a former concentration camp commander, now a judge, escaped prosecution for his wartime activities by hiding in the basement of his family's home. On the eve of his retirement he muses:

> For ten years I was hiding
> then it was time to see the daylight again
> Who would have thought
> that I would end my career as Chief Justice
> and retire with an enormous pension[7]

In Stuttgart, the Baader-Meinhof trial deteriorated into bizarre histrionics. In prison the defendants were isolated from one another and barred from private consultations with their lawyers. The measures became part of the expanded antiterrorist legislation of the Judicature Act (*Gerichtsverfassungsgesetz*), which led to widespread protests by leftists and liberal intellectuals against the restriction of individual rights. In the excessively politicized climate, a nervous public and law enforcement agencies saw the civil rights demonstrators as terrorist sympathizers.[8]

On May 9, 1976, Ulrike Meinhof hanged herself in prison. Her death immediately triggered suspicion of foul play. Twelve days before her death Albert Camus's play *Les Justes,* about Russian terrorists during the tsarist regime, opened at Peymann's theater. The production ended with the dropping of a white curtain. As the opening-night audience applauded enthusiastically, a film was projected onto the curtain. To the accompaniment of music by Mozart, it showed a leisurely trolley ride from the Stuttgart theater to the Stammheim prison. The applause turned into protest.[9] Peymann commented later: "The theater scandal happened. What was perceived as justified and just in the interest of Russia and against the tsar was not permitted in connection with the Baader-Meinhof group and Stammheim, against Vietnam and the media tsar Axel Springer. The fissure in the spectator's conscience was painfully exposed."[10]

In June 1976 Peymann was one of about sixty artists and intellectuals across Europe to receive a letter from the mother of the Stammheim prisoner Gudrun Ensslin, asking for contributions that would help pay the group's dental bills. The prisoner's mother was a resident of Stuttgart. Peymann posted the letter on the theater's bulletin board with a handwritten note inviting contributions. He raised 600 marks, 100 of them his personal contribution. The transaction did not gain the media's attention until the following fall, after the Red Army Faction kidnapped Hanns Martin Schleyer, the president of the federal employers' association and member of the executive board of Daimler Benz, from his Stuttgart home on September 5, 1977.

Filbinger's party, the Christian Democratic Union, demanded Peymann's dismissal on the grounds that in his case "the borderline of artistic freedom had been not only reached but grossly transgressed." The Socialists argued that there were no legal grounds for the dismissal. Peymann declared he would not accept his dismissal without notice, but neither would he renew his five-year contract. The administrative board of the Württemberg State Theater, government members all, stated that "it is irresponsible to use the platform of a public institution for such activities." If Peymann was unwilling to "accept this reprimand," it was up to him whether he would stay until the end of his contract or leave. In any case, his contract would not be renewed.[11]

In the meantime, the drawn-out and finally bungled negotiations between the Red Army Faction and the German government concurrent with the trial led the terrorists to hijack a Lufthansa plane on October 13, 1977, in Mallorca. The Frankfurt-bound plane was diverted to Rome, Cyprus, Bahrain, Dubai, and Aden (where the hijackers killed the pilot), and finally to Mogadishu, Somalia. There a special unit of the German Border Guard stormed the plane and freed all eighty-six hostages. Three of the four hijackers were the only ones to die in the attack. On October 18, Andreas Baader and the two other hijackers were found shot to death in their cells. The fourth survived her suicide attempt. Her account contradicted the official version of a suicide plot and fed suspicions of a government conspiracy. On October 19, 1977, Hanns Martin Schleyer's kidnappers, in an announcement in the French daily *Libération,* informed Chancellor Helmut Schmidt, who had refused to ransom the industrialist, that Schleyer's body could be found in the trunk of a green Audi parked in the French town Mülhausen.[12] Schleyer's burial in Stuttgart on October 25 concluded what was later termed somberly a "German autumn," which had begun with his abduction fifty days earlier.[13] The German government's sacrifice of Schleyer under Chancellor Schmidt, a Socialist, led to a heated debate about each individual's right to life versus the "common good." It was a painful self-examination that tested the Germans' understanding of democracy against their persistent yearning for the protective authority of the state.

The following winter, the Filbinger affair erupted. In February 1978 the internationally esteemed *Die Zeit* published an excerpt from a forthcoming book by Rolf Hochhuth, best known for his play *The Deputy,* which exposed Pope Pius XII's tacit complicity with the Hitler regime. His novel *A German Love Story* told of a wartime affair between a German woman and a Polish POW that led to his execution. Based on an actual event, Hochhuth's account was interspersed with references to the present political situation in Germany.

One paragraph printed in *Die Zeit* targeted Filbinger: "The present minister president of our state, Dr. Filbinger, as Hitler's naval judge, prosecuted a German sailor under Nazi laws even after Hitler's death. Naval judges, more cunning than their colleagues in the army and air force, having destroyed their files at the end of the war, one must assume that the fearsome upholder of the law is a free man only thanks to the silence of those who knew him."

The accusation was based on Hochhuth's painstaking research into the sentences passed by military judges under the Hitler regime, which he also dramatized in great detail in his later play *Juristen* (Lawyers).[14] Filbinger had sentenced the sailor in question to death for alleged desertion, and he was hanged. Filbinger filed a libel suit against Hochhuth and the influential magazine *Der Spiegel,* which documented several cases of desertion still pending after Germany's capitulation. Filbinger claimed that he couldn't remember the death sentences imposed on deserters, because the men had been tried in absentia and none had actually been executed. Knowing that the sailors escaped to Sweden, which did not extradite deserters, he imposed the death sentences only as a deterrent, to prevent panic in the chaotic last days of the war. Therefore they slipped his memory.

Filbinger's ongoing attacks on the liberal press (which he saw as conspiring with East Germany against conservative politicians) and his evasive, contradictory responses only made matters worse. One day before the verdict was reached, *Der Spiegel* produced a paper that Filbinger had written as a law student in which he discussed the new Nazi penal law. The magazine's headline, "Keeping the Community of Blood Pure" (*Die Blutsgemeinschaft rein erhalten*), was a quote from his text, in which he argued for the priority of the "community of the people" (*Volksgemeinschaft*), the "real covenant of the will of a nation" (*der reale Willensverband einer Nation*), over the individual, who "is no longer seen as a singular person but as a link in the totality and only as such receives protection under criminal law."[15] His line of argument sent chills through a nation that had not yet worked through the implications of Chancellor Schmidt's decision not to give in to Schleyer's kidnappers in the interest of the state at the expense of individuals.[16]

The "community of the people," the law student went on, had to be secured "in its natural existence and according to its religious and moral ideas." Good student that he was, Filbinger argued that "according to the National Socialist view, the community of the people is first of all a community of blood." In other words, the element of blood is of greater importance than historical, national, or linguistic-cultural elements. "This community of blood must be kept clean and the racially valuable components of the German people systematically developed." Whether he actually believed what he was saying or was mouthing what was expected of him, his words came to haunt a population of "good Germans" who were trying to put their Nazi past behind them and their enraged heirs who demanded the truth.

In Bernhard's *Eve of Retirement* the judge sleeps with his sister to celebrate Himmler's birthday. Incest is the aging Nazi's grotesque final solution to the problem of preserving the purity of blood.

In its ruling against Filbinger the court noted that he could have helped the men he condemned to death. Hochhuth had to delete only the clause about naval judges being cunning enough to destroy their files. He did not have to retract his description of Filbinger as a "fearsome upholder of the law."[17]

Die Zeit deplored the fact that Filbinger, instead of giving a thoughtful account of his responsibility, responded in generalities about "guilt and fate in the theological definition of guilt, as articulated by the Russian writer Dostoyevsky: 'All of us are guilty of everything and responsible for everything.'"[18] Filbinger's party, the conservative Christian Democratic Union (CDU), demanded his resignation as governor, less because of his past than because of his way of dealing with it after it became widely known. He did resign, but then became honorary chairman of the Baden-Württemberg CDU and was awarded the federal medal of honor for distinguished service (*Bundesverdienstorden*); he also holds a high honorary rank in the French Foreign Legion. At the age of seventy he received the title of professor. In 1995, at eighty-six, Filbinger still blamed his fall on the machinations of East Germany's infamous Stasi and the liberal media of West Germany.[19]

The 1978 New Year's Eve supplement of *Die Zeit* published one of Thomas Bernhard's "dramalettes," *The German Lunch Table*.[20] It features the Bernhard family, "Herr and Frau Bernhard, their daughters, their sons, their grandchildren, their great-grandchildren, and their closest relatives"—ninety-eight people in all—gathered around the traditional oak table. Instead of noodles, all they can find in their soup are Nazis. "Our new president is a Nazi," screams the second-oldest great-grandson. "And our old president/also was a Nazi," the third-oldest great-great-grandson shouts back. The readers knew what they were shouting about.

Walter Scheel, the president of the Federal Republic during the Filbinger affair and a member of the Free Democratic Party, also had a spotty past. Scheel's predecessor, Heinrich Lübke of the Christian Democratic Union (CDU), had allegedly participated in the construction of concentration camps.[21] Scheel's membership in the Nationalsozialistische Deutsche Arbeiterpartei was brought to public attention by his eventual successor, the conservative Karl Carstens, whose own membership in the Nazi Party and service in the Wehrmacht had become known in time to endanger his bid for the presidency in 1979. His later justification for his career-conscious arrangement with

the Nazis was typical of the excuses made by the majority of the contemporaries who voted for him: "In retrospect, that phase of my life seems to be
marked by an inner schism that can't be fathomed by today's generation. Basically, I tried to avoid membership in the party through tricks, but I avoided
an open conflict, which got me involved against my inner conviction. My mo-
tive was, I wanted to become a lawyer and I believed that I could reach my —
surely not dishonorable — goal by the steps described above." [22]

Hans Kiesinger, Filbinger's predecessor as governor of Baden-Württemberg and later chancellor during the Christian Democrat–Socialist coalition,
was known as a *Gelegenheitsnazi,* an opportunist or fellow traveler. A director
in Goebbels's propaganda ministry from 1942 to 1945, he was interned from
1945 to 1947 before launching a successful career as a CDU politician in 1947.
Unlike Filbinger's, his career was not derailed by his Nazi past. Despite public
protests and against the apprehension of the Socialists, he became chancellor in 1966, with Willy Brandt, former mayor of Berlin and future chancellor,
as his foreign minister.[23] Brandt, a returned anti-Nazi émigré, now a prominent cabinet member under the leadership of a former Nazi, later described
the coalition of divergent past and present political interests as "an absolutely
truthful . . . representation of German reality." [24]

"Nazi soup / Nazi soup / Nazi soup," screams Herr Bernhard, the *German
Lunch Table*'s presiding patriarch, and slams his hand angrily into his soup.
Bernhard subtitled his farcical end-of-the year summation of German politics *A Tragedy for a Burgtheater Tour of Germany.* The minuscule vignette of
seventy-five spoken lines is not complete without the wry suggestion that the
honorable company, with its mythical Habsburg legacy, should apply their
histrionic skills to the performance of the quintessential German family, to
which Bernhard lent his name. It encapsulates Austria's convoluted relationship with Germany. Here are Austrians showing the Germans (once again,
this time as farce) that they can play Germans better than the Germans. Yet
it would also have been quite appropriate for Burgtheater actors to deal with
the Nazis in their soup (a task that Austrians habitually leave up to the Germans). The Burgtheater had its own track record of accommodation to the
Nazi regime; some of its most prominent current members had been ardent
admirers of Hitler. By wrapping his own name around the German lunch
table, Bernhard includes himself in the situation he satirizes, in marked contrast to Hochhuth, whose moralistic grandstanding absolved him. There was
no Burgtheater tour at that time. Peymann presented the dramalette in Feb-

ruary 1979, his last season in Stuttgart, then in Bochum, and finally with the Burgtheater in 1987. That production toured in only one city, Mainz, in 1993. It stayed in the Burg's repertory until Peymann's departure in 1999. With a total of 245 performances, it was the most frequently performed production in the theater's history.

During Peymann's tumultuous tenure in Stuttgart, from 1974 to 1979, he commissioned and staged a new play by Bernhard every season. *Minetti,* Bernhard's twisted homage to the actor, opened the 1976–77 season. *Immanuel Kant* followed in the spring of 1978. For Peymann's last season Bernhard wrote another play for Bernhard Minetti, *Der Weltverbesserer* (The World Improver, or Utopian; it has not yet been translated into English). When Minetti became ill, the production had to be canceled (it premiered in Bochum two years later), and Bernhard offered to come up with another play, "something that fits."[25]

It didn't take him long to come up with *Eve of Retirement,* subtitled *A Comedy of the German Soul.* Judge Rudolf Höller, about to retire, sleeps with his older sister, Vera, once a year, on the birthday of Heinrich Himmler, leader of the SS and chief of the Gestapo. Clara, his younger sister, a wheelchair-bound Socialist, was crippled as a child in an American bombing raid. To celebrate Himmler's birthday, Vera irons Rudolf's SS uniform, polishes the frame of Himmler's photograph, and dresses Clara in a concentration camp shirt (all hidden the rest of the year). As the obligatory conclusion to an elaborate dinner prepared by Vera, she brings out the family photo album. The photographs cover their childhood through Rudolf's Nazi career, from soldier to substitute camp commander. This time Rudolf has a heart attack. In the play's final moments Vera calls their Jewish doctor, then tries frantically to get her brother out of his old SS uniform before the doctor arrives.

When the play opened in Stuttgart on June 29, 1979, Filbinger was gone; Peymann was on his way out; the Federal Republic's new president, Karl Carstens, who had survived a close look at his political past, was on his way in. The rescue of the hijacked plane in Mogadishu was a great political success for Chancellor Helmut Schmidt. Though terrorists staged a few more attacks, they had lost their stranglehold on the country's political system. Public demonstrations protesting the statute of limitations for crimes committed under Nazi laws went on. Set in 1969 at thirty years for murder, the limitation was finally revised on July 3, 1979, to permit continued investigations of Nazi crimes. According to the Central Office for the Investigation of National So-

cialist Crimes, of 2,450 procedures against Nazi criminals still pending, 696
were introduced in 1979. Since the end of the war 8,498 persons had been
identified as felons, of whom 6,446 had been sentenced, 6 in 1979.[26]

Against this backdrop Bernhard constructs a chillingly recognizable
world of decent middle-class burghers striving to be model citizens, misunderstood Nazis all of them. Vera laments to her brother:

> And yet the majority thinks just like us
> the majority hides that's what's so terrible
> it's really absurd
> The majority thinks like us and must do so secretly
> Even if they insist on the contrary
> they are still National Socialists all of them
> it's written all over their faces
> but they don't admit it
> I don't know anyone who doesn't think like us
> . . .
> That is the horror Rudolf
> that we don't show the world who we are
> we don't show it
> instead of showing it quite openly [27]

The last four lines hit upon the truth, but not as she intended. It is part
of Bernhard's brilliant strategy throughout the play that the meaning of his
characters' speeches can be reversed. Nazis should admit their past, but for
reasons opposite those Rudolf envisions. He assures his sister:

> Just wait and see
> the time will come for us to show it again
> Everything indicates that we will show it again
> and not only show it

Vera takes heart:

> Then again we do have a President now
> who was a National Socialist (204)

The aging Höller children look like a nice family. They function within the
comfortable rituals of upper-middle-class life, as they can afford to do, thanks
to Rudolf's position and the substantial pension he will receive, like many

of Germany's postwar judges whose careers began under the Nazis. (Many young Germans at that time were outraged that, according to the Decree on Radicals, students with a brief past in the rebellious movements of the 1960s could be barred for life from any job supported by the federal government, while Nazis held high government positions and received generous pensions.)

Vera and Rudolf do the right things: they honor their parents' memory; they take care of their handicapped sister instead of putting her in an institution; they appreciate good art and good music. Vera praises Rudolf's popularity with children. His victory in court on Himmler's birthday seems to be a triumph for the ecologists: he has prevented the construction of a factory that would produce a hazardous gas. But it was primarily an act of self-interest and a bizarre repetition. The factory was to be built across from their house. During the Nazi regime Himmler had intervened to prevent the construction of a plant to produce poison gas for a different purpose on the same site.

There is a dark underside to all the tidy surfaces of the Höllers' treasured domesticity. Their mother committed suicide. "Sometimes I wonder/if it wasn't the right time she killed herself," muses Rudolf (104). Unlike his colleagues at Auschwitz, who didn't mind "sending thousands and thousands into the gas," Rudolf had to force himself to do so (195). Nevertheless, Vera tells her paralyzed sister

> I know you don't like hearing this
> . . .
> Your father was a Jew hater
> like ninety-eight percent of the population
> only very few admit
> that they are anti-Semitic
> but the Germans hate the Jews
> even as they claim just the opposite
> that's the German nature
> in a thousand years the Jews will still be hated in Germany
> in a million years
> if there'll be any Jews left at all
> that's what Rudolf says (138)

If the aging Höller children appear to be the nice people next door, they have terrible secrets. In Bernhard's sarcastic vision they have much in common

with the equally nice neighbors from whom they hide their secrets, although
they actually share them.

Paradoxically, it is their past that keeps them going while it corrodes them
from the inside. In their strenuous efforts to preserve their past according to
their ideals of decency, loyalty, and integrity, which they pervert in the process, they are not much different from Bernhard's archetypal characters, who
are obsessed by one idea and pursue it single-mindedly until they collapse
under the strain. The outrage of *Eve of Retirement* was not the suggestion that
the majority of Germans are incurable Nazis but the implication that fascism
is just another symptom of an innate obsessiveness that also drives scholars,
scientists, and artists. Whatever their accomplishments, failures, or crimes,
the result is invariably madness and death. Underneath the timely political
farce, *Eve of Retirement* is a deeply disturbing existential tragedy.

Peter von Becker observed in *Theater Heute:* "Never before had the
lost Nazi time been retrieved on the stage more banally and viciously."[28]
Benjamin Henrichs of *Die Zeit* recalled Bernhard's remark about a production of Chekhov's *Cherry Orchard,* "This could have been written by me. Only
I would have done it much better," and found parallels also with *The Three
Sisters.* In both plays three siblings mourn a more beautiful past (their "Mos-
cow") and the cutting down of trees is a sign of brutally changing times. The
prominent critic found the play Bernhard's best so far, and his most complicated and "spookiest" — not because it's about Nazis, past or present (it's
not), but, more important, because, like all Bernhard plays, it's about himself in a potentially self-incriminating setting.[29] Self-references surface in the
characters' habits and obsessions (such as the paralyzed anarchist sister writing letters to the editor). Not to be confused with a public confession, the
play includes the author in what it dramatizes: the way language reanimates
history and keeps us entangled in its processes. The characters' speech patterns, inflected by Austrian idiom, eerily echo time-honored "family values"
preached to all children with a solid *Kinderstube.* As Bernhard Minetti put it
after opening night, "It all looks so familiar."[30]

When Peymann moved to Bochum in the fall of 1980, he brought the
production along with a majority of the Stuttgart theater's resident company,
including dramaturgs and designers. Beyond Peymann's inspired artistry, it
was Filbinger and the political pressure of his administration that bonded
his ensemble. Peymann reflected years later, "It was lucky for us that we had
Filbinger . . . , who always saw the West as endangered and who finally was

exposed as a perfidious liar and Nazi lawyer."[31] The dramas on stage and in the public arena mirrored and activated each other. Throughout his career, Peymann continued to insist (with intentional naiveté) that "the theater is a place of opposition—in certain times to the point of subversion."[32]

As Bernhard was writing *Minetti* for Peymann's Stuttgart theater, he articulated his own program of opposition. "As a former and probably lifelong so-called acting student I have always been interested only in writing *for* actors against the audience, as I always did everything *against* the audience, against my readers or my spectators, in order to save myself, to discipline myself to the utmost, highest degree of my capacities."[33] His Minetti says:

> The actor's biggest enemy
> is his audience
> Once he knows that
> he grows in his art
> Every moment the actor has to tell himself
> the audience will storm the stage
> That's the state he has to act in
> against the audience
> against human rights you understand
> All my life I performed
> against the audience
> so I could bear the tension
> so as not to weaken
> My father the magician
> was my teacher[34]

The actor's quixotic bravery was Bernhard's answer to Peymann's politicized theater. If his play about an actor opening the 1976–77 Stuttgart season seemed blatantly oblivious of the escalating political crisis in the city and throughout the country, its political subtext was in the casting. The real Minetti, the actor who lent his name to the title character, who is also an actor, began his career in Berlin during the Weimar Republic and continued there as a popular actor throughout the Nazi regime.[35] Minetti the stage character was banished from the stage because he "refused the classics." A dig at the German theater, which reconstructed the country's post-Holocaust identity in the classical tradition of Schiller and Goethe, the line is also a compliment to Minetti, a classical actor who at an advanced age made himself available to the avant-garde. While

Minetti the stage character hid in his sister's attic for thirty years, the real Minetti kept quiet about his acquiescence in Hitler's Germany to advance his budding acting career. He accepted a role in the notorious anti-Semitic film *The Rothschilds.* As late as 1944 he directed a so-called *Durchhaltestück,* a propaganda play that urged the continuation of the war to the bitter end, *Die Wölfe* (The Wolves), by the Nazi protégé Hans Rehberg, who "seduced him" into staging it in Breslau after even Gustav Gründgens, Göring's darling, and other favored Berlin directors rejected it for its problematic message.

"I could not be a hero. That was my decision" was Minetti's explanation for staying in Berlin, for knowing about the concentration camps (though not of the killings), for not speaking out. "I only know that I was not a Nazi," he said.[36]

After the war he became a wanderer. Unlike most German actors who were associated with one theater throughout their careers, Minetti had various short-term acting engagements at various repertory theaters. In countless classical roles he imitated his old successes. "Minetti reminded one of Minetti," as one critic put it succinctly.[37] Minetti was well aware of his stagnation and never denied it.

The turning point in his postwar career came in 1957, when he was cast as Hamm in the German-language premiere of Beckett's *Endgame.* His experience with Beckett whetted his appetite for more of his plays, and he became known as a "Beckett actor." Beckett himself had little taste for Minetti's virtuoso acting. According to widespread theater gossip, "he considered Minetti an insufferable madonna and took to referring to him as 'Madame Minetti' behind his back. To those who knew Beckett, this seemed unusually catty for such a reflexively polite Irishman."[38] Nevertheless, Minetti aged into a pioneering performer of innovative "difficult" playwrights, such as Jean Genet, Harold Pinter, and finally Bernhard. While he was writing *Minetti,* Bernhard praised him as "probably the greatest . . . living actor," a *"Geistestheaterkopf"*—one of Bernhard's inimitable composite nouns, suggesting a head (or mind) attuned to a theater of thought.[39] Minetti in turn found it "eerie" that Bernhard knew so much about him, although they had very little personal contact. In 1980 Minetti estimated that his personal exchanges with Bernhard amounted to "a total of three hours."[40] Their limited interaction after Minetti's definitive performances in three Bernhard plays sheds light on Bernhard's reserve even with people he deeply respected.

While critics praised Bernhard's *Minetti* and above all Bernhard Minetti for capturing the essence of an actor's existence, they did not mention the undercurrent theme of an actor's — and by association *that* actor's — survival. If the play focuses on existential questions of performance, Bernhard Minetti's performance incorporated his past. The silence about it was part of it. It reflected, for better or worse, the state of the culture that produced it. Jewish directors, such as the returning refugees Fritz Kortner and later Peter Zadek, the son of German émigrés, loved to work with Minetti. If Minetti's wartime career made them uncomfortable, they were won over by his total immersion in his art. That was the kind of existential madness Bernhard recognized, beyond his appreciation of Minetti's acting skills. Minetti was a Bernhard character before Bernhard invented him. Bernhard became a master at staging the actor inside his performance.

Both Peymann and Bernhard learned from Minetti's approach to acting, which Bernhard's stage Minetti articulates as playing "against the audience." The word *Gegenspieler,* opponent or antagonist, contains the definition of his playing against the audience (*gegen das Publikum spielen*). Minetti was an unmatched master at it. His "playing against" defined the audience as an opponent, as in sports, and performance as a match. His performances were matches against the audience, which he played with all the tension and enjoyment of a player in a good game.

Two contrasting productions of *Der Weltverbesserer,* Peymann's original staging with Bernhard Minetti in 1981 and a production in 1998 at Berlin's Deutsches Theater with the eminent East German actor Jürgen Holtz, strikingly illuminate Minetti's superior strength and courage in creating a Bernhard character (and his audience). The "world improver" is a tyrannical old man, a nihilistically optimistic utopian. Like Schopenhauer, he lives with his housekeeper-mistress. His world-famous treatise on the improvement of the world suggests its annihilation. Unable to walk, or at least insisting that he cannot (he forgets for a moment), he is confined to a chair. In the Berlin production, the plain, straight-backed chair evoked the image of Martin Heidegger's *Gestell,* (a framelike supportive contraption that represents the metaphysical dimension of technology). In Bochum the then seventy-six-year-old Minetti, haughty and angular, a hawk both lurking in ambush and trapped himself, held forth in a thronelike chair. The image recalled his distinguished career as a classical actor as well as his role of Minetti, the actor who "refused himself to the classics" with the sole exception of Lear. Beckett's Hamm is the more recent ancestor.

With Minetti, actor and audience never became chummy. The audience felt no pity for the character Minetti performed. Rather, it was awed by the performance—both the actor's and that of the character as he performed against death and oblivion. Minetti had his own way of playing against the audience. During one touring engagement of the production the audience's laughter seemed excessive to Minetti. He softened his voice until the audience had to strain to hear. With the softer voice came a quieter, less virtuoso performance. As Minetti made it tougher for the audience, the character became more vulnerable, but on the actor's terms: not as a concession but, as in a sports match, a countermove. Minetti won.[41]

In Berlin the owlish-faced Jürgen Holtz, altogether softer around the edges, took in the audience with his finely tuned psychological approach to the character. His performance was transparent—it allowed the spectator to take possession of the character, as it were, to make him one's own and fill him with one's private experiences. Strangely, the audience disappeared. So, ultimately, did the stage character. He became one with the audience, a recognizable relative. Holtz won the audience's heart; Minetti won the match.

Holtz's performance, in a radically cut version of the play, ensured its accessibility through his character's familiarity. The cutting of repetitions was aimed at distilling what actors term the psychological through-line. Such an approach might even make the play—or any of Bernhard's plays, for that matter—more bearable for an uninitiated audience. Without the repetitions, however, the most essential aspect of Bernhard's approach to language is lost. His characters are constructed and go on constructing themselves through their iterative speech acts. Cut off from their performative speech acts, Bernhard's characters collapse. They are framed by language, hooked up to a mechanism of repetitions as their life support. Heidegger's *Gestell* is animated by the technology of grammar. Differing fundamentally from the Aristotelian character who reveals himself in decisions that produce an action, Bernhard's characters, mostly old men, are no longer "active" in that sense. They do not reveal themselves in physical acts. They produce themselves in obsessive speech acts that keep the performance of identity in action. In fact, this "action" is the only action of a Bernhard character and in a Bernhard play. What they reveal is the culture that produced them and that they in turn keep producing. The play's real action, which manifests itself in performance, is the production of the culture in the interaction with the audience, rather than just its representation onstage.

Bernhard's and Minetti's adversarial relationship with the audience is not to be confused with the aggressive tactics of Peter Handke's actors in his *Offending the Audience* (also first introduced by Peymann). They attack the audience directly with their provocative criticisms and put-downs. Bernhard's actors, by contrast, even when they are introduced by their own names, are presented in the act of performing someone else (Minetti as Minetti). Nevertheless, their real names foreground their real-life identities. Actors and audience appear to be starting from the same place. The scene recalls Louis Althusser's dramaturgy of interpellation: Someone calls, another turns around. His response constitutes his identity on the caller's terms. In Althusser's terms, the caller subjects the other to "the Law." [42] In Bernhard's subversion of the Aristotelian "law" of the theater, the actor's "interpellation"—his performance —rather than subjecting the audience through emotional identification, produces it as his antagonist. In Bernhard's early explorations of the theater, punishment comes swiftly. A slim, grim tale inserted into *Amras* tells of an actor playing the wicked sorcerer in a children's play who turns the young lovers— the children's favorites—into animals. After the intermission, the children "jump from their seats and onto the stage, and it seems as if there weren't just three hundred of them, but three thousand, as if there were a million of them. . . . Although the actor as sorcerer cries behind the sorcerer's mask and implores them to stop beating and kicking him, they aren't listening and continue to beat him (with hard, sharp objects, scissors and knives) and trample him until he is motionless, until he is *dead*. . . . Having killed him, the children break out in laughter so overpowering that all present lose their minds in it." [43]

German has one term for magician and sorcerer: *Zauberer*. As an acting student, it will be remembered, Bernhard played a sorcerer/magician in a children's production. His stage Minetti mentions in passing that his father, a magician, taught him how to play "against the audience/against human rights you understand." The equation, a bit farfetched under the circumstances, smacks of an actor's swashbuckling pathos. In a typical Bernhard move, the bold assertion undermines itself in performance while flagging the authoritarian nature of art (and Bernhard's own ambivalence toward it). The match isn't even after all. It is the actor's performative power that produces the identity of his audience. Still, the outcome is open: unlike the author, the performer onstage is directly exposed to the audience he produces. He may create a monster that can undermine his authority at any moment and attack him "against human rights," as the children attack the hapless actor who plays the wicked sorcerer. The theatrical space envelops both actor and audience. It replaces Althusser's notion of an overarching ideology that maintains a precarious balance between caller and respondent.

Against the general trend in the theater of the late 1960s, Bernhard did not attack authority. His characters, most of them authoritarian tyrants, regardless of their obsession with art, philosophy, science, or Nazi politics, are neither shown in a critical light nor punished for their delusions. (Death is not a punishment but a fact. That his aged, ailing characters did not come to the appropriate conclusion and kill themselves much earlier makes their efforts at living the stuff of comedy.) Bernhard's theater demonstrates the mechanism of authority in the interplay with the audience. Those reviewers who acknowledged the mechanism in his leading actors' domineering performances but missed a clearly stated political agenda mistrusted the ambiguity of what on the surface seemed so familiar and criticized Bernhard as a reactionary.

The delayed East German premiere of *Eve of Retirement* in 1986, at East Berlin's prominent Deutsches Theater, strikingly illustrates the disastrous results of using Bernhard's stage for ideological purposes.[44] For a long time the East Germans dismissed Bernhard as yet another representative of a moribund capitalist society, his nihilism useless to the Communist project of "world improvement." His memoirs were his only works available in East Germany. With their scathing accusations against Austria's perniciously intertwined Catholic and National Socialist traditions and their continued dynamic in postwar Austria, they seemed to fit, like *Eve of Retirement,* the Communist project of *Auseinandersetzung mit dem Faschismus,* coming to terms with fascism—the West's coming to terms, that is. From the East German perspective it wasn't their problem, since Communists had always opposed the Nazis (that this was also a delusion would surface after the fall of the Berlin Wall). But *Eve of Retirement,* like all Bernhard plays, lends itself neither to streamlined politicizing nor to pointed psychologizing. East German critics who saw the play as an exploration of West German decadence wondered what it had to do with their lives. Those who expected a clearly defined political point of view together with a blueprint for change deplored the lack of "socialist realism." West German journalists suspected that to their East German colleagues it was as good a play as any to prove, if nothing else, the depravity of the bourgeois *Klassenfeind.* Nonplussed theatergoers kept walking out during performances.[45]

Bernhard's dramaturgy needs the shared cultural memory of actors and audiences. The play's "action," its playing with and against the audience, is its message. It makes for its claustrophobic tensions, which are ultimately self-destructive. Bernhard shares this fate with many Austrian writers. Their razor-sharp observations and criticism of conditions at home are deeply rooted in local traditions. Austria's language makes it seem misleadingly German, so that in the larger German context, the more specifically Austrian concerns seem irrelevant or, as we have seen, exotic at best, so that an observer can maintain an uninvolved if bemused distance. In the case of many Austrian playwrights, however, language adds another anthropological divide in what is generally known as "German drama." Local idiom, let alone its pronunciation onstage—often chosen for some sort of alienating effect against the elitist elocution of highbrow theater—is nearly unintelligible north of the Danube. With a few exceptions, Austrian theater remains confined to Austria. Here it works fabulously. The whole country, because it is so small, becomes a stage with everybody participating in one way or another, inside the theater or in the media or out in the streets. When people walk out of shows, it's not a public relations disaster (theaters are generously subsidized anyway). Their responses validate the play's view of them. And the show goes on in one way or another.

In plays such as *Minetti* and *Eve of Retirement* Bernhard and Peymann tested the ground for setting up their performative matches with the audience, against the culture at large. But it was on Bernhard's home ground, in Salzburg and particularly in Vienna, that they had the greatest impact. As in European soccer, the championship match would continue in the streets.

CHAPTER EIGHT

Writing Wittgenstein
Thinking in Action

What thinks is never what it thinks about.

—Paul Valéry, *Monsieur Teste*

IN 1970 BERNHARD WROTE TO AUNTIE, "The decade ahead of me is my decade. Then nothing will interest me anymore and nature will do its part."[1] Though counteracted by its terseness, the statement smacks a bit of Romantic pathos—the *Dichter*'s musing about his brief worldly glory and willed descent into oblivion, his resolve to beat nature to his demise, as it were. Typically, in its bluntness it both highlights and obfuscates Bernhard's ongoing struggle to come to terms with the certainty of an early death.

The 1970s turned out indeed to be his decade. Altogether, ten plays had major productions, each one eagerly awaited and heatedly discussed. His early short stories "Der Italiener" (The Italian) and "Der Kulterer" (Kulterer) were made into television films. His award-winning novel *The Lime Works* was followed by another major novel, *Correction*. In hindsight it falls into place as the summation, the apex of his earlier prose. After that, he concentrated on his autobiographical project. As we shall see, he would continue to do so ever more ferociously. The majority of his plays were produced during that period. His preoccupation with the theater during that time had a profound effect on his fiction.

In his brief early piece "Ist es eine Komödie? Ist es eine Tragödie?" (Is It a Comedy? Is It a Tragedy?) the narrator articulates Bernhard's lifelong obsession: "The theater study, one day the theater study! One describes well what one hates," and he elaborates: "First section: THE ACTORS, second section: THE ACTORS IN THE ACTORS, third section: THE ACTORS IN THE ACTORS OF

THE ACTORS, etc. . . . . fourth section: STAGE EXCESSES, etc. . . . . Last section: SO WHAT IS THEATER?[2]

Performance replaces psychology in Bernhard's thoroughly theatricalized presentations of the vanishing (human) subject long before performance studies became an academic fashion and performance a catchall for postmodernists in search for their lost (theoretical) subject. His early short stories are preparatory studies of performative strategies as they apply not only to actors but to narrative postures that he perfected in his later novels.

Bernhard's preoccupation with performance is informed by the increasing influence of Ludwig Wittgenstein. If Wittgenstein posits that the (thinking) subject can exist only in speech, Bernhard in his short stories demonstrates that a subject's speech acts are not identical to the speaking subject. Bernhard the performer upstages even Wittgenstein: the speech that constitutes the subject is not necessarily his own. Bernhard's speaking subject is defined through another's speech acts, which he quotes in what amounts to an accomplished performance.

Wittgenstein's close scrutiny of language had a tremendous impact on the post–World War II generation of Austrian writers as his hitherto unpublished works appeared in print over the years after his death in 1951.

From the approximately 12,000 pages of manuscript and 8,000 pages of typescript, the reclusive philosopher's work and persona emerged during the 1960s and 1970s in bits and pieces as a fascinating narrative in progress, constructed by the trustees of Wittgenstein's estate. Bernhard was quick to pick up on the drama of the "discovery" of Wittgenstein and the problem of constructing a deceased person from his notes.

In his introduction to *Philosophical Investigations* (published after his death) Wittgenstein calls the work an *Album,* a scrapbook, and says that what he has to say consists of *Bemerkungen,* comments and observations. Bernhard adapts the format in his early work. *Amras* is put together as a compilation of the narrator's thoughts and letters and his dead brother's fragmented writings—his legacy, as it were. The subtitle of the story "Watten" (1969) is "Ein Nachlass" (An Estate).[3]

Another story, "Ungenach" (1968), deals with the distribution of an inherited estate of that name in Austria by the sole surviving heir, who is a professor at Stanford and also the narrator.[4] Ludwig Wittgenstein, it will be remembered, gave away his family inheritance to his siblings and poets. The beneficiaries of "Ungenach" are an odd assortment of local characters, peasants, foresters, and patricians. These passing acquaintances and family friends, many of them isolated iconoclasts or stranded intellectuals, are the forerunners of the stock characters in Bernhard's existential theater. The text is structured in three parts. The first foregrounds the narrator's lawyer, Moro, as quoted in the narrator's enactment of their meeting in the lawyer's office. The second part lists the beneficiaries, with some background information on them. The language here is detached, shorthand. It reads like a playwright's preliminary character notes, or as if a camera zoomed in on files and notes on the lawyer's desk, followed by another close-up of the lawyer, as quoted by the narrator. The concluding part focuses on the notes and letters of the narrator's brother, who was killed somewhere in Africa during an unspecified revolutionary war. The lawyer's speeches are reflections on the estate, its owners and history. As quoted by the narrator, they become the enactment of his own history; that is, ultimately of himself. The process is theatrical: by enacting another person the narrator presents himself through the eyes of the other (whom he also impersonates). In his performance of the other, he is performing himself.

In his next story, "Watten" (1969), Bernhard again toys with bits and pieces of Wittgenstein's biography. Its narrator, a country doctor, has sold his inheritance and given the money to a scientist known for his work with recently released prisoners, who has used it to buy an old castle to convert into a home for ex-convicts. The narrator, who has moved to an old dilapidated shack next to the family manor, has stopped participating in the weekly round of *Watten,* a card game, with the locals in a nearby tavern. His license to practice medicine has been revoked, presumably because of his abuse of morphine.

The story unfolds in his recounting of his conversation with a fellow player, a trucker, who stopped by to persuade him to play cards again. The "real" drama is the suicide of one of the players on the way home. In the narrator's enactment it is staged as a dialogue, which begins as an agon, a verbal contest: the trucker wants him to play cards, the narrator resists. Their encounter becomes a storytelling contest that pits gossip and perception against each other. Bernhard explores narrative perspectives with theatrical tools.

In another story, "Der Wetterfleck" (The Loden Cape), Bernhard begins to touch on one of Wittgenstein's central concerns, the correlation of thinking and speaking. Here the narrator is an attorney. After twenty years of passing the same man on the Innsbruck street where his office is located, he notices that the man wears a loden cape that is identical to the one his brother wore. It was missing when his brother was found drowned in the river. One day as he is once again preoccupied with the man's loden coat, he finds its wearer waiting to consult him on a family matter. He is the owner of a *Bestattungswäsche-geschäft,* a store that specializes in "funerary accessories." The business and his house have been taken over by his son and greedy daughter-in-law, who drove him from the first-floor apartment to the second floor and now to the third floor. While the man recounts his plight, the attorney thinks about the loden cape that frames its wearer. Shortly after their encounter the man jumps to his death from the window of his third-floor apartment. It turns out that he had found the loden cape washed up on the shore several years earlier. Bernhard employs theatrical techniques: substitution (of the dead owner of the loden cape), enactment of another's speech acts to dramatize the clash between inner and outer action. The story that involves two tragic deaths becomes quite comic in the narrator's enactment of the discrepancy between what was going on in his head (where did the man get the loden cape?) and what he was listening to with undiminished attention. The actor's defining skill, says the celebrated actress in David Hare's play *Amy's View,* is saying one thing while thinking another.

In the story "Am Ortler" (On Mount Ortler) Bernhard sharpens the interplay between inner and outer action by juxtaposing the movements of the body and the mind. Two middle-aged brothers climb Mount Ortler to a *Senn-hütte,* an Alpine dairy hut, which they inherited from their parents. Not having visited it before since they were children, they have decided spontaneously to stay there for two years. Their strenuous climb to the peak is riddled with painful childhood memories. The forty-eight-year-old narrator is a scientist, his fifty-one-year-old brother a circus performer; one is an artist of the body, the other an artist of the mind. What their occupations have in common is, not surprisingly, *Vortragskunst,* the art of performance or presentation.

"He wouldn't hesitate to claim that in all his calculations the art of presentation is the most important issue," says the scientist about the circus performer. "'Where would my routine be without my performance skills and where would philosophy be and mathematics and the natural sciences and all of humanity and all of humankind without the art of performance?' he says" (385).

The circus performer's paean to the art of performance is Bernhard's theatricalized application of Wittgenstein's claim that whatever can be thought can also be spoken. Speaking is performance. The circus artist's profession led him to insights that go far beyond his profession. It made him a philosopher, someone who lived rather than wrote philosophy. Both the tightrope walker's and the scientist's professions are founded on the art of observation and breath control. (While the scientist explores the atmosphere, the circus performer's survival depends on correct breathing.) Both functions are the foundation of an actor's craft. The circus performer seems to have a professional advantage over the scientist performer in the absence of fear in the act of performing. Though the tightrope act may be preceded and followed by fear, there must be no fear in the performance of it. "You always were frightened by your tightrope act, I said. Fright *before* the act, fright *after* the act. No fright *in* the act. Your tightrope fright, I said. And you are frightened by your work, by the results of your research. Always frightened, he said. . . . Not *in* the act, he said, not *in* the act. But your nonstop fright, he said. And I: I always was also afraid for you. During your tightrope acts" (386).

Being *in* the act, as in Wittgenstein's picture, precludes self-observation. Fear is the result of projection and reflection. Fear during the performance would be deadly. It is impossible to step outside the picture, says Wittgenstein, just as it is impossible for language to speak about itself. The scientist brother of the tightrope walker as his observer is outside the picture. Safe on the ground, he has no respite from fear. That is what saves him in the end. Used to his fear, he can live with it. His older brother loses his mind when they reach their goal only to find that nothing is left of the hut but a heap of stones. Without the opportunity to overcome his fear—of confronting each other and their parents' legacy represented by the hut—without such respite from fear as the reward for their dangerous mountain climb the circus performer's mind short-circuits from the overload. The scientist-narrator's performance is in the writing. Articulation is survival by the skin of one's teeth. "In a flash I was conscious of the fact that one must practice continuously not only having thoughts and simply practicing those thoughts, one also has to practice continuously to speak those thoughts at all times, for unspoken thoughts are nothing" (387). They are what Wittgenstein calls "private language," which cannot assert understanding. The circus performer's mind collapses under the effort. In his characteristic quasi-private manner of speaking he tries to formulate why they cannot go back to the village and the inn where they had stayed so often with their domineering parents.

"You know his manner of speaking and I don't have to point out its pecu-

liarity to you" (394), says the narrator as he tries to quote his brother, presumably to the psychiatrist in charge. Performing the other, enacting his road
to death, is a moment's triumph over death. As long as one stays an actor, as
long as one knows one's part, knows the lines that precede the speaker, one
survives.

The text the brothers share is inscribed in the landscape. As children
they were forced up the steep, strenuous climb by their parents. "The father,
experienced with mountains, ruthless, crazy about mountains. The mother
subservient." The Alpine territory contains memory, both historical and personal, that sustains and destroys its inhabitants. "Around Razoi, everything
was familiar to us, tree, brook, everything. Even under changed atmospheric
conditions and therefore different soil conditions, sir, we recognized more and
more details, inconspicuous objects, roots, rocks, unchanged. And connected
with these objects, these root formations, these rocks, our parents' threats of
punishment" (398). The circus performer's pathography is inscribed in the
landscape, which triggers his collapse. "So much landscape! So much mental illness! he said suddenly. When I think it's enough, the landscape appears
again" (396). But even stronger is his fear of "the emptiness in our head and
of the emptiness of the landscape brought out by the emptiness of the head"
(403). Bernhard spotlights his characters in scenic environments, which are
barely described in visual details, only in terms of their impact on the minds of
their inhabitants. If the landscape contains the script and the performer loses
his lines, he finds himself in a void. He has literally lost his mind.

At the beginning of "his decade," in 1971, he was invited by a close friend,
the writer and critic Hilde Spiel, to contribute a piece on Wittgenstein to the
publication *Ver Sacrum,* which she edited. He declined. I quote his letter here
at length because it offers a revealing glimpse not only into Bernhard's way
of thinking but into his writerly posturing at that time. The self-conscious reluctance to accept the challenge, cloaked in a convoluted syntax of thoughtful
humility, coyly suggests his worthiness of the impossible task precisely because he is sensitive enough to bow out. The awkward tone reflects his still
strained attempts to negotiate his position within and against his own cultural
conditioning.

Writing about Wittgenstein's philosophy, above all his poetry—for in my
opinion, in the case of Wittgenstein we are dealing with a thoroughly

poetic mind (BRAIN), that is to say a philosophical BRAIN, not a philosopher—presents the greatest difficulties. It is as if I had to write something (propositions!) about myself and that's not possible. It is a state of cultural and mental history, which defies description. The question is not: Do I write about Wittgenstein. The question is: *Am* I Wittgenstein for one moment without destroying him (W.) or me. I cannot answer that question and therefore I cannot write about Wittgenstein. In Austria, where philosophy and poetry (mathematical-musical) are a mausoleum, *we* look at history vertically. That's terrifying on the one hand, progressive on the other, in a word: In Austria, in contrast to other countries, philosophy and art exist not in the consciousness of its people but in the consciousness of its culture of philosophy and poetry etc., which is an advantage for the philosopher and the poet if he is conscious of the advantage. As far as Wittgenstein is concerned: he is the purity of [Adalbert] Stifter, the clarity of Kant all in one and the greatest since Stifter (and along with him). What we didn't have in NOVALIS, the German, we now have in Wittgenstein— one more thing: Wittgenstein is a question that cannot be answered— that puts him on the level that excludes answers (and answering).

Our contemporary culture in all its unbearable manifestations is one that would be easy to answer, if one wanted to get into it—it is different only with Wittgenstein.

And the world is always too stupid and doesn't understand a thing, that is why it is always completely without concepts—the concepts just stand for themselves as concepts. This is deadly for the MASSES of heads, but one mustn't show any consideration for the masses of heads. Consequently, I do not write about Wittgenstein, because I cannot do it, because I do not have an answer for him that would make everything fall into place.[5]

The notion of philosophy and art as no longer generated by a living culture but freeze-dried in tradition and acknowledged by just a few in the know highlights the snobbism of a cultural elite, whose acceptance Bernhard coveted as much as he despised it. However strained Bernhard's relationship with the official cultural administrators at the time, his emphasis on a self-contained consciousness of high culture uncontaminated by the masses of (empty) heads fitted in their efforts to reconnect to the cultural achievements of Austria's pre-Nazi past. Hitler then could be considered an aberration and Austria's artistic and intellectual tradition strong enough to bridge the rupture he caused. Thus culture became an effective tool of *totschweigen* — the conspiracy of silence about the recent past. The works of the first generation of postwar writers — Bernhard's immediate predecessors, most prominent among them his mentor and friend Ingeborg Bachmann — show the struggle to confront the unspeakable. Traditional rural metaphors of a cyclically decaying nature provided the link to a more distant past. One could appropriate and subvert them to imply the trauma of the Holocaust without directly naming it. Stifter's minute descriptions of the ordinary offered a useful model. The unpretentious clarity of his writing preceded Wittgenstein's dictum that language is a picture of the world.

However cynical, Bernhard's perception of cultural consciousness as a mausoleum would provide him with a refuge in which to stage his ghostly spectacles of reconstituted language after the catastrophe. In a world that is extinct, life is simulated in performance. Performance is imitation and repetition. Language is the thin threat that connects — for better or for worse — to the past across the chasm of the Holocaust. Bernhard's characters are marionettes on the tattered strings of language, hanging on to the ruptured memory of culture.

Bernhard's argument about the impossibility of writing about Wittgenstein, however strained, goes to the core of his preoccupation with performance and the performative aspects of writing. It does reveal, in the end, his deep affinity to Wittgenstein's demand that language show rather than tell. Saying anything about Wittgenstein in a Wittgensteinian manner is not a matter of writing about him but rather of writing him, not of describing him but of performing him. The challenge and impossibility is to find a language that performs the movement of his mind. One would have to get inside Wittgenstein's head. Here Bernhard's experiments in performance overlap and collide with the question Wittgenstein pursues in his *Philosophical Investigations:* the impossibility of private languages. In his early works Bernhard tried to get at the language of genius and madness, a language that turns in on itself and at some point stops communicating. To write Wittgenstein one would have to get to the source of the genius that activated his performance, the articulation of his perceptions and thoughts. Bernhard would have had to enter Wittgenstein's private language, which, according to Wittgenstein, is not possible. Bernhard would have "destroyed" Wittgenstein by violating the results of his

Investigations. And he would have destroyed himself by losing himself, his own language, in Wittgenstein's head.

On the other hand, if he were to write *about* Wittgenstein, he would not share his language. What Bernhard is saying, then, is that he cannot write anything critical about Wittgenstein. A critique is a response, a response from the outside. But Bernhard, who is after the actor inside the actor, needs to get inside the other person. According to Wittgenstein, that is not possible. Writing about Wittgenstein, he would have to "write something (propositions!)" about himself, which is impossible. If he wrote about himself, Bernhard would have to get outside himself, so the self he would be writing about would be someone other than himself. He would have destroyed himself and Wittgenstein in the process. Bernhard's letter demonstrates to Hilde Spiel that having taken Wittgenstein at his word, he cannot write about Wittgenstein, not in the kind of drama he investigates in both his fiction and his theater works.

His letter notwithstanding, in "Walking" Bernhard probes deeper into the workings of a Wittgensteinian mind as he further explores the correlation between physical and mental motion. Karrer and Oehler used to take walks together on Mondays. Their regular outings, always through the same streets in Vienna, were also intense thinking expeditions. During one of their walks Karrer has a mental breakdown.

Oehler relates the experience to a third man, his walking companion on Wednesdays, who is also the narrator. The narrator enacts both Oehler and the absent man as he quotes Oehler quoting Karrer. He also takes the dead man's place as Oehler's walking companion on Mondays in addition to their customary Wednesday rounds. Substituting for the absent man, he listens to his companion's account of the events and conversations that preceded and followed Karrer's collapse. In the narrator's account they are replayed several times from various perspectives, including that of Karrer's psychiatrist, who interrogates Oehler.

Wittgenstein is first slipped in surreptitiously in a thought mentioned by the narrator, who quotes Oehler quoting Karrer. "You have to know, says Oehler, that every statement that is uttered and thought and that exists is at the same time correct and at the same time false, if we are talking about proper statements." [6]

Oehler's ruminations about propositions are triggered by conversations he had with Karrer about the nonexistence of reason, and as he recounts the

conversations to the narrator, he rages against people who just "make children
. . . because the faculty of reason was suspended" (13). The topic of "making
children" was triggered by some children playing in the street. Their presence asserts the workings of "Nature," which "excludes actual thinking" and
confirms Oehler's argument.

> What we call thinking has in reality nothing to do with the faculty of rea-
> son, says Oehler, Karrer is right about that when he says that we have no
> faculty of reason because we think, for to have a faculty of reason means
> not to think and so to have no thoughts. What we have is nothing but a
> substitute for the faculty of reason. A substitute for thought makes our
> existence possible. All the thinking that is done is only substitute think-
> ing, because actual thinking is not possible, because there is no such thing
> as actual thinking, because Nature excludes actual thinking, because it
> has to exclude actual thinking. You may think I'm mad, says Oehler, but
> actual, and that means real, thinking is completely excluded. But we call
> what we think is thinking thinking, just as we call walking what we con-
> sider to be walking, just as we say we are walking when we believe that we
> are walking and are actually walking, says Oehler. What I've just said has
> absolutely nothing to do with cause and effect, says Oehler. (13)

"Walking" dramatizes the unstable relationship of imagined, remembered, and experienced reality. The familiar city street, the solid ground Bernhard's men are walking on, is pulled from under them in their simultaneous
pursuit of thinking. The endgame of Wittgensteinian thinking is choreographed as a pas de deux for Beckett's clowns on the sidewalks of Vienna.
Karrer collapses under the strain of appearances, the clash of multiple realities, which is, in the final analysis, the legacy of Wittgenstein's fin-de-siècle
Vienna.

Snippets of Wittgenstein-inspired reflections surface among layers of remembered thought processes only to disappear in the web of walking, thinking, and quoting. Only toward the end of the narrative is Wittgenstein mentioned by name. "Oehler tells me that Karrer's proposal to explain one of
Wittgenstein's statements to him on the Friedensbrücke came to nothing
because he was so exhausted, Karrer did not even mention Wittgenstein's
name again on the Friedensbrücke." After Karrer's "complete nervous breakdown" Oehler himself was no longer able "to say the word Wittgenstein on
the Friedensbrücke, let alone say anything about Wittgenstein or anything

connected with Wittgenstein, says Oehler, looking at the traffic at Friedensbrücke" (54–55). Ironically true to the letter of the *Tractatus,* Wittgenstein's
name comes up under circumstances that made it impossible to talk about him.
True to the spirit of the *Tractatus,* Wittgenstein, without mention of his name,
was present throughout in the men's intellectual preoccupations. Those were
not about Wittgenstein, but were true to his dictum that the subject has to
show itself.[7]

"Walking" examines the correlation of thinking, speaking, and walking. If
the movement of thinking is physicalized in the action of walking in sync with
speaking, the convergence of all three actions is an illusion. Staged in layers
of remembrance and repetition, past and present intersect and fragment the
identities of speakers. The picture comes together like a Cubist painting of a
thought presented from different angles, in a montage of overlapping planes
of reality.

Bernhard's dramaturgy of memory brings to mind Wittgenstein's teacher
Bertrand Russell. In his *Analysis of the Mind* Russell examines the correlation between "memory beliefs" and the objective reality of past events. Since
memory acts stage the past in the present, logically it is not necessary for the remembered past event actually to have happened that way, or to have happened
at all. Norman Malcolm writes:

> In investigating memory beliefs, there are certain points which must be
> borne in mind. In the first place, everything constituting a memory be-
> lief is happening now, not in the past time to which belief is said to refer.
> It is not logically necessary to the existence of a memory-belief that the
> event should have occurred, or even that the past should have existed
> at all. There is no logical impossibility in the hypothesis that the world
> sprang into being five minutes ago, exactly as it then was, with a popula-
> tion that "remembered" a wholly unreal past. There is no logically neces-
> sary connection between events at different times; therefore nothing that
> is happening now or will happen in the future can disprove the hypothesis
> that the world began five minutes ago. Hence the occurrences which are
> called knowledge of the past are logically independent of the past; they
> are wholly analyzable into present contents, which might, theoretically,
> be just what they are even if no past has existed.[8]

What counts for Bernhard is the simultaneity of events, as remembered,
projected, and staged in the theater of his mind.

In "Wittgenstein's *Philosophical Investigations,*" which Bernhard may have known in translation, Malcolm focuses on "Wittgenstein's treatment of the problem of how language is related to inner experience."[9] Wittgenstein's attack on the traditional idea that "there is only a contingent and not an essential connection between a sensation and its outward expression" (97) is a problem Bernhard had staged in his writing since *Frost.* It is central to actors' task of communicating the inner lives of their characters, not just through their speech but through their actions and behavior. Malcolm's approach to Wittgenstein recalls the Aristotelian idea of the audience's identification with the characters onstage:

> In order to appreciate the depth and power of Wittgenstein's assault upon this idea you must partly be its captive. You must feel the strong grip of it. The passionate intensity of Wittgenstein's treatment of it is due to the fact that he lets this idea take possession of him, drawing out of himself the thoughts and imagery by which it is expressed and defended — and then subjecting those thoughts and pictures to fiercest scrutiny. What is written down represents both a logical investigation and a great philosopher's struggle with his own thoughts. The logical investigation will be understood only by those who duplicate the struggle in themselves. (98)

The power of Malcolm's description comes from his personal contact with Wittgenstein, who had been his teacher. His advice on understanding Wittgenstein describes Bernhard's work, which is an ongoing effort to duplicate Wittgenstein's struggle in himself.

Bernhard didn't have to read all of the *Investigations* to pick up the drama of the mind behind it. And if he didn't read all the essays in Malcolm's volume, he would have followed the critical discussions about them in the literary sections of the major newspapers and weekly magazines to glean what he needed for his own literary investigations. The first volume of a Wittgenstein edition to appear in German in 1960 after the philosopher's death in 1951 contained the *Tractatus,* his journals between 1914 and 1916, and the *Philosophical Investigations.* The compilation of the material evokes a drama in three acts: the rigorous, airtight construct of the *Tractatus* is made transparent and eventually undermined by the following insights into the detours of the thinking processes behind it. Not unlike Oedipus, who in his self-assured hubris is led by Tiresias to questions that undermine his error-proof construct of self-identity, Wittgenstein veers in his journal entries between unequivocal logical assertions and deeply personal questions about the existence of God. The *Investigations* conclude the volume like a powerful final act that reveals the humbling of the initially aloof genius and his appreciation of the ordinary. The dramaturgy of this volume would provide the structural and thematic model for Bernhard's *Correction,* the novel in which he mastered the challenge of writing Wittgenstein.

In Bernhard's radical fictionalization, Wittgenstein's progression from the *Tractatus* to the *Investigations* becomes Roithamer's road to suicide. His notes on his family history and the design of the cone-shaped building as the perfect home for his sister add up to a blueprint for his suicide, not as the result of a psychological progression from cause to effect but rather as the ultimate performance of his scientific project. The cone, built in a clearing at the center of the Kobernausser Forest, was to represent perfection, mathematically and existentially. As an attempt at perfect communication, his ultimate gift to his beloved sister, that was intended both to enclose and to represent her, the cone turns out to be a catastrophic failure. The sister dies after she has seen the completed edifice. But the tragedy also verifies his memory concerning Altensam, the family estate, and the interactions among the family. The pressures of substitution and repetition in the ongoing recasting of roles in the genealogical theater leave no way out for the descendants to survive on their own terms. If the cone fails to communicate the intended message, it does succeed as a representation of its truth content, which is ultimately communicated by the death of its author.

The unnamed narrator of *Correction* confronts the task of "sifting and sorting" the legacy bequeathed to him by his friend. The two men had grown up together in rural Upper Austria, Roithamer in Altensam, the family's historic estate on the hill, the narrator, the son of the local doctor, in the village below. Both moved to Cambridge, where Roithamer, a natural scientist, has studied and taught for the past sixteen years. The obvious details appropriated from Wittgenstein's biography, such as Roithamer's privileged background and his academic career in Cambridge, frames the drama of thinking that is at its center. Rather than tell about Wittgenstein, it stages the drama of Wittgensteinian thought processes, the relentless lifelong effort of rethinking and revising. Wittgenstein's literary legacy, in the words of David G. Stern, "is an intricate network of multiple rearrangements and revisions."[10] Contrary to widely held opinion, the trajectory from the *Tractatus* to *Philosophical Investigations* is not a linear path from one philosophical viewpoint to its reversal.

Rather, what emerges from the legacy is one singular quest to track the workings of the mind and map the errors in their representations.

Such an approach must include a critique of one's own philosophical pursuits at every stage in the process. In Bernhard's radical dramatization, this inevitably leads to self-elimination — on the abstract level, in Roithamer's text — and its execution in the existential, physical realm. Bernhard's dramatic vision precedes by two decades scholarly insights based on more information about Wittgenstein's work habits. The narrator's precarious struggle to enter Roithamer's mind without losing his own dramatizes Bernhard's relation to Wittgenstein.

While they were studying in England, all the narrator could think "was Roithamer's thoughts, as Roithamer himself had frequently noticed and found inexplicable, and consequently also unbearable, he said, to have to see me so subjected to his thinking, if not entirely at the mercy of his thinking." And Roithamer warned his friend "not to give in to this tendency, because a man who no longer thinks his own thoughts but instead finds himself dominated by the thoughts of another man whom he admires or even if he doesn't admire him but is only dominated by his thoughts, compulsively, such a man is in constant danger of doing himself in by his continual thinking of the other man's thoughts, in danger of deadening himself out of existence." [11]

To begin this project the narrator moves into the same garret where Roithamer conceived his design and from which he supervised the construction of the cone in the middle of the forest. The garret belongs to the house that another school friend, Hoeller, a taxidermist, built for his family right in the Aurach gorge, a site no one else would have considered suitable for a home. It inspired Roithamer to pursue his own, equally impossible building project.

The bookshelves in the garret are filled with Roithamer's research, his notes tacked all over the walls. The narrator is quick to realize that "whoever enters here has to give up everything he ever thought prior to entering Hoeller's garret, he must make a clean break with all of his past thinking and start completely afresh, at once, thinking only *Hoeller-garret-thoughts,* to stay alive even for a moment in Hoeller's garret it's not enough merely to keep on thinking, it must *be Hoeller-garret-thoughts,* thinking solely about everything to do with Hoeller's garret and Roithamer and the Cone" (15). Here the translation problematically softens the original. The term "Hoeller-garret-thoughts" elegantly contracts the meaning of the belabored literal translation:

"whoever enters is forced to ... think only those thoughts that are permissible in Hoeller's garret."[12] Too whimsical under the circumstances, the contraction eliminates Bernhard's chilling assessment of the room, which reads like the warning inscription at the entrance to hell. The narrator was fully aware that "to penetrate Roithamer's mental state prematurely was dangerous, it had to be done warily, with great care, and above all while keeping watch over my own mental state, which is, after all, also and always a precarious state of debility, as I was thinking during those first moments and hours of contact" (24).

The English "moment of contact" does not imply the tender sensual quality of the German *Berührungsaugenblick,* an ever so brief moment of a first touch that leads to *Berührungsstunden,* hours of touching. For the narrator, entering Roithamer's garret is an erotic act.[13] "I even went so far as to state that this garret is Roithamer" (15). Roithamer's *Denkkammer,* his "thinking room" in the attic, is an opening into Roithamer's head, which the narrator had tried to penetrate throughout their friendship. Bernhard's (and Wittgenstein's) homoerotic intellectual bondings are charged with that kind of desire.

Paradoxically, the narrator also discovers "that when I stepped into Hoeller's garret, I suddenly stepped out of my long years of captivity, if not incarceration, within Roithamer's thought-prison — or Roithamer's thought-dungeon" (26). The liberating separation from Roithamer is not simply a consequence of his death. As the narrator finds himself surrounded by the products of his admired friend's head, it appears to be turned inside out. The seductively elusive thought dungeon of Roithamer's perceived genius is now splintered into tangible objects. Rather than mimic him, the narrator is now in a position to construct him.

In his rucksack the narrator carries the legacy Roithamer willed to him, "consisting of thousands of slips of papers with Roithamer's handwriting plus a bulky manuscript entitled 'About Altensam and everything connected to Altensam with special attention to the cone.'" When he empties his rucksack onto the sofa, the pile of papers begins to slip and he watches the pages slide down "from the top of that heap of papers, which was still in motion as I watched it from the window, where there were still some air spaces left in the heap of papers, these air spaces caved in and more papers slid to the floor. I clapped my hand to my mouth to hold back an outcry and I turned around as if in fear of being seen in this horrible, this farcically horrible situation." He frantically stuffs the papers into the desk drawer. "I went over to the sofa and grabbed handful after handful of the Roithamer legacy and crammed the desk drawers full of it. Again and again I grabbed a handful of papers and crammed it into a drawer, until the last sheet of paper was inside, in the end I had to use my knee to force the drawer shut which, being the last drawer, I had crammed full to bursting" (132–33). Roithamer's garret, a thought prison with no exit, resembles Sartre's hell, where Bernhard mimics a frenzied comedy routine of hiding a dismembered corpse. The intended sequence of the papers (if there ever was one), like that of Wittgenstein's legacy, was lost. It is up to the designated heir to piece his friend back together again.[14] The narrator's daunting task, like that of Wittgenstein's trustees, parallels the taxidermist's: the method of assembling the dead friend from his work resembles Hoeller's deceptively lifelike reconstructions of dead animals.

At one point during his long night in anticipation of the project, he thought that "in giving me this task [Roithamer] may well have meant to destroy me . . . because I was so entirely part of his development, as he felt" (116). His fear echoes Bernhard's of giving himself over to a Wittgenstein project. Roithamer wants his friend to give himself over to him as uncompromisingly as he had tried to give himself over to his sister. The challenge is to arrive at a perfect understanding of the other, which he can achieve only by completely penetrating the other's being. Proof and fulfillment of that understanding was to be the Cone, the most obvious symbol of phallic penetration. The question is a Wittgensteinian one: how to verify one's perception of the other. The quest is the stuff of tragedy; its performance produces farcical excess: the crumbling of the Cone in the middle of the forest is restaged in the collapsing pile of papers the narrator pours on the sofa from his bulging rucksack. The narrative of the Cone's construction and collapse in the context of the family history spills all over the quintessential Freudian prop. Talk of oversaturated signifiers! Bernhard hams up his infantile Freudianism in the midst of tragedy only to deflate both on the spot.

Roithamer's intense desire for his sister to inhabit his Cone and for his friend to inhabit his mind is the excess of the solipsist's terror of the other. To overcome his panic he seeks to incorporate the other in himself, an obsession that only increases the terror. It is a response familiar to Bernhard as it was to Wittgenstein, his fellow solipsist. Bernhard, the trained actor, turned his panicked obsession into a powerful performative tool. Acting himself in the other, he would overcome his fear of the other and himself again and again, in ever more virtuoso performances.

In his approach to Wittgenstein, Bernhard heeds Roithamer's advice to his friend "not to do himself in by his continual thinking of the other man's thoughts" so as not to "deaden himself out of existence" (37). Through Roithamer, Bernhard can meet Wittgenstein halfway. He can encounter Wittgenstein as another, Roithamer not as Wittgenstein but in a Wittgensteinian performance. According to Wittgenstein's assertion that the world is the sum of all possibilities, Roithamer is one possibility among many of performing/representing Wittgenstein. (The German verb *darstellen* means both to perform and to represent.)

Bernhard performs himself in both Roithamer and the narrator. The narrator enacts one possible approach to the overpowering other; Roithamer becomes the conduit for Bernhard's feelings about family, culture, and politics. Rather than lose himself in Wittgenstein, rather than destroy himself and Wittgenstein in the process, Bernhard, always tracking the actor within the actor within the actor, constructs a dense interplay of performances. With the skills of the trained actor who knows better than to try to identify with his character, Bernhard creates a performance model for the workings of a Wittgensteinian mind.

Heimat IV. Excursion

1. Paul Wittgenstein

It was also in his decade that Bernhard emerged on the Austrian scene as the classic fool, the postmodern court jester, claiming the fool's privilege in the fledgling republic that resuscitated the dramaturgy, the pomp and circumstances of an empire that had fallen in every sense. Shy, withdrawn, and secluded, abrasive in his (still) rather rare public appearances, outrageous in his frequent letters to editors, he constructed an aura of personal impenetrability, a sort of intellectual virginity enforced by illness, in a perpetual state of arousal over the world's moral bankruptcy. Like the virgin in the fairy tale, he was fiercely guarded by the proverbial dragon, alias Auntie, who made sure no one got too close to her reclusive genius.

Appropriately enough, he honors her in *Wittgenstein's Nephew*. A sequel to his autobiographical project, it begins in the summer of 1967 in Steinhof and extends to Paul Wittgenstein's death in 1979, three years after the publication of *Correction*. Ostensibly a recollection of his friend, it examines survival, both physical and social, in the private sphere of relationships and the public sphere of recognition, the art

of it and the cost of it, primarily in the private sphere. In the mirror of
Paul's antics Bernhard articulates the dramaturgy of his own success
and survival.

> For decades Paul played the madman, so I played the victim
> of lung disease; and just as he exploited his role for his pur-
> poses, so I exploited my role for mine. Some people spend
> all their lives cherishing some great possession or some ex-
> ceptional art, daring to exploit it by every possible means and
> making it, for as long as they live, the sole content of their
> lives: in the same way Paul spent all his life cherishing and ex-
> ploiting his madness and using every possible means to make
> it the content of his life. Similarly, I cherished and exploited
> both my lung disease and my madness, which together may
> be said to constitute my art.[15]

Illness performed is illness aestheticized. Dying is transformed
into a performance act that is life-confirming. People who met Bernhard
for the first time were amazed at his vivacity, in contrast to his death-
obsessed writing and his media image. Performance is perceived as
entertainment. Bernhard became a master at it—and abandoned Paul
when Paul had wasted all his performative resources.

By all accounts, Bernhard wasn't as close to Paul as the book
might lead one to believe. Then again, what did closeness mean to
Bernhard? There was the affinity between two obsessive personalities.
One episode in *Wittgenstein's Nephew* tells about their frantic search
for an issue of the *Neue Zürcher Zeitung,* which begins in nearby
Gmunden and would have taken them to Zürich had they not been exhausted after driving 220 miles. They shared a deep love and knowledge of music. Paul's was much more flamboyant than Bernhard's, who
appreciated his friend's outrageous fanaticism. He tells of Paul's hailing
a cab in Vienna and asking to be driven to Paris to catch the performance of a celebrated soprano. The fare was paid by his brother. To the
Wittgenstein clan, it was a good enough reason to have him once again
committed to Steinhof. Whether the incident really happened or not, it
was part of Paul's repertory of anecdotes with which he entertained
friends and strangers in splendid self-performances during night-long
rounds of Vienna's cafés and night clubs. Whether the story was true
or not, in his performance it made up a part of his truth. It was the kind
of truth Bernhard was after. Vienna's musical tradition played an impor-

tant part in Paul's upbringing. He loved to tell about the rift between his mother's and father's families, the former devotees of Hugo Wolf, Anton Bruckner, and Richard Wagner, the latter of Johannes Brahms. Bernhard would recycle the familial culture war in his play *Elisabeth II*. Paul loved to brag about making and breaking music performances all over the world with his histrionic responses. A popular anecdote has him attending a Wagner opera conducted by Herbert von Karajan, who took over the post of musical director of the Vienna Staatsoper from Karl Böhm in 1956. The story has Paul running down the aisle toward the orchestra pit after the performance with resounding shouts of "Bravo!" As the maestro slowly turned around with benevolently outstretched arms, Paul exclaimed, "Bravo Böhm!"[16]

Tall, thin, and handsome, he was impeccably dressed, even if his elegant dark suits became the worse for wear when he ran out of money, and the dirty white sneakers he wore with everything added a Bohemian touch to the old-time aristocratic dandy. White chrysanthemum in his lapel and cigar in hand, he was a familiar figure in Vienna's demimonde, a pedigreed patrician whose shady past got ever more decadent in the telling: university dropout, gigolo in Berlin during the Weimar years, black-market dealer in Vienna's underground economy after World War II. He also was manic-depressive, famous for outrageous escapades that were a constant source of embarrassment to his rich and famous family. If for once they failed to commit him to Steinhof, he checked himself in. To his friends he spoke enthusiastically about "the pavilion," the cottage-like building that Bernhard named for Paul's philosopher great-uncle. (There is no Ludwig Pavilion at Steinhof, just as Paul wasn't there at the time of Bernhard's surgery.)

A mathematical wizard with an extraordinary memory, Paul boasted that his magnum opus, *Good Equals 13: A Meditation on God, Sports, the Theater, and Music,* was finished in his head, and as proof quoted long passages from memory. A lifelong soccer fan, he dazzled his entourage with his flawless recital of countless team line-ups and scores. His favorite team was Prague's Rote Rosen (Red Roses). One favorite story was aimed at the historic Viennese prejudice against Czechs and their *Herkunftskomplex,* their absurd denial of their Czech ancestry. When the line-up for an important game between Vienna and Prague was announced, it turned out that all the Viennese players had Czech surnames and the Czechs' names sounded German.

It was easy to goad Paul into one of his stories. Getting him angry by contradicting him was a popular sport among his hangers-on. Insist that a celebrated player left Vienna's popular soccer team Rapid in 1931 and Paul would explode, "You're crazy. That was 1933!" The outburst would be followed by salvos of anecdotes, most popular among them those about the Wittgensteins' private lives, such as his aunt Clothilde's tryst with a stagehand in the family's opera box. Another version features Vienna's famed and feared music critic Eduard Hanslick, the inspiration for Wagner's Beckmesser, in the same encounter. Poor Clothilde's father committed her to a mental institution for a year. Paul boasted that in 1926 he was first in his family's social circle to invite a black man to dinner. The guest was a tap dancer whom he had met in a jazz club. His father had warned him that his favorite aunt would be deeply hurt if he showed up with a black man. He did, and in time his insubordination cost him an inheritance of three million marks. According to Paul, Bernhard observed, "For three million marks you bought your freedom from the white race."[17] Paul's version of *Guess Who's Coming to Dinner* was far less genteel. The clan was aghast, but they did not admit to their shock. Their grudging hospitality made for the comedy in Paul's cutting account of the event. Nevertheless, he also rhapsodized about his parents' elegance and the cultured lifestyle of aristocrats.

Paul's good friend Theodor (Teddy) Podgorsky, a popular Austrian TV personality and operetta star, found him "mischievous as a mandrill, but not a fighter. He said a lot of stupid things. He was sick, superintelligent, and he was a swindler. A broken, run-down, seedy wreck of a dandy, he also had poise."[18] Such contrariness made him the darling of the avant-garde. But, says Teddy, who knows a lot about working a crowd, Paul's histrionic skills made it impossible to turn him into a literary character. He had already invented himself. Bernhard understood that. He respected his friend's vulnerability—and guarded his own. He kept his distance.

Paul was used as much as he used people. He lavished his inheritance on idols, friends, and strangers until the Wittgensteins cut off his supply and he went to work as an insurance clerk at the age of sixty. The job in no way cut down on his public performances of cultured extravagance. If he ordered a lavish champagne breakfast for himself and a friend, he didn't hesitate to let his friend foot the bill. Bernhard once had to pay for his three-hour taxi ride from Vienna to Gmunden.

Paul is remembered quite differently in Upper Austria, cut off from his urban audiences, where the descendants of the Wittgensteins still

live. In the rural environment not far from Bernhard's home, his behavior lost the appeal of charming decadence. Friends and neighbors
were more concerned with Paul's illness. Their sympathy went to his
family, and still does. They still respect the Wittgensteins' privacy and
are much more guarded in their response to Paul than his downtown
devotees.

Bernhard came across Paul through both his contacts in Vienna's
art scene and his patrician friends in Upper Austria. Paul's antics, bril-
liance, and devastation provided him with a performative key to Wittgenstein's philosophical spirit. As an ongoing provocation and contradiction of unquestioned existential and intellectual norms, Paul's life
constitutes philosophy in action. It demonstrates that "it is far from certain that a philosopher can qualify as such only by writing down and
publishing his philosophy, as Ludwig did: he remains a philosopher
even if he does not publish his philosophizing, even if he writes nothing
and publishes nothing."[19] Paul introduced Bernhard to the Wittgenstein
experience in an existential clown's inversion of the mystique. It happened at the appropriate moment. Bernhard's maturation as a writer
coincided with the piecemeal publication of Wittgenstein's papers in
the 1950s and 1960s.

2. An Irishman at the Habsburg Court

The geography of *Correction* was inspired by the estate of Gabi
O'Donnell, an Austrian descendant of Irish nobility and a mutual friend
of Bernhard and Paul Wittgenstein. The O'Donnell family home, a converted hunting lodge in a spectacular Alpine landscape above the Aurach valley, inspired the haunting scenarios of *Correction* and *The Hunting Party.* The estate stretches into densely wooded hunting grounds
in the surrounding mountains. The present owner inherited it from his
mother, of the local Überacker family, whose name is still associated
with wealth, class, and prestige. The lodge was built by Frau Überacker's father on top of Mount Hochkreut, about 5,000 feet up the Alpine
foothills, at a time when there were no roads there. Her husband, the
"old" O'Donnell of ancient Irish blood, proudly refused modern trans-
portation and insisted on hiking up the mountain to his lodge well into
his old age. Bernhard had been close to him since his student days.
Ingrid Bülau, Bernhard's close friend at the Mozarteum, remembers
him introducing her to the white-haired old gentleman, who appeared

elegant despite his shabby clothes. "He looks like a count," she said
to Bernhard. "That's what he is," he replied. Gabi O'Donnell insists
that Bernhard loved his father not because he was an aristocrat but
because he was an eccentric. The old man was one of the "strange"
people who fascinated him.

Hochkreut is about ten miles west of Bernhard's farm. The sign
leading off the Autobahn also indicates a turnoff to Roitham. Bernhard's names are deeply rooted in the landscape. The road leads past a
house with huge lettering on one side advertising its occupant: Hoeller,
taxidermist. His shop is on the ground floor. An assortment of stuffed
birds is displayed in the window. The house is nestled in a bend of
the Aurach River. Contrary to Bernhard's dramatic setting, there is no
Aurach gorge. Usually the river winds gently between meadows and
rolling hills. Only after heavy rains does it turn into a powerful tor-
rent. Nevertheless, the spectacular mountain peaks lining the hori-
zon suggest the forbidding cliffs and threatening drops that Bernhard
condensed in his topography to suit Roithamer's state of mind. From
Hoeller's workshop a bridge crosses the river and the road winds up the
3,000-foot Mount Aurach to an Alpine game park run by Gabi O'Donnell. The instructions for gaining entrance to his home are elaborate.
From a phone booth at the gate of the zoo the visitor has to announce
her arrival to the Indian couple who are in charge of the premises.
They run the inn on the ground floor of the weathered two-story log
cabin at the summit, against a dramatic backdrop of towering mountain
ranges to the north and overlooking Lake Traunsee, with Mount Traunstein to the south. The couple also guard the privacy of the O'Donnells'
second-floor residence. Their probing gaze and soft inquiries at the
door, against the din of tourist chatter in the back and the secretive
silence above, add to the impression that one is about to enter a time
warp. And so one does.

The husband takes the visitor around the house to another staircase, where she is handed over to Gabi O'Donnell, a short, stout man
in his seventies with an owlish face, thinning hair, and an impish smile.
He wears an old rural jacket over a worn shirt with frayed cuffs and col-
lar, a leprechaun gone Alpine in hunter green. Short breath and a shuf-
fling gait betray his frail health. He takes the visitor up the stairs and
across creaking wooden floors through a dark maze of nooks and corners that wrap around wood-paneled rooms with massive tiled stoves
and heavy old-fashioned furniture. Stuffed birds and animals are

perched on bureaus and suspended from the walls, flanked by heads of other animals and antlers of various shapes and sizes. A fox lurks in a corner. A stuffed white owl is mounted next to a painting of a relative who was a minister under Napoleon. An elk's giant antlers jump out from another corner. After the labyrinthine passage through dark, musty rooms the entrance to the large living room is dramatic. Galleries of windows along two sides of the vast rectangular space surround it with a dazzling vista of snow-capped peaks. The panorama's coldly majestic silence asserts its commanding presence even inside. The visitor feels oddly suspended far above the ground, just another species among the other animals on display inside an observatory turned diorama in the sky, where the awe-inspiring view seems to metamorphose into an all-encompassing glacial gaze. The eerie sensation of being watched while watching recalls the experience of Roithamer's friend in Hoeller's garret. Bernhard's Aurach gorge is the inverted model of the high-altitude scenario on Mount Aurach.

A 1977 dissertation at the University of Vienna traces the O'Donnell clan in the northwest of Ireland to the third century.[20] One 1767 genealogy mythologizes them as descendants of King Megalesus, who ruled Spain in 1263 B.C.; his son Irus is said to have taken over Ireland. Be that as it may, the family with their epic Irish heroes and Habsburg pedigree amid the clutter of ghostly hunting trophies, fading documents, and historical mementos in their Alpine habitat fed Bernhard's imagination from his earliest artistic endeavors throughout his life.

Gabi O'Donnell proudly points out the framed document signed by James I, pronouncing his forebear Rory O'Donnell earl of Tyr Connel and baron of Donegal. He was installed by the British crown as ruler of his county in 1603. (In the following century the O'Donnells were elevated to dukes.) When a new decree made the members of Rory's clan subject to taxes to be paid to the king, they rose up against him A suspicious James I accused Rory of conspiracy and threw him into the Tower of London. He eventually escaped to the continent. As the host tells the story of his Irish ancestors, he opens an antique music box that cranks out the Habsburg imperial anthem and segues into the epic of the O'Donnells' Austrian line. Throughout the centuries the O'Donnells produced outstanding soldiers in the bloody battles against the English. To escape retribution, they frequently ended up in continental armies; in the eighteenth century Karl O'Donnell joined Empress Maria Theresa's forces, became a hero in the Habsburgs' Seven

Years' War against the Prussians, and established the Austrian line of the family.

An Alpine museum added onto the lodge offers information about the area's geology and history. There is a display of exquisite rifles, one set belonging to a Habsburg duke, a celebrated hunter, the other to a legendary poacher. The museum is also an odd continuation of the zoo, featuring antlers or preserved animals that died there. Some Arabian sheep perished in the harsh climate. There are two exquisite sets of horns, one curved, one straight and pointed, that belonged to different species of mountain sheep. During the mating season they locked horns. But the former was no match for the latter, who impaled his rival during their battle.

It is up to the visitor to decide whether the O'Donnell home-cum-museum is a tribute to history, both natural and cultural, or to the taxidermist's art. In any case, it captured Bernhard's view of life in contemporary Austria as a perversely lifelike reconstruction of cadavers. From the taxidermist's skill of preservation it is just a small step to theatrical animations both onstage and in "real life." Bernhard's play *The Hunting Party* has a quote from Heinrich von Kleist's *On the Puppet Theater* as its motto: "I inquired about the mechanism of these figures and how it was possible, without myriad strings on the fingers, to control the separate members and their tie points as the rhythm of their movements or dances required." [21]

The milieu and characters of the play are intimately connected to the O'Donnell experience. The prince and the princess are the muted relics of royalty. The wife of the general who fought at Stalingrad is modeled after Gerda Maleta, who as a child attended the progressive nursery school run by Frau Überacker, Gabi's mother. Bernhard's writer stand-in is a taxidermist of the theater. He will preserve the decline of his hosts and their land in his play. It will be a comedy. Paul Wittgenstein, whose mother was a close friend of Gabi's mother-in-law, played out the Wittgenstein legacy as tragic farce. He performed the heroes and madmen of history from his unwritten book. Ludwig Wittgenstein borrowed a quote from Johann Nestroy, Austria's finest comedic playwright, as the motto of his *Philosophical Investigations,* the book he worked on for twenty years and never finished: "Anyway, that's the thing about progress, it always looks so much bigger than it really is." [22] If the quote is intended to reflect on the progress of Wittgenstein's thinking from the *Tractatus* to *Investigations,* it also applies to Bernhard's

view of the progress of Austrians through the catastrophes of the twentieth century. The general of *The Hunting Party* has not outgrown his
imperial roots, nor has he moved far from Stalingrad. The only sign of
"progress" is his deterioration. If Wittgenstein represents the noblest if
no less terrifying possibility of intellectual progress, his nephew acted
out its carnivalesque excesses. Paul was the consummate performer of
Wittgenstein, the name, the genius, and the legacy of both. He opened
the way for Bernhard to write Wittgenstein in performance.

CHAPTER NINE

Self-Projections/Self-Reflections

Truth is tradition, not the truth.

—Thomas Bernhard, *Gargoyles*

MOST OF THE STORIES COLLECTED IN *Erzählungen* (Tales) revisit the Austrian scene of ancestral estates and isolated family farms with a cast of descendants who, like Wittgenstein, left home and Austria for the great universities of Britain or the United States. Like Wittgenstein, they end up giving away their inheritance. If they stay at home, they suffocate in their Alpine fastnesses, cut off from the intellectual life that can be found only in the cosmopolitan and academic centers outside Austria. The native scene, saturated with history, is always a site of resonant memory, which is compulsively reenacted through the centuries by an interchangeable cast of surrogates, or effigies, as Joseph Roach would call them.[1] In Bernhard's theatricalized perception of contemporary existence, effigies become marionettes, suspended on the strings of their cultural and biological conditioning. Their aliveness is an illusion. The source of their animation is outside themselves. The only control they have is over the strings that keep them in motion: they can cut themselves off. But that won't destroy the overall mechanism. An early inspiration for Bernhard must have been the Salzburg Marionette Theater, world-famous for its repertoire of Mozart's operas. He was quick to subvert the exquisite artifice into a grotesque scene of the dying suspended on syringes in his youthful perception of the terminal ward in which he had been hospitalized. The characters in his plays are pulled by the strings of language and gestures, with their long problematic history of both greatness and guilt. In his fiction, the land, with its history of ownership and its continued feudal economy, becomes Bernhard's theater at large. His performance space is all of Austria. The script is inscribed in the landscape, in its ecology: the daily and seasonal rituals of its cultivation that continue its history. His patrician narrators have no choice: no matter how far away they go, they are still suspended on the strings of culture and memory. Not even death can cut through them. The theatrics of the funeral reinstates the renegade in the ancestral continuum.

In Bernhard's 1970 film script *Der Italiener* (The Italian), a forerunner of his great valedictory novel *Extinction*, the master of Wolfsegg shoots himself either accidentally or by design after the dress rehearsal of the annual performance of a play written for the occasion by the children in the family. The dead man is displayed in the greenhouse, on the platform where the performance was to have taken place. His sister, about to wash the naked body, looks at her dead brother. "She thinks: There lies my dead brother, for the first time in my life I control him."[2] In her expert preparation for the funeral she makes sure that tradition will assert itself in a glorious performance.

Elaborate funeral ceremonies play an important part in Bernhard's dramaturgy of substitution. Their theatricality epitomizes what's left of life in Bernhard's Austria: a mechanical passing on of inherited functions and the gestures and language that go with them. In mortuary ritual, as Roach points out, "the three-sided relationship of memory, performance, and substitution becomes most acutely visible."[3] A will usually is the script of substitution that ensures continuity. But Bernhard's fathers are more cunning than that. The son they pick to inherit their ancestral possessions is usually the one most likely to bring them to ruin. In fact, the fathers have prepared for the destruction in their function as progenitors, a motif Bernhard borrowed from Chekhov. Many pick wives solely for breeding purposes, women who are vulgar, of lower social standing, and insensitive to the cultural traditions of their spouses. In Bernhard's post-Holocaust geography of collective guilt the male descendants — more often than not there is a sole surviving heir to a patrician estate — struggle against their predicament as substitutes.

Women do not exist at all in many of the stories. When they are introduced, they serve the traditional functions of birthing machines and caretakers of culture in this post-Habsburg performance of imperial patriarchy. If they are cultured themselves, they are destroyed in the process. If they are outsiders, they are the misplaced parts that ruin the mechanism from the inside. In either case, they never speak for themselves. Ghostlike shadows or fierce avengers, they move in and out of the memory of the male narrators. Their bodies are inscribed in the landscape. Their silence is part of the ecology.

In the film script of *The Italian,* the new inheritor of Wolfsegg is in his early thirties—not old enough to know how he will come to terms with his legacy. He seeks out an Italian guest at the funeral, a cultured man, with whom he takes a walk through the property and lingers in a clearing that had been the children's favorite play area. The Italian visitor elaborates on Hegel's introduction to his *History of Philosophy.* The heir explains that the clearing is the site of a mass grave of two dozen Polish soldiers and officers. At the end of the war German soldiers massacred them in the gazebo, where the family's annual theatrics have taken place since time immemorial. This is also the place where the father presumably shot himself and where he is now laid out. He used to call the gazebo the slaughterhouse in reference to the massacred Poles.

The film script grew out of a much earlier story fragment, "The Italian," written in 1963. This brief tale focuses exclusively on the walk of the two men. In that version, the son and heir, around thirty at the time of the funeral, studies the communists' attempt at revolution in Germany. Six years later, when the film was scripted, his preoccupation with the early revolutionary martyrs, such as Rosa Luxemburg and Klara Zetkin, had given way to listening to his cultured friend's discourse on Hegel. The bloody tragedies of individual resistance had been eclipsed by reasoned theories of change as Bernhard himself, together with his narrator double, reached middle age and Germany had passed from the postwar generation's confrontation with their elders' Nazi past to the bloody excesses of terrorists who appropriated Nazi tactics.

Over a decade later, the forty-eight-year-old heir of *Extinction,* unlike his younger predecessor in both versions of "The Italian," has found the solution for Wolfsegg. Like the narrator of "Ungenach," the narrator of *Extinction,* knowing that he has only one more year to live, wills the family's ancestral estate "and everything that comes with it" to Vienna's Jewish community. "Everything that comes with it" (which had been the stipulation for the distribution of the properties of "Ungenach") includes the beauty of the land, its cultivation and culture, and its heavy burden of historic guilt. The heir is burdened with the responsibility of both maintenance and retribution. The novel's spectacular funeral unfolds as a macabre carnival parade. Following the coffins of the parents, who were killed in a car accident, are Austria's highest clergy, followed by the relatives, who in turn are followed by the former gauleiters and other National Socialist grandees who were hidden by the family after the war. They make their appearance in full Nazi regalia, bespangled by medals, and are followed by the League of Comrades, Nazi veterans, some of them crippled and on crutches. All of them "come with" the estate. Completing the procession is the narrator's old friend and "soulmate" Eisenberg, the rabbi who will administer the problematic gift. In Bernhard's funerary dramaturgy the doomed heirs are cast as the tricksters of the will. Posthumously, Bernhard triumphed as the ultimate trickster in the staging of his own will. Subverting the inherited curse without escaping it, the trickster becomes the tragic hero in Bernhard's post-Habsburg theater of devastating ridicule.

Wolfsegg castle not only actually exists, not far from Bernhard's Ohlsdorf residence; Duke Franz St. Julien, his sister, Mariette, and their eccentric mother, Odile St. Julien, were his longtime friends. He loved to visit them for meals, invited and uninvited.[4] In 1972 he even bought an old farmhouse across the fields from the village, at the edge of the woods, with a splendid view of the aristocratic homestead. It was his third investment in real estate. In 1971 he had bought another small historic farmhouse, which served as a guesthouse for a few select friends and colleagues. While his fictional characters gave away their inheritance, Bernhard made himself an heir. Ironically, this was at a time when his attacks on Austria were becoming more and more incendiary. It seems as though he needed to acquire his birthright. Born out of wedlock, out of Austria, he had literally to earn his homeland if only to dramatize his outsider status.

Underlying the evolution of "The Italian" from story fragment to film script and to the grand finale of *Extinction* over almost a quarter of a century is a bildungsroman in three parts. It documents Bernhard's increasingly self-assured self-dramatization as an aristocrat. The son in the earliest version is the same age Bernhard was when he wrote the story. He is eager to impress his older guest (the Italian is forty-eight), who finds him "mysteriously young." On their evening walk across the property they stop by the shed attached to the greenhouse where the costumes and musical instruments for the family's annual summer performance are stored. There are great pride and affection in the young man's description of the family's amateur theatrical tradition as he shows his cultured visitor the exquisite costumes, which are historic treasures. This is the world Bernhard knows best. The conversation becomes more animated and erotically charged. The young man takes his guest to the clearing. He hesitates, uncertain whether he should tell him "that he and I were standing on two dozen hastily buried corpses." This is the world to which Austrians are heir. In this early version the father is set apart to some degree from the guilty Germans. He offered shelter to adolescent (*halbwüchsige)* war deserters, "fifteen-year-olds, sixteen-year-olds." [5] The film script, by contrast, describes them as "common soldiers" and "officers." Presumably they had been Polish prisoners of war working the Wolfsegg fields. The son, "although only twelve years old at the end of the war," still remembers the Poles. They were "put up in the gazebo, they waited out the war in the gazebo, they sought refuge in the gazebo," he tells the visiting Italian.

> From my father's stories I knew that two weeks before the end of the war they were shot by Germans who suddenly appeared from the forest at night. Apparently the corpses were lying in the gazebo for two weeks and spread "a tremendous odor," the people in the house were prohibited from entering the gazebo. The Germans had apparently threatened to shoot my father and anyone else who took the corpses from the gazebo and buried them. . . . I said that I heard the screaming, on the day of the murder I heard the screams of the Poles from the gazebo all the way to my room. For years I heard those screams in the vicinity of the gazebo and everywhere in the world. For two decades, until today, I had to fight with those screams, which automatically got louder as I approached the gazebo. "All my life," I said, "I kept thinking I would never be able to escape the screams of the Poles lined up against the wall." [6]

In *Extinction* the constellation is entirely altered. It is no longer during but after the war that Wolfsegg serves as a refuge — now not for the victims but for the perpetrators. The gazebo becomes the children's villa where the father hid the war criminals who would later show up for his funeral. The emphasis shifts from the young Bernhard's early perspective on World War II, shaped by his childhood experiences, to the mature writer's increasing preoccupation with Austria's Nazi legacy. The relationship between the Italian and the heir has also been reversed in the novel. Now the Austrian is forty-eight years old and the teacher of the much younger Italian, whom he instructs in anarchy and the destruction of the world.

In his film version, Bernhard observes the activities on the day before the funeral in Wolfsegg village and Wolfsegg castle, a sprawling estate overlooking the village and the fields, many of them belonging to the castle. Its feudal history surfaces in the funeral rites, which connect the peasants in the valley to their masters on the hill. The mailman, the baker's assistant, the merchants of funerary paraphernalia, the altar boys bring their goods and business to the castle. In the inn the local band rehearses a funeral march. A cow is being slaughtered on camera. (Here Bernhard seems to have been influenced by the Austrian artist Hermann Nietsch's controversial experiments in ritualistic performance art. Nietsch, Bernhard's contemporary, owns a castle in Austria where he lives and works.)

Inside the castle compound, everyone knows his or her part, from the cook who prepares breakfasts, luncheons, and dinners for the countless guests from all over the world to the young peasant who kills the fowl for her to the mailman who keeps returning with stacks of letters of condolence. It all happens under the expert direction of the dead man's sister, who prepares his body, dresses the catafalque for his display, and oversees the setting of the table. Etiquette and proceedings have been passed on through countless generations and practiced many times. Bernhard's script lovingly guides the camera along the facade of the main building, up the staircase, into the kitchen and dining room, as well as outside past the various buildings into the gazebo. One can't help suspecting that he does so in order to show off his own intimate knowledge of this privileged world and its codes of conduct. Rarely does he permit himself to show such affection for his surroundings. Usually any signs of vulnerability, love, and tenderness are buried under layers of despair, cynicism, and, later on, outrageous histrionics and hyperbole. Here Bernhard registers the guests arriving in their Bentleys and Jaguars, their impeccably tailored coats and suits, their ease in the beautifully cultured setting with a melancholy that reveals both the outsider's desire to belong and the sadness for a world long gone. It continues to exist only in performative events.

In *Extinction,* the melancholy surfaces once again, but there it is anchored in the ambivalent emotions of its dying heir. The middle-aged narrator's return to the landscape of his childhood elicits some of the most poignant descriptions of the castle's geography. Like Hamlet, he keeps himself hidden for a while when he arrives at the family estate to watch the proceedings. They follow a centuries-old family ritual whose every detail is still driven by the ancient feudal dynamics of the region's customs, its economy, and accordingly its social hierarchy.

In the narrator's grotesquely painful outrage over the Wolfsegg legacy, there is also much affection in his painstaking descriptions of the layout and architecture of the buildings, the main house, the orangery, the stables, the children's villa, the hunters' lodge, and the farmhouse. Perfectly fitted into the shape of the hilltop so as to be discretely hidden from view, the estate is the commanding center that shapes the life of the surrounding area. The quietly functioning order based on historic hierarchies has an oddly seductive aura, and the surviving heir has to take drastic measures to extricate himself from complicity in it.

The film script provides the narrator — in this case Bernhard as himself — with the camera as another opportunity to hide. Bernhard's film version is not a conventional script. His narrative introduces the camera as a visible partner and recounts its interaction with the environment. The camera's perspective is counterpointed by another set of eyes suggested by the ubiquitous land surveying instrument. While the camera documents the continuity of ritual, the surveyor's lens intimates change. The camera asserts life over the disruption of a catastrophic death; the surveyor's instrument extends the catastrophe to the land, suggesting that the redistribution of property precipitated by the master's death will affect not only the heirs but the villagers, dependent as they are on the castle's feudal economy. Shakespeare nods to Chekhov in the interplay of lenses that circumscribe the liminal stages of Bernhard's funerary dramaturgy, between extinction and continuity, memory and performance, models and doubles.

In *Extinction,* his final novel, Wolfsegg has become Austria and its last surviving heir Bernhard's double. Not unlike Roithamer, this narrator, about ten years older than he (each is the author's age at the time he wrote the story), works on an account of his family legacy that culminates in its "correction" through his bequest of his entire inheritance to Vienna's Jewish community.

As an act of reparation, the narrator's penance and revenge for the sins of his fathers abruptly ends the narrative on a deeply disturbing note. If the Jewish community accepts the gift with "everything that comes with it," including its lethal legacy of guilt, ambition, repression, and self-delusion, will it once again cynically affirm the cycle of the victims as heirs of the criminals? Finally, a strong biblical scenario emerges from the text's many subverted images of Catholic tradition. In the patriarchal context of the culture, the family line is extinct. What's left is a barren post-Holocaust landscape of guilt and retribution. Is it the desert, once again, through which the modern tribes of Israel have to pass yet another time to pave the way to the promised land for everyone? Or is it Bernhard's equivocal answer to a Jewish joke?[7]

In 1973 Bernhard expanded another story, "Der Kulterer," into a script for a television film.[8] It, too, is a bildungsroman of sorts, the story of a convict's coming of age as a writer, the precarious transformation from imprisonment to inner freedom, which in the end is threatened again from the outside. The quietly touching story of the emergence of a writer in an oppressive institutional environment reflects Bernhard's own experiences. The short story, published in 1969, is based on an even earlier story, "The Mailman," which appeared one time only in 1962, in an anthology of German stories.[9] It was Bernhard's first attempt at a longer story. The Kulterer of the title is Franz Kulterer, who has been imprisoned for a year and a half for an unspecified crime.[10] The short story goes further than the film script in explaining it as "a crime that he committed as if in a radically suicidal state of unconsciousness."[11]

Story and film focus on Kulterer's last days in jail as he prepares for his release. In a sense it is also a preparation for a funeral—the burial of the person he had become in jail. "He was afraid that once he was free, rid of his inmate's clothes, he would no longer be able to write anything or think anything, he was afraid that, discharged and exposed without restraints, he would no longer be" (49).

The passage appears twice, at the beginning and the end of the film script. After Kulterer changed into his civilian clothes, he "bent over his still warm institutional clothes and cried" (119). He was mourning a double death: of the person he had become, whose body warmth would soon evaporate from his inmate's uniform, and of the person who was about to walk out. The latter is a substitution. The person he was had died, or rather had killed himself with his crime, "which he committed as if in a radically suicidal state of unconsciousness." In the earliest version, the mailman throws himself under a train as soon as he is released. His suicide is a duplication, which the more experienced writer deleted in his later version.

To pass the time in jail and make himself think of something other than his inner resistance to the oppressive system, Kulterer begins to tell himself stories and eventually to write them down. Reminiscent of Bernhard himself, particularly in his early period, he "sometimes had ideas for extremely funny stories, which made him laugh, but he never could write them down. He hadn't written one single funny story. Why can't I write a funny story? he often asked himself. A story with a balloon, for example, with a sailor in rolled-up sleeves, with a trampoline, a carousel?" (102).

In prison Kulterer learned to think. "The invention of a thought inside a human being seemed to him the most precious thing of all" (22). Thinking provides the mirror that reflects his observations and captures reality. In his early fiction Bernhard brushes against Wittgenstein, the young philosopher's picture theory: thinking produces the sentence that produces the picture that touches reality.[12]

Once Kulterer can register reality in pictures, which become his stories, it is no longer threatening. He doesn't have to fight it, he absorbs it. In a sense, he himself becomes invisible — and invincible — in the process:

> No one found anything the least bit special about him, aside from the fact that they simply considered him a remarkably modest person. Inconspicuous as he was, they never found him ridiculous. If they met him with indifference, they often had the feeling that they should help him, even though they never knew *how*. But he disappointed such feelings, inasmuch as they gradually discovered as they were getting used to him that in almost every respect, especially the most simple things, which didn't matter at all and therefore were the most important, he surpassed them by far.

The passage continues quietly with a compassionate tenderness that Bernhard rarely permitted himself to show so openly. Syntax, tone, and the gently instructive stance show the influence of his grandfather.

> It was strange: they treated him as if he was not to be taken quite seriously and yet they felt respect whenever they got in contact with him. In their ludicrous predicament, they found countless opportunities to yell at each other and humiliate each other where there was nothing left to humiliate; in their despair, which sometimes got the better of them and drove them into a rage, they often woke up to find him standing in the shadows of the almost completely darkened room; turned toward them he told them: "Yes, yes, I know." In such moments even the men who burst with coldblooded muscularity, whom one would never have thought capable of such feelings, were overcome by shame. One could take that thought much further and claim that Kulterer often prevented serious physical harm, if not murder. He was the counterbalance to the filth and idealism gone sour, to the obscenities, vilifications, and greed. (98)

Never again would Bernhard expose himself so openly. His soft, circumspect voice, echoing his grandfather's, has the experienced calm of a village elder. Perhaps the mailman's self-inflicted violence in the earliest version erupted from Bernhard's vulnerability at that time. Artistically it was the most crucial period of transition—just after the Tonhof debacle and before *Frost*—from a gifted young man with multiple talents to the writer with a distinctive "difficult" voice and vision. Perhaps the brutally abrupt ending reflected Bernhard's melodramatic response to his own experience of institutionalized life, in boarding school (the prison in his story had once been a monastery), in various hospitals, and in the Mozarteum, before his release into the destructive freedom of the bohemian Tonhof scene. In any case, his own life experience may have changed his mind. By 1969 he had proved himself not only as a serious writer but—as his victories over illness and the dramatic controversies accompanying his success have shown—as a successful survivor on all counts. Not that the revised version allows much hope: as he leaves, Kulterer can hear the supervisor beating an inmate. "As quickly as he could, he got away from the penitentiary into the open country; hilly, brown, and gray, it steamed with hopelessness." The film script encloses the story's last sentence in quotation marks. Bernhard is quoting himself, as if to show that the film, based on the earlier story, is also a reflection on his much younger self from the distance he has come. The film script is structured to emphasize multiple levels of self-reflection. Each also reflects on the theme of reflection, which is an essential function of the medium itself.

In contrast to *The Italian,* which has no narrator, *Der Kulterer* introduces the calm voice of an actor commenting on the proceedings. It is the voice of the actor who plays Kulterer. As Kulturer he speaks only a few lines. The voice-over, severed from the body, describes his movements and thoughts. The detached voice-over establishes an emotional distance from the character. On camera, as imagined in his cinematic narrative, Bernhard can stage his earlier prose experiments in correlating the motions of the mind and the body. Specifying an actor for the third-person narrator's voice isn't just a reference to the obvious (who else would narrate a film?). It isn't just any actor or another actor, it is the voice of the actor who also plays Kulterer on the screen. Although the same person, the off-screen actor is different from his on-screen character. By telling the audience about the character while he is also playing him on screen, the actor is sharing his process with the audience. With no alteration of the lines, the original story's conventional narrative strategy of the all-knowing third-person narrator is transformed into a character, "the actor." His quietly observing voice communicates how an actor prepares, the questions he asks himself about the character he is playing, how he constructs the character's biography, arrives at insights that justify his actions and permit him to visualize him in different situations. The strategy personalizes the detached voice as a legitimate character. Rewriting his story for a performative medium, Bernhard subtly appropriates an actor's technique that legitimizes getting inside Kulterer's head from the outside, through the perception of another. Bernhard the actor outwits Wittgenstein's persistent question regarding the verification of another's perceptions or feelings. "Der Kulterer" was his last short story that featured an all-knowing narrator with privileged insights into his subject's mind. Its evolution into a film script eleven years after the original version maps the development of Bernhard's technique from narrative to performative strategies.[13]

The two film scripts that grew out of his early stories show the two worlds Bernhard straddled in his life and work: one in which he had been cast by circumstances, the other in which he more and more insistently would cast himself. While he projects himself into the Italian's pedigreed culture, Kulterer reflects the experiences that shaped him.

In 1978 Bernhard published a collection of brief pieces under the title *Der Stimmenimitator* (The Voice Imitator).[14] It is a collection of terse, deadpan anecdotes in the style of news briefs, journalistic "about town" vignettes, greenroom and tavern gossip, coffeehouse stories. In these mini-monologues in the laconic first-person plural, Bernhard casts himself as the man of the world and world traveler. Without a defining home, he is at home everywhere: in scholarly circles, at receptions for former kings and reigning dignitaries, among performers of all kinds, en route through the hinterlands of Austria. The stories add up to a darkly witty assessment of the world Bernhard constructed and traversed during the decade he called his.

Among the quasi-journalistic anecdotes, news-in-brief-style reports, commentaries, and more eccentric fables is a report of a fateful encounter between reader and adored writer, titled "Verehrung" (Worship; "Respect" in its American translation). The account, quoted here in its entirety, is a timely self-parody.

Our respect for a writer whom we never in our life dared approach was without doubt at its peak when we stayed in the same hotel in which the writer whom we admired had been living for some time, and were introduced on the hotel terrace once day — through the good offices of a friend — to the man we admired. We can remember no better example of the fact that to approach actually means nothing more than to withdraw.

The closer we came to our writer after the first meeting, the more we distanced ourselves from him — and with the same intensity — and the more we got to know his personality, the more we distanced ourselves from his works; every word he spoke to us, every thought he thought about us, distanced us from the same word and the same thought in his works. He finally disgusted us totally, took us apart, dissolved us, and put us back together again. When we left the hotel — and the only thing that made us happy about that was that we could still make do without the writer — we had the impression that the writer had destroyed his personality in our eyes as he had his work. The author of those hundreds of thoughts and ideals and perceptions, whom we had served for decades with our understanding and to whom we had been loyal in our love, had, by not refusing our acquaintance but ultimately by seeking it against our will, destroyed his works. Whenever we heard his name after that, we were repelled.[15]

The anecdote catches the flavor of the collection's overall style. At that point in Bernhard's career, which had reached its midpoint pinnacle, it was considered a departure — disappointing to some readers — from the dark, pain-ridden vision of his major works. The resounding existential rage to which his readers were accustomed not only qualified him as one of the most important contemporary writers of "serious literature"; it also helped them understand and accept Bernhard's difficult personality. Bernhard Lite was a slap in the face. The laconic raconteur of ostensibly mundane absurdities denied his admirers the personal despair that would have absolved him of his offensive personal idiosyncrasies.

Many of the tales in *The Voice Imitator* are ironic responses to some of Bernhard's own preoccupations and aspects of his career and reputation. There is the famous playwright who for the first time in his life attends the opening of one of his plays. Afterward he sues the artistic director of the theater, demanding that he as well as the actors and audiences, "nearly five thousand of them, who had already seen his play return to him what they had seen."[16] Another a vignette about the theater introduces a playwright who hid in the balcony and "put a bullet through the head of every member of the audience who had, in his opinion, laughed in the wrong place. At the end of the performance only those members of the audience whom he had shot, and who were therefore dead, remained seated in the theater. The actors and the theater manager had not allowed themselves to be disturbed for a moment by the self-willed author and the events he had perpetrated."[17] The "famous dancer" of another piece "had collapsed in mid-performance on the first night of Handel's *Raphael,* which had been specially choreographed for him by Béjart, and he had been paralyzed ever since." According to the dancer, "for the first time in his career he had thought about the complexity of a combination of steps that he had been afraid of for the whole fifteen years of his career and that had taken him to all the great opera houses of the world. A dancer, in his opinion, ought never to think about his dance while he is dancing; he should only dance, nothing else."[18] Actors and athletes know the importance of "staying in the moment." In Wittgensteinian terms, the dancer stepped out of the picture. He was literally out of his mind. Losing consciousness was inevitable. To Bernhard as to Wittgenstein, the key to philosophy is in performance.

If many of the anecdotes are about performers, the collection with its telling title adds up to one solo performance. The narrating voice, objectified as the royal "we," introduces a raconteur in the coffeehouse tradition of fin-de-siècle Vienna who has listened and knows how to mimic a variety of voices: the courtroom reporter, the gossip columnist, the dandy and satirist, the show-off and cynic, all of them, like Bernhard himself, denizens of Viennese coffeehouses and rural inns.

Geographical references and name-dropping establish cosmopolitan savvy and cultural insider status. Maurice Béjart choreographed the dancer's fateful ballet. The dancer established his fame at the Paris Opera. The encounter with him took place in Maloja. He is accompanied by "a young Italian from Castasegna." Other stories tell of encounters with "a certain Princess Radziwil"[19] and "a certain Prince Potocki, a nephew of the famous Potocki who wrote the Saragossa manuscript."[20] The narrator knows and stays at the best hotels in Warsaw and Taormina. They distinguish the connoisseur from the tourist. He has seen the pyramids of Giza, been to Alsace, tells a story about Montreux, and knows a man who disappeared in the Austrian Alps and reappeared in Lima. He has traveled widely in Eastern Europe and keeps returning to Northern Italy, to areas that once were Habsburg territories.

At a reception given by the German ambassador in Lisbon, he met the former king of Italy, Umberto, as well as the Communist leader Alvaro Cunhal. He rubs elbows with world-famous scholars, and if he doesn't know some of the distinguished people himself, he has relatives or friends who do. He travels to Shiraz and Cairo, where he spends an evening at the French embassy with "a hundred people who spent most of the evening talking about

Baudelaire's *Fleurs du Mal.*" To be sure, that evening, like most of the other episodes, ends in tragedy. An elevator filled with departing guests crashes down the shaft.[21] But behind Bernhard's unrelentingly death-bound scenarios and their deadpan delivery is the snob dramatizing his sophistication.

Not unlike Bernhard's fictional stand-ins, whose libraries include Schopenhauer, Nietzsche, and other giants of the canon (which doesn't mean that they or Bernhard, for that matter, have read them), and some of the characters in his later fiction (most prominently the Auersbergs of *Woodcutters*, who buy the "right" books as well as people), Bernhard shows off his "culture" by dropping the appropriate names.[22] He also swiftly punishes himself in effigy, as it were, in his characters' absurdly tragic predicaments.

Back in his native province, the narrator's observations are laced with the global citizen's laconic bemusement, which affords him an outsider's perspective on well-trodden native territory. There is the *Auszügler,* in local idiom the oldest member of a farming family, who, according to native custom, is moved out of the main house into a smaller house or hut on the property. In this case he is "an invalid who had lost his right leg in World War II in the Caucasus and had received the Iron Cross Class One for bravery in the face of the enemy." Totally neglected by his son and daughter-in-law, who had brought him no firewood in months, he had "finally thrown his wooden leg into the open fireplace, as the police discovered in their investigation, but in spite of this he froze to death when the fire burnt out." [23] There is the story of a member of a village's outstanding fire department who pulls the safety net out from underneath a suicide at the moment he jumps.[24]

In "The Italian" Bernhard showed his intimate knowledge of the aristocratic culture. "Der Kulterer" revisits Bernhard's early life-shaping experiences of institutional and cultural imprisonment. Both works are driven by the longing for insider status. In *The Voice Imitator* Bernhard stages himself as the ultimate insider, who flaunts his outsider status as an exile at home and abroad. His cameo routines are travel reports that establish him as a man of the world. They are also laced with the self-questioning of the seasoned impersonator, whose fictional double, with duly melodramatic flair and self-pity in the guise of satire, can mimic so many voices but not his own.[25]

In his play *Immanuel Kant,* which premiered in the same year *The Voice Imitator* was published, Bernhard carried the notion of a voice imitator to its extreme.[26] Immanuel Kant, a professor of philosophy, sails to New York to receive an honorary degree at Columbia University. Of course, Bernhard's

Immanuel Kant is not the historical Immanuel Kant. He is a contemporary surrogate, an impersonator who *naturgemäss* does not really get an honorary degree from Columbia University. Instead, upon his arrival in New York he is received by "the doctors of a New York lunatic asylum." Bernhard's Kant is accompanied by his parrot, Friedrich, who keeps shouting "Imperative Imperative" and *"Urheimat Urheimat,"* when he is not repeating some quasi-Kantian phrases of his master. When a millionaire widow, who is traveling to New York to get the *Titanic* raised so she can retrieve her family treasures, asks him, "How do you remember all the philosophies in your head?" Kant replies:

> I stored everything
> I ever thought
> in Friedrich's head
> if I lost Friedrich
> I'd lose everything [27]

He wants to get Friedrich's head opened, because

> such an operation
> would prove everything
> that's ever been said to him
> an operation that would make it possible
> to look inside Friedrich's head
> I'd have the perfect proof [28]

The image is Bernhard's revenge on Wittgenstein after years of wrestling with his challenge. He may also have learned a thing or two from his friend Paul about impersonating a famous philosophical name.

The widow says to Kant, "The bird is the most important thing you've got" — "Der Vogel ist das Wichtigste, das Sie haben." In the vernacular, *einen Vogel haben,* to have a bird, means "to be crazy." Under the circumstances, it's anyone's guess what *Vogel* she is referring to. With a nod to Luigi Pirandello's *Enrico IV,* Kant's performance commands the participation of the ship's crew and passengers. Their performances leave one wondering which one belongs in a mental institution, a theater, or a university. In Bernhard's philosophical cartoon, Friedrich the parrot starts Kant's lectures for him. The parrot as the ultimate voice imitator impersonates Foucault's absent author.

Given the multiple levels of impersonations it is quite consistent that this

Immanuel Kant sails to America, the land of substitution, reproduction and performance. Perhaps it wouldn't be so farfetched after all that a mad fake would be honored with a degree from a distinguished American university. In any case, this Kant's life consuming performance deserves credit as a philosophical act.

Bernhard's 1978 short novel *Ja* (Yes) marks the transition from the (re)-construction of a person from sources such as letters, notes, and gossip to his later, full-length "performance prose."[29] The narrative opens with a breathless, 477-word sentence (503 in the English translation!) that reflects the narrator's state of mind (and health) at the moment he decides, after three months of total seclusion in his house, to run to his friend Moritz, the real estate agent, to reveal his desperate condition.[30] He continues in more or less one breath while the structure and rhythm of his syntax reflect his gradual calming down as he tells the story. He recounts his encounter in Moritz's house that day with the "Persian woman" at this critical point in his life, when his illness, in this case his mental condition, had reached a frightening, life-threatening stage. While his ensuing two-month friendship with the cultured foreign woman extends his life, he abandons her, albeit at her wish, at the point when she can no longer be saved. Although fictionalized, the intensely autobiographical content is barely disguised. As we saw earlier, the work is a tribute to his former (and abruptly abandoned) friend Hennetmeier. The narrator's relationship with the "Persian woman" also suggests patterns of Bernhard's behavior as surrogate husband to the wives of several friends. As fictionalized self-dramatization *Yes* stages a harrowing self-examination in regard to friendship, loyalty, responsibilities to oneself and others, and finally puts into question as it affirms the narrator's determination to survive, the leitmotif of his concurrent autobiographical work *In The Cold*.

In relation to the fiction that follows his memoirs, *The Voice Imitator* and *Yes* can be seen as exercises in performance prose, which he perfects in his next work, *Concrete*. Given the performative thrust of his fiction, it is quite obvious why Bernhard resisted the term "novel." Theatrical terminology and technique also inform the subtitles of some of his later works (routinely omitted from the English publications). They point not just to a state of mind, a static condition, but to a process — in actor's parlance an "inner action," such as *eine Erregung*, an agitation, or *ein Zerfall,* a disintegration (the subtitles of *Woodcutters* and *Extinction,* respectively). By contrast, *Comedy,* the subtitle of *Old Masters,* seemingly a misnomer for a work of fiction, dramatizes the poetics of comedy.[31] Even without subtitles, his titles denote an active process, if not a drama: *Holzfällen* (literally cutting wood), *Der Untergeher* (translated as *The Loser;* the German term connotes someone who is in the process of going down or under), *Auslöschung* (extinction as a gradual if inevitable process).

Bernhard's grand "performance prose" texts were preceded by a prolific period of playwriting, thanks to the continued patronage of Claus Peymann in the theaters of Stuttgart and Bochum. The theater not only provided Bernhard with a diversion from the intense immersion in his fiction projects; against critics' increasing charges that he was repeating himself, it honed his dramaturgical skills to turn self-imitation into deliberate self-performance. The fragmentation of his earlier fiction gives way to full-length monologues. If the tragedy of history repeats itself as farce, Bernhard repeats himself as a farcical solo performer in the persistent darkness of his worldview. Writing itself becomes a philosophical performance act.

CHAPTER TEN

Theatermacher

Plays and Histrionics

*But, Doctor, I am speaking about myself only in quotation
marks, as you know; everything I say is said only in quotation
marks.*

— Thomas Bernhard, *Gargoyles*

Der Theatermacher IS ONE OF BERNHARD'S most popular plays. It also
is his tongue-in-cheek self-definition, which is lost in the play's English title,
Histrionics. "Theater maker" suggests a show-off, someone who makes a
show of everything, especially of himself. "Mach doch nicht so ein Theater,"
Austrians say: "Don't make such a theater," meaning relax, don't make such
a fuss. And when the pressures of reality intrude, they shrug and say, "Ist
ja alles ein Theater"—it's all just theater, it's all just a show. In that sense,
Theatermacher became a synonym for Bernhard.

At its Salzburg premiere in 1984, the play with its real dunghill onstage
as an odorous metonym for Austria infuriated the then finance minister and
later chancellor Franz Vranitzky, who is said to have suggested that "people
with a vision should see a doctor." The publication of Bernhard's roman à
clef *Holzfällen* later that year set off another round of political histrionics that
turned everybody into a *Theatermacher*. Bernhard's old friend Gerhard Lampersberg thought he recognized himself in the novel's failed artist Auersberg
and filed a libel suit. A court order removing all copies of the first edition from
Austrian bookstores led to a boom in books smuggled across the border from
Germany. Bernhard's next work, *Old Masters,* added more fuel to the simmering culture war. Enraged by the text's renewed diatribes against Austria, the
minister of culture and education, Herbert Moritz—none other than Bernhard's old editor on the local beat of the Salzburg *Demokratisches Volksblatt*—

suggested on national television that the author was a case for science, not
literary studies. Austrian writers protested and demanded but did not get an
apology for the insinuation that artists were pathological—an equation made
by the Nazis on their rampage against"degenerate art."

While all of Austria became Bernhard's stage and Bochum his theatrical
sanctuary, Germans watched, bemused, bewildered, and somewhat envious
about so much ado about culture in the tiny Alpine republic. In Germany,
particularly in the starker northern landscapes, where all things south of the
Danube have a whiff of the exotic, Bernhard became a cult figure of sorts. His
political attacks, although they certainly didn't spare the Germans, were different enough in form and temperament to be amusing. The graying oddballs
onstage, familiar as they seemed in their domesticity, had enough mannerisms
in speech and bearing to keep them foreign. Not too foreign, to be sure, but
just strange enough to keep them fascinatingly intriguing rather than downright offensive. Bernhard's new plays were recognized as comedies. Arguably,
Bernhard's perceived turn to comedy had more to do with audiences who had
grown accustomed to his idiosyncrasies than with a profound change on his
part. Be that as it may, this development was applauded by some but frowned
upon by others who strictly distinguished between good "serious" theater and
the vulgar pits of entertainment, the so-called boulevard theater. Going for
laughs was one of the worst offenses a serious writer could commit in the eyes
of Germany's haloed guardians of high culture. Nevertheless, it was in Germany that Bernhard was discovered as a writer of comedy in the tradition of
the nineteenth-century Viennese playwrights Johann Nestroy and Ferdinand
Raimund and as heir to the apocalyptic fin-de-siècle satirist Karl Kraus.

While his career as a playwright reached its apex in Bochum, Bernhard
spent much more time in Vienna. He became a familiar sight in the fashionable cafés of the city's historic hotels, the Sacher, Ambassador, and Imperial,
and at the Bräuner Hof with its smoky mirrors and threadbare velvety décor,
a popular hangout of writers, scholars, students, and artists. His newfound
urbanity was reflected in his fiction. Like Bernhard himself, his narrators had
grown up. They were adults, in their middle years. No longer hopelessly mired
in the infectious squalor of Alpine decay, they became skilled survivors of terminal diseases. Like Bernhard, they know their time is limited. They tell their
stories in one breath, before death can catch up with them. Their perspective,
although they may live in the country, is urban. Narcissistically, they watch
themselves perform their agonies of outraged estrangement and despairing

quests for genius. Knowing that their performances are matches with death, they enjoy the antics of the game. What makes them survive their genuine pain is their skill at sustaining the game at match point, as it were, the thrill of their own mastery. Not uncertain about the imminent outcome, they, like Bernhard, claim all the classic fool's privileges. Their hyperbole is reality rendered from the margins of temporality. Performance is all — self-performance, that is, which includes the art of watching oneself perform and watching oneself watching oneself perform. Bernhard leaves no doubt about who is the *Über*-actor in and of his works, and ultimately of himself. His self-presentations in his rare and calculated appearances on television suggest the casual, world-traveled elegance of his narrators. Those who expected to meet a pensive man marked by his illness and literary preoccupation with death were surprised to meet a spirited, charming gentleman with a special fondness for being silly.

He didn't mind being pegged a "negative writer," he claimed in a television interview that became legendary as the "Mallorca Monologues," after their location and the ultimate outcome of the "conversations," a marathon soliloquy that went on for several days. "I am quite comfortable in that role, it doesn't irritate me at all that people say I am a negative writer, yet at the same time I am a positive human being. So I'm pretty safe, right? I don't know but I find everything very pleasant, especially when I am far from home, and there are pleasant people around me and palm trees and a bit of a breeze and good coffee." [1]

Typically Bernhard makes a mock-serious assertion and instantly plays on its banality, which fits the specific circumstances of the interview. He maintains this attitude throughout. In response to people's reactions to his books, beginning with his first novel, *Frost,* he wonders: "I don't know, don't people have any sense of humor or what? I don't know. It always makes me laugh, even today. Whenever I am bored or there is some sort of tragic period, I open a book of mine. That'll most likely get me to laugh" (43).

To illustrate the pressure of death in his life, he points to his right shoulder:

> I constantly feel it — the pressure — right here. That's why, you see — if you look carefully — one of my shoulders is lower, from the pressure of death. No one can take it away from me, not even by surgery, really. And this is my fear, sitting on my right shoulder, like a — a — well, like a little death bird, right? It built its nest here for good. Of course, one could say

the whole thing very seriously, as I was about to do. If—instead of little death bird—you simply say death. A terse definition, you can serve it to the world like a cup of coffee—but now, that's not serious either. Comparing death to a cup of coffee can't be serious, right? Although, of course, everything can be compared to anything. (143-44)

In an interview for *Die Zeit,* his interlocutor pressed him on the issue of suicide, which is always present in his work but not followed through in his life. "I'm not against life," Bernhard quipped. "Nonetheless," insisted the reporter, "there are people who perceive your books as an invitation to suicide." "Yes, but no one has accepted it," Bernhard countered, and he described in local dialect his recent encounter with a woman who suddenly stood in front of his window and said she had to talk to him.

So I said: Why would you want to talk to me? I was in bed at that time with a terrible flu. And she said: Before it's too late. So I said: Do you want to kill yourself? And she said: No, but you do. So I said: Not me, that's for sure. Be reasonable, go home. And she said no, she has to come in. So I said, that's not possible, because I can hardly stand up straight, I have to lie down right away. And she said: You don't need to worry, I have a husband, I don't want to go to bed with you. . . . All that took place in front of the open window and when I wanted to close the window, she put her finger in between. So I said: I'll smash your finger. So she pulled it out and I closed the window and went back to bed. After a while I looked out, she still stood in the courtyard. But at some point she was gone and then she wrote me a letter that on such-and-such a date, it was a Monday, at 8 P.M. she would meet me at the cemetery, at the right gate, which was her favorite place. But I wasn't even home that day. And then she wrote me another letter, sixteen pages long, in which she told me her entire life, about her husband, whom she married too soon, things like that. She probably wanted to kill herself with me in that cemetery. You never know what you trigger in people.[2]

Bernhard's banter was in no way intended to break the ice in the commonly understood sense. It was a trap that many people who had occasion to talk with him fell into. The ice broke all the way and his unwitting partners in conversation would find themselves splashing about in the deep, chill waters of utter nonsense. Any attempt at a meaningful, intimate, in-depth literary or personal conversation was parried with deadpan humor. When a reporter decided to press on further, Bernhard brushed him off with brusque defensiveness. The more successful strategy was to surrender, at the risk of making a fool of oneself, to his oddly flirtatious foolery.

The 1981 *Mallorca Monologues,* edited for television by Krista Fleischmann from her interviews with Bernhard and published in its entirety after his death, is an excellent example of Bernhard's conversational tactics. Behind his gentlemanly, worldly demeanor was the fool waiting in ambush to send up his interlocutor's adoringly trusting sincerity. Her questions, those not edited from the film altogether, were reduced by Bernhard's maneuvers into timid cues for his stream-of-consciousness performance. Revealingly enough, except for a couple of barely audible off-screen interjections, the interviewer completely eliminated herself from the broadcast version. Her presence was merely suggested by a second cup of tea on the table. The published version of the unedited conversation in the original sequence over several days testifies to Bernhard's masterful dramaturgy in leading his partner on through mock-serious, mock-flirtatious, and downright nonsensical free association, from which there was no return. "Before you keep putting me on any more, let's stop it right now!" the exasperated interviewer exclaims in an attempt to finish one such riff (28). It had started on the topic of dreams and nightmares, which led to Freud and spun into innocuous banter on beards and fame. "Do you have anything against beards?" asks Fleischmann. "No," says Bernhard, "but most people call men with big beards—well, let's say relatively big beards—great; the bigger the beard, the greater the man" (21). Her query whether he thinks that psychoanalysis is a fraud triggers a stream-of-consciousness improvisation on the theme of fraud that segues into a routine on heaven.

> I always believed in heaven, even as a child. The older I get, the more I believe in it, because heaven is something quite beautiful. In heaven they always wear freshly cleaned, white clothes. There is no dirt, there is no chemical industry, no hygiene, because everything is fresh and clean to begin with. . . . I don't believe in hell. It's too dirty for me, too hot, too black, too awful. Heaven isn't like that at all. And you will certainly be an angel in that heaven. I'll be flying toward you in a white shirt with pretty embroidery. And if the shirt rips, you'll mend it maybe, if you feel like it, with the right thread, the heavenly thread. (23–24)

And so it goes on for some time yet (most of it cut on screen), until the interviewer notices: "I am a pretty good medium for you, am I not? I act as if I knew nothing about you or anything, and I look pretty stupid with my questions." "There are no stupid questions, only stupid answers," Bernhard winningly concedes, and that is the end of that day's conversation (28–29).

In another round he offers his theory of humor: "The material for a joke is always there, where there's a need for it, where there is a defect, some mental or physical deformity. No one laughs about a joker who is normal, right. Instead, he has to be one-eyed or limp or fall every third step or [he laughs] his ass explodes and a candle shoots out of it or something like that. That's what people laugh about, defects and terrible handicaps. No one ever laughed about anything else, right?" (38–39).

He goes on in that vein until he remembers his interviewer: "But you wanted to say something meaningful." "I didn't want to say anything meaningful," she replies girlishly, "I just wanted to humbly ask: Do you want to get people to laugh sometimes with your writing?" Typically, Bernhard answers with an instant negation followed by a qualifier that allows him his own variations on the theme. "No, but that comes all by itself, I don't have to make a special effort. I laugh out loud myself occasionally and I think to myself, well, that's something to laugh about. But those places that make me laugh out loud — and I'm already laughing while I am writing and afterward, when I read the proofs — other people don't find them funny at all" (42).

There are other great minds, known for their seriousness, who make him laugh — Pascal, Schopenhauer, Kant. He calls them "the great laugh philosophers." That subject eventually gets him to the birth of his brother. It all begins with that first scream,

> when you jump out with the help of some midwife, of course, slippery and disgusting, and right away you piss into the world. If you're a boy, it's straight out . . . birth always makes me think of my brother, when he was born — we had a midwife, my mother never was in a hospital when she had children — and when the midwife put him on the table, he pissed in my face. That was his first hello. That was something to laugh about. We all doubled up laughing, because in my excitement over my brother I opened my mouth, naturally, and first thing, that jet of pee-pee got into my mouth. (45–46)

The story's setting is Bernhard's invention. A snapshot shows him with his stepfather outside the hospital where his mother was in labor. And according to his memoir, he was far away from his family, in a "home for maladjusted children" in Thuringia, when his brother was born.[3]

Another peeing episode comes up in their conversation about religion. As a child Bernhard was so terrified by threats of hell and damnation that he peed in his pants in the confessional and all he could think of in his shame was the puddle of pee the next confessing sinner would find there. "The church has a human life on its conscience," he declared. "How so?" asked his interviewer. "Well, because it provoked me to make pee-pee in the confessional" (61). Bernhard's obsession with peeing goes back to his humiliating childhood experiences as a bed-wetter.[4]

In deference to his interviewer's and viewers' expectations of a serious writer, he suggests a visit to the cemetery. The trip to the cemetery would be featured in his novel *Concrete.* In one of their conversations on the hotel terrace, Bernhard and his interviewer were briefly joined by a young Bavarian widow who would inspire the tragic character of Anna Härtl in the same novel. "Do you often go to cemeteries?" Fleischmann inquires, and she is rewarded with: "I would love to go with you, in the dusk. I would hide with you, from you, behind a gravestone." In the published version Fleischmann comments: "I try not to respond to the coquettish tone and pick up instead on an earlier conversation." She asks him about the role sickness played in his life. None, he says. "Why do you ask such intense questions? Such intense stuff will get you right into intensive care. You could ask, 'How's your tea?' or 'Do you like the tablecloth?' or 'Did you spill something on you today or not?' But you ask, 'What role does sickness play?' It's such an outrageous sentence, one gets crushed under so much bombast. There is nothing one can say to that" (65–66).

So instead, he asks her—in Austrian dialect, which he corrects to high German, since "there are no other Austrians around"—whether she wants another cup of tea, and discusses the word for "cup" in various regional Austrian dialects. He feels "left alone" by his interviewer. "I keep saying, 'Don't you think' and you don't say anything, probably because it's so stupid," he baits her. "Maybe because I am so stupid," she parries flirtatiously. "No, that's out of the question," he assures her, "the half moon is right behind you." She tries to get back to Bernhardian subjects, such as the imminence of death. "If

you knew you had only a very short time left to live, what would you do?"
(67). He free-associates his way out of that subject into a riff on inhibitions,
drives, and the dropping of all inhibitions, which finishes the conversation,
but not the evening, according to the interviewer. Bernhard insisted that she
have dinner with him. Later that night, off camera, they danced in the hotel bar
and after midnight Bernhard sang, "with and against the band, operatic arias,
operettas, and popular songs, loudly and clearly, carried away by the vast number of lyrics he knows by heart." All the while she "resisted the temptation"
to film him (73).

Bernhard's late-night escapades carried over into the mock intimacy of
subsequent rounds of talk. One went straight to the subject of hugging — not a
person but a sort of lettuce that was featured on the menu. It didn't look good
enough to make Bernhard "want to hug it." Does he want to hug anything?
inquires his companion. Predictably, he denies that he does: "I have my arms
not for hugging, but for writing and tying my shoelaces and eating and dressing." In that day's conversation (mostly cut in the televised version) he merrily
trashes Austria. "Almost all Austrians talk about 'gassing' without giving it
much thought. 'That one got away from Hitler' or 'These people should be
gassed.' And if someone wears the wrong high-heeled shoes or doesn't walk
the way they think is right, they should be gassed as well." He kicks at Switzerland for good measure, but for different reasons: "They only have fat bellies
but no geniuses," whereas "Austria always had more geniuses than the Swiss,
but also more criminals. The Swiss prevented both" (88–90).

The subject of corruption brings him back to the Church and even the
pope, whom he doesn't like. But he can see her falling in love with the pope
and sneaking into his residence at Castel Gandolfo, then climbing up to the
pontiff's bedroom on a ladder or even pulling herself up on a vine, the way
Austrian peasant boys get to a girl's bedroom, so why shouldn't girls try it
too? Fleischmann's inquiry whether he would like to be pope is rewarded with
an emphatic yes. Maybe, Bernhard speculates, she could poison the present
pope and then he could climb after her and slip into the pope's nightshirt and
undergo facial surgery and emerge as the pope. He would be the first to change
his name while in office, to Pope Thomas I (96–101).

That day's session culminates in a marathon routine on women (nineteen pages in print [107–26], not aired). In the great theater of world politics
women "appear only briefly, and when they do they get dragged offstage right

away, because they always appear at the wrong time and miss their cues" (107). Furthermore, bright voices aren't good for great drama, and the female pitch, if not altered by too much alcohol, "is usually too high for great drama, right." His interlocutor meekly wonders whether he has anything against women, which he denies with a salvo about women not being able to endure anything except the weltschmerz of giving birth—"That of course is horrendous and hurts a lot" (109). Women have their roles to play, and it wasn't history but nature that cast them. If the laws were made by men, why don't women change them? "Because they lack the courage in the end," Bernhard answers himself. The few female representatives in the Austrian parliament are the living proof. As his argument gets sillier and sillier, his contradictions get more and more outrageous and he obviously has a great time busting his interlocutor's chops. Her interjections of rudimentary feminist tenets ("Laws were made by men"; "In the Christian structure of society women are second-class beings"; "History was written by men"; "But for centuries, really, woman has been repressed and degraded by men") barely surface as faint gasps for breath from under his verbal rapids and sound as ridiculous as his outré misogynist rant (110–27).

Surprisingly, the entire section on women was cut in the broadcast version. One is left to wonder whether the interviewer, quite obviously smitten by her subject, was more eager to protect his public image than her own. In any case, the performative force of Bernhard's comedic routines turned his interlocutor into his willing subject, quite in the sense of Foucault's *assujettisse- ment*. She submitted to his dramaturgy. Her questions turned into echoes of his self-performance. They became unnecessary in the broadcast version, in which the screen became the medium of (self-)reflection. Uncannily, Bernhard so thoroughly incorporated his interviewer that she allowed herself to disappear. Their bizarre exchange on women served only to prove the point. If Bernhard appeared a childish fool, his invisible interviewer and by extension the viewers pushing for earnestness were made fools of. In any event, it was Bernhard who controlled the level of the foolishness. The *Mallorca Monologues* acquired the status of another Bernhard work sui generis.

Bernhard appreciated Fleischmann's self-effacing submission to his self- dramatization. He was pleased with the film and conscious "of its lasting im- portance for posterity," as the blurb on the videocassette cover informs the prospective viewer. As a result, he agreed to another video collaboration with her, a portrait in a series titled *Settings in World Literature,* filmed in June 1986. Lest he be labeled an "Austrian *Heimatdichter,*" he summoned her to Madrid and staged himself as a citizen of the world in settings, including a bullfight, chosen by him.

That the desolate, arid highlands around Madrid suggested Bernhard's vision of nature was highlighted by the voice-over of Bruno Ganz reading excerpts from the recently published novel *Extinction.* In contrast to the mischievous, lighthearted fool of Mallorca five years earlier, Bernhard now cast himself in a cynical and ruthless vein. His face, somewhat puffy from medication and elongated by his large reddish nose, projected a misleadingly jolly good nature in a performance that was an eerily unsettling demonstration of his ultimate mastery in exploiting his illness. Gaunt and visibly weakened, he presides as an avenging jester who settles once and for all with the deadly stupidity by which he saw himself pursued all his life: "All intellectuals are assholes digging themselves into the mouse holes of their definitions; politicians, if one waits long enough, disappear by themselves, into old age, sitting on a park bench after a stroke, talking to the sparrows and little children, 'old-age sauce' dribbling from the mouth" (243).

Bernhard didn't say why he wanted to be filmed at a bullfight. Perhaps he saw his roles of jester, moral scourge, and clinical observer merge in the bloody arena of a spectacularly staged death. His remarks accompanying the thrusting of the pics recall the doctor's minute elaboration on the dissection of a corpse in his play *The Ignoramus and the Madman.* (The role of the doctor, it will be remembered, was originated by Bruno Ganz, the narrator of the Madrid project.) Whether Bernhard intended to confront his audience with the reality of the killer instinct ("the human ur-drive, which goes through all humans" [217]) on display in a stylized dance of death or saw himself as the martyred bull, the spectacle exceeded his clinically, cynically distanced curiosity. The speechless horror in his face finally belied even his professed intimacy with dying and death.

His silent, invisible interviewer once again took on the role of the taciturn listener to the obsessive speaker, a familiar configuration of characters in Bernhard's plays. Over the years, both he and Fleischmann had perfected their parts to his complete satisfaction. He made plans to work with her on his eulogy; those plans were cut short by his death (279).

Bernhard kept his public persona under strictest control. When he agreed to a rare printed interview, the reports by some of Germany's most feared crit-

ics burst with adolescent excitement about the adventure. There was the journey to the remote Austrian village with its quaint inhabitants who showed them
the road to the odd *Dichter.* And if he wasn't home, they could point them
to a couple of inns where he might be. First-time visitors from Germany approached the author's habitat and his compatriots' cultural peculiarities with
the ethnographer's fascination. "A beautiful summer day in the hinterland of
Salzburg. Between pear trees, next to the corn fields, the sign 'Ohlsdorf.' Right
next to it another colorful board: 'Grüss Gott in Ohlsdorf' [the equivalent of
'God bless,' the customary greeting in Catholic Austria]," begins one typical
account.[5] Asked for directions, the local innkeeper explains to the journalist
from Germany that although Bernhard's address reads Ohlsdorf, he lives in
Unternathal, which is part of Ohlsdorf but has its own name. Actually, the
reporter still got it wrong. Bernhard lived not in Unternathal (Lower Nathal)
but in Obernathal (Upper Nathal). The confusion could have come straight
from a peasant farce. The directional prefixes suggest exactly the kind of provincialism that Bernhard loved to satirize. If the visitor actually managed to
meet him in his cloistered farmhouse, there was the strain of living up to the
great man's trust, of proving one's own literary and existential mettle. Most
strenuous of all was the effort to prove oneself a worthy writer. The tone of
such reported encounters with Bernhard, full of admiration, begged for his
admiration in return.

Over the years there developed, especially in Germany, a distinct style
of Bernhard journalism. Reports about him were usually structured in fragments — to indicate the difficulty of approaching such a complicated subject — laced with self-deprecating irony and interspersed with appropriations
of Bernhard's idiolect. In the process, many rarefied, archaic terms that Bernhard revived, appropriated, or invented became idiomatic in contemporary
usage.[6]

Peter von Becker, the esteemed editor in chief of *Theater Heute,* tells about
his visit in a third-person narrative, subtitled "A Story in 15 Episodes":

Late afternoon. The taxi with the critic from Germany had already left the
poet's estate when a second car approached over the hill in front of the lake
and the mountains. It carried Z, a nephew of the famous philosopher and
logician from Vienna. Occasionally the nephew had an urge to dive into
Lake Traunsee and conduct, way, way out in the lake. It was the *Dichter*
who saved him from the ultimate fulfillment of his desire. That day, a spe-

cial wind had been blowing in Vienna and the logician's nephew, filled with his own desire for literature, wanted to see the poet to philosophize with him—alas, he was almost penniless.

Bernhard has to pay for the taxi ride from Vienna's Peter's Square to the Salzburg area and back, reluctantly. Thus he dismissed the visitor, who was no stranger to him, in a friendly manner, after a few hours of terror.[7]

Z, the philosopher's nephew, is of course Paul Wittgenstein. The oblique reference establishes kinship between fellow aristocrats, by *Bildung* and birth or both. The visiting critic, whose surname is preceded by an aristocratic "von," tightly circumscribes the territory of insiders and populates it with a few more select allusions, such as to a famous director and a cardinal, who is a friend of a friend of Bernhard (and will appear later in his novel *Extinction),* all unnamed. Named, however, are the geniuses, from Beckett to Foucault, from Heidegger to Sartre and Wagner, whom the critic quotes to find his way through the maze of the *Dichter's* brain. It is the code by which he qualifies himself as at home with Bernhard and the informed reader in the pantheon of culture.

Von Becker sees Bernhard as Sartre's dandy, a stoic who defies categorization by others and watches the show he makes of himself as his own most merciless judge.[8] "Stoic ascesis" (which Sartre attributes to his model dandy Baudelaire) is also part of Bernhard's mystique, a peculiar state of tension, which makes it hard for the outsider to distinguish the enormous effort he puts into being true only to himself from the comedy act he makes of and for himself. However blurred the lines, the sensitive Bernhard critic strives to prove himself worthy to penetrate the comedic veneer to the heart of darkness and beyond, to the stoic hero inside the actor inside the actor, and so on—a solid German classic after all in the guise of an Austrian *Kasperl.* That hero, however, refused to be nailed. His elusiveness was an ongoing irritation in the Bernhard reception.

Rolf Michaelis, a critic for *Die Zeit,* worked hard to earn the admired writer's respect. Before the Salzburg opening of *Am Ziel* (1981) he set out on a pilgrimage to Ohlsdorf. To prep himself for the visit he brought along a copy of Bernhard's play *Über allen Gipfeln ist Ruh,* which had just been published. He describes his encounter with the master with the sort of awed flirtatiousness that Bernhard's inhibited, awkwardly unpredictable graciousness elicited from his invited and so presumably trustworthy visitors. He is rewarded with discretion and a tone of gently ironical shyness to reflect his. "The 'dramatic writer' is a friendly host," writes Michaelis. Bernhard "fetches from the cellar gray bottles of cool pear cider, performs with ironic dignity the part of 'the author at leisure.' Pro that he is, he knows all the questions, acts at times as if he hasn't yet thought through the answer: 'My plays are skeletons, the meat has to be added by the reader himself. That's why I find punctuation so ridiculous in plays. Where one [actor] needs an exclamation mark, another goes right on and pauses later—and discovers entirely new things, "improving" the text as it were.'"⁹

Before he leaves, the critic asks, "Will we see each other in Salzburg?" The answer is no. "Just like his stage character," Michaelis observes, and he quotes from the play: "[He] doesn't bow for curtain calls/that's not his way." Ever so discretely, he indicates that he left late that evening:

> On the way to the car, which is covered with night dew, in the dark, these sentences: "Of course one reads what one has written, but one always hates it, can't hear it anymore. That's why I'd be happy with one performance only, with the best actors. One time and then never again. But opening night . . . that evening belongs to the actors, with good reason. What's there for me to say? During rehearsals one can't change anything—and shouldn't. I talk with the people [about the play] before they begin."
>
> So when that little play is finished one should push it out like a little boat and stop drilling, otherwise it'll just sink.

In his meandering review cum travel report, Michaelis quotes Bernhard directly only in the above passages. The discretion does not go unnoticed, since all evidence suggests that they talked long into the night. The final light-hearted shoptalk suggests an intimacy that wasn't betrayed in the article. Access to Bernhard's farmhouse was a rare privilege honored and emphasized by the visitor's tactful silence.

As he became the center of journalistic attention, Bernhard, perhaps remembering his own journalistic roots, discovered the newspaper as another performance medium, and he increasingly chose it to stage his dramatic responses to contemporary events.

The *Mallorca Monologues* were aired on November 2, 1981, within a month of a major offensive by Bernhard against a fellow Mallorca vacationer,

Chancellor Bruno Kreisky, in the Austrian news magazine *Profil*.[10] Bernhard's article "The Retired Salon Socialist" was commissioned by the magazine as commentary on a book of recent photographs and sentimental descriptions of the revered if controversial Socialist politician on the occasion of his seventieth birthday.[11] Ironically, in some respects Kreisky was as contradictory as Bernhard. His unmatched popularity in Austria notwithstanding, his shrewdly pragmatic politics was highly controversial. The son of upper-class Viennese Jews, he joined the Socialist Party in high school, became a leading figure in the workers' opposition against Austro-fascism, was arrested twice when his party was outlawed, and finally was forced into exile (in Sweden) by the Nazis. Early in his chancellorship the Socialists gained an absolute majority in Parliament, thanks to his close political ties to the leader of Austria's Freedom Party, Friedrich Peter. When the Nazi hunter Simon Wiesenthal publicized Peter's service as SS *Obersturmbandführer* (which was no secret to anyone but had been tacitly ignored), Kreisky accused Wiesenthal of "posthumously adopting Nazi concepts under reversed conditions," and insinuated that as a concentration camp inmate Wiesenthal had collaborated with the Gestapo. Wiesenthal threatened legal action. Kreisky countered that he would waive his immunity as chancellor to confront Wiesenthal in a court of law, if only to initiate a special investigation of Wiesenthal's "mafia methods" and connections to the state police.[12] Wiesenthal withdrew his suit. Peter was rehabilitated as a man who had completely changed since the early 1940s and continued his political career. The Freedom Party continued to attract members with outspoken nostalgia for the Nazi past. The party grew in popularity with the spectacular rise of its charismatic leader, Jörg Haider, who unabashedly catered to aging Hitler veterans, young neo-Nazis, and disgruntled blue-collar workers (traditionally Socialist voters) with his calculated remarks (for which he later apologized) that members of the Waffen SS deserved credit as devoted patriots and that concentration camps were mere "punishment camps."[13] Haider's xenophobic platform helped his party to a stunning victory in 1999, when it replaced the conservative People's Party as Austria's second strongest party and the two parties formed a coalition government. Ironically, the Freedom Party's rise to the status of a governing party, which unleashed a storm of protest around the world, was due in part to the election reform that won a parliamentary majority in 1970 thanks to the collaboration of Kreisky and Peter.

In 1979 the Jewish chancellor caused an international uproar when he rec-

Hans Leinberger, *Little Death* (ca. 1520), Ambras Castle

Thomas Bernhard, 1970

(top) Thomas Bernhard
plays Twenty-one, 1974

(bottom) Thomas
Bernhard with Amalia
Altenburg

Am Ziel, Salzburg Festival, 1981: Marianne Hoppe as Mother
and Kirsten Dene as Daughter

Steinhof. Otto Wagner's fin-de-siècle church towers over the rows of pavilions. The pavilions to the right of the church belong to Baumgartnerhöhe, where Bernhard was hospitalized; those to the left belong to Steinhof. In the background is Vienna.

Paul Wittgenstein in 1977.
(inset) Paul Wittgenstein, ca. 1948

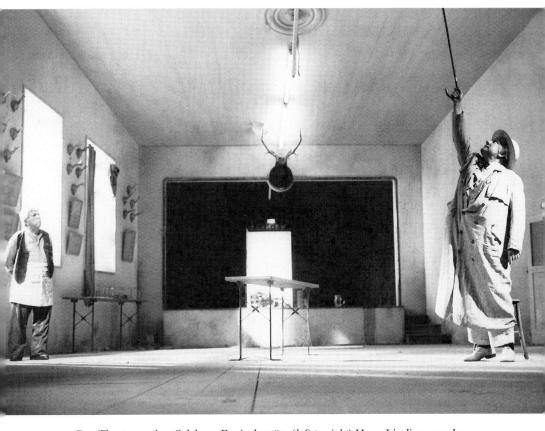

Der Theatermacher, Salzburg Festival, 1985: (*left to right*) Hugo Lindinger as the innkeeper and Traugott Buhre as Bruscon

Oskar Werner as Hamlet, Salzburg Festival, 1970

Ritter, Dene, Voss, Salzburg Festival, 1986: Ilse Ritter and Gert Voss

Glenn Gould in 1955

Glenn Gould in 1980

Bernhard and children on Graben, Vienna

Bernhard at the Café Bräunerhof, Vienna

Bernhard and his sister, Susanne Kuhn

The Burgtheater in flames: photomontage in a *Kronenzeitung* insert,
November 4, 1988

Heldenplatz, Burgtheater, 1988, scene in Volksgarten with Burgtheater in background:
(*left to right*) Kirsten Dene as Anna, Wolfgang Gasser as Robert, Elisabeth Rath as Olga

Thomas Bernhard and Claus Peymann take a curtain call after the opening of
Heldenplatz, Burgtheater, November 4, 1988

ognized the Palestine Liberation Organization and met in Vienna with Yassir
Arafat and Willy Brandt.

Over the years, Kreisky and the corruption of Socialist principles during
his regime had become one of Bernhard's favorite targets. His *Profil* article
is a volley of invective punning in nearly untranslatable composites of slang,
political jargon, and tabloid clichés. Irate about the book's sentimental portrait of the chancellor as a "pampered pensioner," which belies the "horror of
many" over his continued political tenure, he calls him a demimonde socialist
(*Halbseidensozialist*), a "rosy-red appeasement uncle" (*rosaroter Beschwichti-
gungsonkel*) and "global palm reader" between Teheran and New York, Palma
de Mallorca and Unterkleinwetzdorf—"Lower Little Wetzville," an invented
name with the gleeful implication that few Austrians, despite their bourgeois
background, can shake their provincialism, while Bernhard, though born into
it, rose at least far enough above it to recognize its pitfalls. It goes hand in hand
with "the cactus plant in the living room, the gnome sculpture on the lawn,
and the dream of a charter flight," all "mercilessly written in his face." Dropping the names of great artists and great minds, Kreisky actually shakes hands
only with "the small-minded" (*Kleindenker)* and minor entertainers (*Klein-
künstler,* the usual term for a cabaret performer). The "Sun Chancellor," as he
was called in allusion to the Sun King, Louis XIV (and to sunny Mallorca, his
favorite vacation spot), is at best the king of "the tanning studio's quartz lamp"
(*Höhensonnenkönig*). To top it off, "he is not a GREAT Jew, he is, as we know,
not a GOOD JEW. He is (and has been for a long time now) a bad chancellor." [14]

Bernhard's cadences and resounding hyperbole turn his critique into a
dark stand-up routine, closer to Lenny Bruce than, say, Art Buchwald. When
read as a performance piece rather than as political commentary, the lines between the performer and his target get blurred. If laughter is a curative, a social corrective, it also is (intended or not) a self-corrective. The performer is
present in his routine. Bernhard's "philosophical" comedian knows that the
laughter he elicits is also aimed, if not primarily, at himself. He cannot extricate himself from his targeted subject. He becomes the stand-in for his subject
and thus the object of ridicule.

Bernhard's satire, his anger, was directed less against Kreisky than against
his representation in the book. Bernhard saw the gushy writing, intended as
homage, as an exposure of the hypocrisy of performance. However, Bernhard argued, Kreisky wasn't even a good performer. If he had been, he would
have made a "good" Jew, who at that point in history wouldn't have frater-

nized with the Palestinians. Not being a good Jew, he made the right (and unsentimental) political compromise, which in the eyes of the world reflected badly on the Austrians' attitude toward Israel. Not being a GOOD Jew, Kreisky couldn't be a GREAT Jew. Bernhard's terminology was deliberately provocative at a time when Austrians were still quite self-conscious about referring to someone as being Jewish, which they whispered discretely or, better yet, avoided altogether. Kreisky was the great exception. Despite his emigration to Sweden during the Hitler years, he continued to feed into the silence that persisted in Austria about the Holocaust. He was the Jew Austrians could love, thus avoiding the need to truly confront their past.[15]

Perhaps there was more affinity between Bernhard and the chancellor than first meets the eye; perhaps the literary performer had more sympathy for the predicament of the political actor than he was willing to acknowledge. "An aging, smug state clown," he called him on another occasion, true to the adage that it takes one to recognize one. It might even have been his preoccupation with Kreisky that turned Bernhard's attention from the Nazi perpetrators and their heirs to the predicament of the victims. While his plays and other works had been marked from the beginning by the legacy of historic guilt, it was only in his late works, particularly in *Extinction* and *Heldenplatz,* that he approached the problems of Jews in contemporary Austria head on. Kreisky's contrary personality and the complexity of his negotiations as an Austrian Jewish politician fed into the controversial portrayal of the Schusters, the upper-class Viennese Jewish family of *Heldenplatz.* The last and dying heir of *Extinction* wills the ancient estate of Wolfsegg, "with everything that comes with it," to the Jewish community of Vienna. Wolfsegg stands for Austria. It is the postwar Austria that Kreisky, the returned Jew, inherited, "with everything that comes with it," while Bernhard watched how he negotiated its problematic legacy. Kreisky, in any case, reacted to Bernhard's assaults in good spirits: "I heard that kind of railing is supposed to be good for his health. I'm glad if that's the case."[16]

Vienna's legendary coffeehouses provided Bernhard with the sort of aggravation he needed for his writing: a wide selection of local and international newspapers, which one was free to peruse as long as one liked for the price of an espresso. The newspapers' so-called feuilleton section, roughly equivalent to the Arts and Ideas section in American newspapers, offered another outlet for Bernhard's political histrionics. Fetishized in the German-language world as the principal forum for intellectual exchange, the feuilleton had become the breeding ground and battlefield of major culture wars. For international recognition, Austrian as well as Swiss writers and artists need the attention of the German feuilleton, with its much larger readership. The term connotes both the section and the individual article. The Viennese critic and editor Karl Kraus was a notorious foe of the dilettantism, vacuity, and vanity of feuilleton writers, whom he blamed for deterioration of language and thought. In full agreement and quite consistently, Bernhard made the German feuilleton his performance space, a fool's paradise, where he upstaged all serious discourse with his outrageous satirical sketches, open letters, and guest commentaries.

The German Lunch Table, his 1979 New Year's gift to *Die Zeit,* opened a barrage of minifarces lampooning the ubiquitous Nazi spirit in contemporary Germany. *A Doda, a Doda* (A Corpse, a Corpse, spelled phonetically in Bavarian dialect) appeared the following December in the same paper.[17] It depicts two peasant women walking home from church along an empty country road. They discover a big package shaped like a body wrapped in brown paper. It turns out to be a bundle of swastika posters that slipped from the moped of the husband of one of the women.

The May 1981 issue of *Theater Heute* featured *Alles oder Nichts* (All or Nothing), a TV game show devised by Bernhard for the leaders of the Federal Republic: President Karl Carstens, Chancellor Helmut Schmidt, and Foreign Minister Hans-Dietrich Genscher. They participate in inane races and games, such as hitting their heads or crawling through an empty (but not yet scrubbed) manure drum to pick up their ballots at the other end. Finally, there is the crucial question in front of viewers "from the entire German-language world/and the whole world": "In your heart are you/A National Socialist?" All three shout back ("like a shot"), "Yes!" and "the audience raves, the music blares" (145).

Bernhard added four more "dramalettes" and Claus Peymann presented all seven in a six-hour extravaganza of political farce at his Bochum Theater, which opened November 11, 1981. Titled *Our World,* the event lasted well past midnight. One-act plays by Dario Fo, Heiner Müller, Howard Brenton, and Trevor Griffith were performed simultaneously in various performance spaces in the Bochum Theater complex. Bernhard contributed some more sketches on German families, which pick up on motifs from *Eve of Retirement.* *Maiandacht* (Vespers in May) is dedicated to Bernhard's "childhood town, Traunstein." Two women come out of the village church after the prayer service and watch a gravedigger at work. He is burying an old man who was run over by a car. The driver is said to have been a Turk. Soon the women launch into a tirade against Turkish and other foreign laborers, with the conclusion that all of them should be gassed. *Match* depicts a taciturn policeman at home in bed, watching a soccer game after a day of controlling protest rallies. His talkative wife, ready for sex, suggests that he is too soft on student demonstrators. He should shoot right into the crowd. *Eis* (Ice Cream) features two vacationing governors of federal German states and their wives in their cabanas on the shore of the North Sea. The men reminisce nostalgically about their experiences in World War II, bombing London and invading Russia, at the cost of the lives of so many of their comrades, all war heroes. Because they don't want to spoil the fun of travel, one couple avoids any country where German heroes are buried. "But then you can't go anywhere / there is no place to go," observes the other man. The ice cream vendor they had been waiting for passes by and shoots them all (103).

Freispruch (Acquittal) features a dinner party of three judges and their wives, who are celebrating one judge's acquittal of charges of Nazi criminality at a trial presided over by one of the others. "We are a conspiracy against Jews / Tonight let's celebrate the acquittal / We've all been acquitted / at this particular moment of German history," says the judge who found his colleague not guilty, and he adds, "should you have really killed a few thousand Jews / it certainly was too few" (89–90). The statement, deeply offensive as it is even in the context of political cabaret, is characteristic of Bernhard's all-or-nothing strategy of crushing facades. What made Bernhard so troublesome was his shameless delight in demolishing the walls of silence, digging obscenities out of the rubble, and shouting them at the top of his lungs. Barking dogs don't bite, the saying goes. The argument about Bernhard's political bite continued. As one critic remarks in his defense, Bernhard's brief pieces are not drama, they are cabaret. "Cabaret texts are oppositional. Bernhard's texts ridicule every opposition as well as every affirmation. They are endgames of cabaret."[18] The same critic found it wrong to stage the pieces at a theater festival, with spectators milling about between playing areas, balancing plates of goulash and chewing on their hot dogs. The director "should have noticed that Bernhard's texts, all of them about fascism in one way or another, are not just for laughs, they are also terrifying." *Theater Heute*'s critic also blamed the director for failing to establish the connection between Bernhard's satire and contemporary events, such as the Arab terrorists' kidnapping and killing of the

Israeli athletes at the Olympic Village in Munich and the increase in neo-Nazi activities across West Germany.[19]

From the perspective of Vienna's coffeehouses, Bochum was a remote mining town somewhere in the German north, shrouded in coal dust and obscurity among the larger cities that cluster in the Ruhr area. But even though the relatively small city in the heartland of West Germany's coal and steel industry was far from the cosmopolitan centers of culture, it had a resident theater company with a long tradition of excellence. The Socialist government of the state of Nordrhein-Westfalen, to which Bochum belongs, took great pride in its support of the arts. Its resident theater was established in 1918 by the legendary Hans Schalla, who brought it to national prominence and ran it successfully through World War II until 1950. There were only two other artistic directors before Peymann took over: Saladin Schmitt, who maintained the theater's acclaimed traditional style, and Peter Zadek, one of the brilliant enfants terribles of German postwar theater. The son of Jewish refugees, Zadek grew up in England, graduated from Cambridge, and rose to prominence in Germany with productions that lightened the fashionably heavy Brechtian *Verfremdung* with Anglo-Saxon flair and his own brand of eroticized politics. Although he was too erratic and demanding an artist to make a good administrator, his bold innovations paved the way for Peymann's experiments.

The climate in West Germany had changed when Peymann arrived in Bochum. With the end of the Baader-Meinhof tragedy, terrorism gradually subsided. The government lost its dramatic function as the "external enemy" of individual freedom and political dissent. "Theater workers," as the leftists of the "68 generation" styled themselves, had to turn their attention elsewhere. (In the 1980s Bernhard's ambivalent term *Theatermacher* offered itself as a fitful sobriquet for the graying revolutionaries.) Critics fretted that with the vanquishing of the "external enemy," the theater of opposition—the trademark of Germany's directorial elite—had lost a formidable motivational force. The general feeling of "external insecurity" in the face of terrorism and the countermeasures that shaped the German theater season only two years earlier "gave way to internal insecurity," noted the critic Günther Rühle in *Theater Heute.* "Questions as to what the theater means, is, and could be, where it goes, whether it has a future and if so what kind, hadn't been asked in a long time with such urgency and pain," he observed.[20] Star directors such as Peter

Stein and Peter Zadek tried to break out of their established mold and test themselves in new waters. Robert Wilson, the American avant-garde director largely ignored at home, was discovered by Germans as the new visionary of postmodern theater. His stunning slow-motion mega-tableaus, in which performers served to animate the space rather than create characters, promised an antidote to the overpoliticized deconstructions of the classics popular in both Germanys at that time. Nevertheless, his radical formalism further rattled the institutionalized elite of enfants terribles now approaching midlife crisis. The 1960s theater of revolt had become stagnant. Peymann, courtesy of Hans Filbinger, was the last director lucky enough to squeeze out another season motivated by "oppositional audacity." According to Rühle, the law-and-order politician's extraordinary denouement inspired one of the few remarkable plays of the season, *Eve of Retirement*. Moreover, it sustained the creative spontaneity that was Peymann's trademark, in marked contrast to the strained efforts of other directors to conceptualize the Baader-Meinhof tragedy in their staging of classic dramas (*Antigone* was the most obvious choice).

In Bochum Peymann was quick to articulate the shifting concerns in the post-Stammheim era. "It was quite revealing that in the autumn of 1977 we directly experienced the external enemy who built walls around the theater. Now we get to know the internal enemy, who does the wrong construction job on the theater itself," he said in an interview five months into his first season. He continued to insist that "the theater is a place of opposition—in certain times to the point of subversion."[21]

Peymann's new internal enemy was the stage unions and the politicians who tried to cut the arts budgets in an effort to stem the threatening economic crisis. That an incoming director would bring with him his core company of actors and key members of his artistic and administrative staff was unprecedented in the German theater. In the interest of maintaining a permanent resident ensemble, most institutions provided lifelong employment for their members, who were, in effect, state employees. As public servants they were the beneficiaries of the generous pension and welfare system. Peymann's move necessitated the firing of thirty members of the Bochum Theater, twelve of them actors, at a time when the unemployment rate in West Germany was climbing perilously and Bochum's blue-collar population was especially hard hit. It made for a rocky beginning with the theater's municipal administrators and the public at large. Seven years later Peymann would restage the controversy in Vienna when he brought his Bochum company to the Burgtheater. Although in numbers his Bochum company barely made a dent in the Burg ensemble of 144 permanently employed actors, his clash with the resident company erupted into a full-scale culture war fought out on the stage of the entire nation. It resuscitated ancient conflicts and problematic bondings between Austrians and Teutons, Germanophiles and Germanophobes, monarchists, neo-Nazis, Socialists, Catholics, and nativists.

As the Viennese were quick to point out, Bochum was a far cry from Vienna. Its stodgy earnestness was no match for Vienna's histrionics and intrigues. Bochum was a traditional stronghold of socialism. That Peymann, an outspoken leftist, took on the unions and demanded the costly reconstruction of the theater and a larger budget to support his artistic vision demanded some explanation. "The work we are doing now is still subversive, even if we are paid—albeit not bought—by public funds," he claimed three years later. Furthermore,

> artists have a completely different foundation, their legitimacy goes so much deeper than that of politicians. That's why I have no bad conscience about accepting the subsidy of seventeen million marks the city of Bochum still spends on its theater, although not without a struggle. I accept this money . . . without hesitation, because I know that a society that no longer invests in exploring its future and confronting its past dies on the spot. If we lived in a time of great political utopias and dreams, in times of new beginnings, art could perhaps step back a bit; but in times such as ours, an epoch of glacialization, of militarization, the public art of theater has a function that I fully accept.[22]

Bernhard's stage utopians, their hypostatization of artistic genius, had clearly rubbed off on their stage director by then. Peymann's post-Brechtian, post-Stammheim theatrical utopianism makes him a bona fide Bernhard figure, a maniacal fool, ultimately—and luckily perhaps—a figure of the theater. His oppositional stance remained, for better or for worse, confined to theatrics.

By 1984, when Peymann accepted the position in Vienna as of September 1986, he completely identified with Bernhard's dramaturgy of the fool: "In the final analysis, art, even if financed by the state, is hostile to the state. Art and especially theater, this wonderful communal art, always serves to ridicule the powerful. . . . An extremely difficult as well as thrilling situation: the play of fools against the king who finances those fools and still lets them bash his head," he said in an interview.[23]

Peymann fought on all fronts and, unlike Bernhard's characters, succeeded brilliantly. His political savvy owed much of its finesse to Bernhard's political theatrics. Peymann's histrionic warfare with politicians, like Bernhard's verbal bombardment of Austria, depended on the stability and support of the very institutions he attacked. If Vienna and with it all of Austria would eventually offer the ultimate stage on which the entire population joined in the play of fools against the king and the king's men, it was in Bochum, the harsh, unglamorous mining town, that Peymann perfected the minimalist elegance of his Bernhard productions. They became, in the words of the most influential critic, Henning Rischbieter, "the contemporary cornerstone of the Bochum repertory." [24] It was a groundbreaking repertory that turned the Bochum Theater into an outstanding model of the German Stadttheater. The function of a city theater with a regional artistic mission suggested a welcome shift of emphasis from the earlier model of one National Theater that evoked disquieting associations with fascist cultural politics.

In Bochum, Peymann programmatically focused on contemporary German-language drama in marked contrast to the overwhelmingly classical repertory of other prominent German theaters. German directors generally preferred to gain attention with provocative reinterpretations of well-known classics — a fact to which Bernhard alludes in the banishment of Minetti — the stage character — for resisting the classics. Bochum's repertory did include a core of classic plays, to be sure, particularly the German classics. In the aftermath of the upheavals of the past two decades, Peymann and his team revisited Goethe, Kleist, and Büchner to reexamine the past in light of the present unease.

Brecht was the most performed playwright, with nine productions, closely followed by eight Bernhard plays and seven by Heiner Müller. Brilliantly imaginative productions of *Baal, St. Joan of the Stockyards, The Mahagonny Songspiel, The Mother,* the very early one-act play *The Wedding, Mother Courage,* and *Puntila and His Servant Matti,* as well as two evenings of poems and songs, offered an opportunity to follow Brecht's development in the context of his political journey and the present conditions in East Germany. There were four new plays by the Bavarian playwright Herbert Achternbusch, two each by Thomas Brasch, Franz Xaver Kroetz, Gerlinde Reinshagen, and George Tabori, one by Botho Strauss. If *Eve of Retirement,* in a total of fourteen performances, played disappointingly to half-filled houses, all Bernhard productions together reached a total of 84,500 spectators, almost as many as all of the other nineteen productions of new German plays, which had a total audience of 94,500.[25]

Renowned East German directors, such as Adolf Dresen, B. K. Tragelehn, Manfred Karge, and Matthias Langhoff, joined the company as visiting artists. Along with Heiner Müller, who directed his play *Der Auftrag* (The Task),[26] Brecht's former pupils and collaborators infused their reinterpretations of the classics with glaring images of Western consumption and Eastern disillusionment with communism.

Peymann and his artistic team continued their political activism. Much to the dismay of the city fathers, performances were followed by the reading of a letter to Chancellor Helmut Schmidt signed by prominent German writers, among them Thomas Brasch, Günter Grass, and Peter Schneider, urging him to resist U.S. armament policies and the placement of Pershing missiles in West Germany. Audiences were invited to add their signatures. The dramaturg Hermann Beil could be spotted downtown, distributing flyers against conservative politicians. The company joined young squatters in their protest against the demolition of an abandoned factory that served as a youth center and was also used by the Bochum ensemble as a performance space for Brecht's *St. Joan of the Stockyards*.[27] The standoff with municipal agencies climaxed in Peymann's declaration that he would bring his bed to the factory and spend the night there with the squatters. (He lost. The building was torn down.)

While Peymann staged his kind of political drama in the streets, his theater was focused on reflection — of itself, its function in a specific area at a specific time and in Germany's troubled history. Presented in alternating repertory, the Bochum productions, both of contemporary plays and of innovative reinterpretations of the classics, explored questions of memory, responsibility, and self-understanding in a divided Germany as they measured the distance both Germanys had come since World War II. The growing acclaim for their work advanced Bernhard's status as a playwright and prepared, ironically if predictably, for his return to Vienna's Burgtheater.

The subversive element of the Bochum repertory was in the form and production aesthetics of the plays rather than in their content. Heiner Müller's condensed, fragmented, intensely poetic constructions lent themselves to innovative scenic elaborations. At the opposite end of the spectrum was Bernhard, whose subversion of contemporary concerns with the props of Viennese operetta imposed its own kind of alienation effect on German reality.

While Müller, with agonized cerebral macho, extracted his pain from deconstructed fragments of canonical texts, political manifestos, and commercial
slogans, Bernhard laughed at the inflated egos that pronounced operetta sentiments the ultimate truths without denying the tragic consequences of their
histrionics. His repetitive speech arias deliberately mined the conventions of
grand opera and virtuoso acting only to wrap themselves around a bottom-
less Beckettian silence. *Der Weltverbesserer* (The World Improver or Utopian)
and *Der Schein trügt* (Appearances Are Deceiving), which premiered in 1980
and 1984, respectively, both written for Minetti, borrow Beckett's isolated old
men and expand their endgames into querulous tirades against an ignorant
world. Like hamsters in a barrel, Bernhard's despotic clowns cannot wriggle
themselves free from the wheel of handed-down language, which keeps them
running in place.

Am Ziel (1981) and *Über allen Gipfeln ist Ruh* (1982) appropriate the Bochum ensemble's self-reflective mode on a personal level. Both plays feature
a writer, a playwright and a novelist, respectively. Through both characters
Bernhard pursues a coyly self-referential dialogue with his critics and audiences:

> A dramatic writer
> is by nature
> an arrogant megalomaniac
> They get applause and have
> delusions of grandeur
> or they sneak out
> the back door
> with their heads down

comments the wealthy patroness of *Am Ziel*.[28]

Some critics were charmed; others caught him at his game. "Bernhard
. . . speaks about himself and his work as never before and lets the reality
of our times enter his closed theater world," rhapsodized Rolf Michaelis in
Die Zeit.[29] Urs Jenny of *Der Spiegel* was not impressed. "Thomas Bernhard
presents himself as a writer who now simply flirts, albeit with great gusto, with
everything that once was a painful wound to him."[30]

Like many of his colleagues, Michaelis tried to articulate the balance between seriousness, silliness, and a profound sadness. He insisted that in the
context of the recently published memoirs, one couldn't simply laugh off

Bernhard's blunt attacks on contemporary theater, such as "More and more crap on stage/. . . Yes of course the young have talent/but the old sleazes of the theater . . ." The "dramatic writer's" comment that "the theater is one of the many possibilities to survive" should be taken quite seriously as the "most horrifying, most honest" statement in the play. If performance was the key to Bernhard's existence, he indeed had the highest stake in the integrity of theatrical work. The play's sadness, Michaelis concluded, had to do with the general state of the theater. He blamed Peymann's production for not hearing the melancholy and instead letting it evaporate in a steam of rage.

If mixed messages were coming from the play, they may have reflected Bernhard's ambivalence about his return to the Salzburg Festival. Not only was he still in the process of exorcising the city's mean spirits in his memoirs; he had turned his back on Austrian theaters and made his theatrical home in Germany. Ironically, it was the West German press and the Germans' ethnographic fascination with their Alpine neighbors that produced Bernhard's fashionable "Austrianness" and generated a boom in Austrian literature in Germany. One widely quoted critic feared the "Austrianization" of German literature.[31] Bernhard came to represent the intriguing paradox of the archetypal Austrian as Anti-Austrian (as in Antichrist). Ostracized in his own country and lionized abroad, he was the Last Austrian, propagating the extinction of the culture he embodied. His contradictoriness fed the dialectically schooled imagination of German critics.

Am Ziel had been commissioned by the Salzburg Festival for the summer of 1982. Bernhard pushed for a production in the summer of 1981, immediately after he finished the script. A new play by Peter Handke was also scheduled for the summer of 1982. Perhaps Bernhard wanted the stage for himself as Salzburg's more or less native playwright. (His play's Dutch setting ironically foregrounds his geographical birthplace while satirizing his Salzburg roots.) Handke, by contrast, was born and raised in Carinthia, studied in Graz ("dullness/that's Graz," "only old and stupid people live in Graz," Bernhard says in his last play, *Heldenplatz*), and lived many years in Germany. Such were the jealousies of Austria's two leading writers, who lived barely an hour's drive from each other, that Siegfried Unseld, who published both, couldn't tell one of them that he was also visiting the other on the same trip.

In any event, Peymann's acclaimed production prepared the way for his own and Bernhard's take-over of the Austrian theater from their Bochum stronghold. It was a shrewdly strategized maneuver. In the spring before the festival opening, he was invited to bring his production of *Der Weltverbesserer* with Bernhard Minetti to the Vienna Burgtheater for a few performances. Thus two German productions of plays by an Austrian—the only ones Bernhard permitted at that time—were showcased back to back in Austria's foremost theaters. National pride overcame the international humiliation Austrians had to endure from Bernhard's pen. If they couldn't recoup Bernhard from the Germans, they would import his German sponsor. Soon Peymann was approached as to his interest in the artistic leadership of the Vienna Burgtheater. Negotiations were successfully concluded in 1984, with his term to start in the fall of 1986. In the meantime, he commissioned and co-produced with the Salzburg Festival two more Bernhard plays. *Der Theatermacher* premiered in July 1985, *Ritter, Dene, Voss* in the summer of 1986. After their subsequent runs in his Bochum repertory, they opened Peymann's first Vienna season. While *Der Theatermacher* had caused another political skirmish in Salzburg, the dust (or manure) on its iconic dunghill could settle in Bochum and finally gather the canonic patina of the imperial capital, where it became a staple of Peymann's repertory throughout his embattled twelve years there. For better or for worse, at the start of his epic voyage through the stormy waters of Austria's cultural politics, Peymann invested Bernhard as his flagship poet.

CHAPTER ELEVEN

Stand-Up Writer

To be in the audience and on the stage, that is the odd fate.
— Paul Valéry

THE AUSTRIAN WRITER ELFRIEDE JELINEK IMAGINES the late Thomas Bernhard speaking his texts out loud into the typewriter. He may even have dictated them, she speculates.[1] All of his works, not just his plays, evoke the immediacy of a speaking voice. Wieland and Erika Schmied recall one of Bernhard's last visits, a few weeks before his death, when he told them about his next project. Intended as the sixth installment of his memoirs, it was to deal with his early days in Vienna, when he drove a delivery truck to supplement the rigidly restricted allowance he received from Auntie. The way he told the story, it seemed finished in his head. After his death they inquired whether he had left a draft or notes, but apparently his estate contains nothing of that sort. Jelinek calls Bernhard "a poet of speaking" (*ein Dichter des Sprechens*) rather than of writing.[2] Even if Bernhard didn't act out his texts while he wrote them, they resound with the motion of fingers hammering the spoken words into the typewriter (not unlike Glenn Gould, the fictionalized catalyst of one of his last novels, humming to himself the piece he is playing on the piano).

The nonstop book-length monologues of his late works suggest the writer traversing the room as if it were a stage, in a state of extreme agitation (which is the subtitle of his *Woodcutters*). The narrator, ostensibly observed by yet another narrator in the act of writing, asserts himself as a solo performer: ". . . writes Rudolf" is the frequent interjection in *Concrete*. The opening sentence of *Extinction* sets up the narrator in the process of writing ("writes Franz Josef Murau"). The act of writing is introduced in the present tense. The agitation that produces the impulse to write comes through in grammar and rhythm, which in turn reiterate the mental and emotional states he writes about. Writing is not descriptive but performative. Ultimately it is of course Bernhard himself who performs the role of the narrator and watches himself in the process both of acting the part of the dying writer and of writing the text *about* the dying writer. That Bernhard is aware of the limited time he has to live does not mean that his work is autobiographical in the sense that he is Murau (or Rudolf). It is another role the trained actor writes for himself, writes himself into, as it were, which the accomplished writer performs in the act of writing, while watching himself in performance.

One of Bernhard's early influences, the French writer Paul Valéry (1871–1945), speaks of the ideal text as a "concert for a solo mind," as "scores for thinking." [3] He called his fragmented *Monsieur Teste* — one of Bernhard's declared favorites — a "comedy of the intellect." Bernhard found and perfected his own unique method of scoring thought processes. On several occasions he spoke of his early interest in *Monsieur Teste,* first published in 1896: "It's a book that's been read to pieces [*das völlig zerlesen ist*] and I had to buy it again and again, because it always was a mess, read through and through, frayed and ragged," he said in a 1970 television interview.[4] It had a considerable influence on the evolution of his theater of the mind.

Valéry was preoccupied throughout his life with Teste as his alter ego, "the life of a man who watches himself live," [5] an intellectual Harvey of sorts for highly abstract conversations with himself. Decidedly not a full-blown fictional character with distinct features and a biography, the figure of Teste was to serve as "witness *against* the infernal power of the body and the world and, above all, *of* the inner reaction of the mind." [6] Valéry's lifelong preoccupation with what his English translator called "the drama of consciousness," which amounts to a lifelong exercise in self-observation, was not lost on the solipsist in Bernhard.[7] The notion of constructing an alternative existence, of "writing against," was close to Bernhard's efforts to overcome his illness and break through the literary conventions of his earliest poems and prose. Teste's thoughts on pain must have struck a chord in the young Bernhard, for they reverberated in all his writing: "A pain we could clearly conceive and somehow circumscribe would become a sensation without suffering . . . a knowledge that on the order of that we find in music. Pain is something very like music, one can almost talk about it in musical terms. There are flat and sharp pains, some are andante and others furioso, sustained notes, rests, arpeggios, progressions, and sudden silences, etc." [8] Little known in the United

States, Valéry's experiments in poetry and prose, influenced by Edgar Allan Poe, Stéphane Mallarmé, and the drawings of Edgar Degas, had great influence on writers in French and German, such as Hugo von Hofmannsthal and Rainer Maria Rilke (who translated his poems), in the early twentieth century.[9] Paul Celan translated his grand poem *La Jeune Parque* and took great interest in the translation of *Monsieur Teste* into German.[10] *Monsieur Teste* (the name is a composite of the French *tête*, head, and the Latin *testis*, witness) is a purely cerebral construct. Pieced together from perceptions of others — the author, Teste's wife, a letter from a friend to Teste — and "extracts from Monsieur Teste's logbook," it was later expanded by entries from Valéry's notebooks. "I have tried to invent synthetic human beings . . . this meant sacrificing "'the interest' of action and adventure," reads one of those added entries.[11] Teste was pieced together as the model of a mind that contained the possibilities of many roles but refused to be objectified in one. "Could any man bear to look at himself at every moment of his life and rethink, as a witness, all he has thought, all that has come into his head, into his whole being?" Valéry as Teste asks at one point, and he elaborates: "Who would not hate himself, not wish to blot out what he was, not so much from want of success, or the effect of certain acts he has committed, but simply because of the particular person whom these have little by little defined, and who shocks his full sense of possibility. Our history makes of us Mr. So-and-So — and this is an offense. What is more ridiculous than SOMEONE?" (147–48). Bernhard couldn't have agreed more.

Valéry's method of fragmentation was to diffuse such categorization and destabilize the notion of a unified self that could perceive itself as such. "No one could accept himself as he is if some miraculous circumstance offered him a full knowledge of what he was and what he is. Man recognizes HIMSELF only . . . in another" (148). For Valéry as for Bernhard, however, that "other" is yet another role he has constructed for himself in order to recognize himself in his "comedies of the intellect." "Comedies of vanity" detractors might call them, appropriating the title of a play by Elias Canetti, narcissistic performance acts in the halls of mirrors of their minds. The fragmentary, open-ended structure of Valéry's text served as a model for Bernhard's early experiments in (re)constructing a character from his notes in conjunction with observations and quotes of others. Teste's highly idiosyncratic view of the world, his solipsistic use of language, provided Bernhard with a mold from which to cast his early characters.

Valéry extols "sadisms of the mind" committed by "those who exercise the abstract faculties and seek enjoyment of the intellect — in nonnatural ways. Thus, certain mathematicians, and the syntactical sadism of Mallarmé. . . . For man is excess, abuse . . . this is his very essence" (146). Such thoughts left their mark on the language of Bernhard's earliest characters, such as Strauch, the mad painter of his first full-length novel, and most prominently on Prince Saurau, whose monologue constitutes the second part of *Gargoyles*.

Like Valéry, Bernhard eschews physical descriptions of his leading figures. Valéry envisions Teste's exterior as nondescript to the point of invisibility (all the better to refract the world around him in its multiple possibilities). His alter ego's attitudes, however, in tandem with his own, suggest an intellectual arrogance, cultural elitism, and solipsistic genius that blend easily with Bernhard's favorite role models, from Schopenhauer to Ludwig Wittgenstein, from his grandfather to Paul Wittgenstein. "Valéry never recovered from his amazement about the spectacle of his own intellect," mocks E. M. Cioran.[12] If one replaced "amazement" with "laughter," the statement could apply to Bernhard.

Valéry calls Teste a monster (a "somewhat monstrous self-caricature," clarifies René Wellek).[13] As his creation ages with the author and is quoted more frequently and extensively, it — or they — seems to become even more monstrous, reduced to a "severed head" that "looks at things just as they are, the pure present, without meaning, without high or low, without symmetry or features" (119). One is reminded that *Köpfe* (Heads) is the title of Bernhard's first produced one-act play (with music by Gerhard Lampersberg). The surrealist fairy tale features a queen and her sister guarded by three dwarfs who make an occasional appearance to demand in menacing choral repetitions, "Off with their heads!" A later televised production was set in a cagelike structure that suggested a theater of the mind. If Bernhard's mise-en-scènes of the mind are not directly inspired by the cephalic (un)nature of Monsieur Teste, there certainly is a strong affinity between them, both indebted as they are to Schopenhauer's idea of the world as representation of an ubiquitous, nondefinable will.

A firm believer in unfinished, fragmented works that reflect thoughts in process, Valéry would have to resist on principle the completion or closure of his textual "scores." Bernhard, the trained singer and actor, applied his practical understanding of a score not only to his plays but also to his fiction, without losing the element of process, or, as Valéry would have it, the presence of unrealized possibilities. Bernhard's operatic and theatrical training provided him with the necessary foundation for his performative textual strategies. A stage character as text is always just a possibility until the actor fleshes him out. And even in performance a character is fully realized only in the perception of the audience, which represents a wide range of possibilities. Furthermore, by making a choice in the building of his character, the actor is fully aware that he eliminates other possibilities. They remain present, however, in the very act of their exclusion (as well as in the audience's memory of other actors performing the same role). No doubt Bernhard's ongoing affiliation with Claus Peymann's theater further sharpened his awareness of performative strategies. Valéry remained a poet of writing; Bernhard, a poet of speaking, perfected his poetics of performance.

Bernhard's fiction up to *Correction* shows the structural influence of Valéry's montage technique. Furthermore, the characters that emerge in his novels and stories, in bits and pieces of testimonies and other documentary material, have the intellectual characteristics of Monsieur Teste. All live in their heads, so to speak. They aspire to the highest, which can be realized only as perfection; that is, never. So then, quite *naturgemäss,* the industrialist of *Gargoyles* tears up in the evening what he wrote during the day and Konrad of *The Lime Works* never begins writing. In the spirit of Valéry, they remain open-ended, unfinished, in daily intercourse with their possibilities, their potential kept intact by their failure.

Valéry speaks of Teste as "jealous of his best ideas, of those he considers his best—at times so personal, so much his own, that to express them in ordinary impersonal terms can give others only the faintest and falsest notion. . . . Who knows whether one's true 'philosophy' is communicable? . . . Jealous, then, of his individual insights, Teste thought: What is an idea that is not given the value of a state secret or a secret of art? . . . and about which, also, one is not reserved, as if it were a sin or an offense. Hide your god, hide your demon" (69). Bernhard's characters of the period discussed here do not publish their studies or coordinate their notes for publication. When they face their writings, their "demon," the consequences are disastrous.

In one remarkable instance, however, Bernhard the performer asserts himself against his novelistic function as a witness, a self-conscious assembler of evidence. His Prince Saurau is a fully realized stage character, a completed masterpiece with all the possibilities of his consciousness fully realized and played out in his mind over and over. Valéry describes Teste as "a man ob-

served, watched, spied on, by his ideas, by memory." But he is the opposite of
a madman, because "aberration — so important in nature — " is conscious in
his case (68). If Bernhard's Saurau is not pathologically insane, his resolve to
live out the "drama of consciousness" makes him an existential madman. He
speaks the language of Teste, but unmediated by his author's interjections.
Unlike Teste, Saurau is never out of his mind, as it were. Freed from the con-
straints of theoretical abstraction, he comes to life in a brilliant performance in
the theater of his head. As soon as Bernhard went beyond Valéry's structural
model, he found his own Teste, so to speak, the archetype of his later pieces.
All concerts for a solo mind, they are scripted speech acts, scores that track
the movement of thought against the movement of the body. The ideal reader
is a theatrical observer. Like the musical listener with the perfect ear who is
able to read a score and hear the entire concert (a gift Bernhard shared with his
favorite pianist, Glenn Gould), the reader can see the writer's entire mise-en-
scène. "Reading books one looks over the author's shoulder," writes Valéry.[14]
Bernhard stages himself as the writer, first reader, and first spectator of his
performance. What the Bernhard reader sees is a virtuoso performance of a
solo mind refracted through several mirrors. Not surprisingly, Bernhard also
named Genet, the dramatist of fluctuating, performed, and mirrored identities, as one of his early influences.[15]

Valéry wanted to write the "comedy of the intellect." Bernhard did — over
and over again. His artistic *Herkunft* clearly was the theater. It asserted itself
from his first novel, *Frost*. Its narrator, a twenty-three-year-old medical intern
at a provincial hospital in Austria, has been assigned to observe a disturbed
former painter in the Alpine hinterlands. In daily journal entries the student
painstakingly records his subject's utterances for twenty-seven days. Quoting
him at length, he gets drawn deeper and deeper into his language. It begins to
"perform" its narrator, who gradually appears to enact his subject rather than
document his ways. Right from the start the student exhibits considerable theatrical talent. His account opens with a passage that immediately jumps off
the page, like the prologue to a play. It is his impassioned defense of his decision to accept the task he is about to begin on this "First Day," as indicated in
the brief chapter heading. Since it hasn't been published yet in English, the
opening is quoted at length.

An internship, after all, is more than watching complicated intestinal sur-
geries, more than cutting open the peritoneum, clipping lungs, and saw-

ing off feet, surely it's more than closing the eyes of the dead and dragging
children into the world. An internship isn't just that: sawed-off arms and
legs, whole or parts, tossed over the shoulders into the enamel bucket.
Neither is it the constant dawdling behind the chief of surgery and behind
the assistant and the assistant's assistant, the living tail of the daily rounds.
There has to be more to an internship than pretending, not just me saying:
"The pus will dissolve in the blood and you'll be well again." And telling
hundreds of other lies. Not just me saying: "It'll be all right!" — though it
won't. An internship isn't just an exercise in cutting and sewing, in clamp-
ing and enduring. An internship has to also reckon with extracarnal facts
and possibilities. My task of observing the painter Strauch forces me to
deal with such extracarnal facts and possibilities. To explore something
unexplorable. To uncover an astonishing range of possibilities. The way
one uncovers a conspiracy. And it could be, after all, that the extracarnal,
by which I do not mean the soul, that which is extracarnal without being
the soul about which I know nothing, whether it exists, of which I expect
nonetheless that it exists, that this thousands-of-years-old hunch is the
thousands-of-years-old truth; it could certainly be that the extracarnal,
namely that without cells, is that out of which everything exists and not
the other way around and not only one out of the other.[16]

Before turning the page one could envision this chapter as an opening
monologue in the classic Viennese comedy tradition of Johann Nestroy and
Ferdinand Raimund. The youthful energy of its outrage evokes Nestroy's
feisty apprentices of *Einen Jux will er sich machen,* his defensiveness Raimund's disarmingly rambunctious characters, who are straightened out by
interfering fairy-tale authorities. The verbal pratfalls in the paradoxical attempt to articulate the soul's nonexistence address themselves to an audience
that appreciates philosophical propositions twisted into the acrobatics of a
Promethean clown. Above all, it is the musical texture of the language that
places the moment on the popular stage that gave birth to Mozart and Emanuel
Schikaneder's Papageno and the vain attempts, even by magic threats, to shut
him up.

As in the works of his theatrical ancestors, a dark undercurrent drives
the comedy. In *Frost* it is language, the language of his subject, Strauch, to
whom he keeps referring as "the painter" although Strauch has long given up
painting and has torn up all his canvases. His is a language of madness that

defies clinical definition. Its syntax produces fragmented representations of the world that do not have to be torn up like his paintings; they self-destruct and take their speaker with them on his road to suicide. They also hook the young observer, who begins to speak like his subject, and pull him into a maelstrom of colliding possibilities. The student's project turns into an increasingly obsessive process. His voice, hesitant at first, astonished, awed, struggles to maintain a scientific distance from the landscape and its population until he is nearly subsumed by his subject's language. "Is this still language?" he asks himself on the fourteenth day and attempts to articulate his impressions: "Yes, it is the double ground of language, hell and heaven of language, it is the uprising of the rivers, 'the steaming word-nostrils of every single brain that is desperate beyond measure and shame.' Sometimes he speaks a poem, tears it apart instantly, reassembles it into a 'powerhouse.' . . . His sentences are rowing strokes that would advance him were it not for the strong current" (137).

But what he doesn't realize as he quotes the painter for scientific documentation is that he lends his own voice to his subject. The lines between speaker and witness get blurred. What he has been hearing from the beginning is himself, mimicking the painter like an actor representing another. Who lends his voice here to whom and where does it ultimately come from? It's a sort of Mephistophelean enterprise that catches up with him in the end. Trying to get a grip on those "extracarnal" properties that have replaced the notion of the soul, he tunes in to his subject's language and is in danger of losing his own, of losing himself, as it were. On the twenty-third day Strauch tells him, "It is terrible for me to know that I might possibly infect you, you know, with my disease, and, equally terrible, to feel how I need you" (258). And the narrator writes to his teacher: "I thought that I would remain unaffected by your brother. Now I feel myself overcome by his disease, by this consistently progressing disease" (305). The choice of words is interesting: "von seiner Krankheit erfasst," overcome by his disease, which literally means "taken over by his disease." Erfassen can also mean to understand, so he might be saying "I feel myself understood by his disease"; in other words, "I feel myself found out by his disease." All along, the relationship between observer and observed has evolved on a lie: the medical student told Strauch that he was studying law. Whether intended or not, their unbalanced relationship intimates a stab at Freudian analysis, which is also an exchange of spoken language. The narrator's choice of expression suggests a classic Freudian slip.

It leads, like Ariadne's thread, along dreams, childhood traumas, and more or less obvious symbols embedded in labyrinthine sentences straight to the heart of Bernhard's fellow Austrian, the Minotaur of unconscious meanings. At the center of the maze is Theseus/Wittgenstein stabbing at a phantom with his unequivocal dictum: "The boundaries of my language are the boundaries of my world."

Freud's netherworld of the unconscious collides with Wittgenstein's uncompromising demands of grammar: "Whereof one cannot speak, thereof one must be silent."

> What kind of language is this, Strauch's language? What do I do with these shreds of thoughts? What seemed to me torn, disconnected at first, has its "really horrendous connections," the whole thing is a terrifying word transfusion into the world, into the people, "a ruthless proceeding against stupidity" in order to talk to himself, an "incessant tonal cataract worthy of regeneration." . . . How to write this down? What sort of notes? Schematic, systematic to where? Those outbursts come down on me like falling rocks. Suddenly what he says breaks off with the explosive outcry of ridiculousness that he "superinvents onto the world" and himself. It is a heart muscle language, Strauch's language, a heinous language against the brain-pulse-beat [*pulsgehirnwiderpochend*]. (137)

Clearly, this is not the kind of text the student had been asked to submit to his teacher, the doctor. It is an outcry. The narrator himself has turned into a performer. In the process of quoting his subject's "text," he, like an actor has identified with it. Like an actor, he examines the language he now speaks, where it comes from. This enables him to speak it "as intended" by the text. As he acquires his subject's language, he is in danger of becoming the character.

Where science doesn't offer categories for Strauch's condition, the theater offers the only appropriate model, the Fool. "Outside I saw the painter, he was wearing his red artist's smock. 'I want to terrify myself once more today,' he said. 'Terrify myself and the world. When I wear this red smock, I feel like the biggest fool of all time. And people believe me that I am the biggest fool of all time'" (134).

As a painter, Strauch could present the world as he saw it. But that didn't mean that he could actually relate to the world as he perceived it. Not surprisingly, then, he burned all his paintings. As a performer of himself he could turn the whole world into a stage simply by consciously inhabiting it as such.

That way, there never is any doubt that the world, as perceived, is nothing but a representation. To take it for real is foolishness. It can be enjoyed at times as an absurd comedy; to experience it for what it is, is tragic. The only consistent way out of this predicament is suicide. "The pain, you must know, the pain in my head pulls my earlobes down to my knees," says the painter (258). The image, painfully grotesque, highlights the ears as points of contact with the world, the Other, and therefore of excruciating pain. It also instantly evokes the classic fool with the ears reaching the knees like a two-pointed dunce's cap.

Above the first day's entry there is a quote without specific reference to its source: "'What do people say about me?' he asked. 'Do they say: the idiot? What do people talk?'" (7). Later it turns out to be a quote from the painter. As an introductory motif it suggests Bernhard's own preoccupation. Performance begins as soon as we begin consciously to observe ourselves in relation to the world. There is no fool without the Other.

Four years before Peter Handke's pathbreaking play *Kaspar,* Bernhard's breakthrough work also deals with the acquisition of language. The name Kaspar, based on Kaspar Hauser, the historic model for the stage character, instantly evokes the figure of Kasper, or its diminutive Kasperl, the stock clown character of Austrian puppet plays, the so-called *Kasperltheater.* Handke, no less obsessed than Bernhard with Wittgenstein and the mechanism of the theater as a useful paradigm for philosophical investigations, brilliantly exploits this fortuitous coincidence. Handke's Kaspar is drilled and ultimately subdued by the public language of media slogans and reconstituted as a mechanized, standardized stock character. Bernhard reverses the process. The world of his narrator, tightly constructed from the professional language of his medical training, is gradually corroded by the painter's grammar, the artist's vision, unmitigated by the safety mechanisms of sanitized, standardized naming. "I will sit opposite the chief of surgery rather helplessly, unable to tell him anything," the medical student notes on the thirteenth day:

> He imagines I'll get to Schwarzach after a while and put everything I observed right in front of him: Look here, that's what it is. That's the way he said it. And that's how I observed it! Error-proof! Sadness is not the way I imagined it but that is how it goes! Do you understand? No. I certainly won't be able to say even two or three coherent words. Even though there is clarity. And what clarity! And then silence, nothing will happen that would apply. And how differently everything will present itself when I'm reading what I am writing down just now. Completely different. Be-

cause what's written down isn't right. Nothing that's written down is ever right. It has no claim to anything. Not even precision, even though everything has been established conclusively, to the best of one's knowledge, under the assumption to know something about a perfectly obvious matter. Always just less wrong at best. Different. Untrue then. (129)

The passage is staged like a monologue in which the speaker acts out a dialogue between himself and his supervisor. It contains an important clue to the development of Bernhard's future dramaturgy in his fiction. If "what's written down is never right," because in its unalterable rigidity it suggests an authenticity of meaning that doesn't exist, the only viable medium communicating language is the theater. As actors speak the words of another written by yet another in performances they repeat every night without ever being quite the same, they are closest to the truth, at least a truthful representation of the impossibility of ever getting at the truth. It is a performer's technique through which he arrives at insights that reveal themselves in the act of quoting, but cannot be described. As he quotes, he is "inside the picture" and can observe neither himself nor his subject. If he were able to do that, to split himself into performer and observer, into a spect-actor, to borrow the writer-director Augusto Boal's definition, he would go as mad as the painter in his fool's smock. Eventually Bernhard would dramatize this split in the seamless, book-length solo performances of his narrators.

Frost, his first grand narrative, is a bildungsroman in performativity, a coming-of-age novel that documents the performative impact of language on the listener. It also reflects Bernhard's testing his ways with language. The process of its acquisition is a theatrical one. It begins with rehearsing the language of another. The narrators of the fiction works following *Frost,* up to and including *Correction,* incorporate and in the process embody the languages of various subjects of their observations and investigations. In a similar process, Bernhard himself appropriates his own literary models. His early nicknames, Alpen-Kafka and Alpen-Beckett, suggest the enactment or reinterpretation of well-known roles in a novel setting. It is not until his memoirs that he commits to his own voice only and makes himself the primary subject of observation. That perspective is maintained and theatricalized in all the fiction that follows.

By the time *Concrete* was published, Bernhard had already written twelve full-length plays. He had learned enough about the theater to integrate its resources fully into his nontheatrical writing. From now on the split between self-performer and observer will be staged in the persons of his narrators, all of whom are consummate performers. To make sure no one misses the real actor here, he infuses his own performance as a writer into the antics of his self-performing writing subjects. The author and his stand-in merge in their roles as narrating spect-actors.

In German, *Concrete (Beton)* begins with a mammoth 197-word sentence that reverberates with and calls for a spoken voice. The English version cuts this breathless overture into three sentences with a total of 237 words.

> From March to December, writes Rudolf, while I was having to take large quantities of prednisolone, a fact which I am bound to record here, against the third acute onset of my sarcoidosis, I assembled every possible book and article written by or about Mendelssohn Bartholdy and visited every possible and impossible library in order to acquaint myself thoroughly with my favorite composer and his work, preparing myself with the most passionate seriousness for the task, which I had been dreading through- out the preceding winter, of writing — such was my pretension — a major work of impeccable scholarship. It had been my intention to devote the most careful study to all these books and articles and only then, having studied them with all the thoroughness the subject deserved, to begin writing my work, which I believed would leave far behind it and far be- neath it everything else, both published and unpublished, which I had previously written in the field of what is called musicology. I had been planning it for ten years and had repeatedly failed to bring it to fruition, but now I had resolved to begin writing on the twenty-seventh of Janu- ary at precisely four o'clock in the morning, after the departure of my sister, who was due to leave on the twenty-sixth, and whose presence in Peiskam had for weeks put paid to any thought of my starting work on Mendelssohn Bartholdy.[17]

Through the specific gestures of language, the Austrian-baroque excesses of inspired self-indulgence are clipped by an Anglo aristocrat's stiff upper lip.

The present tense of "writes Rudolf" highlights the immediacy of the event. Its urgency to the (fictional) writer is underscored by the manic speed of the syntax, which further suggests that the narrator, in the process of writ- ing, reenters the state of mind that finally, after many detours, drives him to the typewriter. Yet the tense of the interjection "writes Rudolf," reminiscent

of a stage direction, also suggests the presence of the (real) author, either looking over his subject's shoulder or reading the text to an assumed listener. The
function of the narrator is split into two roles, that of the writer and that of the
first reader, the latter suggesting yet another role: that of investigative reporter
or a witness called to present his evidence in court. Bernhard, after all, began
his writing career as a court reporter. The readers in turn are addressed as an
audience in the theatrical sense. They are drawn in by the pitch and rhythm of
the speaker's voice in a highly agitated state of mind, which shows itself in the
flow of the speech rather than in a description of it. An actor would recognize
it as the speaker's "inner action," the subtext underlying the visible action.
The reader of a Bernhard text then must first of all be an expert listener, like
the narrator of *Yes,* who can read a music score and hear it in his head more
perfectly than in a concert hall.

But the author as impersonator of the writer does not simply identify with
the agitation of his fictional character. The insertion "writes Rudolf" introduces another voice, that of the first reader or the author in the role of first
reader and witness, whose own state of mind and emotional responses, though
barely distinguishable on the surface, run in tandem with his subject's. The
opening monologue merges two voices. They have become interchangeable,
like the roles they represent, as the text proceeds. Bernhard, in the part of the
reader, functions as *enactor* of and on behalf of his subject, who also splits
himself into performer and spectator of himself.

To enact, according to the *Oxford English Dictionary,* is to "enter in a
public record; chronicle," as well as to "represent (a scene, play, etc.) on or
as on a stage; play (a part); take part in (a drama or scene in real life)." Bernhard's earlier narrators function as chroniclers, researchers, or reporters who
collect notes of another person, who frequently is diseased. In the process of
assembling and presenting the material to the reader, they enact the deceased.
By themselves, those notes could be viewed by the reader like a corpse. The
presence of another (the narrator) presenting these notes makes the dead man
come to life. The narrator enacts the words of the diseased as an actor delivers
the words of his role, which in the case of the classic European theater tradition are the words of a dead playwright in the mouths of long-dead characters.
Knowing that Bernhard's narrator is suffering from a life-threatening disease,
we can assume that he too will be dead by the time his text reaches us. As we
know, at the time of the writing, Bernhard knew he would die an early death.
With relentless consistency, he cast himself as his text, which can be viewed

as a corpse or heard and therefore enacted in the head of the reader with a musical ear and perfect pitch.

> I went upstairs but didn't immediately sit down at my desk. I looked at it through the door of the thirty-foot upstairs room, standing about twenty-five to thirty feet away from it, to see whether everything on it was in order. . . . I looked steadily at the desk until I could see myself sitting at it, as it were from behind. I could see myself bending forward, because of my illness, in order to write. I saw that I had an unhealthy posture. But then I'm not healthy — I'm thoroughly sick, I told myself. Sitting like that, I told myself, you've already written a few pages on Mendelssohn Bartholdy, perhaps ten or twelve. That's how I sit at the desk when I've written ten or twelve pages. I stood motionless and observed the motion of my back.[18]

Splitting himself into multiple roles, Bernhard himself takes center stage in his text as the satirist of his own predicament as a writer, dramatized in the fictional writer observing himself, all under the watchful gaze of the "real author," who occasionally asserts his presence with autobiographical details, like an actor in an aside, still in performance. The author's work then becomes a series of performance acts, validated as such by himself in yet another role, perhaps the most central role, that of his ultimate spectator.

The scene is a gem of overlapping glimpses into comedy routines. For ten years the narrator has tried in vain to begin his study of the composer Felix Mendelssohn Bartholdy. The attempt always fails right from the start, because he is unable to find the first sentence. Starting to play a piece of music on an instrument and messing it up almost instantly is, of course, an old comedy shtick. The autosuggestive effort of projecting himself to his desk creates a role he can't fill. Moreover, it is doomed to failure from the start, since it is perceived as a role, a performance act, split from the would-be writer, who is reduced to his own spectator, concentrating on his failure rather than his vocation: "I must have made a pitiful, if indeed pitiable impression on an observer, though there was none — unless I am going to say that I am an observer of myself, which is stupid, since I am my own observer anyway: I've actually been observing myself for years, if not for decades; my life now consists only of self-observation and self-contemplation, which naturally leads to self-condemnation, self-rejection and self-mockery."[19]

Rudolf knows that he has only about one or two more years to live. The knowledge of his imminent death provides the seriousness as well as the madcap frenzy of his daily actions. The concern that he may not be able to begin his work about Mendelssohn Bartholdy, let alone finish it, tragic as his failure to do so may be, might be less important than the underlying fear that his whole life is completed once its purpose has been accomplished. The obstacles that prevent his life's work may also delay his death. In any case, he is making a fool of himself and there is a perverse delight in watching himself do so. First it is his sister's prolonged stay at the family house in the country, which he inherited and she is entitled to use. After her departure he first has to air out all the rooms to get rid of her aura and his irritation. Then the climate in the depth of winter in his native landscape evokes his family history, which triggers once again his ambivalent responses to his descent, which avalanches into his increasing agitation about the state of affairs in Austria, which leads to the sudden thought that he should leave the country for a while. That he should make a trip had actually been suggested by his sister, all the more reason for him to utterly banish the thought only to counter it instantly with obsessive thoughts as to whether or not he should go to Mallorca, his favorite place, with a climate beneficial to both his health and his work, followed by inspection and then lengthy contemplation of the two suitcases he would take, one crammed with books related to his work and necessary for the survival of his mind, one for clothes to ensure the survival of his body. All medication, however, would go into the so-called mental suitcase.

Within three days of his sister's departure and 170 printed pages later, he finds himself in Mallorca, much too exhausted, as expected, to begin his work. In that time span, the minimal mechanism of his physical movements proceeded in negative proportion to the revved-up motor of his mind. Correspondingly, the concrete environment of his farmhouse, which suggests many similarities to Bernhard's home, provides the stage for a compulsively repetitious choreography. It takes him up the stairs into his study, down to the kitchen, up to the bedroom, down to the hallway and into the doorway, accented by deep breathing, occasional laughter in response to a thought or to the occasional lines he says or shouts to himself, a result of his many years of solitary existence, all the time under his own vigilant gaze. While his physical performance is duly confined to a quasi-Aristotelian one-set space, his mental acrobatics confound all notions of time and space. They take him from the hypocrisies of Viennese society to Mallorca—both in his projected stay and in the remembrance of previous sojourns—from attacks on the Austrian chancellor (Bruno Kreisky) to mental checks and double checks of all the chores that would have to be done before he could leave. Elements of time and space are further scrambled in the process of writing, which ostensibly takes place in Mallorca, propelled by the haunting memory of a young German woman he had met by chance during his previous stay in Palma. Apparently dozing off in his chair in a sidewalk café, he recalls, in cinematic vividness, her agonized story of her husband's suicide during their desperate vacation in a run-down hotel. The chilling remembrance of a nightmarish event in the past takes on the physical reality of a nightmare experienced in the present, which at the same time puts into question the factual context of the memory. This ambiguity drives him, as soon as he finds himself awakening as from a dream, to the local cemetery of concrete graves shared by the poor, to which he had accompanied her in search of her husband's burial place. There he finds her name added to her husband's. The woman's death engenders a narrative that once again delays his life-consuming study of Mendelssohn. Like the conventional melodramatic hero, he escaped his own death by a hair's breadth through pure chance, which put another death in his way on his way toward his own. From the dawn of storytelling, the tricking of death, at the core of Bernhard's stand-up tragedies, has always been the beginning of yet another tale.

Schopenhauer, in his *World as Will and Representation,* offers the conceptual tool for Bernhard's poetics of comedy:

> The life of every individual, viewed as a whole and in general, and when only its most significant features are emphasized, is really a tragedy; but gone through in detail it has the character of a comedy. For the doings and worries of the day, the restless mockeries of the moment, the desires and fears of the week, the mishaps of every hour, are all brought about by chance that is always bent on some mischievous trick; they are nothing but scenes from a comedy. The never-fulfilled wishes, the frustrated efforts, the hopes mercilessly blighted by fate, the unfortunate mistakes of the whole life, with increasing suffering and death at the end, always gives us a tragedy. Thus, as if fate wished to add mockery to the misery of our existence, our life must contain all the woes of tragedy, and yet we cannot even assert the dignity of tragic characters, but, in the broad detail of life, are inevitably the foolish characters of a comedy.[20]

In Bernhard's dramaturgy the serious seeps through the cracks in his split-screen comedian's routine. The narrator sees himself in action or rather in the action of being inactive, which captures the underlying action of his ongoing battle with a terminal illness. Between what he does and what he wants to do and what lies behind what he doesn't do and what he will end up doing, which is writing a text about not writing a text, lies the abyss, or, as Schopenhauer sees it, "a very great incongruity between our concepts and objective reality."[21] It rings with the mocking laughter of those who watch what we are doing, which Bernhard anticipates as his own most merciless scourge.

Most important, *The World as Will and Representation* provides the radical dramaturgical model for Bernhard's revisionist view of the Shakespearean world as a stage conceived, perceived, and manipulated from within the individual's skull as playwright, director, and audience. Schopenhauer's concept of *Vorstellung*, as the representation of an all-pervasive will, provides Bernhard with a paradigm that he continues to mine for all its signifying potential from idea to representation to performance. *Vorstellung* denotes idea, representation, performance, and also imagination. While the English term "representation" has a performative aspect, the German *Vorstellung* refers directly to a theatrical performance. Bernhard, obsessed by the histrionics of existence, makes Schopenhauer the butt of his own philosophy, as it were. Bernhard's world is a *Vorstellung* in every respect. It is based on the philosopher's vision of the world as representation of the thinking subject, who simultaneously projects himself into his imagined world, where he performs and watches himself in performance perched in the private box of his mind. Pathetic enough to believe that it is he who masterminded the whole spectacle in fulfillment of his desires, he is in fact nothing but a puppet manipulated by a Schopenhauerian will: ". . for the will performs the great tragedy and comedy at its own expense, and is also its own spectator."[22]

The notion of *Vorstellung* as performance, both imagined and executed, is the central theme of *Wittgenstein's Nephew* and *The Loser*. Each features a consummate performer: the former Paul Wittgenstein, the latter Glenn Gould. Both are geniuses, virtuoso performers in very different ways, one as a madman, the other as a pianist. Both are caught in the discrepancy between the imagined perfect performance and its flawed if not impossible execution. Gould was notorious for his slouched position at the piano, his flailing arms, and above all his humming along as he played. What was often perceived as tacky showmanship was the struggle to match his perfect inner hearing with the actual performance.[23]

Typically (*naturgemäss*), Bernhard's Gould is not identical to the pianist. He too is the project of *Vorstellung* on every level. Bernhard's musical ear matches Gould's. Reading a score, he can hear it played. On the inner stage of the mind, reading as hearing produces a perfect performance. Like Gould's physical distortions during performance, Bernhard's writing scans the collision between inner perfection and outer representation. It is the drama at the heart of the narrative not only in terms of its subject matter but also as an inherent working problem. How does one write about music? As the text's last gesture, the narrator puts on Gould's recording of Bach's *Goldberg Variations*. It is up to the reader to hear it in his mind.

Both the narrator of *The Loser* and his friend Wertheimer were promising pianists until they met Gould during a (fictitious) summer class taught by Vladimir Horowitz at Salzburg's Leopoldskron Castle. Needless to say, Gould never studied in Salzburg. Horowitz never taught a master class there. However, there are affinities between Gould and Bernhard in their histrionic impulses and delight in *blödeln.* What links Gould to Horowitz is a recording in which he parodies the much older Russian pianist's return to the stage after a hiatus of many years caused by an emotional breakdown. In the 1980 CBS release *A Glenn Gould Fantasy,* in which Gould takes on Horowitz, whom he did not like, in the guise of several fictional critics, with names such as Karlheinz Klopweisser and Sir Nigel Twitt-Thornwaite. The perfect New World equivalent of Bernhard's Old World voice imitator, Gould had developed his impersonations over the years in his articles and radio programs to discuss his thoughts on music in the protective guise of another. For his famous self-interviews he would impersonate a fictitious interlocutor. He loved to perform in a heavy German accent, satirizing his genuine interest in German culture. (Note that Bernhard's Gould speaks perfect German.) In Gould's hilarious impersonation of Horowitz, the pianist makes his comeback on an oil rig in the Arctic Ocean. A narrator announces that during his performance, Gould/Horowitz's piano stool has been swept out from under him by a wave, which has also pulled the entire audience out to sea. In a Bernhardesque finale, the lone virtuoso continues playing the piano on his knees to the clapping and barking of a lonely seal.[24] The "real" Gould triumphed at the 1959 Salzburg Festival with his legendary performance of Bach's *Goldberg Variations.* It followed his Salzburg debut the previous summer with the Concertgebouw Orchestra playing Bach's D Minor Concerto under Dimitri Mitropoulos. Gould blamed the draft in the Festspielhaus for the cold he came down with afterward, which developed into a painful throat infection, which forced him to cancel a concert in Salzburg and part of his European tour. Bern-

hard would certainly have seconded his accusation. Gould's reasons for can-
cellations alone, at least as argued by his longtime friend and biographer Peter
Ostwald, predestined him to be a Bernhard character. As Ostwald, a psychiatrist and violinist, sees it, an upper respiratory infection would not normally
interfere with a pianist's performance; but Gould's "singing was integral to
his piano playing, so that an upper respiratory infection or the loss of his voice
might be considered a legitimate handicap." Furthermore, "he was so tuned in
to disturbing sensations anywhere in his body that this quickly led to a general
feeling of malaise, distracting him from playing as well as he wanted." [25] Finally,
with Gould's disdain for concert performances, he probably welcomed the
opportunity to avoid them. His eventual retreat to the recording studio, with
its state-of-the-art technology that allows for repeated corrections, brought
him closer to his idea of perfection. Undoubtedly Gould's obsessive temperament makes him the perfect double of a Bernhard character—so perfect that
he does not need to be duplicated. Biographical details have already become
so legendary that they are brought into play by the name alone. Gould's hypo-
chondriac preoccupation with his body and his obsessive use of drugs, his
eccentricities and solitary life, all in the service of music, also make him an
Untergeher like his fictional friend in Bernhard's novel, in the sense of someone irreversibly set on his own destruction. It takes one *Untergeher* to know
another: Bernhard's Gould knows what he is talking about when he coins
the term for his friend Wertheimer. The English translation, *The Loser,* not
only misses the point but actually reverses the meaning. That said, both the
narrator and Wertheimer are losers by their standards of artistic perfection.
Wertheimer eventually hangs himself, "for there's nothing more terrible than
to see a person so magnificent that his magnificence destroys us." [26]

In contrast to Bernhard's idea of Gould as perfection, his text is about
failure. It includes Gould as well as his author, whose account ends with his
narrator putting the *Goldberg Variations* on the record player. Music cannot
be represented in words.

Bernhard's Gould aspires to become the piano, like an actor who dreams
of total identification with his part: "Basically we want to be the piano, he said,
not human beings but the piano, all our lives we want to be the piano and not
a human being, flee from the human beings we are in order to completely become the piano, an effort which must fail, although we don't want to believe
it, he said" (81).

Photographs of Gould at the piano vividly illustrate how closely Bernhard's terse lines capture the essence of his performative style. One 1955 photograph shows the twenty-three-year-old Gould playing the piano, sitting very low in his customary bent-over posture. The left half of his face almost touches the keyboard as he plays with his right hand. His open mouth suggests that he is singing along. His eyes are focused on his fingers as if to draw out the sound of them and have it merge with the sounds that pour from his mouth. The curve of his back, extended by his neck and head and a lock of hair circling over his forehead toward the keyboard cover, seems to flow right into the piano and reemerge in his fingers. The line continues through his bent arm to his shoulder, thus completing the circle that is circumscribed by his body and his instrument. Player and piano have merged. His taut body and the expression on his face, completely focused on the act of listening and singing, suggest a state of complete alertness in the act of prodding the instrument to release its music from deep inside. In a 1980 photograph, by contrast, the movement seems reversed. The aged pianist seems to want to dig himself into the piano. His head is now sunk between his shoulders. Arms and body are one dark, chubby, spherical mass with only his hands sticking out of it. His fingers seem to burrow into the keyboard, followed closely by his head. Shown in profile, his lips and nose appear sharply pointed, also ready to dig into the instrument. Dark-rimmed spectacles throw their circular shadow onto his face, completing the overall impression of a mole burrowing into the earth. In the first instance the young player cajoles the music from the body of the piano. It is as if he wanted the piano to become him. Close to his death he wants to move inside it. Now he wants to become the piano.

Unlike an actor, whose body is his instrument, Bernhard's Gould seeks to embody the instrument that produces the author's voice; that is, to leave behind humanness, which means, of course, to die. Bernhard's Gould dies from a stroke during a performance of the *Goldberg Variations*. His Gould *had* to die while playing the piano. Transcendence has its boundaries, even for genius. The rest is silence. Bernhard's narrative ends in the middle of an action: the surviving friend puts on his dead friend's record of "Glenn's Goldberg Variations." The real story begins where the text cuts off. Death and perfection are beyond the reach of words. Whereof one cannot speak, thereof one must be silent. In the end, the writer, like his subject, must surrender to his own idea of perfection.

If *The Loser* is not about the real Glenn Gould, it is about *the* Glenn Gould, the depersonalized idea he had come to represent. "Suddenly Glenn was *Glenn Gould,* everybody overlooked the moment of the Glenn Gould transformation," says the narrator, Glenn's former friend and roommate. *The* Glenn Gould had become public property that could be appropriated by anyone. As the idea of perfection, he drove Wertheimer to death. Bernhard comes closer than any biographer to the truth of the genius madman virtuoso. His Gould wants to become the piano, to depersonalize himself. "I want to be the Steinway, not the person playing the Steinway, I want to be the Steinway itself" (82). By turning himself into a music machine he would eliminate himself, the subject, and with it chance, spontaneity — the contingencies that interfere with perfection. (Valéry struggled with the problem, which was at the heart of modernism's claim to universality.) The real Gould withdrew from public performance and turned to recordings in order to produce pure music. "In the end people like Glenn had turned themselves into art machines, had nothing in common with human beings anymore, only seldom reminded you of human beings, I thought" (92).

Anyone who saw Gould perform on his special low chair, humming along, his hands reaching the keys from below, from inside the instrument as it were, will appreciate Bernhard's grasp of the full drama played out in his performance. Playing the music, he could give birth to himself as pure music. Gould's mother, herself a gifted pianist, prepared him for such a feat before he was even born. During her pregnancy she sang and played the piano to the fetus, along with recordings of the great composers, in the belief that this would influence the unborn's musical development. (Some scientists have begun to support this assumption.)[27] His earliest sensation, then, would have been a womb of music. His mother also became his first piano teacher. As soon as he was ready to sit, she would put him in her lap and prop him up at the piano as close to the keyboard as possible, her fingers guiding his across the keyboard, humming or singing along with the sounds they elicited together from the piano. Mother, child, and piano merged into one and kept Gould in a womblike setup. The psychiatrist Peter Ostwald suggests that this may be the origin of his later posture at the piano.[28] That Gould's special chair, with its short legs, was made by his father completes Ostwald's revised Freudian scenario (reconceived, as it were, in a Heideggerian parental *Gestell*) of Gould's birth as music.

Vorstellung as idea is embodied in *Vorstellung* as performance that transcends embodiment. The term *Vorstellung* visualizes the confluence and thus suspension of all its meanings. Bernhard's Gould had to die at that point.

No wonder the real Glenn Gould shunned performances and perfected instead the (disembodied) recordings of his work. To Bernhard, this is lived philosophy.

Similarly, Paul Wittgenstein, in Bernhard's notion of embodied philosophy, was as much a philosopher as his famous great-uncle: ". . it is far from certain that a philosopher can qualify as such only by writing down and publishing his philosophy, as Ludwig did: he remains a philosopher even if he does not publish his philosophizing, even if he writes nothing and publishes nothing." [29] Indeed, if perfection is possible only as an idea, who is the true philosopher and who the fool? Paul in his real and performed madness, an aristocrat of the spirit and the full-blown clown of an aristocrat, playing out all the contradictions between appearance and reality, is nothing if not the incarnation of the quintessential *Homo bernhardus.* And *naturgemäss* Bernhard takes full advantage of this "found character" and appropriates him as "his" Paul: "I stress the word *my,* for what is set down in these notes is the picture I have of my friend Paul Wittgenstein, no other." [30]

He introduces him like a found object in a context that heightens his "realness" and at the same time the absurd unrealness of what's accepted—and tolerated—as real. Bernhard stages their encounter in the dramatic setting on Wilhelminenberg, their "hill of destiny" between the mental institution and the sanitarium that they both experienced, albeit at different times. Thoroughly true to life, it is so well fictionalized that it could have happened that way. In tongue-in-cheek deference to Paul's intellectual lineage, he puts his friend in the Ludwig Pavilion. The name is Bernhard's invention, in contrast to the Hermann Pavilion, which actually does exist. The observer keeps himself anchored in reality; his friend, placed in an ever so slightly reimagined site, becomes the subject of art.

Both Gould and Wittgenstein, in Bernhard's perception, embody philosophy beyond expounding it. Both are performance artists in and of their lives. "We are art products, the piano player is an art product," says Bernhard's Gould. [31] As lived art, their lives have become philosophy as well as the subjects of philosophy, not unlike the work of Marcel Duchamp and its impact on the visual arts in the twentieth century. [32] Accordingly, the lives of both Gould and Wittgenstein constitute philosophical productions. As such, they are open to being redefined and reimagined. Bernhard appropriates their names as existential algorithms of sorts, which can produce a variety of hypothetical, fictionalized lives from the original paradigm.

Wittgenstein's Nephew is also about failure. The book's subtitle, *A Friendship,* points to the heart of the failure. In contrast to Paul, whose failure to
produce a text supports his philosophy, Bernhard fails not as a writer but as
a friend. Paul's mental imbalance scared him. Ruthlessly self-protective as he
was by his own admission, he kept the necessary distance. If his text is an
homage to Paul that highlights the selective affinities between them, it also
foregrounds Bernhard's self-absorption. He runs away from Paul as soon as
he realizes that he is marked by death.

> From time to time, without his suspecting it, I saw him in the city cen-
> ter, walking along laboriously, yet trying hard to maintain his accustomed
> bearing. . . . He was only the shadow of a man, in a very real sense, and
> this shadow suddenly frightened me. I did not dare to go up and speak
> to him. I preferred to have a bad conscience rather than to meet him. . . .
> Quite deliberately, out of a base instinct for self-preservation, I shunned
> my friend in the last months of his life, and for this I cannot forgive my-
> self. Seen from across the street, he was like someone to whom the world
> had long since given notice to quit but who was compelled to stay in it,
> no longer belonging to it but unable to leave it. Dangling from his ema-
> ciated arms—grotesque, grotesque—where the shopping nets in which
> he laboriously carried his purchase of fruit and vegetables, naturally ap-
> prehensive that someone might see him in this wretched state and afraid
> of what they might think.[33]

The image suggests one of Picasso's emaciated mountebanks playing out the
conclusion of one of the theater's most poignant evocations of the world as
voiced by a philosopher-fool: "Last scene of all,/That ends this strange event-
ful history,/Is second childishness, and mere oblivion,/Sans teeth, sans eyes,
sans taste, sans everything."[34]

As a meditation on human and artistic failure, both *The Loser* and *Wittgenstein's Nephew* prepare for the savage attack on the self-betrayal of artists in
his next work, *Woodcutters.* A thinly disguised roman à clef in a thoroughly theatricalized milieu, it turns Shakespeare's wistful equation of the world as stage
into a pretentious travesty. "Ist ja alles nur Theater," "It's all just a show," is
the Austrians' knee-jerk reaction to reality. "Everything about them has always
been show; their social relations amount to nothing but show, and the same
is true of their relations with each other, their marital relations: they've always
put on a show of marriage because they've never been capable of sustaining

a real one, I thought, sitting in the wing chair. And it's not only the Auers-bergers who've always lived a life of pretense: all these people in the music room have only ever made a pretense of living—they've never had the courage or the strength or the love of truth that is required for real living." [35]

What sets off the breathless furor that triggers the writing is a dinner party, a "so-called artistic dinner" in honor of a well-known actor at the Vienna Burg-theater, hosted by the Auersbergers, former intimate friends of the narrator. To the insider, the cast of characters is easily identifiable as Maja and Gerhard Lampersberg and their entourage of Austria's former bohemians of the 1950s. Thirty-some years later they are the graying representatives of state-supported artistic mediocrity. No wonder the book hit a nerve, and not just in the people who recognized themselves. The questions raised beyond the ruthless expo-sure of former friends concerned an entire generation that came of age during or shortly after World War II. Burdened with the enormous responsibility of coming to terms with the legacy of guilt, they started out with youthful self-confidence to do better than the preceding generation and settled instead into the same patterns, which served their own vanities rather than the artist's com-mitment to truth.

The publication of the book triggered a scandal when a Viennese critic passed on his review copy to his friend Gerhard Lampersberg, who initiated a libel suit against Bernhard and his publisher, Siegfried Unseld, and secured an injunction against the distribution of the book in Austria. Television audi-ences watched policemen pull copies of *Woodcutters* from booksellers' shelves. Bernhard retaliated with the demand that Unseld stop the distribution in Aus-tria of all his books published by Suhrkamp so far (about thirty) until the expiration of the copyright. Although there were no legal grounds for such a demand, Unseld complied—for the moment, anyway—to show his soli-darity with his author (and boost sales in Germany). Austrians crossed the border to get their copies, with the result that sales of a Bernhard book rose to unprecedented figures. A Suhrkamp ad in *Die Zeit* about six weeks after the seizure of *Woodcutters* announced that 60,000 copies had been sold. (By comparison, the total sale of *Frost* up to that time was 30,000 copies and of *Concrete* 16,000.) The controversy dragged on for six months, from August 1984 to February 1985. After a court ruling against the ban on sales and dis-tribution, Lampersberg withdrew his suit. [36] The public drama of hurt egos, legal issues, questions of artistic freedom, integrity, and censorship seemed to flow seamlessly from the book, which provided the first act for a quite consistent second act, played out in (and by) the media. The real people acted out their fictionalized doubles with astounding consistency, which proved, if nothing else, the realism of Bernhard's hyperbole.

In his book, he stages himself as a spectator. For the better part of the evening, Bernhard's narrator stand-in is seated in a wing chair in the ante-room, where he has an optimal view of the arriving guests passing through to the music room. In the semidarkness of his post, between the door to the apartment and the entrance to the brightly lit music room, he observes the goings-on as if from a theater's wings. From his vantage point all the world's reduced to a show, or rather its vulgar sham in the strained dramaturgy of Vienna's cultural elite.

The repeated interjection "... I thought, sitting in the wing chair" points to the real action and setting inside the spectator's head. In slight variations, the reference appears on almost every page, sometimes as often as six times on one page, syncopating the narrator's state of agitation, measuring his heartbeat as it were, in response to the action in his mind, which refracts the mock-up reality around him. The image could have been visualized by Magritte: the spectator as leading actor carrying the stage and following the action inside his head. The rest is fake: Vienna's fin-de-siècle elite aspired to transform every-day life into art. Their heirs heading toward the next fin de siècle reduced the utopia of a lived *Gesamtkunstwerk* to pathetic imitations of lifestyles and art-ists. The Auersbergers' city apartment, furnished in Biedermeier and Empire antiques, simulates aristocratic distinction. They even shortened their name to Auersberg to make it sound like the name of an aristocratic dynasty, the Auerspergs. The historic Palais Auersperg in Vienna is now used for chamber concerts and exhibitions.

The name prescribes the role. There are those who adopted the pose of another famous name. Joana, the failed movement artist who hanged herself, was born Elfriede Slukal. Jeannie Billroth sees herself as Vienna's Virginia Woolf. If her early writing was inspired by her role model, it eventually froze into an empty gesture. Anna Schreker, the so-called Austrian Gertrude Stein, keeps imitating her imitations of her role model. The host himself, once a promising young composer hailed as the successor to Anton von Webern, never found his own voice. Interestingly, having changed the names of the other characters from those of their real-life models, Bernhard kept both the birth name and adopted stage name of Elfriede Slukal. Much more radical than her friends who adopted literary poses, she renamed herself to reinvent her life in her professional self-image. Her suicide was already staged in the dropping of her birth name. The pretenses of her friends are the travesty of her tragedy.

Bernhard cast himself as the narrator among the *faux artistes* of his generation. The strategy suggests that he saw himself as one of them. The ferocity of his attacks against old friends, which put off some of his most tolerant admirers, is ultimately directed against himself. Like his former friends, he impersonates another, albeit in a much more convoluted and inspired manner. He is the voice imitator of none other than himself. Promise is eclipsed by self-betrayal. By 1984, when *Woodcutters* was published, he was well past "his" decade, which would also mean, according to his own prediction, past his prime. What he wrote to Auntie in 1970 may have come to haunt him now: "Then nothing will interest me and nature will do its part." His career so far, topped by the unqualified international success of his autobiographical project, was a tough act to follow. His memoirs brought down the first-act curtain to thundering applause. In 1983 the publication in one volume of the twelve full-length plays he had written so far could but reinforce the sense of closure. Furthermore, the collection highlighted the repetitiousness of his writing. All the plays feature the same minimalist dramaturgy and obsessive rhetoric. Play after play introduces an aging maniacal speaker in lifelong pursuit of some self-imposed absolute standard of quasi-transcendental perfection, which more often than not cripples any concrete endeavor right from the start or ends in madness or death. The political and institutional targets of Bernhard's critical attacks remained the same throughout, as did the philosophical aesthetic ruminations, all delivered in interminable sentences without punctuation marks. Subdivided instead into short lines of subclauses, the printed text becomes a graph that plots the emotional pitch and rhythmic variations in the trajectory of thinking. Did Bernhard create a body of drama sui generis or did he merely repeat the same formula over and over again? At midpoint in his career, the issue was publicly debated with increasing urgency amid speculations as to whether his memoirs suggested a caesura, if not a turning point of sorts. But in fact the novels that followed are an extension of his autobiographical project. *Concrete* parallels the stage of Bernhard's diagnosed terminal illness. *Wittgenstein's Nephew,* overtly autobiographical, picks up on an earlier time in his life when the threat of his imminent death followed the completion of a major literary work. And *Woodcutters* examines his artistic beginnings, which put in question all middle-aged accomplishments.

Thematically, his later prose works, much like his plays, continue to cover the same familiar territory seen through the eyes of an aging narrator: Austria as the central cesspit in a decaying Middle Europe of shattered values, standards, lifestyles, and beliefs; the references to the same thinkers, writers, and artists (all dead) that serve as cues for the reader to complete the work's utopian *Lebensraum* for the ontological tragedy of being. What is noticeable in his later fiction, however, is a marked shift of emphasis from the perplexing experience of the tragic to the comedy in the persistent acting out of the tragedy. The role of the actor merges with that of the writer, whose very act of writing constitutes this kind of comedy.

A review of *Concrete* in the *Süddeutsche Zeitung,* one of Germany's most influential papers, captured most succinctly the increasingly ambivalent response to Bernhard's ongoing writing project:

> For years I devoured every sentence Bernhard published. But at some point it simply got too much. I couldn't help myself: I had to laugh. I read two pages, laughed about the brazenness with which Bernhard kicked up his mad virtuosity yet another time — and put the book away. Maybe Bernhard had to laugh himself; perhaps he got tired of his own virtuosity. . . . He turned to the theater. In addition — it must have been refreshing despite all the pain — he wrote his five-volume autobiography of childhood.
>
> Now . . . *Concrete* was published. A text without a definition of genre, it speeds breathlessly without paragraphs through 212 pages. The first sentence is one and a half pages long and gathers, like a good overture, all of those Bernhardian trigger words that prepare for their impact on form and subject matter. I had to laugh again. The way one laughs meeting a good friend after a long time who still has his old ticks and peculiarities.[37]

After writing so much for the theater, Bernhard had learned his lesson well. All his writing became a stage with all the players none other than himself. No matter what the writing is about, it inevitably closes back in upon himself in the self-observing act of writing, which becomes increasingly aggressive against the world that stands between him and his death. Ultimately, it is a self-suffocating process. Inevitably (*naturgemäss*), in the process of such self-performances, he was imitating himself over and over again. Not surprisingly, then, the Godot of *Woodcutters,* in Bernhard's mise-en-scène of waiting, is reduced to a professional actor. Leave it to Bernhard's delight in infantile *blödeln* that the actor comes to the Auersbergs' "artistic dinner" in his honor after his performance in Ibsen's *Wild Duck*. And he gets roasted like all the other party guests, with the narrator stewing in his own brew of reconstituted *Duck Soup*. It is brought to a boil by the Groucho-mustached specter of another fateful actor in Austria's troubled cultural scenario, Martin Heidegger. At the end of the long-delayed dinner the guest of honor unexpectedly delivers an incensed tirade against one guest's insistent insults, which is punctuated by his repeated exclamation "The forest, the virgin forest, the life of a woodcutter." This gains him, quite unexpectedly, the narrator's respect, at least for the moment, for his transformation from a "gargoyle into a philosophically minded human being, if not from a driveler into a philosopher." [38] The jarring non sequitur signals to the observer not senile sentimentality but mental clarity. What causes this sudden outburst of nativist imagery, now admired for its philosophical acumen?

The title offers more than a hint, which is followed by verbal clues scattered throughout like so many crumbs to mark a path through the forest to the philosopher's ghost hidden in the closet of Austria's silenced past. Martin Heidegger's 1935 lecture "The Origin of the Work of Art" was published in 1950 in a collection of his writings with the German title *Holzwege*, woodcutter's paths. The German title of Bernhard's book is *Holzfällen*, cutting wood. Heidegger's *Holzwege* begins with a brief explanation: "Wood [*Holz*] is an old name for forest. In the woods, there are paths, which mostly end up overgrown, where no one has set foot [*im Unbegangenen*]. They are called woodcutters' paths. Each one runs separately, but in the same forest. Often one appears to be like the other. But it only appears to be that way. Wood gatherers and foresters know these paths. They know what it means to be 'on the woodcutter's path.'" [39]

According to George Steiner, Heidegger's woodcutters "seek to hack out a path to the clearing," the luminous "thereness of being." [40] But Bernhard is quick to bring Heidegger's lofty philosophical ennoblement of peasant chores back to a more Wittgensteinian appreciation of the linguistic savvy of common folk. In German vernacular, *auf dem Holzweg sein*, to be on a woodcutter's path, means to bark up the wrong tree. What is certainly true of Heidegger's troubled political life can be said of the artistic careers of Bernhard's party guests. Most of them came of age at the time *Holzwege* was published. The redemptive impact of Heideggerian angst on this generation, left in a metaphysical void by the war, cannot be overemphasized. Ironically, all of them ended up on such *Holzwege* turned moral impasse. In the case of Joana, the dancer, it led to suicide in the appropriate rural environment.

Heidegger's silence after World War II about his association with Nazi ideals is paradigmatic for the great silence in Austria up to the controversial presidency of Kurt Waldheim. The real scandalous impact of *Holzfällen* was less the outrage of one insulted individual than the suggestion that Austrian artists, by coveting state sponsorship, acquiesced in the continuation of cultural politics that had its ideological roots in the 1930s.

Ironically enough, the more Bernhard attacked his culture, the more he got involved in it. In *Woodcutters* there are hints of the incoming artistic director of the Burgtheater. Elevated by Claus Peymann to near-mythical status as the Burgtheater's poet laureate, Bernhard became a cult figure in Vienna and all of Vienna his stage. He could be sighted at the same hours in the city's legendary cafés, a solitary figure reading his newspapers (a quasi-restaging of well-known autobiographical hints in his writing). Wieland Schmidt-Dengler, one of the leading scholars of Austrian literature and head of the University of Vienna's department of German studies, an astute Bernhard expert, made it a point not to introduce himself to his subject of study. The only exchange he ever had with Bernhard was in the Café Bräunerhof. Bernhard had approached the professor he didn't know, who sat at another table reading some newspapers, to ask whether he could take the *Frankfurter Allgemeine Zeitung*. The Bernhard expert said yes and that was that.[41] The theater historian Wolfgang Greisenegger, the head of the university's Institut für Theaterwissenschaft, passed Bernhard on his way to the Café Bräunerhof almost every morning as he walked to work. They exchanged looks that registered their daily encounter without ever getting into a conversation.[42] Both professors had been overseeing thesis projects and dissertations on Bernhard for years. Keeping their scholarly distance, they played into his existential mise-en-scène and helped him sustain the aura of impenetrability that had become part of the Bernhard myth. Though he attacked the phony theatricality of Viennese life and helped subvert the Burgtheater's stodgy traditionalism, Bernhard was susceptible to the city's worship of greatness, still suffused by imperial dimensions and haunted by those elusive "highest standards" that had been imbued in him since earliest childhood. The potent blend of the extinguished empire's vestiges infused the vision and mise-en-scène of Bernhard's last works with a melancholy that belies the performative furor of his own race against death.

Bernhard planned the publication of *Extinction* as his final grand narrative, to be published posthumously.[43] Apparently he had given the manuscript to his brother to keep for him, then changed his mind. It appeared as his last published novel. In fact, he began writing it in 1982, around the time *Concrete* was published. Like Bernhard himself, the narrators of both novels are driven to write in a race with death. Appropriately enough, the second part of *Extinction,* titled "The Will," is devoted to the staging of a spectacular funeral. The two-part book is the ultimate testimony to Bernhard's theatrical genius, which manifests itself more fully when he is not writing for the theater but rather using its tools to animate his philosophy. In that sense he becomes a philosopher like his Paul and his Glenn. Performance onstage is no match for the theater in his head. While the first part of *Extinction* is an outrageous stand-up routine, the funereal scenario of the second part is the apotheosis of Bernhard's lifelong obsession with playing dead. For all but two pages of the first part's 154 pages Franz Josef Murau is poised at the window of his Rome apartment, absorbing the news of his parents' and older brother's sudden death. With his mind reeling back and forth between Rome and his native Austria, the news triggers torrents of overwrought reminiscences, neurotic resentments, and replays of scenes dreamed and imagined, fed by highlights of his recent intense encounters with his Roman pupil, whom he instructs in political anarchism while expounding the glory and decline of Western culture, both spawned in Bernhard's Austria and eroticized by his passion for the ancient beauty of Rome, which sublimates his attraction to his young charge. Philip Roth's term "diatribalist" captures this Alpine Lenny Bruce with the emperor's first name, suspended on a cliff above the dark woods of a Grimm fairy-tale childhood that is haunted by the ghosts of gauleiters, braided and bedirndled matrons, and gorgeously costumed cardinals, among them the lover of the narrator's beheaded mother.

In the second part Franz Josef Murau has returned home for the funeral. He keeps himself out of sight for a while to observe the goings-on unnoticed.

I stopped in front of the big gateway by the Home Farm and peered between the enormous branches of chestnut trees into the park and across to the Orangery, for it was there from time immemorial the dead of

Wolfsegg had always lain in state. And indeed the Orangery was open; in front of it the gardeners walked to and fro, carrying wreaths and bouquets. . . . I was again struck by the calm demeanor of the gardeners and their characteristic way of moving as they silently carried the wreaths across from the Home Farm to the Orangery. They also brought buckets of water across from the stable. A huntsman appeared and seemed about to enter the Orangery, but then he turned back and disappeared in the direction of the Farm. I stood pressed against the wall in order to get a better view. . . . The gardeners continued to cross from the Farm to the Orangery, carrying wreaths and bouquets, buckets of water and wooden planks. Large wooden tubs containing cypresses and palms had been placed in front of the Orangery, as well as one of the agaves that had been carefully cultivated by the gardeners. . . . The theatricality of the proceedings in front of the Orangery was suddenly borne in upon me. It was like watching a stage on which the gardeners were performing their parts with wreaths and buckets. But the main character's missing, I thought; the real play can't begin until I make my entrance as the principal actor, so to speak, who has come hotfoot from Rome to take part in this tragedy.[44]

The quiet beauty of the setting is in sharp contrast to the narrator's preceding inner turmoil. Like Hamlet returning to Denmark, Murau secretly observes the preparations for a burial and delays the time of his reentry into the unfolding tragedy, which is his own. Like Hamlet the last of a historic family line, Murau will also die soon, albeit a natural death. Like Hamlet he will have his revenge, above all for his mother's betrayal—she kept up a thirty-year affair with a dashing papal nuncio whom Murau himself admires as a substitute father figure with quasi-incestuous infatuation. But for a moment time is suspended in the serene perfection of thoroughly mechanized motions rehearsed since time immemorial.

I felt like the principal actor preparing himself for his entrance, reviewing all the possibilities, not to say subtleties, recapitulating what he had to do and say, going through the lines again and mentally rehearsing his movements, while nonchalantly watching the others engaged in their own supposedly secret preparations. I was surprised at my nonchalance as I stood by the gateway reviewing my role in the drama, which suddenly seemed to be no longer new but to have been rehearsed hundreds if not

thousands of times already. . . . This play, this tragedy is centuries old, I
thought, and everything enacted in it will be more or less automatic.[45]

Granting his character time out in the wings for a while gives Bernhard the opportunity to dream himself into a privileged childhood cradled in the beauty
of "time-honored" feudal traditions.

> I now heard, wafting up from the village through the trees and shrubs
> on the hillside, the strains of a familiar piece by Haydn played by a wind
> band. They're probably rehearsing the music for tomorrow's funeral in
> the Music House, I thought, the Music House being an old building next
> to the school. . . . As a child I loved to listen to the villager's music making,
> especially the wind band, and I still do. . . . This music by Haydn was
> in tune with the noontide atmosphere, with the shimmering air and the
> movements of the gardeners, carefully carrying the wreaths and bouquets
> from the Farm to the Orangery, unflustered and unfaltering. I was re-
> minded of the many afternoons in my childhood when the sound of the
> band, playing the same piece, probably in the same scoring, had wafted
> up to my room from the village.[46]

Bernhard's infatuation with an elite he publicly ridicules, his self-
absorbed confessional stance, and his social satire that includes himself as a
target makes him the unlikely relative of Woody Allen. Both are equally at odds
and in love with their respective tribes. Both cultivate the image of the urban
sophisticate trapped, misunderstood, in a social environment he derides, yet
to whose trappings he is perversely attached. Feeling guilty about it, but indulging all the same in his predicament, he uses all that guilt to seduce not only
his young object of desire but his voyeuristic, equally urban-chic audiences.
Typically, the works of both Allen and Bernhard continue with the same cast of
characters. While Allen has occasionally ventured beyond the comic boundaries of his New York neuroses into Northern European alienation, Bernhard
gradually transposed his landed obsessions into the satiric pitch of Vienna's
Jewish cabaret artists. Allen has his shrinks to confess to; Bernhard doesn't
need such mediators to reach his audiences. The confessional mode is part
of a national heritage that theatricalized national and literary discourse. It is
vented in many forms, from self-flagellation to rebellious provocation and ob-
stinate chutzpah. In the more worldly environs of Vienna's coffeehouses the
sublimated Catholic confessional reflexes mix with the equally sublimated

rabbinical fervor of the Jewish literati. The result is a highly idiosyncratic literary—as well as conversational—style. To outsiders its pernicious humor
may be puzzling, even off-putting, but it pierces the well-bred silence in which
Austrians drown out any unwanted criticism.

Jean Paul's novel *Siebenkäs* is mentioned several times in *Extinction.* The
quirky book by the early nineteenth-century German writer heads Murau's list
of recommended readings for his beloved pupil, Gambetti. Typically, Bernhard doesn't go into the content, but offers the title as bait. It is up to the reader
to pick up the clue. *Siebenkäs* is the story of a man who exchanges identity
with his best friend and goes through an elaborate mock funeral for himself
in which he observes the grief of his wife and relatives. As a child Bernhard
played dead to scare and punish his mother. In his thirties, Granny Hennetmair became a supporting actor in the ritual. That was also the time when
The Italian, the forerunner of *Extinction,* was filmed, affording him the opportunity to actually watch himself at the game. Voyeuristically, he guides the
camera with Schiele-inspired clinical precision over the father's naked corpse
being washed by his daughter. Anticipating his own death, he dreams himself
into the other's. The other represents Austria's old nobility. Staging himself
in their deaths, Bernhard dreams himself into an aristocracy whose historic
demise has long been completed. His literary playing dead fulfills two functions. He distances his death as a work of art and he performs himself as aristocracy. Both processes are reflected in his biography. By rewriting himself as
a nobleman he assigned himself the part of a dead man. His texts, all heavily infused with personal experiences, prepare for the postmortem examination of
his corpse. Reading equals viewing his body. Reading the texts with a perfect
inner ear, as Gould read music, amounts to a performance: Now the reader
becomes Bernhard's voice imitator. Disembodied, Bernhard returns to the
stage he perfected, locked inside the head.

For his real death, he wanted no stagy funeral. He didn't need it. He had
already gone through it—many times. He would not allow others to ruin its
perfection and enshrine his absence to boot. No one would cut short his self-
performance, which he so shrewdly immortalized.

CHAPTER TWELVE

Questions of Genius

Since I saw my grave, there is nothing I want but to live.
—Heinrich von Kleist, *The Prince of Homburg*

THE SETTING OF BERNHARD'S PLAY *Der Theatermacher* is a run-down inn in an Austrian village of two hundred–some inhabitants where the actor Buscon presents his touring production of *The Wheel of History,* which he wrote and staged, starring himself and featuring his wife and his son and daughter. The summer before the play's publication in 1984 the Austrian actor Oskar Werner, once a brilliant young stage actor and internationally admired film star, now aged sixty and ravaged by alcohol, staged and played Heinrich von Kleist's youthful *Prince of Homburg* on a makeshift stage in a beer hall in the Austrian village of Krems. Werner's inspired performances at the Vienna Burgtheater and his budding film career in the mid-1950s, together with his notorious temper and fondness for alcohol, made him Austria's most talked-about actor at the time Bernhard became interested in the theater. Werner, adored by several generations of cineasts as the eternally young Jules in François Truffault's 1961 cult movie *Jules and Jim,* saw his career sky-rocket after World War II as the young genius of Vienna's Burgtheater, where he had been hired at the age of eighteen, untrained and inspired, in 1940. With his exquisite talent and seraphic beauty he was the perfect embodiment of the Phoenix that rose from the ashes of the bombed-out imperial theater, which reopened in 1945 in its temporary home, a former vaudeville theater. When the old Burgtheater was restored to its prewar glory in 1955, Werner triumphed in its first season as Schiller's Don Carlos, one of the most presti-gious roles, the equivalent of Hamlet in the German-language theater. It was the first time he had played a leading role opposite his beloved mentor, Werner Krauss, one of the greatest—and most problematic—actors in the history of

German-language theater. Krauss had starred in the most rabidly anti-Semitic Nazi propaganda film, *Jud Süss*. Lithe, blond, and luminous, Werner could be worshiped by his morally and physically drained postwar audiences as the resurrection of the classic ideal of nobility, whose youthfully impassioned genius purified anyone within his aura. He soon left the stage for a meteoric movie career in internationally acclaimed films such as *Ship of Fools, The Spy Who Came In from the Cold, Fahrenheit 451*, and *Voyage of the Damned*. The camera extracted from Werner's angelic beauty the mystique of the damned.

An uncompromising purist in his vision of artistic integrity, impassioned, temperamental, and notorious for his drinking, he didn't last in the film industry. Theatrical producers were also wary of hiring him. It was the Salzburg Festival that brought about the decisive turning point in his career, when in 1970 he played Hamlet at the age of forty-eight in a disastrous production, which he also directed. After the painful fiasco he completely withdrew from the stage for the next thirteen years. Like Bernhard's Minetti, he "withheld" himself from the classics and isolated himself in his house in the mountains of the tiny state of Liechtenstein. Like Glenn Gould, Werner shunned live performances. Unlike Gould, who could realize his notion of the perfect performance electronically, Werner could communicate only through the presence of his body. Every now and then Werner emerged to recite poetry. While Bernhard's Minetti recited Lear in front of a mirror in his sister's attic in Dinkelsbühl, Werner recited his favorite poets in the mirror of his audiences, who reflected their expectations of the artist as the eternally young man. Like Bernhard, he became a master of the monologue. His body became his portable stage, haunted by the figures from an actor's memory, which spans centuries. It was bound to become overloaded. The process was bound to attract Bernhard's attention. His *Theatermacher,* Bruscon, wrote, staged, and performed many parts in a play that features figures who shaped the world's history, from Caesar and Nero to Metternich, Napoleon, Stalin, Churchill, Hitler, and Madame Curie. The performance takes place in the dance hall of a shabby country inn. Rehearsals are interrupted by the grunting of pigs. If history the second time around plays itself out as farce, its representation on stage, repeated over and over again, becomes the farce of a farce of a farce. And the world leaders, demons and saviors alike—the actors within the actors within the actors—are reduced to what they are: shabby stock players. The farce is what's tragic in Bernhard's universe.

Oskar Werner returned in the summer of 1983, the sole producer, organizer, director, and star of his "private festival" in Krems, the "Prince of the Beer Hall," as *Der Spiegel* brutally put it. His myth—the tragic decline of genius blinded by megalomania and alcoholism—preceded him. The magazine reported "rumors about a drunken Werner who skipped rehearsals for the local pub, where he himself sold tickets to his drinking buddies and waited for the hour of truth." As a prelude to the opening of *The Prince of Homburg,* the actor, "emaciated, ravaged, drunk," gave a poetry recital at the nearby castle of Schallaburg to a pitiful audience of twenty-three, whom he invited to the opening free of charge. Rumors of the pathetic spectacle attracted a sell-out crowd for opening night, who came to see "the myth Oskar Werner self-destruct in a brewery hall." One prominent critic pleaded that for the sake of his youthful achievements he should be protected from himself and not be allowed to proceed with the production.[1]

During the two-month run the audiences dropped from 350 to 7. Chairs were taken out for other municipal events. Werner insisted that performances continue nonetheless. It is said that at times only the fire marshal, a policeman, and a few local habitués of the inn were in the hall.

Bernhard's Bruscon says:

> Two hundred thirty inhabitants
> that won't even cover
> expenses
> But things have been worse
> Once in Merano there were less than three
> only a cripple
> who had himself wheeled
> to the front row
> by the cloakroom attendant
> The only time
> we canceled[2]

Oskar Werner died in October 1984, at the age of sixty-two. Bernhard's immediate reaction to the actor's death was characteristically contradictory, instantly negative (he was no good anyway, all that pathos, those indulgences, a good thing he's dead), then in the same breath acknowledging Werner's great art (he really could act).[3]

Bernhard's Bruscon, on the surface at least, has little in common with Oskar Werner. A tyrannical shabby entrepreneur, he is a pathetic old man and as such vintage Bernhard, at least as presented on stage. (The part was first offered to Minetti, who rejected it. Another bona fide Bernhard actor, Traugott Buhre—he originated the role of the judge in *Eve of Retirement*—wrapped the character's dictatorial histrionics in well-nourished gemütlichkeit). Werner, thin and frail, his angelic features ravaged by alcohol, seemed eerily translucent. His Homburg, stumbling and awkward, reviled by critics and spectators, nevertheless reached moments of transcendent serenity, suspended as he was between life and death.

Bernhard, better than anyone else, would have understood Werner as the product and victim of their shared cultural environment. After all, Werner's decisive failure was at the Salzburg Festival. Bernhard's good friend Hilde Spiel called his Hamlet a "theatrical catastrophe" of unprecedented magnitude in Salzburg's memory. The fledgling director embarrassed his audience with pretentious, disjointed conceptual ideas and stagy tricks. He was the perfect Hamlet "as long as he stands quietly on stage, thin, pale, blond, red-eyed, radiating a 'casually soft' but ever alert intelligence." But as soon as he speaks the first words, "pointed, through the nose, one starts to doubt the potential of his approach. . . . When he starts to go for effects, he sobs and rages, bellows and croons, and generally prefers to deliver his monologues lying on the floor." [4] The star critic Ivan Nagel observed that this highly talented actor stuck to the period in which he stopped growing as an artist.[5] Nagel didn't have to go into detail to explain that this was the Vienna Burgtheater's prewar tradition of classical acting, which continued unbroken through World War II into the 1950s and beyond. In the German theater the old heroic acting style (associated with the actors popular in the Nazi era, to whom Werner was indebted in many ways), had been superseded by the innovations of the 1960s, in rebellion against their Nazi fathers. The work of the new postwar generation (with Claus Peymann in the vanguard) was based on the model of Brecht (whom Werner despised) and influenced by the American avant-garde.

For the older generation, Werner continued to embody a myth. His spiral into disaster was part of it. Despite the dismal production and highly flawed performance, Werner's Hamlet garnered standing ovations in sold-out houses. The headline of the *Süddeutsche Zeitung* review read "Hamlet, or the Living Corpse." Bernhard followed Werner's career with ambivalence, both admiring his great gifts, particularly his supple voice and exquisite sense of language, and dismissive of his "exalted" acting.[6] While he must have appreciated the actor's affinity with the obsessive, self-destructive pursuits of his own fictional characters, he had little sympathy for his unbridled flights of inspiration.

Two years after Werner's Hamlet, Bernhard's *The Ignoramus and the Madman* opened at the Salzburg Festival. It explored the pathology of genius and the deadly discipline of perfection. His Queen of the Night, the coloratura soprano blessed with a perfect voice and driven to superhuman exertion by the self-perpetuating mechanization of technique, is the operatic counterpart to Oskar Werner. Her precarious mental condition mirrors the aging alcoholic actor's predicament, torn as he was between his own sense of perfection and the public's expectation of a living myth, suspended between ignorance and madness. Not unlike Bernhard's doctor who describes in minute detail the dissection of a body, Werner's critics dissected his "living corpse" and audiences flocked to see it. Werner's relation to Mozart, from the ridiculous to the sublime, has Bernhardesque dimensions. Early in his career he played Mozart in one of those cheap, kitschy postwar films with which the modestly emerging Austrian film industry tried to comfort an entertainment-hungry public that was eager to find relief from the memories of war and the toils of reconstruction.[7] In his later isolation, Werner was said to perform — on the telephone — the entire *Magic Flute,* playing all instruments and all parts. He shared a fondness for interminable phone monologues with Glenn Gould, who would serve as the catalyst for Bernhard's exploration of genius and its victims. "When we meet the very best, we have to give up," says the narrator of *The Loser* about his first encounter with Glenn, long before he became "Gould."[8] Bernhard, the trained actor who did not pursue an acting career, didn't need such an overwhelming encounter to evaluate his acting talent and arrive at the same conclusion while still in search of his own genius. The young actor Oskar Werner was already a national idol when Bernhard studied at the Mozarteum. If the ecstatically inspired (indulgent) acting style of the celebrated Burgtheater star wasn't exactly to his taste, Bernhard would have appreciated its underlying force. The self-conscious pathos of his characters' rhetoric owes much to the grandeur of the imperial acting tradition. Werner, however, could exist only in his own universe, where he lived his characters beyond the control of a director or his fellow actors, luminous and terrifying at the same time. Bernhard's plays called for the superb acting machine — the consummate actor reigned in by his intellect rather than a volatile medium of genius.

At the time Werner attempted his comeback on a makeshift stage in a brewery hall in 1983, Bernhard's career was well past its midpoint, something

he must have been keenly aware of as his health deteriorated. He had accomplished everything he set out to do, as indicated in his letter to Auntie, and
even more: He had "written Wittgenstein." As nature began to take over as
predicted, he began to take account of his *Herkunft* in his autobiographical
project. Memoirs, by definition, mark a caesura, a looking back on a period
finished. What comes after is, by necessity (*naturgemäss*), a comeback. Like
Oskar Werner, Bernhard staged his comeback, his return from his childhood,
on a makeshift stage in a community hall in the hinterlands of Austria. Unlike Werner's, his run-down stage was only a set—on the stage of the exquisite Salzburg Landestheater. By poignant coincidence, it also was the site of
Oscar Werner's catastrophic Hamlet. Theaters are haunted by memories and
cursed by comparisons. Bernhard, like his *Theatermacher,* was a survivor.
Oskar Werner was not. Bernhard's play is a farce of survival born from the
tragedy of a broken genius. Werner went where Bernhard chose not to go:
to a life of unbridled abandonment to his art, to the point of abandoning the
profession (or being ostracized by it). Bernhard, coming out of his memoirs,
returning from the search for his origin, came back as a *Theatermacher.* From
now on he would repeat his history as farce. The farce is in the writing. Observing himself in the act, the writer turned *Theatermacher* makes a show of
(and for) himself. A *Macher* is also a manipulator, a somewhat unsavory entrepreneur. As long as he writes, as long as he puts on that kind of show, Bernhard
is his own entrepreneur, the manager of his survival—even beyond his death,
as his testament and the ensuing theater around it would show. His work in
the 1980s was also a preparation for that testament, an examination of genius,
failure, and legacy. Oskar Werner was not that kind of *Theatermacher.* He was
a failed genius. Bernhard in the end was a brilliant *Theatermacher.* He was
not a genius. In the sense in which his Queen of the Night was a coloratura
machine, he turned himself into a writing machine. Plays were commissioned
and finished on time. He was said to make major purchases in order to force
himself to write to make money to pay for them. He was a pro. His works in
the 1980s were also an accounting with himself. While his memoirs were attempts to come to terms with his life, the works that followed were attempts to
come to terms with his calling. The novels that follow his memoirs obsessively
circle back to the promise of genius and its destruction, as if to scrutinize his
own claims and literary legacy. Rudolf of *Concrete* attempts unsuccessfully to
begin his study of Felix Mendelssohn Bartholdy, the beloved composer whose
status in the pantheon of genius was often disputed. *Woodcutters* exposes the

betrayal of youthful promise and the grotesque spectacle of compromised success. Paul Wittgenstein embodies the potential of genius, never realized.

The narrator of *Extinction,* Bernhard's middle-aged Hamlet, is the same
age as Oskar Werner's Salzburg Hamlet. Both return from self-imposed exile.
Werner lived out the life of a Bernhard character, Bernhard didn't have to
write him. He couldn't write him the way he thought he couldn't write about
Wittgenstein, by becoming Werner the actor. It would have destroyed him,
probably a long time ago, had he chosen to become an actor. He became a performer instead. Werner was not a performer. There was not an actor within the
actor within the actor. He was the actor through and through, a naive, unsentimental genius in Schiller's definition of "sentimental," meaning "reflective."
No, *Der Theatermacher* is not about Oscar Werner. There was no way to write
about him — that is, to reflect on that kind of genius in Bernhard's dramaturgy
of performance. Using the setup of Werner's final devastating performance
only serves to highlight the fact that Bernhard's *Theatermacher* isn't about
him and in that sense becomes all about him — about the world in which he
couldn't function. It is the farce of genius.

> We give our all
> but that's not understood
> the more we give of ourselves
> the greater our mental exertion
> we perform all our lives
> and no one understands us
> . . .
> Theater prison for life
> without the least chance of parole
> yet never quit
> Penitentiary as theater
> Tens of thousands of inmates
> none of whom has the prospect
> of parole
> The death sentence is their only certainty.[9]

Laugh lines from the mouth of a pathetically pompous old ham capture the
tragedy of the sixty-year-old Oskar Werner reimagining the young Prince of
Homburg through the prism of experience and an unbroken performative
innocence.

The director Hans Jürgen Syberberg watched videos of Werner's performance over and over in preparation for his inspired cinematic homage to the actor. His sensitive appreciation of Werner's vulnerability and cruel reception captures the tragic counterpart to Bernhard's grinning mask of comedy.

Retreat and tower existence of Oscar Werner mean fourteen years of solitude. After his last performance in Salzburg, the "market of the flies" (Niezsche), the meat flies of the industry, which was ten years after his exit from the Burgtheater, where he came from. As Kleist wrote in Homburg: Mountains as partners and the land from morning till night, year after year, more than a quarter of a century. . . . And when he came back to the people, down the mountain, like Zarathustra, they did not forgive him that their young postwar Mozart had reached the *Requiem* and asked for forgiveness, while still alive, for not having finished." [10]

In the *Theatermacher*'s project, the deeds of the heroes and demons of history deteriorate into histrionics, as Bernhardian excesses sink to an all-time low. But just when it looks as if the bottom is reached, it drops out completely. The audience gets to glimpse the fathomless pit of historic nightmares. Nero, Caesar, Churchill, Hitler, Einstein, and Madame de Staël are introduced as theatrical costumes on tailors' dummies to be used in the performance of *The Wheel of History,* a comedy "that contains all comedies that have ever been written."

Smells and grunts waft through the preparations in the dilapidated hall, which still features a framed photograph of Hitler, nearly unrecognizable under crusts of dirt, and the traditional inscription on the doorpost, *K + M + B*, for Kaspar, Melchior, and Balthasar, with which Austrian Catholics mark each passing year on January 6, the feast of the Epiphany. In this case, however, the date hasn't been changed since 1945.

Bernhard allows only a brief quote from Buscon's play within the play. It is a fragment of a line that Bruscon rehearses with his daughter. He instructs her how to speak it "very softly" and shows her how to do it.

> Very softly this passage
> you hear me
> you'll think
> no one will hear you
> but they have to hear you

>you'll speak so softly you'll think
>that they won't hear you
>but you'll speak very clearly
>   (*shows her how*)
>If we don't have beauty
>and our minds and souls
>are sick and barren through and through

His daughter tries several times, first the whole passage, then less and less of it, until "If we don't have beauty" reverberates like an incantation led by the shaman's exhortations:

>What you miss
>is the devotion
>with which you must speak
>you must speak with utter devotion
>This way
>If we don't have beauty
>and our minds and souls
>lightly softly lightly
>devotedly my child . . . .[11]

Against the *Theatermacher's* overbearing patriarchal terror the moment is surprisingly tender. Soon enough the fragile grace of the bare fragment of a line is quickly drowned in the cacophony of his histrionic posturing. Nevertheless, the quiet genuineness of longing restores, if just for a moment, a sense of beauty, if only as our loss. It evokes in a flash the spirit of Oskar Werner and the sadness of his loss.

Shortly after this magic moment Bruscon proudly declares, "I am a classic actor," and elaborates a few lines later:

>I sacrificed my passion for alcohol
>to high art
>that is the truth
>not a drop of wine for thirty years
>hardly a glass of beer
>Crazy
>if not insane
>a completely senseless renunciation

> High art or alcoholism
> I've chosen high art [12]

The obvious connection to Werner's alcoholism may be purely coincidental. The statement has autobiographical roots, indicating the choice Bernhard made as opposed to the options available to him, at the Tonhof and in his early, heady days as a writer. By all accounts a hearty drinker in the 1950s and 1960s, Bernhard later cut down his alcohol consumption to keep his illness in check and to realize his promise as a writer in the limited time available to him.[13] Knowing that his death is imminent, he chose life. Werner, the icon of eternal youth, took the fast road to death.

On the intimate stage of cultural memory, particularly in Salzburg and Vienna, the actor's myth became part of its stock, to be used imaginatively or routinely, as a convenient prop. Bernhard, as we have seen, was an accomplished master at doing both. Werner's glory and self-destruction, played out on the same stage as *Der Theatermacher,* deepened the shadows cast by Bernhard's farce. Bruscon repeatedly insists that the hall must be completely dark at the end and frets about the fire marshal. This is, of course, a reference to the debacle of *The Ignoramus and the Madman* (also at the Salzburg Landestheater). Unlike Peymann in 1972, Bruscon gets his way. But at the moment of utter darkness, lightning strikes and the inn is engulfed in flames. What seems a cheap in-joke climaxing in melodramatic thunder also establishes a deeper connection to the darkness of the earlier play. Both are backstage plays. Both ask the question of genius, *The Ignoramus and the Madman* more in the bizarre vein of the theater of the absurd, *Der Theatermacher* in the milieu of a *Bauernschwank,* a peasant farce. The former, about a brilliant singer at the point of breakdown, ends in total darkness, while the latter, about a traveling actor at the end of his road, goes up in flames. This time the darkness is not final. On the metaphoric level, the theatrical thunder and smoke produce a fire that is the opposite of the darkness of the earlier play. It suggests a flame that continues to burn, the flame of genius, however destructive, however buried in cheap theatrics it may be. The memory of Oskar Werner's genius, his final decline and recent death, adds substance to the gimmick that connects the Queen of the Night to the *Theatermacher.*

If Peymann's infamous dunghill onstage set off another episode in the cloak-and-dagger drama of Austrian politics, the scatologically sensualized scenario of local provincialism wasn't all that irked its illustrious representatives. It was again the Nazis Bernhard kept finding in their soup. In an insidiously deadpan scene Bruscon discovers Hitler's photograph on the wall. In German, the brief exchange between Bruscon and the innkeeper mimics the rhythm of Papageno's first encounter with Papagena in Mozart's *Magic Flute*. Expecting to meet a young woman, he is shocked to find an old hag (Papagena in disguise). The innkeeper's repeated reply "Ja freilich" (Yes of course) to Bruscon's inquiries echoes Papagena's "Ja, mein Engel" (Yes, my angel).

BRUSCON (*questioningly*): Isn't that Hitler's picture

INNKEEPER: Yes of course

BRUSCON (*questioningly*): And it still hangs here

INNKEEPER: Yes of course

BRUSCON (*questioningly*): All those years

INNKEEPER: Yes of course

BRUSCON: One has to look quite closely to recognize Hitler
It's so dirty

INNKEEPER: That never bothered anyone

The motif is wrapped up in a nasty ditty that invites comparison with the bucolic scenery of Austria's national anthem's "land of mountains, rivers, and streams, the homeland of great sons":

> Where there was a forest
> now there is a quarry
> where there was a meadow
> now there is a limeworks
> where there was a person
> there is a Nazi [14]

Austria's politicians responded on cue, as described earlier. By the time *Der Theatermacher* opened Peymann's first season at Vienna's Burgtheater in 1986, Kurt Waldheim, steadfastly denying involvement in Nazi deportations, had been elected the new president of Austria, to the outrage of the international community. Once again Austrian politics seemed to imitate Bernhard's theater.

Bernhard's play *Ritter, Dene, Voss,* about the histrionics of philosophy and the presence of the actor, arrived at the Burg three nights after *Der Theater-*

macher. The inspiration for it went back four years. In 1982 Bernhard drove to Cologne to see a production of *Am Ziel,* which he didn't like except for the performance of Ilse Ritter in the role of the daughter. He went on to Bochum to see Peymann's celebrated production of Kleist's *Hermannsschlacht.* Not a fan of the play, he loved the performances of Gert Voss and Kirsten Dene. Two years later, with Ludwig and Paul Wittgenstein on his mind, he wrote his play for three "intelligent actors."

The actors' names are not the names of the characters they play. The cast list reads: Voss, Ludwig; Dene, his older sister; Ritter, his younger sister. Accordingly, Ritter, Dene, and Voss are introduced as themselves — or rather, as the actors their audiences have come to know — and also as their designated roles. Their named presence destabilizes the identities of the roles they are playing. In telling contrast, Ludwig is identified only by his first name and the actor playing him only by his last. In the course of the play the stage character emerges as a composite of Ludwig and Paul Wittgenstein. The sisters are Bernhard's contributions from his stock of female companions to tyrannical, madly inspired males. (They have very little in common with the philosopher's sisters. Perhaps this is one of the reasons they have no names.) The interplay of names in the presence of the actor becomes even more intricate in productions with different actors. Would they have to perform Ritter, Dene, and Voss performing Ludwig and his sisters? The problem gets more complicated (or perhaps less so) in places where no one knows or remembers the persons behind the names in the title. Will the actors be playing Ritter, Dene, Voss, *and* the characters Bernhard intended them to play? Or should the names in the title simply be replaced by the names of the performing actors? The performance market is acutely aware of an actor's drawing power. Did the audiences come to see *Hamlet* or Oskar Werner as Hamlet, and whose tragedy did they see? So why not call the event *Werner* (or, say, *Schwarzenegger* rather than *Terminator,* to stay with Austrian icons)? If, on the one hand, Bernhard's title was an homage to the actors as well as a way to ensure their being cast, it also can be read as a stab: Voss (who became Vienna's most beloved actor during Peymann's tenure at the Burgtheater) would be Voss no matter what parts he played (Othello or Shylock or Richard III, to name just a few of his signature roles). His mannerisms remained the same or became more pronounced as his vanity grew along with his popularity. Especially in Vienna audiences go to the theater to see an actor, "the Werner," "the Dene," "the Voss," no matter what the play. They are willing to ignore the play, but they don't forgive an actor. While *Ritter, Dene, Voss* is not about those actors, it is about their acting and the overlap as well as disappearance of identities in performance. In most productions (save for the sort of postmodern deconstruction most dreaded or ridiculed in the United States), the problem will most likely resolve itself in performance. Audiences will respond to the relationship of three siblings who are caught between genius, madness, and incestuous desires (as an American press release might suggest). Nevertheless, Bernhard provided a blueprint for his lifelong explorations of the actor within the actor within the actor. The riddle is inscribed in the title. Each name multiplies into an infinite number of roles as the audience's memory of a given actor's previous roles interacts with their perception of his present one. Correspondingly, the actor himself carries all those roles inside his head. In Bernhard's dramaturgy the mind is always a stage for a vast repertoire of interactive roles. The visible "individual" character is a product and the continuation of that dynamic.

In this confusion of identities, Bernhard stages, fittingly enough, the blurring of lines between genius and madness. Ludwig, propped up by incidentals from Ludwig Wittgenstein's biography, stands for genius. His performance, inspired by Paul's antics and illness, indicates clinical madness. Like Hamlet, Bernhard's Ludwig is a virtuoso performer of insanity. Unlike Hamlet (but like Paul Wittgenstein), Bernhard's Ludwig is a bona fide clinical case. At least, he is a regular patient at Steinhof. The performative aspect of madness — whether pathological or faked — is framed by the profession of Ludwig's sisters: both are actors at Vienna's Josefstadt Theater. (Typically Bernhard undermines their professionalism and ridicules the theater for hiring them, as Ludwig insists, only because their father is its majority shareholder.)

In Vienna, the name Steinhof is synonymous with insanity, just as the name Voss stands for actor. (If he — the actor Gert Voss — stays long enough in Vienna, preferably until his death, he will become an institutionalized icon, an immortal sign for "actor," like so many of his legendary predecessors.) Bernhard's Ludwig has no last name, for the same reason the narrator of *Der Untergeher* distinguishes between Glenn, his fellow student at the Mozarteum, and *the* Glenn Gould he became. Ludwig is still on his (dubious) way to becoming Wittgenstein, a brand name for genius.

> Your brother will be very famous one day
> and then people will say
> here in Steinhof
> is where his work was born

and we hope that then they will also say
that here in Steinhof he completed it,[15]

the director of Steinhof tells the older sister, who is identified only by the
name of the actress who plays her. Unlike the real Ilse Ritter and Kirsten Dene,
who in the past have distinguished themselves in performance (and who, performing in *Ritter, Dene, Voss,* are in the process of doing so again), Ludwig's
sisters, both mediocre actresses, have not made names for themselves. Bernhard sticks to the letter of the idiom, thus proving himself worthy of Ludwig
Wittgenstein, who urged that close attention be paid to vernacular expres-
sions for the truths that are easily overlooked in their simplicity. Bernhard, like
Wittgenstein, knows that this is also the stuff of comedy. Wittgenstein chose
a quote from Nestroy, Austria's best comedy playwright, as the motto for his
Philosophical Investigations, the work in which he explored simple language
games to lead him to the structure of language and the communication of intent. Bernhard mines the structure of language for opportunities to undermine
its intent.

Dene calls Ludwig the "counter-Kant." The definition not only applies to
her (or Ludwig's) self-understanding, it also works in juxtaposition to Bernhard's earlier play *Immanual Kant.* Bernhard's Kant was just a madman.
Even as a stage character he was not the real Kant. Ludwig is not yet *the*
Wittgenstein. Voss, however, *is* a brilliant actor. His performance invites the
accolade "genius," at least in its broader vernacular application, which Bernhard quickly undermines. "An actor is never a genius/interpreters are not
geniuses/least of all actors," says "Dene" as the actress sister (117). This is
also the author speaking as the former acting student who chose to become a
writer rather than an "interpreter." Ultimately, both "Ludwig" and "Voss" are
actors. The unease about actors and madmen, both inhabiting and producing an illusory reality, is as old as the theater. Prompted by Shakespeare and
Pirandello, Bernhard's madmen turn everyone around them into a performer.
(The ship's passengers help play up a madman's illusions of being Kant and
the former camp commander's sisters supply him with the props of the Nazi
era.) Accordingly, Ludwig's mad performance undermines any claim to genius
he may have or those playing along with him may grant him. But Bernhard
borrowed from Shakespeare not only the madman but the fool. He is the existential genius, embodied by Paul Wittgenstein, who is also part of Bernhard's
Ludwig. Rather than the performer/interpreter of madness or the victim of

illness, Bernhard's fool, taking his cues from Shakespeare and Ludwig Wittgenstein, is a master at subverting language games into a jumble of perceived realities that mirror the madness of the world. The fool doesn't succumb to madness because he doesn't look into the mirror (at himself). Rather, he looks in the same direction as the mirror, he becomes the mirror, the world passes through him in an ongoing game of mutual reflections, but he throws the world back on itself. The fool's mirrored madness is in constant flux, it becomes what to Bernhard is lived philosophy rather than interpretation. The fool, as existential genius, may be the only true genius. A genuine *Lebenskünstler,* an artist at living, he is the counterpart to Bernhard's frequently introduced *Überlebenskünstler,* a survival artist (like himself), a descendant of the ancient trickster.

Old Masters, Bernhard's last novel, is his (self-)portrait of the (survival) artist as an old man. The self-consciously contradictory subtitle, *Comedy* (in German the article is intentionally omitted), sets the stage for the trickster rather than the fool with his deep roots in tragedy. The eighty-two-year-old Reger has been going to Vienna's Kunsthistorisches Museum for thirty-six years. Every other day he sits in the same room, the so-called Bordone Room, in front of Tintoretto's *Man with a White Beard,* where he has been meeting the narrator, Atzbacher, for many years.

Bernhard stages the scene in his accustomed manner: The narrator arrives early one day and from the adjacent room observes the old man facing Tintoretto's portrait on his customary bench in the Bordone Room. As he recapitulates in his mind some of their earlier conversations, Reger becomes present through the performance of the narrator, who quotes extensively from his friend's lucid diatribes on genius and art and their abuse in Austria—in short, Bernhard's pet peeves.

Reger has been studying the old masters for the flaws in their paintings and has concluded that there is no perfection: "There is no perfect picture and there is no perfect book and there is no perfect piece of music, Reger said, that is the truth, and this truth makes it possible for a mind like mine, which all its life was nothing but a desperate mind, to go on existing" [16] In other words, even geniuses are doomed to fail. Perfection is only in the mind. The moment anything is realized, exposed to the eye, its flaws become visible. Even Goya, according to Reger, had a weakness: he couldn't paint human hands. Thus Reger, a music critic for the London *Times*—that is, an interpreter—can hold his ground vis-à-vis the creative artists, the geniuses. "A good mind is a mind that searches for the mistakes of humanity and an exceptional mind is a mind which finds these mistakes of humanity, and a genius's mind is a mind which, having found these mistakes, points them out and with all the means at its disposal *shows up* these mistakes" (20).

At long last, Bernhard's grumpy old men, the critics, the grumblers in the tradition of Karl Kraus—in short, the archetypal Viennese—are elevated to the status of genius, in charge of questioning the real geniuses, as it were. For no one can endure "the whole or the perfect. That reassures me. That makes me basically happy," says Reger. "We have to travel to Rome to discover that Saint Peter's is a tasteless concoction, that Bernini's altar is an architectural nonsense. We have to see the Pope face to face and personally discover that all in all he is just as helpless and grotesque a person as anyone else in order to bear it. We have to listen to Bach and hear how he fails, listen to Beethoven and hear how he fails, even listen to Mozart and hear how he fails. And we have to deal in the same way with the so-called great philosophers, even if they are our favorite spiritual artists" (19).

The moment anything is exposed to the eye, the flaws become visible. Implicit in his condemnation of all visualization is a post-Platonic condemnation of the theater, *theatron,* a place to see. Glenn Gould knew that and drew the radical conclusion: he never performed again. Bernhard keeps staging his best theater inside the head and performs in his novels. His plays are always also a travesty of theater, the pompousness of its corporeality.

Reger's stripping of genius doesn't stop at painters, architects, and composers. He extracts the flaws of the great writers and thinkers with an exuberance that surpasses even his forerunners among Bernhard's disenchanted diatribalists. Adalbert Stifter, the writer whom Bernhard in his 1970 letter to Hilde Spiel put next to Wittgenstein for his accurate descriptions of nature, is now ridiculed as a "a literary fuss-pot" who "makes nature monotonous and his characters insensitive and insipid," who "knows nothing and . . . invents nothing, and what he describes, because he is solely a describer and nothing else, he describes with boundless naiveté" (38). Stifter's affinity to nature takes Reger to Heidegger's proto-Nazi nature worship. The "Black Forest philosopher," a "ridiculous Nazi philistine in plus-fours," gets an encore to his show-stopping appearance in *Extinction* as a "feeble thinker from the Alpine foothills," a "genuine German ruminant, a ceaselessly gravid German philosophical cow . . . which grazed upon German philosophy and thereupon for decades let its smart little cowpats drop on it" (42).

The old masters of the museum get their come-uppance for providing nothing but state art, "pleasing Catholic state art," Lotto, Giotto, Velázquez, even Rembrandt, and above all "that dreadful proto-Nazi and pre-Nazi Dürer who put nature on his canvas and killed it" (29). Artistic freedom is a myth.

> The so-called old masters only ever served the state or the church, which comes to the same thing, as Reger says time and again, they served the emperor or a pope, a duke or an archbishop. Just as so-called free man is an utopia, so the so-called free artist has always been an utopia, Reger often says. Artists, the so-called great artists, I believe, are moreover, says Reger, the most unscrupulous of all people, they are a lot more unscrupulous even than politicians. Artists are the worst liars, even worse than the politicians, which means that the art artists are even worse liars than the state artists, I can hear Reger say again. This art invariably turns towards the all-powerful [*der Allmächtige,* the Almighty] and the powerful, and away from the world, Reger often says, therein lies its baseness. (29)

The "art artists" (*Kunstkünstler*), in contrast to the "state(-supported) artists," delude themselves into believing they are "free artists," uncorrupted by the powers (clerical or secular) that support them.

All art, then, according to Reger, comes down to the art of survival (*Über-lebenskunst*). It is just "an attempt to cope with this world and its revolting aspects," and that's possible only "by resorting to lies and falsehoods, to hypocrisy and self-deception" (151). Accordingly, even the best of artists are tricksters—like Bernhard himself, who accepted government subsidies and denied doing so, whose plays were produced in one of the Catholic Church's most formidable centers of power by one of the world's richest festival organizations, which paid astronomical fees to its artists. In short, he himself had become an "old master." If there is any implied self-criticism, the trickster nonetheless has the last laugh: the inclusion of himself among the inspired liars also elevates him to their status.

Not that Bernhard hadn't fired off his attacks many times before, but this time it was the last time he would do so in a novel. And he probably knew it would be. Perhaps that is why he did it with such graceful ease. It seems as if he consciously wrote his valedictory performance. Rather than referring to a genre, the subtitle *Comedy* indicates an action. It suggests what he (in the role of Reger) does to the old masters: he makes them ridiculous. While *Extinction,* subtitled *A Disintegration* (*Ein Zerfall*), stages the end of the Habsburg dynasty, *Old Masters* takes another step to ensure its total (perfect) annihilation by debunking its cultural products. If the former takes care of nature, the latter finishes off culture. It makes sense that *Old Masters* was actually written last, as the satyr play to the trilogy that includes *Woodcutters, The Loser,* and *Extinction,* the trickster's last tour de force.[17] Bernhard's performance resembles a popular Viennese folk hero, the *lieber Augustin* (dear Augustine), a medieval street musician who survived the plague. According to legend, he got so drunk that he passed out. Taken for dead, he was dumped in a pit with the corpses. He woke up, unruffled, picked up his bagpipes, and continued to play on top of the corpses. His unlikely feat of survival has been immortalized in an old song, "Ach, Du lieber Augustin, alles ist hin" (Oh, you dear Augustine, everything's gone). Some say it qualifies as Austria's unofficial anthem, asserting as it does survival when everything is lost.

Bernhard, like Augustine, continued with his performance, if not on a pile of corpses, after the loss of the person closest to him. The "comedy" of *Old Masters* was written after the death of Frau Hede in April 1984. He took care of her during her illness and was at her side when she died.

On the debris that's left of the old masters, Bernhard set his most tender scene, a quiet description of the old man's mourning over the death of his wife. It is a touching memorial also to Frau Hede. After his wife's death, Reger was unable to eat or go out in the street for days, hating everything and everybody.

> I pulled out several drawers and several chests and looked into them and kept taking out pictures and writings and correspondences of my wife and put everything on the table, one item after another, and progressively inspected everything, and because I am an honest person, dear Atzbacher, I have to admit that I wept while doing so. Suddenly I gave my tears free rein, Reger said. I sat there, giving my tears free rein and I wept and wept and wept and wept, Reger said. I had not wept for decades . . . with my eighty-two years I have no need to conceal or to hide anything at all, Reger said, and I therefore do not conceal the fact that suddenly I wept and wept again, that I wept for days. (142)

In its total openness, unprotected by rhetorical bravado, the moment is unprecedented in Bernhard's work. For the first time, in public, he let go in a cathartic release that is free of his customary rage, resentment, and ridicule. The tender stillness of Reger's mourning recalls the old Oedipus returning to Colonus. Like Sophocles' chorus, the old masters and great thinkers on whom Reger has relied all his life are of no help at this turning point. "We always think we can rely on those so-called important and great ones, whichever, but that is a mistake, precisely at the moment which is crucial in our lives we find ourselves left alone by all those important and great ones, by those, as the saying goes, immortal ones, they provide us with no more at such a crucial moment in our lives than the fact that even in their midst we are alone, on our own in an utterly horrible sense, Reger said" (143–44).

Like Everyman, the wealthy man who at the hour of his death cannot get any of his friends to accompany him to his grave, Reger finds himself alone: "We hoard the great minds and the old masters and we believe that at the crucial moment of survival we can use them for our purposes, which turns out to be a fatal mistake. We fill our mental strong-room with these great minds and old masters and resort to them at the crucial moment in our lives; but when we unlock our mental strong-room it is empty, that is the truth, we stand before that empty mental strong-room and find that we are alone and totally destitute, Reger said" (144).

Like the medieval Everyman, he looked at his own grave when he stood at his wife's open grave. And he did not want to die. He looked for his friends to accompany him awhile longer. They abandoned him, with the exception of Schopenhauer, but not without a struggle: ". . . quite simply I abused him [Schopenhauer] for the purpose of my survival" (144). In Bernhard's customary shorthand, the reason Schopenhauer saved his life is never explained. The name stands for the ferocious will to survive that permeates all nature.

As Everyman was saved by his very fragile good deeds, Reger is saved by a fragile moment of mourning, a painfully simple insight:

When you have lost your closest human being everything seems empty to you, look wherever you like, everything is empty, and you look and look and you see that everything is really empty and, what is more, for ever, Reger said. And you realize that it was not those great minds and not those old masters which kept you alive for decades but that it was this one single person whom you loved more than anyone else. And you stand alone in this realization and with this realization and there is nothing and no one to help you, Reger said. You lock yourself up in your flat in despair, Reger said, and from day to day your despair grows deeper and from week to week you get into ever more desperate despair, Reger said, yet suddenly you emerge from that despair. (144–45)

Everyman, set on the threshold between the Middle Ages and the Renaissance, is the last anonymous representative of a vanishing Christian cosmos. He could ensure, by a hair's breadth, eternal afterlife for his soul by the saving grace of his good deeds. Reger, the more or less anonymous interpreter of Bernhard's vanishing culture, is also one of its last relics. He sought out eternity in this life, in the undying genius of the old masters and thinkers, in the timeless lives of their products. He is saved by his acceptance of death without salvation, without the saving grace of genius. Paradoxically, his acceptance of death enables him to go on living. If death is tragic, its ongoing repetition makes survival comic. Comedy (without the article) stands for life itself— as a repetition of survival acts. The awareness of it makes life a comedy—a theatrical experience for the subject observing itself in the act of living.

"The performance was terrible" is the final statement of Bernhard's "comedy," his last novel. With his narrator's final response to a performance at the Burgtheater of Heinrich von Kleist's comedy, Bernhard set the coda to his life and work.

CHAPTER THIRTEEN

The Staging of a Nation

Austria itself is nothing but a stage
on which everything has gone to rack and ruin
a population of extras bound by mutual hate
six and a half million people left all alone
six and a half million retards and maniacs
who keep screaming for a director at the top of their voice
The director will come
and throw them into the abyss once and for all
six and a half million extras
pushed around and bullied every day
and finally thrown into the abyss
by a few criminal leading actors who sit
in the Imperial Palace's government suites

—Thomas Bernhard, *Heldenplatz*

WHEN PEYMANN APPROACHED BERNHARD TO WRITE a play for presentation in conjunction with the commemoration of the fiftieth anniversary
of Austria's annexation to Hitler's Reich in 1938, he declined. He insisted that
he had said it all before, at a time when there was general silence about the Nazi
pasts of prominent politicians. For the same reason he never commented on
Waldheim's presidency. It would have been redundant and expedient to boot
to join the chorus of protesters. He refused to write on command on any given
issue, never signed joint political statements, and shunned demonstrations. If
Peymann and the city of Vienna, which sponsored a year of commemorative
events, wanted to theatricalize the theme of the Anschluss, they should forget
about plays and other moralizing works of art. Instead, Bernhard suggested, all
stores in Vienna that had been owned by Jews before Hitler's take-over should

display a sign saying *Judenfrei* (free of Jews), the way it was done during the Nazi regime.

At Peymann's insistent urging, however, Bernhard finally wrote *Heldenplatz*. The unprecedented uproar it caused may have been more than even Peymann had bargained for. Bernhard himself, no stranger to scandals, was deeply shocked by the intensity of the hostility directed at him. He died three months after the opening. His will, with its prohibition of all new productions of his plays in Austria until the expiration of the copyright, seventy years after his death, indicated the depth of his hurt. Some say it was Austria that killed him, and that his will was an act of revenge. Others see his ban on productions as directed against Peymann, whose unrelenting ambition drove Bernhard into the *Heldenplatz* debacle and accelerated his death.

There may have been other reasons for Bernhard's initial resistance to writing a new play for Peymann, who had just begun his tenure as artistic director of the Vienna Burgtheater. He had already written one, *Elisabeth II,* and submitted it early in 1987 with the expectation that Peymann would produce it in his first season at the Burg. He was used to that sort of flexibility in his preferred director. But Peymann postponed the project for a year. Bernhard turned his sadness and hurt into a comic outcry: "Now that I've given you my play *Elisabet II,* I think I've put it in a coffin, all I can do is wait one year for the funeral. That thought isn't just depressing, it's paralyzing. It would be deadly for any other author, for there aren't many who would come out strengthened from such ghastly constellations."[1]

Elisabeth II was the second new Bernhard play in a row that Peymann did not put into production. The earlier, *Einfach kompliziert* (Simply Complicated), was written for Bernhard Minetti, who had joined Berlin's Schiller Theater and starred in its 1986 premiere production. Bernhard was incensed that Peymann initially rejected even a proposed guest performance of the Schiller Theater's production at the Burg with the explanation that it was just a paler, thinner version of the kinds of plays he had written for Minetti before. The play's only speaker is a retired actor, over eighty years old, widowed for more than twenty years. His only contact with the outside world is an eleven-year-old girl who brings him milk twice a week. Once a month, on the second Tuesday, he puts on the crown of Richard III. It gets stuck on his head as the girl arrives. With its fleeting recapitulations of familiar Bernhard motifs, the play seems as fragile as the old man, who is introduced simply as He. (Minetti's performance would have made any other name superfluous any-

way.) Eventually the Berlin production starring Minetti was included in the
Burg's repertory; Peymann delayed and eventually dropped plans to produce
Elisabeth II. He later claimed that he was generous enough to let the Schiller
Theater have it so that Minetti could play the leading role of the industrialist
Herrenstein, an eighty-seven-year-old patriarch with artificial legs, memory
lapses, and dentures served to him on a silver platter by his servant. It seems
quite likely that Peymann didn't consider the play strong enough to follow the
success of *Der Theatermacher* and *Ritter, Dene, Voss,* with which he opened
his first season at the Burg. Nevertheless, it was clearly conceived as a play
for Vienna. The setting is Herrenstein's elegant third-floor apartment on the
Opernring (Opera Ring, part of the grand avenue encircling the old inner
city), with a view of the State Opera. People he hasn't seen in years arrive to
watch the state visit of Queen Elizabeth II of the United Kingdom from his
balcony, which collapses under their weight when the royal procession passes
by. Herrenstein's name, profession, and musical tastes allude once again to the
Wittgensteins, in this case their founding patriarch, with anecdotes supplied
by Paul.

> The Herrensteins made Hugo Wolf
> they despised Brahms
> as children we had to go out on the balcony before breakfast
> and say in unison
> "Wolf is the greatest composer
> Brahms is a flop"
> . . .
> every day every single day
> all of Ringstrasse waited for us
> to recite our saying
> It was our real morning prayer
> "Wolf is the greatest composer
> Brahms is a flop"
> . . .
> When they played Brahms at the Musikverein
> we hung a black flag
> from our balcony
> even if it was just a small composition they played[2]

Paul Wittgenstein's friends had heard the story many times.
    Buried in Herrenstein's acid verbosity is another take on the *Woodcutters*

scandal. Herrenstein hints at an affair between his servant Richard and a certain Dr. Schuppich in the Herrensteins' Altaussee villa. Schuppich, who never
makes an appearance, is a descendant of an old Nazi family "who published
that disgusting book/in which I am featured/Whatever that doctor wrote
about me in his book/is not true/and yet . . ." (108). In one breath, Bernhard
alludes to himself in both Dr. Schuppich, the absent author, and Richard, the
rich man's servant, who wants to leave his master (as Bernhard left Gerhard
Lampersberg) for a mysterious lover. Only a small circle of insiders would
remember that the president of the Austrian Bar Association at the time of
Lampersberg's libel suit had been Dr. Walter Schuppich, who argued that one
has to examine "whether the description is in fact so unequivocal that not only
the person in question recognizes himself, but everyone in his vicinity knows
who is meant."[3] The fact that the same Dr. Schuppich also declared himself
to be an avid Bernhard reader may have earned the name a mention in the
play.

Many of the motifs that would become so explosive in *Heldenplatz* are
introduced here in passing. There is Herrenstein's "philosophical neighbor,"
Dr. Guggenheim. A forerunner of the Schusters of *Heldenplatz*, he taught at
Oxford. Like them,

> he shouldn't have come back from England
> the disappointment wasn't long in coming
> the Austrians are a rotten people
> the Austrians hate the Jews
> and deepest of all those returning from emigration (51)

Even Dr. Guggenheim's death at the end—he drops to his death with all
the other guests on Herrenstein's collapsing balcony—-prefigures Professor
Schuster's jump to his death from the window of his apartment. The Opernring, where the Herrensteins have their apartment, becomes Burgring, which
turns into Dr. Karl Lueger Ring, the probable location of the Schusters' apartment, with its view of Heldenplatz and the Burgtheater. One of the Herrensteins' country estates is in the fashionable resort of Altaussee (not far from
Bernhard's and Paul Wittgenstein's homes), a "Nazi nest," as he describes it:

> Austria's most beautiful spots
> always attracted the most Nazis
> Salzburg Gmunden Altaussee
> are nothing but Nazi nests (51)

The Burgtheater, "that perpetual horror theater" (*Schauerbühne*), and its new German head, Claus Peymann, get their share early in the play. *Schauerbühne* is a pun on Peter Stein's legendary Berlin Schaubühne, which Peymann left after a brief stint as co-director.

> A new artistic director people keep saying
> but he's also a charlatan
> the Germans come in as a breath of fresh air
> and soon enough it's the gaping void again
> and boring as ever
> How many directors have I experienced
> at the Burgtheater
> and nothing changed basically
> that perverted play-destruction machine
> the new faces become the old ones within the shortest time
> and the new spirit is from yesteryear
> this theater has always been out of date (29–30)

Rumor has it that these lines were the reason Peymann dumped the play. In any event, the rebuff must have driven Bernhard into the state of agitation that finally inspired him to write *Heldenplatz* (and possibly also his will).

Elisabeth II was produced by the Schiller Theater in November 1989, the season after Bernhard's death, but without Minetti, for whom it was written. Bernhard's will had made it impossible for Peymann to stage the play in Austria. The following summer Austrians managed to reclaim the play with their proverbial skill in circumventing the law. In 1990 the Vienna Festival sponsored four guest performances in the Slovak city of Bratislava, on the Austrian border, about thirty miles southeast of Vienna. Special buses provided by the festival transported audiences from the Austrian capital across the border to Bratislava.

Heimat V. An Excursion

The Burgtheater

To fully appreciate the Burgtheater's importance even (or especially) to its most cynical critics, one has to keep in mind the mythical role that the historic institution continues to play in the self-definition of Austrians. Stefan Zweig (1881–1942), the popular Austrian writer,

fondly remembered its civilizing effect on the Viennese even while he
was on the run from Hitler and shortly before he committed suicide in
Brazil.

> The first glance of the average Viennese into his morning
> paper was not at the events in parliament or world affairs, but
> at the repertoire of the theater, which assumed so important
> a role in public life as hardly was possible in any other city.
> For the Imperial theater, the Burgtheater, was for the Vien-
> nese and for the Austrians more than a stage upon which
> actors enacted parts; it was the microcosm that mirrored the
> macrocosm, the brightly colored reflection in which the city
> saw itself. . . . In the court actor the spectator saw an excellent
> example of how one ought to dress, how to walk into a room,
> how to converse, which words one might employ as a man of
> good taste and which to avoid. The stage, instead of being
> merely a place of entertainment, was a spoken and plastic
> guide of good behavior and correct pronunciation, and a nim-
> bus of respect encircled like a halo everything that had even
> the faintest connection with the Imperial theater. The Minis-
> ter President or the richest magnate could walk the streets
> of Vienna without anyone's turning around, but a court actor
> or an opera singer was recognized by every salesgirl and
> every cabdriver. . . . Every jubilee and every funeral of a great
> actor was turned into an event that overshadowed all politi-
> cal occurrences. To have one's play given at the Burgtheater
> was the greatest dream of every Viennese writer, because it
> meant a sort of lifelong nobility and brought with it a series of
> honors such as complementary tickets for life and invitations
> to all official functions. One virtually became a guest in the
> Imperial household.[4]

While Peymann, erstwhile anti-elitist rebel, was well aware of the
irony of taking on the leadership of such an institution, he, like Bernhard (and most Austrians), was not immune to the allure of its myth.
It goes back beyond its present building to Austria's legendary Empress Maria Theresia. During her reign, the "ballhouse," the royal tennis
court in the main compound of the imperial palace, was turned into a
theater for plays and operas. It opened in 1741 as the Royal Theater
Next to the Burg (Castle), under the leadership of a savvy impresario,
Joseph Carl Sellier. For the first time, ordinary citizens could attend per-

formances right inside the imperial court together with their empress. Audiences felt like the personal guests of their maternal ruler. As one of its more recent directors described it, the old Burgtheater "was a part of the home of the emperor, who only had to cross a hallway to get from his suite to his box in the theater. Gathered here every evening was the city's 'good society,' nobility, bourgeoisie, and students." [5] A cherished anecdote tells about Maria Theresia hearing about the birth of her grandson. Immediately she rushed from her suite in the palace across the hall to her box in the theater and interrupted the performance to share the good news with her subjects. [6] In the course of her reign there were quite a few births of imperial heirs to announce, along with less frequent victories in battle. In any event, audiences were made to feel part of the royal household. It is a feeling Viennese still hold. Even without an emperor, their theater, the "Burg" for short, continues the empire, which is inscribed forever in its name.

The old theater's extremely narrow rectangular shape made for close contact between spectators and stage and with each other. Only about 30 feet wide, the auditorium featured three tiers of boxes topped by a balcony with standing room, under a ceiling so low that tall standees had to crouch. With only two spiral staircases to let audiences out from the tiers, it took over an hour to clear the 1,125-seat house. Built entirely of wood, it was a fire hazard. Undaunted, the Viennese gladly risked their lives for their beloved theater. They braved other inconveniences—the house and especially the imperial box, close to the stage, was so drafty that its occupants had to wear heavy woolens over their regal getups. The intimacy between members of the court, the actors, and the bourgeois audience forged an etiquette of performance both onstage and in the audience, a sense of ennoblement through the theatrical experience that has survived into the present. The persistence of that sense, both in the acting style and in the audience's expectations, has made the Burgtheater a notoriously difficult venue for innovative directors and playwrights.

It was Maria Theresia's son, Emperor Joseph II, the inspired ruler of enlightened absolutism, who officially designated the theater Hof und National Theater (Court and National Theater) in 1776. Thus the Burgtheater proper is the same age as the United States. Arguably, to contemporary Austrians their Burg is as important a foundation of their country as the U.S. Constitution is to Americans. The imperial founding father of Austria's Court and National Theater was also its first artistic director. Joseph II made all artistic decisions, including the hiring of the twenty-two actors who made up its resident company. He also participated as much as he could in the daily rehearsals.[7] Thus Peymann (who took over a company of more than 140 actors) could consider himself the direct successor of Emperor Joseph II. If the Burg's artistic leaders have been historically elevated to imperial power, they have also been the victims of courtly pressures and intrigues. The casualty list of embattled and dethroned directors is long, starting with Joseph II himself: his increasing political difficulties forced him to relinquish his theatrical post and transfer the administrative duties to the court chamberlain, who was responsible directly to him.

The imperial status of the Burgtheater director became even more significant after the collapse of the monarchy. The Burgtheater's courtly structure survived the demise of the empire. One could say that from then on the Burgtheater was the empire. How else to explain the establishment in 1927 of the honorary title of *Kammerschauspieler* (literally chamber actor), which nominally suggests an employee of the royal household? Furthermore, the Burgtheater's ban on curtain calls, which was in effect until 1983, continued the actors' status as employees of the court, where only the emperor was worthy of such demonstrations of admiration. Even the repeal of the ban in 1971 did not result in permission to take curtain calls. In 1979 the artistic director, Achim Benning, called for a company vote on the issue and also polled the Burg's subscribers. Since the vote was not unanimous, although the majority was for the lifting of the ban, he let the cast of every production decide whether to bow or not to bow. As the Viennese critic Sigrid Löffler pointed out, audiences that applauded the closed curtain unwittingly cheered a phantom emperor.[8] The ban was finally abolished by Claus Peymann in 1986. The drawn-out curtain-call controversy reflects the persistence of imperial traditions.

During Joseph II's reign most of Mozart's operas premiered at the Burgtheater, although the emperor continued to consider them too difficult for entertainment. "Too beautiful for the ears and quite a lot of notes, dear Mozart," was his famous dictum. It is easily adapted to Peymann's Bernhard productions: too beautiful for the eyes and quite a lot of words. Joseph II can also be credited with Vienna's rich tradition of popular theater. His decree of *Spektakelfreiheit* or *Schauspielfreiheit* (freedom to do theater) broke the monopoly of the court theaters and allowed for the construction of new theaters outside the city walls, where improvisational theater, musical theater, and popular entertainment would flourish. Joseph II, it will be remembered, was also the founder of Vienna's mental institution, the so-called Narrenturm. No wonder his portrait graced one of the conspicuously bare walls of Bernhard's farmhouse.

In the early nineteenth century opera productions were eliminated from the Burgtheater's repertory, which then became Europe's foremost theater for spoken drama, under the guidance of the inspired dramaturg Joseph Schreyvogel from 1814 to 1832.[9] The Burg's fabled reputation for exquisitely tuned ensemble acting dates back to that era. The narrow auditorium allowed for an intimate conversational tone that became all but impossible in the new Burgtheater on the Ringstrasse, which opened in 1888. The latter was designed primarily for the staging not of plays but of audiences. The fights between two renowned architects, the Hamburg-born Gottfried Semper and the Viennese Karl Hasenauer, and the blatant flaws of the finished building were the stuff of a Bernhard comedy. Semper, who worked in Zürich, envisioned a democratic space inspired by the Greek arena rather than the old, rigidly hierarchic box structure. Hasenauer was set on the spectacular representation of the patrons. He won. (Semper died during the planning stage.) The imperial office of the *Obersthofmeister* (the "highest" comptroller of the royal household) insisted that the hierarchic system of hereditary boxes be maintained. The result was a four-tiered auditorium designed in the shape of a lyre, which created enormous sightline problems, particularly for boxes 3, 4, and 5 on all tiers, from which the stage was not visible. The main building was flanked by two large wings. Their sole purpose was to accommodate two spectacular red-carpeted staircases beneath ornately gilded ceilings with frescoes by, among others, the young Gustav Klimt. The wings were connected by a balcony around the auditorium where audiences could show off during lengthy and frequent intermissions. Most devastating were the acoustical problems. The height of the auditorium and the distance of the boxes from the stage forced the actors to push their voices and develop an exaggerated performance style, soon to be derided as the "Burgtheater pathos."[10]

The building was eventually reconstructed, though not substantially improved. It received considerable damage in an air raid in February 1945 before the auditorium and stage were destroyed by fire on April 12, 1945, when the war in Austria was over. The cause of the fire was never determined. It is said that it could not be extinguished because all firemen were ordered to follow the troops retreating westward from the approaching Soviet army.[11] Eighteen days later the company moved to a temporary home, the Ronacher, one of Europe's leading music halls, which had survived the bombs. The inhabitants of the bombed-out capital flocked to the theaters. Moving accounts of hungry, freezing playgoers rushing to rejoin their beloved actors and musicians, survivors together in the war-torn city, persisted into the early 1980s.

On April 27, 1945, a noted critic wrote about the Vienna Philharmonic's first concert after the war in Austria. His breathless pathos reflected the population's desperate hunger for the arts. The speedy resumption of performances in damaged theaters and concert halls provided the assurance—or illusion—of continuity across the devastation. If the arts promised absolution and redemption, they also became an effective means of denial.

> The city is bleeding from a thousand wounds. Tears of bitter sorrow over our city, ravaged by the brown plague until the very last moment, are flowing from millions of eyes. Those who had always bragged and aggrandized themselves as the guarantors of Western culture, as the protectors of art and science, used their wretched departure to almost completely demolish one of the brightest jewels of this culture. Almost—but not completely. Because the eternal remained in this city, the ever-alert spirit that builds its body. They had to leave us more than our spirit. There is one thing they couldn't take from us in their seven years of oppression, and that is our Austrian soul, which took on the shape of our beloved music. Generations have found consolation and a new beginning again and again in music, in Vienna, the musical heart of Europe. We are fortunate to have in our city an orchestra whose quintessence is no less than Austria's musical soul. With the organization of the Vienna Philharmonic we have been given one of the world's most celebrated orchestras; with this fanatic musical community the custodians of the noble and the beautiful are right among us.[12]

With brutal irony the sentiments of such accounts blend seamlessly with Stefan Zweig's sadly nostalgic recollections. As late as 1940, while on the run from the Nazis and two years before his suicide, Zweig paid tribute to the Austrians' passion for the arts in the wake of World War I.

. . . at no time had we ever been so devoted to art in Austria as in those years of chaos, because the collapse of money made us feel that nothing was enduring except the eternal within ourselves.

I shall never forget what an opera performance meant in those days of direst need. For lack of coal the streets were only dimly lit and people had to grope their way through; gallery seats were paid for with a bundle of notes in such denominations as would once have been sufficient for a season's subscription to the best box. The theater was not heated, thus the audience kept their overcoats on and huddled together, and how melancholy and gray this house was that used to glitter with uniforms and costly gowns. There never was any certainty that the opera would last into the next week, what with the sinking value of money and the doubts about coal deliveries; the desperation seemed doubly great in this abode of luxury and imperial abundance. The Philharmonic players were like gray shadows in their shabby dress suits, undernourished and exhausted by many privations, and the audience, too, seemed to be ghosts in a theater which had become ghostly. Then, however, the conductor lifted his baton, the curtain parted and it was as glorious as ever. Every singer, every musician did his best, his utmost, for each had in mind that perhaps it might be his last time in this beloved house. And we strained and listened, receptive as never before, because perhaps it was really the last time. That was the spirit in which we lived, thousands of us, multitudes, giving forth to the limit of our capacity in those weeks and months and years, on the brink of destruction.[13]

The two scenarios, nearly identical in content and separated by only five years, boosted the Austrians' self-image as an especially cultured society devoted to the arts. Ennobled by their dedication to the arts, they and their proud tradition could bridge even the Holocaust.

In the fledgling years of the Second Republic of Austria, Hitler's Reich was perceived as a catastrophic disruption forced upon a dismembered country from the outside and thus an aberration that had best be forgotten as quickly as possible. As Bernhard had frequently pointed out, Austrians were accomplished masters at forgetting. "Glücklich ist, wer vergisst, was nicht mehr zu ändern ist" (Happy is he who forgets what can no longer be changed), teaches a well-known operetta song—the popular culture's answer to Wittgenstein's "Whereof one cannot speak, thereof one must be silent." The Burgtheater was no exception. Returning Jewish artists played side by side with former Nazis, both repentant and unrepentant, fellow travelers and manipulators who helped their Jewish colleagues while representing the regime. Membership in the Burgtheater during the war saved the actors from joining Hitler's army. If they could thus claim that they did not actively participate in his war, they could also be looked upon as privileged outsiders who did not share the forced duties of ordinary people. It was often pointed out that their continued performances until the closing of Vienna's theaters in the summer of 1944 (special events, such as poetry recitals and staged readings, went on until December 26, 1944) gave people in the bombed-out city some comfort and escape. At the same time, some of the productions under the *Reichspropagandaminister*'s extended eye highlighted the need for patriotic heroism in trying times and reinforced the population's commitment to Hitler's war.

The convoluted levels of professional interaction in the immediate postwar years, once again in the service of the "highest" humanist goals, may well have been beyond the immediate comprehension of all concerned. What became even more incomprehensible in time was how long the silence on all sides could be sustained. It was not until the early 1980s that a new generation of scholars began methodically to examine the continuities of the Nazi past in all areas of public life. With an irony that seems characteristic of Austria's baffling synchronicities, their efforts coincided with the campaign of Kurt Waldheim, former secretary general of the United Nations, for the presidency, which he won despite international furor, or rather because of it. His victory was quite consistent with the Austrians' frequently noted delight in spiting their critics and opponents. For better or worse, the Waldheim affair forced Austrians to come out of their political closet. The controversy suddenly gained the leftover republic unprecedented international attention. As a proudly theatrical people, Austrians were keenly aware of their effect on an audience. For better or worse, they suddenly found themselves at center stage. Therefore it became essential for conscientious citizens to speak up, if only to save Austria's image for their global audience. A global mind-set was still part of the shrunken republic's imperial legacy.

The year of Waldheim's victory was also the year Claus Peymann took over the Burgtheater. Politically, it was an auspicious beginning

that boded well for his professed belief in the theater's power to change
its culture. It was also the time when a young upstart politician from
the provinces took over the liberal Freedom Party and changed it into a
populist right-wing party. Jörg Haider's stunning ascendancy to opposition leader in the Parliament and governor of Carinthia was accomplished on a platform that exploited the general resentment over the
corruption of the ruling coalition of Socialists and Conservatives with
a blatant appeal to Nazi sentiments. In the years to follow, Haider's
ever-increasing popularity and unabashed courting of the extreme right
would provide the perfect foil for Peymann's confrontational cultural
politics.[14]

The opening of *Heldenplatz* was scheduled for October 14, 1988, on the
hundredth birthday of the new Burgtheater on the Ringstrasse. The timing
was brilliant. The coinciding anniversaries of the theater and Austria's annexation to Hitler's Reich produced an unprecedented preproduction drama.
The colliding subtexts erupted in a bizarrely convoluted spectacle of past and
present racial dynamics and political agendas. The calculated choice of Bernhard to mark the centennial of the institution that claimed to be the definitive
German-language theater elevated the country's bluntest critic to poet laureate
not only of Austria but of the German language. As was to be expected (*naturgemäss*), the play did not lend itself to the usual self-congratulatory anniversary
celebration of the venerable institution. Set in the present, it begins after the
suicide of Professor Schuster, who jumped to his death from his Heldenplatz
apartment. The professor, together with his wife, their two daughters, and his
brother, had escaped to England and returned to Vienna after the war, only to
find themselves haunted by anti-Semitism. His widow still keeps hearing the
screams of the adoring masses who crowded the Heldenplatz to greet Hitler
and his German army upon their arrival in Vienna. The Burgtheater's problematic adjustment to the Nazi regime was brought into play by its location on
the northern periphery of the Heldenplatz. The stage direction for the second
scene specifies that the Burgtheater is to be seen "in the fog" behind the Volksgarten, the "people's garden," where the scene takes place. The Volksgarten
connects the Burgtheater to the Heldenplatz. Approaching the Burgtheater
from the Heldenplatz, one has a view of the west wing, with the artistic director's office on the second floor. In Peymann's production, the Burgtheater,
at the back of the stage, was in the dark except for the light that shone from
the windows of the artistic director's suite. It drew attention to the direc-

tor's view of the Heldenplatz, which suggested a view similar to the window from which Professor Schuster jumped to his death, which in turn suggested Bernhard's underhanded warning to Peymann (or Peymann's narcissistic self-dramatization) that he might face a similar fate in his embattled position. In any event, the framing of the Burgtheater within the square and the play suggested that it played a significant role in the spectacle of the cheering masses of Hitler supporters.

The architectural circumference of the monumental square delineates a resonant playing area of mutually reflective historic layers. The ghostly dramas evoked by the performative presence of each building grow mellow in the nostalgic glow of the monarchy's reified beauty. Adjacent to the theater's west wing is the former imperial Ballhaus (dance hall), which is now the office of the chancellor of the Federal Republic. Next to it is the seventeenth-century imperial palace, with the offices of the president of Austria—at that time the newly elected Kurt Waldheim. At a right angle, the so-called new imperial tract (completed in 1913) rounds toward the Ringstrasse. Its dominant feature is the balcony where Hitler greeted the throngs of clamoring supporters. Today the building is the home of the Völkerkundemuseum, the museum of ethnography, and parts of the National Library. On the other side of the Ringstrasse, the imposing statue of Empress Maria Theresia is flanked by Vienna's two major museums. Next to the Museum of Natural History is the elegant Palais Epstein, the former home of a prominent Jewish family. It now houses municipal offices. A plan to turn it into a museum of tolerance has been resisted by the Parliament, which claims it as additional office space for its adjacent neoclassical building. Next to it towers the neo-Gothic city hall, which faces the Burgtheater across the Ringstrasse. Ironically, that segment of the Ringstrasse is named after Dr. Karl Lueger, Vienna's beloved mayor from 1897 until his death in 1910. (He won his first mayoral election in 1895 on a populist platform, but Emperor Franz Joseph had little sympathy for his rabble-rousing rhetoric and did not confirm him as mayor of Vienna until two years later, after Lueger had won two more elections.) A prominent spokesman of Pan-German ideas, Lueger qualified his anti-Semitism with the dictum "Wer ein Jude ist, bestimme ich" (I decide who is a Jew). From Dr. Karl Lueger Ring one can see the offices of the president across the rose beds of the Volksgarten. Thus in Bernhard's archaeology of power the circle closes at the Burgtheater. Situated at the crossroads of troubled legacies, it is the connecting link between Vienna's legendary pre-World War I mayor and Austria's most problematic post–World War II president. The Burgtheater's location on the circumference of power was certainly not lost on Peymann. It was he that suggested to Bernhard that the second act be moved outside. Originally all scenes took place inside the Schuster apartment. Surprisingly, Bernhard—not one to have his texts tampered with—made the change. It was his first play with an exterior setting (not counting *Immanuel Kant,* which is set on an ocean liner, with one act taking place on the deck).

Bernhard wrote the part of the professor's widow for Marianne Hoppe, who had earlier starred in his *Hunting Party* and *Am Ziel.* The celebrated actress's biography expanded the text's political resonance. Hoppe (like Minetti) achieved stardom at the Staatliche Schauspielhaus in Berlin, from 1933 to 1945. From 1936 to 1946 she was married to its charismatic artistic director, Gustaf Gründgens, a brilliant actor and director, the protégé of theater buff Hermann Göring, governor of Prussia and as such chief of Berlin's theaters. Gründgens' portrayal of Mephistopheles in Goethe's *Faust* lent the title to Klaus Mann's roman à clef *Mephisto,* a scathing attack on the gay actor's shrewd negotiations with the Nazi administration, which ensured his career at the helm of Germany's most prestigious theater at that time. Both Mann and his sister Erika worked with Gründgens in the Hamburg theater during the 1920s. Klaus was probably his on-and-off lover in that period, while his sister was married to Gründgens from 1926 to 1928.[15]

A scintillating, contradictory figure, Gründgens was criticized for his influential role in the theater of the Third Reich but exonerated by the Jewish colleagues and others whom he used his influence to help. Marianne Hoppe's association with Gründgens was well known and added to her aura. Hoppe's presence introduced by association a controversial director of nearly mythological status in a production staged by a director who was well on his way to constructing his own myth in Vienna. Gründgens, the enigmatic virtuoso of the Nazis' theater, was the anti-father (against Brecht as the father) of Peymann's generation of German directors. By stealing the father's wife, as it were, the son achieved revenge for the political sins of the father in a politically charged production onstage and off in a way that acquired a Freudian twist, appropriately enough in Vienna. Bernhard's early interest in the actor within the actor within the actor led him to perfect, with Peymann's help, the drama within the drama within the drama.

The opening of *Heldenplatz* had to be postponed a few weeks. On May 27, when rehearsals had already begun, *Die Zeit* published a highly incendiary interview with Peymann. Several members of the *Heldenplatz* cast resigned in protest against Peymann's offensive remarks. The majority of the Burgtheater's company refused to participate in the special centennial celebration on October 14. Among other things, Peymann had called actors stupid, his colleague and protégé, the director and playwright George Tabori, a pig, and the Burgtheater so full of shit that it should be wrapped by the artist Christo and torn down. Minetti was an unbearable megalomaniac, the East German playwright Heiner Müller a show-off revolutionary. Max Frisch and Friedrich Dürrenmatt were among the many playwrights who "let their asses be wiped, took on professorships, bought mansions where they sit fat-bellied from all that dining in three-star restaurants before they even turned thirty." Unlike them, Peymann did not have his "ass gilded." Quite the contrary, he never accepted any medals of honor, such as the *Bundesverdienstkreuz* (the cross of merit of the German Federal Republic), which he threw back in the face of President Richard von Weizsäcker.

Furthermore, Peymann proudly asserted that he refused to grow up and was "not ashamed of his diapers," which enabled him to keep his belief in dreams and fairy tales, the stuff of theater, where "the impossible happens, the dream and also the fantastic murder." All theater should be a big party "to celebrate the good, the true, and the beautiful." There was no doubt in his mind that the theater could effect change. As to his background, yes, his father, a teacher, was a Nazi, an *Obersturmbandführer,* and a superb athlete who won a medal at the 1936 Olympics in Berlin. (In fact, his father participated in Hitler's Olympics like millions of others, as a spectator at the opening ceremonies.)[16] During *Kristallnacht,* the elder Peymann went along with his buddies but made sure the stores of his Jewish friends were protected by guards. Peymann's mother was "half an antifascist." As a family they "knew that there were camps where Jews were killed." They "got the soap from Auschwitz." Nevertheless, they hoped to win the war. About his directing style he confessed: "I am a rapist [*ein Vergewaltiger*] in rehearsals." If actors didn't understand what he wanted them to do, he used "the most uncompromising, brutal force. It ranges from shouting to murder. I break their resistance and I know that other directors do the same." President Waldheim, bragged Peymann, was so taken by his staging of *Richard III* that he attacked him from behind with a kiss on his neck to congratulate him in front of everybody in the Imperial Café. There was nothing Peymann could do about it, "it was a rape." He claimed he never spoke out against Waldheim for the simple reason that criticism by a leftist would only win the president more support among conservatives.[17]

The veteran members of the Burgtheater demanded Peymann's dismissal. Even the actors Peymann brought with him from Bochum and his loyal dramaturg and co-artistic director, Hermann Beil, publicly distanced themselves from him in open letters. The conservative press raged about the "de-Austrification" of culture. The prominent Jewish critic Hans Weigel warned about a "pogrom against Austrians" by the "new German cultural occupiers."[18] There were calls not only for Peymann's dismissal from the Burg but also for his expulsion from Austria. The suggestion weirdly echoed the *Ausländer raus* (foreigners out) campaign waged by the conservative press in response to the increase in the numbers of Eastern European refugees, which anticipated the fall of communism a year and a half later.

Peymann, tall, blond, and aggressive, with a clipped North German accent, came to represent leftover Austria's nemesis, the embodiment of the Teutonic genius and megapower bestowed, coveted, and envied by the minirepublic. If Austrians who clamored against the presence of impoverished foreigners from the "Balkans" could be accused of reviving the violent Pan-German sentiments of the First Republic, their simultaneous virulent attacks against Peymann, the "Prussian" usurper of Austria's cultural throne, served as an odd alibi. It would deflect all suspicions of a Germanophile anti-Semitism, which always loomed within Austria's theatricalized politics of classic Freudian *Verdrängung und Verdichtung* (repression and condensation).

Peymann apologized to the company for the transgressions in the interview, but he insisted that he was assigned the mission to "fundamentally" change the Burgtheater by the Austrian government. That task required drastic measures. Peymann's defenders, among them some of the colleagues he singled out for attack, pointed out that the interview was not to be taken as a standard conversation; it should be understood as a performance, an (in part) justifiably enraged, deeply moralistic comedy act. Underlying the blatant untruths and outrageous insults was his willingness to expose himself in the process. All in all, the interview was a daring theatrical project and must be judged as such.

Bernhard apparently did so judge it. One of the publications to which the journalist submitted his interview sent it to Peymann for verification. Peymann claimed he forwarded it unopened to Bernhard for his comments. Bernhard (who was exempt from Peymann's attacks) immediately responded that this was his best interview ever. What was indeed most remarkable about it was the degree to which Peymann, the impassioned Bernhard director, had internalized the dramaturgy of his favorite playwright. Bernhard was quite agitated about Peymann's subsequent public apologies. About two weeks after the interview came out, Peymann agreed to a televised discussion along with some of his accusers. "When I say something, I don't take it back," Bernhard fretted on the day of the live program. "The Viennese are out there en masse, their knives drawn, and he is running right into them." He was concerned about the extended rehearsals for *Heldenplatz*. To his mind, some of the actors were already overrehearsed and all spontaneity was drained out of them.[19] Close friends recall that his health was rapidly deteriorating and he was afraid he would not live to see the production.[20] The opening was postponed to November 4, which brought it close enough to another heavily symbolic date, the fiftieth anniversary of *Kristallnacht*, November 9.

The controversy escalated into a political showdown. As a state-run institution, the Burgtheater fell under the governance of the Socialist minister of culture and education. The majority Socialist Party came under attack both from the rightist members of their junior partners in the coalition government, the Freedom Party, most prominent among them the outspoken Jörg Haider, and by the opposition, the conservative People's Party. An embittered culture war was waged against several state-sponsored artistic projects that dealt with the commemoration of the Anschluss.

Over the summer, a drawn-out dispute over the site for a controversial Holocaust monument came to a boil. The scandal-prone artist and respected professor Alfred Hrdlicka had been commissioned to create a memorial sculpture, and Helmut Zilk, the Socialist mayor of Vienna, approved a location in the center of the city. Hrdlicka, a former Stalinist and furious opponent of Waldheim, was notorious for his wildly contradictory politics and offensively provocative rhetoric. His sculpture depicts a man scrubbing the pavement with a toothbrush. It was to be part of a larger "monument against the war." The stone was to come from the infamous quarry at the Mauthausen concentration camp. Its designated location was an open space left by the World War II bombing of an apartment building, which was occupied at the time of the attack by about two hundred civilians, none of whom survived. The building was so thoroughly destroyed that no efforts were made to retrieve the dead. Situated in the historic imperial compound of cultural institutions and administrative wings across from the State Opera and in full view of the legendary Hotel Sacher, the space was kept as a gaping memorial to the event. Conservatives insisted that it should be preserved as such, to honor the innocent victims of Hitler's war. They suggested another, less exposed site, near the former Gestapo offices. Advocates of the monument's central location de-

nounced the proposal as a ploy to keep the memorial completely out of sight —
yet another thin disguise of the persistent anti-Semitism.

The public outrage over the mayor's approval, staged most prominently
in the *Kronenzeitung,* was ostensibly against Hrdlicka's Stalinist past and the
offensive "ugliness" of his design. It barely concealed the disconcerting sentiments simmering close to the surface. There was the shamed anger over such
in-your-face open-air exposure of the unspeakable humiliation of Jews at the
hands of their fellow citizens, and there was the lingering resentment that the
memory of (non-Jewish) civilian war casualties was eclipsed, if not put in question, by the sculpture.

In this already charged atmosphere, passages from the top-secret rehearsal script were leaked to the press and caused another explosion. The
conservative papers, led by the *Kronenzeitung,* leaped at the opportunity to
let Austrians know that, according to Bernhard,

> conditions today really are the same
> as they were in thirty-eight
> there are more Nazis in Vienna now
> than in thirty-eight
> it'll come to a bad end
> you'll see
> it doesn't even take an extra-sharp mind
> now they're coming out again
> of every hole
> that's been sealed for over forty years
> just have a conversation with anyone
> after a short time it turns out
> he's a Nazi [21]

The nation was

> a cesspool stinking and deadly
> the church a worldwide perfidy
> . . .
> the president a cunning lying philistine
> an altogether depressing figure
> the chancellor a crafty peddler selling off the state" (367)

Furthermore, Austria itself was

nothing but a stage
on which everything has gone to rack and ruin
a population of extras bound by mutual hate
six and a half million people left all alone
six and a half million retards and maniacs
who keep screaming for a director at the top of their voice (359)

Jörg Haider was among the first to voice his outrage. Ironically, Haider's rhetoric against Socialists and the academic elite sounded quite like Bernhard's. The handsome, aggressively nativist heir to vast expanses of "Aryanized" land taken from Jews, Haider had come to represent the blood-and-soil Austrian against the urban corruption and decadence associated with contemporary socialism. To serve his purposes, he shamelessly appropriated sources he would otherwise demonize. His headline battle cry against Peymann, "Hinaus mit diesem Schuft aus Wien," "Throw that gangster out of Vienna!" was borrowed from Karl Kraus, who had directed his recommendation against one of Vienna's most corrupt publishers.[22] Ten years later Haider declared himself an admirer of Bernhard in the shockingly successful campaign that won his party a partnership in a coalition government with the People's Party and forced the long-ruling Socialists into the opposition. Appropriating Bernhard's rhetoric against the state's subsidizing of the arts, he extended it to the universities. Both budgets were drastically slashed by the new administration.

Haider's was not the only voice to call for the prohibition of the production of *Heldenplatz*. The head of the conservative People's Party, Vice Chancellor Alois Mock, suggested that the play came under the *Wiederbetätigungsverbot* (the prohibition against the resumption of Nazi activities). Therefore the Socialist minister of education and culture, Hilde Hawlicek, had the duty to prevent its production by a state institution under her jurisdiction. If the play were to be put on at all, it should be independently produced, without taxpayer support. Peymann should be fired immediately.

President Waldheim offered his idea of the freedom of art: "The freedom of literature and art is one of democracy's great achievements. But if this freedom is abused in the manner of *Heldenplatz*, then the Burgtheater is not the place for that sort of production. I consider this play a crude insult to the Austrian people and therefore reject it."[23] Edward Busek, the cultural spokesman of the conservative People's Party, recommended a boycott of the performances. Austria's grand old Socialist, the former chancellor Bruno Kreisky, advised from his retirement residence in Mallorca that such denigrations of Austria must not go unchallenged. By contrast, the Socialist chancellor in office, Franz Vranitzky, one of the targets of *Heldenplatz*, let it be known that "certain people simply can't offend me."[24] Vienna's Socialist cultural councilor, Ursula Pasterk, who had been instrumental in the hiring of Peymann, was concerned about Austria's image abroad. In the wake of Waldheim's election and the Hrdlicka debacle, the attacks against a play that focused on a returning Jewish family might be perceived as yet another example of Austria's festering anti-Semitism. Conservative voices countered that to have a Jewish character insult Austria in such outrageous terms might well incite anti-Semitic reactions.

What came as perhaps the biggest shock in the preproduction culture war was that the diatribes against Austria, familiar though they were to the readers of any Bernhard novel or play, were spoken not just by any cranky old man but by a Jew.

In Bernhard's Austrian anthropology, Jews were Austrians; simple as that—and as complicated. They spoke the language that constituted Bernhard's *Homo austriacus:* outside the context of the play it simply seemed the language of hate, bitterness, and disgust, a language of cynical nihilism. It also echoed the sentiments voiced in blue-collar beer halls and cheap taverns—places traditionally associated with the rise of fascism.

On November 2, two days before opening night, an arson attack by a neo-Nazi on another controversial Holocaust memorial in Graz, the capital of Styria, seemed to validate Bernhard's most dismal views of Austrians and further aggravated the situation. The German-born American conceptual artist Hans Haacke covered a landmark statue of the Virgin, one of the oldest monuments in the center of the city, to give it the appearance of an obelisk. The statue was originally erected in 1669 to commemorate victory over the Turks. Haacke's construction was a replica of the obelisk the Nazis constructed around the statue in 1938 with the inscription "Und ihr habt doch gesiegt" (And you were victorious after all). It was a quote from Hitler's speech when he declared Graz "the city of resistance" in a ceremony at the foot of the obelisk on June 25, 1938. His statement referred to the defeated Nazi putsch in 1934 in which the Austro-fascist chancellor Engelbert Dollfuss was assassinated. Below the quote Haacke listed the victims of the "victorious" Styrian Nazis: 300 murdered gypsies, 2,500 murdered Jews, 8,000 political prisoners murdered or died in prison, 9,000 civilians killed in the war, 12,000 missing, 27,000 soldiers killed. On November 2 the obelisk was set on fire, and the statue beneath suffered heavy damage. The arsonist was identified as a thirty-six-year-old unemployed man who moved in neo-Nazi circles. The instigator was a well-known sixty-seven-year-old Nazi.[25] Journalists saw parallels between the arson attack and the responses to the opening of *Heldenplatz* two days later. By contrast, the editor in chief of the local edition of the *Kronenzeitung* pointedly criticized the Catholic Church for allowing the wrapping of the statue, thus letting politicians spend the taxpayers' money on such a shameful project. As part of its advertising campaign under the motto "Uns ist nichts zu heiss" (Nothing is too hot for us), the *Kronenzeitung* designed flyers about various controversial issues that were not too hot for its editors. On the day *Heldenplatz* was to open, the flyer inserted in the *Kronenzeitung*'s national edition featured the provocative motto with a photomontage of the Burgtheater going up in flames.

On the same day, the (generally liberal) paper *Der Standard* published a scathing pre-opening review of the text by Peter Sichrovsky with the incendiary headline "Storm Heldenplatz." Raging against a "theater director from Bochum who, with the help of an Austrian writer, makes a Viennese Jew bark like a German shepherd," Sichrovsky holds up as a model the prevention in 1985 of the first performance in Frankfurt of Rainer Werner Fassbinder's *Die Stadt, der Müll und der Tod* (The City, Garbage, and Death), in which an author also used a Jew "to get rid of his own prejudices."[26] Fassbinder's play depicts the corruption of personal, professional, and political morals in Frankfurt in a grotesque spectacle that features, among other lost or depraved urban creatures, a ruthless real estate dealer who is Jewish. The play was written in 1975 in response to a controversial urban renewal project in Frankfurt, where Fassbinder headed the Theater am Turm (the same experimental theater that launched Peymann's career). Large residential blocks were being torn down to make way for high-rise office buildings. Fassbinder left the theater before his play could be produced. Suhrkamp Verlag published it a year later. Joachim Fest, who later wrote a biography of Hitler, attacked it as a glaring example of anti-Semitism on the left. Suhrkamp stopped the publication of the text. In protest against the 1985 Frankfurt premiere, members of Frankfurt's Jewish community, led by Ignatz Bubis (who was a prominent real estate broker in Frankfurt at the time the play was written), occupied the stage on opening night and prevented the performance from going on. The eminent Jewish critic Marcel Reich-Ranicki, a survivor of the Warsaw ghetto, was among the journalists who came to the theater for opening night. Like most people who knew the play, he found it tasteless, ugly, and badly written. Nevertheless, he pleaded unsuccessfully with the demonstrators—among them survivors of concentration camps—to clear the stage to allow the show to go on. (There was one closed performance for a small audience of critics.) The play and the prevention of its presentation raised many sensitive questions about political responsibility versus artistic freedom and the performative force of negative representation, even though Fassbinder's dark, cynically distorted vision was an all-out critique of contemporary Germany. Above all, there was the question whether Fassbinder and his play were anti-Semitic. Despite its obvious shortcomings, Reich-Ranicki considered the play "a characteristic document of its time. No matter how clumsy and brutal, it signals a German problem: the relationship to Jews. It was at that time that the expression 'end of closed season' came up, meaning it was time now to speak about Jews openly and honestly—open season, in a word."[27]

Fassbinder's play has little in common with *Heldenplatz* other than the storm of raw, conflicting emotions that both unleashed over the representation of Jews. The former introduces an offensive caricature that exaggerates the worst sort of anti-Semitic clichés in a grotesque hell of the marginalized, all products and themselves the producers of social clichés that they either exploit or succumb to in the dog-eat-dog world of contemporary capitalism. The latter presents the archetypal Bernhard character. That he is Jewish does not differentiate him from his literary predecessors in their love-hate relationship with Austria. His railing against anti-Semitism, though contextualized by his Jewishness, nevertheless introduces anti-Semitic rhetoric to make his point. The highly emotional controversies about both plays were over the performative force of clichés, which might prove stronger than the intended critique of the circumstances that produced them. Ironically, those fears and the rhetoric in which they were vented actually reinforced the reality of the world the plays depicted.

Sichrovsky argued that the sit-in on Frankfurt's stage to prevent the opening of Fassbinder's play did not amount to official censorship. Rather, it was a "successful prevention." He recommended the same treatment for *Heldenplatz*. The son of Jewish parents who had emigrated to England, Sichrovsky is best known for his book *Born Guilty*, for which he interviewed the children of Nazi criminals. Ironically, his play *Das Abendmahl* (The [Last] Supper) was also commissioned by Peymann for the commemorative year of 1988 and ran in the repertoire of the Burgtheater's smaller house, the Akademietheater. It deals with a young Viennese couple, she the daughter of Holocaust survivors and he the son of Nazi criminals, trying to come to terms with their legacy. The supper at which they had planned to introduce their parents to each other comes to a strained Strindbergian climax in a violent orgy of sexual-political denigration.

Like his play, Sichrovsky's premature critique of *Heldenplatz* was fraught with personal anguish. Fixated solely on the text's reiterative, deliberately outrageous language, he missed the point of Bernhard's performative strategies. Bernhard's texts uncannily get everyone to speak out and reveal himself, observed Wendelin Schmidt-Dengler, the doyen of Austrian literary studies.[28] Instead, Sichrovsky insists on psychological realism and sociological subtleties.

> The play never mentions why Jews returned to Vienna at all; what the real problems are and have been, what it meant to return to this city where they grew up and which drove them away. Nothing about the thoughts and feelings about their children and how they should live after the war. Nothing about how they tried to start all over despite the past and how, in sentimental moments, they call this city home again. Nothing about the disappointments, burdens, and problems of that generation, the desperate efforts to perhaps feel at home again somewhere — nothing, not a word about any of it.[29]

Sichrovsky's call for censorship set off another round of heated arguments. He was not the only one to suggest the prevention of the Fassbinder opening as a useful model. Nevertheless, he wired the Burgtheater company and its director his best wishes for opening night. Remarkably, in 1996 Sichrovsky joined forces with Jörg Haider. As a member of Haider's Freedom Party, Sichrovsky became a representative at the European Parliament in Brussels.

On November 4, 1988, a front-page headline in the *Kronenzeitung* ominously announced "*Heldenplatz* Premiere: Burgtheater under Police Protection." And in fact, 200 policemen, in plainclothes and uniform, were positioned around all entrances before curtain time. The Communist daily *Volksstimme* (People's Voice) pointed out that all this happened a few days before the fiftieth anniversary of *Kristallnacht*. Right-wing activists dumped a pile of horse manure in front of the theater's main entrance in response to the *Theatermacher*'s oversaturated signifier.

All fired-up expectations to the contrary, the four-hour opening performance, occasionally disrupted by hecklers and catcallers, finished without major incident. In the final moment the eruption of *Sieg Heil* choruses in Frau Schuster's head eerily segued into the shouting, booing, clapping, and whistling from the audience. The dissonant ovation lasted forty-five minutes. It was crowned by the appearance onstage of Peymann and Bernhard, hands joined, their arms raised triumphantly. Uncannily, their victorious pose framed by clamoring masses conjured up the semiotics of the historic Heldenplatz scenario.

Things went back to normal in subsequent sold-out performances. Audiences reverted to their tradition-bound behavior in the theater's gilded, plush decor, their respectful silence or discrete boredom hiding perhaps a bit of disappointment that that was all there was to what had promised to be such a scandal.

All in all, the production was anticlimactic after the drama that led up to it. The media war seemed to have drained the critics' resources for dealing with the play. Local reviewers sounded rather listless. Most agreed that this wasn't Bernhard's best play, that it occasionally ran on empty rhetoric and overextended repetitions. German journalists and reviewers supported that view. From their perspective, all of Austria could be viewed as a stage. Not only the play, the whole country was the thing they watched with bemused amazement and a degree of envy that a theatrical event could elicit such passion and trigger such a revealing political spectacle.

Peter Iden, the respected critic of the *Frankfurter Rundschau,* objected most of all to the play's central message: that suicide was the only answer to the persistent anti-Semitism and Austria's irredeemable corruption. Even a society that elected Waldheim could not, must not accept this. Iden questioned Bernhard's sweeping generalization of anti-Semitism in a "frenzy of excessive invectives" as a problematically unpolitical gesture. The attempt to promote political insight onstage, like politics itself, demanded "a critical approach that is capable of differentiating," which Bernhard, caught up in his "all-inclusive anger," sorely lacked. His play's inflated gestures of hatred remain merely literary gestures. Ridiculing the uselessness of any attempt to counter the situation while reveling in its own pessimism, he sent a message that was nothing if not reactionary. If Sichrovsky expected psychological revelations, Iden asked for a political *Lehrstück*. He also was concerned that some Jews might feel exploited by Bernhard's strategy of protecting himself against the scandal his offensive language would inevitably provoke "by putting the words of his renunciation [of Austria] into the mouth of a Jew." Nonetheless, Iden conceded that Bernhard and Peymann's politics of the theater must be credited with exposing the utterly debased state of public discussion in Vienna.[30] Another German critic pondered with some envy why it was impossible to imagine such excitement over a theatrical event in Berlin in 1988, on either side of the wall, since "the German reality is no less stupid than the Austrian. But what [German] author clashes with it so painfully and what theater would follow him—and where is the audience that would be able to take the theater's authority so seriously?"[31]

In an interview with the Austrian *Standard,* Heiner Müller suggested that Bernhard fulfilled the task of a government employee:

> He writes as if he had been hired by the Austrian government to write against Austria. It should qualify him for a pension. Offending Austria is a public service. He should really be employed and paid by the government for his service. It's exactly what Austria needs and the two complement each other fabulously: Thomas Bernhard's subjective sense or feeling or consciousness that he is fighting against Austria and Austria's interest in being fought, in the theater. . . . The scandal [about *Heldenplatz*] is exactly what the government needs. A scandal fulfills the crucial function of a safety valve. It distracts from all the questions that should really be asked in Austria. . . . The disturbance can be articulated that loudly and clearly because it doesn't disturb. That's part of it all, it's all part of the way things work. They wouldn't work without it. Austria without Thomas Bernhard wouldn't even get mentioned in any West German paper. It's almost like an advertisement. There is no better advertisement for Austria than Thomas Bernhard. There would be no Austria in the West without Bernhard.[32]

Müller knew what he was talking about. An outspoken critic of both Germanys, the controversial East German playwright fulfilled an important function for his government as he came to be the most significant writer to emerge from his homeland, then still divided.

The reviewer of the Jewish paper *Jüdische Rundschau,* Robert Singer, strongly defended Bernhard's choice of Jewish characters. To him, the predicament of the Schuster family "paints a moral picture that is terrifyingly close to reality." This critic applauded Bernhard for

> intentionally choosing a Jew as the mouthpiece of his concentrated accusation, because most Austrians still want Jews to be ducking and servile, acknowledging their intermittent toleration with humble gratitude. Jews who speak out and ask for their legal rights in everyday life, who preserve their autonomous identity and confront their surroundings with self-confidence, frighten most Austrians. They want to get to know "the Jews" only in terms of many prejudices: as killers of Christ, Bolshevik revolutionaries, degenerate global conspirators, and greedy, ambitious vultures. What a shock, what blasphemous provocation, to have a Jew sit in judgment on Austria!
>
> But Thomas Bernhard does not abuse Jews and does not stir up anti-Semitism. Rather, he emphatically brings to public attention the conflict that has been smoldering over many centuries, between Jews who acquiesce without resistance and those who actively fight for full acceptance.[33]

As the star critic Benjamin Henrichs put it:

> The people of *Heldenplatz,* who wrangle with Austria, attack Austria, and want to destroy it with their hate arias (which would also destroy their contradictory love for it), are Austrian Jews. As Jews they have the rights of the victims. As Austrians they speak the language of the perpetrators. . . . It is Bernhard's courageous, albeit diabolical construction that he doesn't show the Jews in roles that would move even the hard-core anti-Semite to tears. Not as decent, cultured, attractive victims of barbarity, but — oh my God — as Austrians. And what Austrians hate, whoever they are, is always also who they are and will be, to the end of their days.[34]

Henrichs's observations come closest to the uneasiness that was at the heart of the controversy, over the othering of Jews in contemporary Austria. How and by whom is this otherness constructed and perceived? Against the charges of a persistent anti-Semitism, non-Jewish survivors of World War II and their "born guilty" heirs, starved for sympathetic acknowledgment of their suffering, insist that it is the victims who keep prolonging their privileged status. This sort of argument was also the most incendiary aspect of Fassbinder's grotesquely exaggerated portrayal of the "rich Jew" who openly exploits the taboo status of Jews in post-Holocaust Germany for his corrupt business deals.

The ambivalent perception—and self-perception—of Jewish otherness in contemporary Vienna made for the panicked anticipation of *Heldenplatz*. It permeates the writing itself. In a telling moment Robert reminds his niece Olga how she had recently been spat on by a passer-by in the street, "because she is a Jew [*weil sie Jüdin ist*]." Her sister suggests it might have been a mistake. Robert replies:

> what kind of mistake was it supposed to be
> does someone spit on somebody in the street
> when he doesn't even know the person
> just because he can see she is a Jew [35]

Robert's strong reaction suggests that he is still traumatized by the past, by the enforced wearing of the yellow star. His response raises more questions. What and, perhaps more to the point, who distinguishes Olga as Jewish? Is it Robert? If so, what are his feelings about her apparently obvious racial traits? Or is it the author's own Freudian slip?

Another controversial production in the Burgtheater's commemorative season, which ran in repertory with *Heldenplatz,* Peter Zadek's staging of *The Merchant of Venice,* provoked the question of the visualization of "Jewishness." Zadek's Shylock, brilliantly performed by Gert Voss, is a seductive Wall Street yuppie, indistinguishable from Antonio and his buddies—so much so that Portia's question at the beginning of the trial, "Who is the Jew?" makes sense as genuine confusion rather than a calculated setup. When she mistakes Antonio for Shylock, Antonio recoils for an instant but quickly recovers his professional composure. The moment captures the boundaries of tolerance in contemporary culture. In her concern over the production's aim of "neutralizing" Shylock, the German scholar Ruth von Ledebur raises the question "What happens to our understanding of Shylock if he is disrobed of his 'Jewishness'?" [36]

Disturbingly, Bernhard's play asks what "Jewish" means in post-Holocaust Vienna. Does it stand as a metaphor, a generalized slur on all otherness? Has Robert internalized this perception? Has he, a descendant of Vienna's quasi-aristocratic elite, so thoroughly absorbed the racism of his class that it undermines his own sense of identity? When Anna suggests that her sister was spat on by mistake, is she saying that she was mistaken for another "other" and thereby implying that this makes the act less odious? Typically, Bernhard drops ambiguous hints and leaves their elaboration to the individual spectator. Honi soit qui mal y pense.

Frau Zittel points out to the maid that all of Vienna's superintendents are Yugoslavs.[37] In the city's postimperial multicultural hierarchy they represent the lowest level of undesirable foreigners, the latest victims of discrimination and hate crimes. There are several references to the fact that the Schusters' Heldenplatz apartment has been bought by a "Persian." In the contemporary context of global politics, Iranians represented the latest deadly wave of anti-Semitism. The sale of the apartment eerily iterates the confiscation of Jews' apartments by the Nazis. To the nativist readers of the *Kronenzeitung*, Persians are all nouveaux riches oil magnates, eyed with envy and suspicion. Frau Zittel, who fits the profile of the typical *Kronenzeitung* reader, refers to the buyer as "a Persian rug dealer" who "wants everything changed / next week he wants to start with the renovations" (211). Her remark underscores the buyer's foreignness with a sense of superiority she might well have picked up in the upper-class household. Robert speaks of a "Persian businessman / who lives in Istanbul" (388). His dry appraisal signals the intellectual and bourgeois elite's condescension toward commerce (the play moves into Chekhovian territory here). Presumably the apartment will no longer be the permanent home of its inhabitants, but a business address for its Iranian buyers. After all, OPEC's headquarters are in Vienna. The change represents a threat to the city's historic identity, the loss of tradition and stability to foreigners. There is a sad irony that it is a Jew returned from emigration who clings to Vienna's cultural identity. Robert, by his own admission, is an avid reader of the *Kronenzeitung* and similar sensationalist papers, even though he reviles them for the dreck they publish. Some of it may have rubbed off on him, along with the cheap print. Master and servant are contaminated by the same language.

Bernhard shrewdly plants his cryptic clues. Brief and fleeting as they are, their strategic placement and subtle variations set off an excess of possible meanings. It was the excess that constituted the drama beyond the play, the scene of what Lacan calls "the real," where all of Austria's repressed past and rejected present came into play. That which has been excluded from the symbolic order, from language, enters the real as excess. In Bernhard's linguistically based understanding of his native culture, the excess reenters the symbolic as exaggeration.

Olga tells her uncle that he exaggerates when he claims that his brother didn't expect

> that after the war the Austrians
> were more venomous and much more hostile to Jews
> than before the war
> nobody expected that
> He walked as he himself said so often
> straight into the Viennese trap
> He forgot
> that Vienna and all of Austria for that matter
> is home to falsehood and deceit (373)

As he talks himself more and more into rage, he insists that

> If they had their way
> if they were honest
> they'd love to do what they did fifty years ago
> they'd gas us (375)

Is Bernhard's exaggerated rendering of Austrian anti-Semitism the excess of his own rejection of his early schooling in Nazi ideology, later transformed into Catholic indoctrination, which he described so vividly in his memoirs? Does Bernhard deal with or rather reveal inadvertently, in the deliberate play of sliding signifiers, his own racial ambivalence? Buried in Robert's exasperated verbosity is the information that his father purchased the family country villa, which originally included forty acres of meadowlands, in 1917 (404). The date passes by so quickly that it is easy to overlook its significance: that was during World War I, a period of desperate hunger and poverty all across Europe. Those who pick up on the anti-Semitic stereotype of Jews as speculators and wartime profiteers might take this as an indication of Bernhard's bias or find themselves caught in their own.

Bernhard plays a volatile game with his audience in which it is never quite clear who reveals what about whom. This deliberately cultivated ambiguity is at the heart of Austrian culture. It is not shown in the dramatic action on-stage or in nuanced dialogue that leads to mutual insights, recognition, and character development. Bernhard puts the action inside the language; it is the mechanism that animates the characters from the outside and links them to each other and to the world outside the theater, which is kept in motion by the same linguistic apparatus. Therefore, the actual drama shifts easily to the culture at large, and the line between the real and the theatrical get blurred or can no longer be distinguished at all. Fredric Jameson's prison-house of language turns out to be a theater where Bernhard's mise-en-scène sets up a powerful if cynical model of the performative force of language, or more to the point, citation.

For a long first act, Frau Zittel, the Schusters' housekeeper, talks of the dead Professor Schuster, ironing his shirts and airing out his suits while the maid, Herta(!), polishes his many shoes and interjects a few words here and there. Mostly Frau Zittel quotes the professor. Fifty-seven times she punctuates her citations with "he said" or "the professor said" or "he explained to me"; sometimes "he yelled" some self-explanatory remark. A few times she quotes herself quoting someone else to yet another person. More often than not the professor's quotes are orders—how to iron and fold shirts (meticulously), which books to read to her aging mother (Gogol and Tolstoi), which artists to like (Glenn Gould). He also shared with her his preference in underwear (cotton, not silk), his attitude toward his wife, his children ("my two academic monster daughters . . . my daughters are my gravediggers/and my son Lukas is a loser" [324–35]), his brother ("he hated everybody except his brother Robert" [317]), Frau Zittel herself ("The only one worth anything is you Frau Zittel/he once said/that's something one doesn't forget" [329]), and insights about himself ("I am not a good man/he always said" [316]), the world at large ("One day China will rule the world Frau Zittel/the Asian age has already begun" [316]), and tips for self-protection ("You have to watch out for cripples Frau Zittel he said/above all blind people" [337]). These certainly are not original remarks, let alone noble pronouncements; they are commonplaces, many of which play into widespread fears and prejudices, not unlike the columns in the populist press. In Frau Zittel's quotations Professor Schuster emerges as a misanthropic tyrant, and clearly she is utterly devoted to him. Her monological performance re-presents, quite literally, not only the professor but the shaping of her identity through him. Later we learn from his daughter that Frau Zittel converses in English with the professor. Unlike his wife, a socialite and heiress with no interest in intellectual pursuits, his housekeeper even reads Descartes and Spinoza. Her interactions with the maid make it clear that she has also internalized the language of domination, by which she had been conditioned by her mother. "There was nothing but orders/and all the orders were executed," she says of her upbringing (331).

The second act introduces Josef's daughters, Anna and Olga, and later his brother Robert as they walk home through the Volksgarten after the funeral. In the usual Bernhard fashion, there is a dominating voice and a more reticent listener. First Anna is the obsessive speaker; she has fully absorbed her father's language and, so it seems, his personality. It is never quite clear whether it is her father who comes to life in her speech—a familiar device in plays that unite relatives who remember a deceased family member—or whether her obsessive quotations and reiterations, particularly of his traumatized perception of a Nazi-infested Vienna, continue to produce her own identity. The theatrical context further emphasizes the fluidity of performed identity. Does her performance represent her father or constitute herself? And who is who here, anyway? In the Burgtheater production the part of Anna was performed by Kirsten Dene, who had originated many Bernhard roles of similar obsessiveness. Residues of her previous work as Bernhard characters feed into her present role and merge with the audience's memory of her performances. *Ritter, Dene, Voss* was running in repertory with *Heldenplatz.* So was *Der Theatermacher,* in which Dene plays the title character's ailing wife. In his final season at the Burg Peymann restaged *Eve of Retirement* with the original Stuttgart cast, which included Kirsten Dene as the paralyzed younger sister, Clara. Ten years after Bernhard's death the productions with their aging casts had accumulated exactly the sort of Burgtheater dust Bernhard admiringly ridiculed in *Elisabeth II:*

> That's what makes the Burgheater so appealing
> it has been gathering dust for so long
> and it will continue to gather dust
> any attempt at airing out the Burgtheater
> will only stir up a new orgy of dust[38]

Now Bernhard himself had become one of the anachronistic institution's nostalgically treasured fixtures.

Much of Bernhard's dramaturgy is based on deliberate appropriations from other plays. In his review of *Heldenplatz,* Benjamin Henrichs pointed out the Chekhovian names of the two sisters, Olga and Anna. Uncle Robert introduces an entire Chekhovian scenario. He refuses to protest the construction of a highway right through the apple orchard and forest that are part of the family's old summer home. Some of the professor's features make him a distant relative of Hofmannsthal's charmingly inefficient upper-class Viennese in his plays *Der Schwierige* and *Der Unbestechliche*. A frail elderly gentleman of the old school, he is resigned to a changed world that is plunging toward its own destruction, a development he bemoans for its irreversibility:

> the world today is one ugly
> and thoroughly stupid world
> deterioration everywhere
> devastation all around
> I'd rather not wake up anymore (360)

Sad, infuriating as it may be, the situation also validates his own passivity. He counteracts his outer paralysis with time-honored Viennese rhetoric, a potent blend of *raunzen* and *nörgeln*. The former translates into the Yiddish kvetching, a national pastime; the latter is grumbling or nagging, a much-practiced survival skill, well known to Karl Kraus, who created the character of the Grumbler in juxtaposition to the Optimist, the two lead figures in his mammoth drama *The Last Days of Mankind*.

> I'm not exerting myself
> but every now and then I permit myself to get worked up
> so that you won't think
> I'm already dead quite the opposite
> the body is gone but the mind is reborn
> every single day

uncle Robert explains to his nieces, as he gets himself duly worked up.

> . . . those so-called socialists made national socialism
> possible today
> they didn't only make it possible
> they brought it on
> These so-called Socialists who hadn't been Socialists
> for half a century
> are the true gravediggers of Austria
> that's the horror of it the daily disgust with it
> the Socialists are the exploiters today
> the Socialists have Austria on their conscience
> the Socialists are the gravediggers of this nation
> the Socialists are the capitalists of today

the Socialists who aren't Socialists
are the real criminals against this nation
compared to them the Catholic rabble is insignificant (364–65)

His diatribe against the ruling party appropriates rhetorical devices of both fascist propaganda and Catholic litanies (and served Jörg Haider as a useful primer). Robert's assertion that "the Viennese are Jew haters / and they always will be Jew haters / for all eternity" (356) could have been voiced as easily by a diehard anti-Semite. In *Eve of Retirement* Bernhard had put similar pronouncements about Germans in the mouth of an unreformed Nazi. Bernhard's method of characterization demonstrates the hideous mechanism of language conventions, what Judith Butler calls "an echo of others who speak as the I." [39]

The more he talks himself into his hate speeches against Austrians, the more he asserts himself as an Austrian. It is a vicious cycle: the more Robert gets caught up in his own obsessions about Austrian anti-Semitism, the more he derives his identity as a Jew in reaction to it, which gets him even more wrapped up in his Austrianness. The language that "speaks as" Robert is "a language whose historicity includes a past and a future that exceeds that of the subject who speaks." [40] Perhaps this is why, according to all reports of the Burgtheater opening of *Heldenplatz*, a hush fell over the audience during Robert's scene. Perhaps it was the hush of recognition in Althusser's sense: of the speech act that brings the subject into being, here the audience as Austrians, who participate in the same language and the excess of its historicity.

While cynics suspected that Peymann masterminded even the preproduction culture war, leaks and all, Bernhard's text effectively demonstrates the performative force of the theater beyond the theater. His minimalist dramaturgy highlights the compulsively repetitive speech acts of one or two dominant figures and the submissive silence of their partners. Forced into the roles of listening subjects (in Foucault's double sense of *assujettissement*), they find themselves in a predicament that reflects the audience's (equally enforced) function within the performance. Playing along, as it were, the audience constitutes itself within the power dynamics set up onstage. The stage dynamics do not just reflect but activate anew the power dynamics outside the theater. The public response first in the media and finally inside the theater is the continuation of Bernhard's dramaturgy of *assujettissement*, the subjectivization of the public sphere, in the sense of both constituting and subordinating the subject. The generative force of Bernhard's speech acts staged in his speakers is as much activated by the constitutive grammar of authority as the culture he exposes and reaffirms with masochistic pleasure. Against the utopian notion of a theater that can change society Bernhard constructs a theater that brings out its reactionary resilience. In that sense, the production, in the end, fitted in perfectly with the Burgtheater's historic mission as a guardian of its society's culture and tradition. Not surprisingly, then, shortly after his death Bernhard, the reviled anti-Austrian, could smoothly be appropriated as a national treasure. The scandals made for nostalgic lore, while his will provided the script for the show to go on.

Epilogue
The Drama of the Will

Whoever manages to write a pure comedy on his deathbed has achieved the ultimate success.

—Thomas Bernhard, *"Ungenach"*

TWO DAYS BEFORE HIS DEATH, BERNHARD, weakened by his illness, was driven by his brother and personal physician, Dr. Peter Fabjan, from Gmunden to Salzburg, where he revised his will in the presence of a notary public. He designated Dr. Fabjan his sole heir and co-executor of his will, together with his publisher, Dr. Siegfried Unseld. The income from royalties on his work was to be divided equally between his brother and sister.

On the day of his death he called some of his close friends to say good-bye, among them a duchess and the television journalist Krista Fleischmann. In the evening he went to one of his favorite local inns, polished off a second helping of his favorite dish, drank his favorite cider, and took home an extra bottle to wash down his final medication in the company of his brother. He died in his Gmunden apartment at seven o'clock the following morning. His brother was with him all the time. The funeral was carefully planned in advance. It was to happen secretly, with only his brother and sister in attendance. Dr. Fabjan persuaded him to let his stepfather join them. He was to be buried at Grinzing cemetery in the grave of Frau Hede and her husband. His death was to be announced only after the funeral. On February 16, four days after his death, a local undertaker managed to enter the underground garage of the Gmunden apartment unobserved and spirited his body to Vienna. The funeral took place immediately upon its arrival at the cemetery, one hour ahead of schedule, to avoid any advance notice.

As planned, the news of Thomas Bernhard's sudden death caught everyone by surprise. His will hit the country like a bombshell. It stipulated that

> nothing I published during my lifetime, or any of my papers wherever they may be after my death, or anything I wrote in whatever form, shall

be produced, printed, or even just recited within the borders of the Austrian state, however that state defines itself, for the duration of the legal copyright.

I emphasize expressly that I do not want to have anything to do with the Austrian state and that I reject in perpetuity not only all interference but any overtures in that regard by this Austrian state concerning my person or my work. After my death, not a word shall be published from my papers, wherever such may still exist, including letters and scraps of paper.[1]

Bernhard had talked to his brother about his "posthumous literary emigration."[2] He certainly had rehearsed the staging of an unexpected will over and over again in his narratives. His literary wills, usually made by émigrés, accelerated, for better or worse, the disintegration of the Austrian homeland together with its ambiguous cultural legacies. Bernhard's will, consistent with the main theme of his work, transfers the fate of the land onto the body of his texts. As part of Austria, it must disintegrate with Austria, together with his physical body, which was to be buried in Austrian soil. Rather than an act of revenge against Austria, his will constituted a self-sentence that was far more cruel than anything the state could have plotted against him. As a literary gesture it evokes the ancient drama of Antigone, whom Creon ordered to be entombed alive. The role for which Bernhard was best remembered as an acting student at the Mozarteum was the Speaker in the Mozarteum's production of Anouilh's *Antigone.* His will set the stage for the body of his work to be buried alive in the tomb that was Austria as he had described it all along. Antigone hanged herself in the tomb. In the final analysis, Bernhard's will, like his death, amounts to a suicide plot.

If his physician brother eased the physical process of dying, he finally did not allow Bernhard's literary death in Austria. As this book has shown, the performative impact of Bernhard's language asserts itself fully only in ongoing interaction with his native culture. Hermann Beil, Bernhard's longtime dramaturg. argued persuasively that by 2059, when the copyright would expire, several generations would have grown up without the lived experience of a Bernhard play in performance. His language, banished from the Austrian stage, cut off from the mutually enlivening contact with its native speakers for seventy-five years after his death, would ring dead as well. Ten years after his death, Bernhard's heirs lifted the ban on productions of his plays in Austria—

just in time for Peymann to bring down the curtain on his reign at the Burg with a Bernhard premiere.

The surprise announcement of a new Bernhard production did not reveal its title, only the number 205, to indicate that this would be the 205th premiere during Peymann's tenure. It turned out to be a trilogy of dramalettes written for Peymann over the years, staged by his protégé, twenty-eight-year-old Philip Tiedemann, under the title *Claus Peymann Buys Himself a Pair of Pants and Takes Me to Lunch*. The first piece, *Claus Peymann Leaves Bochum and Goes to Vienna as Artistic Director of the Burgtheater*, had been commissioned by Peymann in his last year as artistic director of the Bochum Theater and was originally staged as part of his farewell party there. It depicts Peymann and his secretary, Christiane Schneider, packing his suitcases with Bochum dramaturgs and actors, discarding others (some of them corpses), and unpacking them at the Vienna Burgtheater. The second, which lent the production its title, was written in 1986 for the annual special edition of *Theater Heute* to highlight the playwright and his director's triumphant, if highly controversial, initial season at the Burgtheater.

The third piece, *Claus Peymann and Hermann Beil on Sulzwiese*, was first published in *Die Zeit* in 1987. It marked the high point of their tenure in Vienna. The response to the production signaled a turning point in the Bernhard reception. He was perceived now as a quirky old man, a dear if nutty relative, whom one visited occasionally to reminisce and keep up family traditions. When Peymann opened his first season at the Berlin Ensemble in January 2000 with a revival of *The Ignoramus and the Madman*, also staged by Tiedemann, the response was similar. His strenuously absurdist production was greeted with benevolent ho-hums and some nostalgic giggles over the familiar jokes of a weird old family friend who wasn't quite up to the challenges that faced the new Berlin. Peymann's faithful revival of his original staging of *Eve of Retirement* turned out to be another case in point.

The drama of Bernhard's will had more political acumen than his plays in performance. The debate over its circumvention continues today. Ethical concerns were politicized when Bernhard's heirs sought the financial assistance of both federal and local governments to alleviate the costs of maintaining the estate, which includes substantial real estate and the cataloging of the papers in a style appropriate to the nation's foremost *Dichter*. The nation, in turn, had discovered its *Dichter* as a profitable tourist attraction. Every village he passed through or named in his writing scrambled for its own Bernhard festival. Modest country inns offer showings of the rooms he slept in, with anecdotes provided by employees who shined his shoes or served him breakfast or answered a casual question. The Austrian countryside was combed for Bernhard spots. His landscape descriptions turned out to be far more naturalistic than he was willing to admit. To everyone's surprise, his pathologized geography yielded wholesome vistas that fitted the aesthetics of glossy tourist brochures.

Ten years after his death Bernhard's fury onstage appeared quaintly theatrical, aglow in a nostalgic halo. His literary output was safely enshrined in academe. His verbal inventions entered the vernacular. His hyperbole set the norm. His peculiar syntax provided a safe conduit for the venting of outrage. His name came to serve as the trademark of the self-righteously disaffected. (At the time of this writing the Bernhard heirs fight the founding of a Bernhard Prize in France for writers who challenge the status quo.)

Bernhard's speech acts modified the German language. It is hard to resist the infectious rhythm of his phrasing. In Austria, the performative force of his speech continues to impact the country's collective psyche. His language, its use and misuse after his death, has become an active part, for better or worse, in the production of his native culture, which in turn keeps producing him.

Chronology

<table>
<tr><td>1931</td><td>February 9, Nicolaas Thomas Bernhard is born in Heerlen, Holland.
In the fall his unwed mother, Herta Bernhard, takes her son to her parents in Vienna, then returns to the Netherlands to work as a maid.</td></tr>
<tr><td>1932</td><td>Herta Bernhard returns to Vienna.</td></tr>
<tr><td>1935</td><td>Herta's parents move with Thomas to Seekirchen, near Salzburg. Herta Bernhard stays in Vienna.</td></tr>
<tr><td>1936</td><td>Herta Bernhard marries Emil Fabjan in Seekirchen. Thomas starts elementary school in Seekirchen.</td></tr>
<tr><td>1937</td><td>Emil Fabjan finds work as a hairdresser in Traunstein, just across the border from Salzburg. Herta brings her son to Traunstein.</td></tr>
<tr><td>1938</td><td>Birth of Peter Fabjan.
Grandparents move to village of Ettendorf, near Traunstein.</td></tr>
<tr><td>1939</td><td>Alois Zuckerstätter, who lives in Berlin, denies paternity of Thomas. He and Thomas are summoned for blood tests to determine the veracity of Zuckerstätter's claim.</td></tr>
<tr><td>1940</td><td>Birth of Susanne Fabjan.
Alois Zuckerstätter commits suicide by inhalation of gas in his Berlin apartment.</td></tr>
<tr><td>1941</td><td>Court of Traunstein, informed of Zuckerstätter's "accidental death," stops paternity investigation.
Thomas is sent to an institution for difficult children in Thuringia.</td></tr>
<tr><td>1942</td><td>Thomas returns to Traunstein and continues school there.</td></tr>
<tr><td>1943</td><td>Thomas is confirmed in a Catholic church in Traunstein.</td></tr>
<tr><td>1944</td><td>Thomas attends a boy's school in Salzburg and stays in a home for boys.
After the heaviest air raids on Salzburg, he returns to Traunstein.</td></tr>
<tr><td>1945</td><td>Back in Salzburg, he now lives at the Johanneum, a Catholic home for boys, and attends Gymnasium.</td></tr>
<tr><td>1946</td><td>His parents with his brother and sister and the grandparents move into a small apartment in Salzburg, where he joins them. Herta's brother Harald Rudolf also moves in with them.</td></tr>
</table>

1947   Thomas drops out of school and goes to work as an apprentice in
            a grocery store.

1948   Continues his apprenticeship and takes private singing lessons in
            Salzburg.

1949   First hospitalization for pleurisy, Salzburg Landeskrankenhaus.
            Grandfather Johannes Freumbichler dies.

            Bernhard is moved to a tuberculosis sanitarium in Grossgmain,
            near Salzburg. He later suspects that he actually caught tubercu-
            losis from the other patients there.

            Two weeks after his release he is admitted to the sanitarium of
            Grafenhof, where he stays from June 1949 to February 1950.

1950   Two days after his release from Grafenhof, on February 26, he is
            informed that his tuberculosis has recurred and he is admitted to
            the Salzburg Landeskrankenhaus.

            On June 13 he is readmitted to Grafenhof, where he stays until Janu-
            ary 1951. In that time he meets Hedwig Stavianicek (born Vienna,
            October 18, 1894).

            On June 16 he publishes his first short story, "Vor eines Dichters
            Grab," under the pen name Niklas van Herleen, in *Salzburger Volks-
            blatt*.

            Herta Bernhard dies, October 13.

1951   On January 11 he leaves Grafenhof and seeks outpatient treatment
            for his tuberculosis by a doctor in Salzburg.

            He publishes another story, "Die Siedler," signed Thomas Fabjan,
            in the *Demokratisches Volksblatt*.

1951–55   Works as a cultural journalist and court reporter for the Salzburg
            Demokratisches Volksblatt; contributions unsigned or signed
            Thomas Bernhard.

            Continues with singing lessons.

1952   Publishes his first poem, "Mein Weltenstück," signed Thomas
            Bernhard, in *Münchner Merkur,* September 20.

1955–57   Studies acting and directing at Salzburg's Mozarteum.

1956   The short story "Der Schweinehüter" (The Swineherd) published
            in the Viennese literary journal *Stimmen der Gegenwart.*

1957   *Auf der Erde und in der Hölle* (On Earth and in Hell), a volume of
            poetry, published by Otto Müller Verlag.

            In hora mortis and *Unter dem Eisen des Mondes* (Under the Steely

Moon), both collections of poems, published by Kiepenheuer & Witsch.

1959   *Rosen der Einöde* (Roses of the Wasteland) published by S. Fischer.

1960   *Köpfe* (Heads) (music by Gerhard Lampersberg) and the short plays *Rosa* and *Frühling* (Spring) produced in Maria Saal.

1962   *Die Irren* (The Insane). *Die Häftlinge* (The Inmates), two poems published privately in Klagenfurt.

1963   *Frost* published by Insel Verlag.

1964   *Amras* published by Insel Verlag.
        Receives Julius Campe Prize.

1965   Buys old farmhouse in Obernathal.
        Receives Bremen Literature Prize.

1967   *Verstörung* (Gargoyles) published by Insel Verlag.
        Has surgery at Vienna's Baumgartnerhöhe.
        Prosa, a collection of stories, published by Suhrkamp Verlag.

1968   Receives Austrian Förderungspreis für Literatur (Little State Prize for Literature).
        Ungenach published by Suhrkamp.

1969   *Watten* published by Suhrkamp; *Ereignisse* (a collection of early stories) published by Literarisches Kolloquium Berlin; *An der Baumgrenze* (a collection of short stories) published by Residenz Verlag, Salzburg.

1970   *Das Kalkwerk* (The Lime Works) published by Suhrkamp.
        Ein Fest für Boris (A Party for Boris) (dir. Claus Peymann) premieres at Hamburg Schauspielhaus; published by Suhrkamp.
        Receives Georg Büchner Prize.
        Films: *Der Italiener* and *Drei Tage,* dir. Ferry Raddatz.

1971   Publication of *Gehen* (Walking) (Suhrkamp); *Midland in Stilfs,* a collection of three stories (Suhrkamp); the film script of *Der Italiener* (Residenz Verlag).

1972   *Der Ignorant und der Wahnsinnige* (The Ignoramus and the Madman) (dir. Claus Peymann) opens at Salzburg Festival; published by Suhrkamp.

1973   Filming of *Der Kulterer.*

1974   *Die Jagdgesellschaft* (The Hunting Party) (dir. Claus Peymann) premieres at Burgtheater, Vienna; published by Suhrkamp.

Die Macht der Gewohnheit (Force of Habit) (dir. Dieter Dorn) premieres at Salzburg Festival; published by Suhrkamp.

1975   *Der Präsident* (The President) (dir. Claus Peymann) premieres at Burgtheater, Vienna; published by Suhrkamp.

Korrektur (Correction) and *Die Ursache* (The Cause) published by Suhrkamp.

1976   *Die Berühmten* (The Famous) (dir. Peter Lotschak) premieres at Burgtheater; published by Suhrkamp.

Minetti (dir. Claus Peymann) premieres in Stuttgart; published by Suhrkamp.

1978   *Immanuel Kant* (dir. Claus Peymann) opens in Stuttgart; published by Suhrkamp.

Der Atem, Der Stimmenimitator, and *Ja* published by Suhrkamp.

1979   *Vor dem Ruhestand* (Eve of Retirement) (dir. Claus Peymann) opens in Stuttgart; published by Suhrkamp.

Der Weltverbesserer (The World Improver) (dir. Claus Peymann) opens in Bochum; published by Suhrkamp.

1980   *Die Billigesser* (The Cheap Eaters) published by Suhrkamp.

1981   *Die Kälte* (In the Cold) published by Residenz Verlag.

Über allen Gipfeln ist Ruh (dir. Claus Peymann) premieres at Ludwigsburg, moves to Bochum; published by Suhrkamp.

Am Ziel (dir. Claus Peymann) premieres at Salzburg Festival; published by Suhrkamp.

Ave Vergil, a collection of early poems, published by Suhrkamp.

1982   *Ein Kind* (A Child), *Beton* (Concrete), and *Wittgenstein's Neffe* (Wittgenstein's Nephew) published by Suhrkamp.

1983   *Der Schein trügt* (Appearances Are Deceiving) and *Der Untergeher* (The Loser) published by Suhrkamp.

1984   *Der Schein trügt* (Appearances Are Deceiving) (dir. Claus Peymann) opens in Bochum.

Der Theatermacher and *Ritter, Dene, Voss* published by Suhrkamp.

Holzfällen (Woodcutters) published by Suhrkamp.

Hedwig Stavianicek dies, April 29.

1985   *Der Theatermacher* (dir. Claus Peymann) opens at Salzburg Festival.

Alte Meister (Old Masters) published by Suhrkamp.

1986   *Einfach kompliziert* (Simply Complicated) (dir. Klaus André) opens in Berlin.

Ritter, Dene, Voss (dir. Claus Peymann) premieres at Salzburg Festival.

Auslöschung (Extinction) published by Suhrkamp.

1987   *Elisabeth II* published by Suhrkamp.

1988   *Heldenplatz* (dir. Claus Peymann) opens in Vienna; published by Suhrkamp.

Der deutsche Mittagstisch (The German Lunch Table), a collection of dramalettes, published by Suhrkamp.

1989   *In der Höhe* (On the Mountain), written ca. 1959, published by Residenz Verlag.

Bernhard dies, February 12.

1990   *Claus Peymann kauft sich eine Hose und geht mit mir essen* (Claus Peymann Buys Himself a Pair of Pants and Takes Me to Lunch) published by Suhrkamp.

1998   *Claus Peymann kauft sich eine Hose . . .* (dir. Philip Tiedemann) premieres at Burgtheater, Vienna.

Notes

PREFACE

1. Thomas Bernhard, *Wittgenstein's Nephew,* trans. David McLintock (New York: Knopf, 1989), 21–22.

CHAPTER 1

Fool on the Hill

1. Thomas Bernhard, *The Cellar: An Episode,* in his *Gathering Evidence,* trans. David McLintock (New York: Knopf, 1985), 204.
2. Thomas Bernhard, *Wittgenstein's Nephew,* trans. David McLintock (New York: Knopf, 1989), 29.
3. *Verstörung* means perturbation; *Gargoyles* is the misleading title of the U.S. publication: Thomas Bernhard, *Gargoyles,* trans. Richard and Clara Winston (Chicago: University of Chicago Press, 1986).
4. Bernhard, *Wittgenstein's Nephew,* 45.
5. Ludwig Hevesi, *Otto Wagners Moderne Kirche* (1909), 249.
6. Elisabeth Koller-Glück, *Otto Wagner's Kirche am Steinhof* (Vienna: Tusch, 1984), 20.
7. Bernhard, *The Cellar,* 89. Hereafter page references are supplied in parentheses in the text.
8. Conversations with Sylvia Dahms and Wolfgang Bauer, respectively, Salzburg, August 1996.
9. Paul Wittgenstein, "Sprüche und Anekdoten," in Camillo Schaefer, *Hommage to Paul Wittgenstein* (Vienna: edition freibord, 1980), 75.
10. Bernhard, *Gargoyles,* 165–66. In her translation of the novel, Sophie Wilkins translates Schopenhauer's *Die Welt als Wille und Vorstellung* as *The World as Will and Idea.* I prefer *The World as Will and Representation,* which has been used by other translators of Schopenhauer.
11. Karl Kraus, *Die Letzten Tage der Menschheit* (Frankfurt am Main: Suhrkamp, 1986), 1: 9.
12. Bernhard, *Wittgenstein's Nephew,* 21.
13. Thomas Bernhard, "Claus Peymann and Hermann Beil on Sulzwiese," trans. Gitta Honegger, *Conjunctions* 31 (1998): 37–38.
14. Karl Ignaz Hennetmair, *Aus dem versiegelten Tagebuch: Weihnacht mit Thomas Bernhard* (Weitra: Bibliothek der Provinz, 1992). The full version followed in 2000: Salzburg: Residenz.

15. Louis Huguet, *Chronologie: Johannes Freumbichler, Thomas Bernhard* (Weitra: Bibliothek der Provinz, 1995), 471–72.
16. Conversation with Karl Ignaz Hennetmair; Ohlsdorf, Jan. 2, 1996.

CHAPTER 2
In Search of Family

1. Conversation with Wieland Schmied, Vorchdorf, Dec. 27, 1998.
2. Thomas Bernhard, *In the Cold,* in his *Gathering Evidence,* trans. David McLintock (New York: Knopf, 1985), 308.
3. Thomas Bernhard, *Correction,* trans. Sophie Wilkins (New York: Knopf, 1979), 170–171.
4. Caroline Markolin, *Thomas Bernhard and His Grandfather Johannes Freumbichler: Our Grandfathers Are Our Teachers,* trans. Petra Hartweg (Riverside, Calif.: Ariadne Press, 1993), 13. The material in the following paragraphs relies on this source.
5. Ibid., 25.
6. Ibid., 43.
7. Louis Huguet, *Chronologie: Johannes Freumbichler, Thomas Bernhard* (Weitra: Bibliothek der Provinz, 1995), 116.
8. Markolin, *Thomas Bernhard and His Grandfather,* 87; translation modified.
9. Ibid., 97.
10. The archival chronology differs from Bernhard's narrative, which cites his mother's pregnancy as the reason for her sudden departure—her wish to keep it secret from her parents and to avoid being ostracized by the Catholic village community. See Bernhard, *Gathering Evidence,* 25. However, if we count the months from her first job search in Holland until Bernhard's birth, we find it would have been too early for her to know that she was pregnant. See Huguet, *Chronologie,* 183.
11. Thomas Bernhard, *Extinction,* trans. David McLintock (New York: Knopf, 1995), 143.
12. Bernhard, *A Child,* 26.
13. Huguet, *Chronologie,* 191.
14. Ibid., 198, 202; see also Bernhard, *A Child,* 45.
15. Huguet, *Chronologie,* 221.
16. Bernhard, *In the Cold,* 306–7.
17. Huguet, *Chronologie,* 461.
18. Bernhard, *In the Cold,* 301.
19. Ibid., 59–60, modified. McLintock's translation omits the multiple stages within stages of Bernhard's memories.
20. *The Cellar* is the third part of the U.S. edition.
21. Bernhard, *In the Cold,* 306. Subsequent page references are supplied in parentheses in the text.

22. Huguet, *Chronologie,* 478–80.

23. Bernhard, *In the Cold,* 307.

24. Conversation with Susanne Kuhn, Grossgmain, June 1997; and Ingrid Bülau, Hamburg, June 1997.

25. Conversation with Dr. Peter Fabjan, June 1989.

26. Bernhard, *In the Cold,* 314. Subsequent page references are supplied in parentheses in the text.

27. "Über allen Gipfeln" is the opening of Goethe's poem "Ein Gleiches" (known in English as "Wanderer's Night Song II"). In Henry Wadsworth Longfellow's translation, the first two lines read: "O'er all hill-tops/is quiet now."

28. Thomas Bernhard, *Am Ziel* (Frankfurt am Main: Suhrkamp, 1981), 17–19. Subsequent page references are supplied in parentheses in the text.

29. In Ludwigsburg, June 25, 1982, directed by Alfred Kirchner. Peymann transferred the production to his Bochum theater the next season.

30. Thomas Bernhard, *Über allen Gipfeln ist Ruh* (Frankfurt am Main: Suhrkamp, 1981), 36.

31. Ibid., 21.

32. Bernhard, *The Cellar: An Escape,* in his *Gathering Evidence,* trans. David McLintock (New York: Knopf, 1985), 183. The horse blanket reappears in Bernhard's novel *Concrete:* "I had meant to begin working at four o'clock and now it was five. I was alarmed by this negligence of mine, or rather this lack of discipline. I got up and wrapped myself in a horseblanket, the horseblanket I had inherited from my grandfather, so tightly that I could hardly breathe. Then I sat down on my desk": trans. David McLintock (New York: Knopf, 1984), 7.

33. Bernhard, *Über allen Gipfeln ist Ruh,* 136.

34. Bernhard, *Extinction,* 146.

35. André Müller, *André Müller im Gespräch mit Thomas Bernhard* (Weitra: Bibliothek der Provinz, 1992), 85.

36. Bernhard, *Concrete,* 11.

CHAPTER 3
The Construction of Origin

1. Thomas Bernhard, *The Cellar: An Escape,* in his *Gathering Evidence,* trans. David McLintock (New York, Knopf, 1985), 339; see also Jens Dittmar, ed., *Aus dem Gerichtssaal: Thomas Bernhards Salzburg in den 50er Jahren* (Vienna: Verlag der österreichischen Staatsdruckerei, 1992), 259.

2. Louis Huguet, *Chronologie: Johannes Freumbichler, Thomas Bernhard* (Weitra: Bibliothek der Provinz, 1995), 288; Herbert Moritz, *Lehrjahre: Thomas Bernhard—Vom Journalisten zum Dichter* (Weitra: Bibliothek der Provinz, 1992), 12.

3. Huguet, *Chronologie,* 324.

4. See Dittmar, *Aus dem Gerichtssaal.*

5. See Moritz, *Lehrjahre,* 13.

6. Kurt Hofmann, *Aus Gesprächen mit Thomas Bernhard* (Vienna, 1988), 43.

7. See, for example, "Die drei Damen sind wieder da," *Demokratisches Volksblatt*, July 22, 1952, on the return of *The Magic Flute*.

8. Dittmar, *Aus dem Gerichtssaal*, 274.

9. Ibid., 141.

10. Huguet, *Chronologie*, 318–19.

11. Dittmar, *Aus dem Gerichtssaal*, 141.

12. Quoted in Jens Dittmar, ed., *Sehr gescherte Redaktion: Leserbrief-Schlachten um Thomas Bernhard*, 2nd ed. (Vienna: Österreichische Staatsdruckerei, 1993), 11–12.

13. Conversation with Wieland Schmied, Vorchdorf, Dec. 27, 1996.

14. Huguet, *Chronologie*, 314.

15. Quoted in Friedbert Aspetsberger, *Literarisches Leben im Austrofaschismus* (Königstein im Taunus: Anton Hain Meisenheim, 1980), 3–4.

16. Ibid., 4.

17. Robert Musil, *Tagebücher,* vol. 2 (Reinbeck bei Hamburg: Rowohlt, 1976), 1242.

18. Friedbert Aspetsberger, Norbert Frei, and Hubert Lengauer, eds., *Literatur der Nachkriegszeit und der Fünfziger Jahre in Österreich* (Vienna: Österreichischer Bundesverlag, 1984), 47.

19. Ibid., 52.

20. Günter Anders, *Die Schrift an der Wand: Tagebücher, 1941–1966* (Munich: C. H. Beck, 1967), quoted in Aspetsberger et al., *Literatur der Nachkriegszeit*, 58.

21. Victor Matejka: "Unverbesserlicher Judenknecht: Notizen zu meiner jüdischen Autobiographie," *Das jüdische Echo,* no. 27, September 1978, 1–10, quoted in Aspetsberger et al., *Literatur der Nachkriegszeit*, 58.

22. See Aspetsberger et al., *Literatur der Nachkriegszeit;* Karl Müller, *Zäsuren ohne Folgen: Das lange Leben der Literarischen Antimoderne Österreichs seit den 30er Jahren* (Salzburg: Otto Müller, 1990).

23. Klaus Amman, "Vorgeschichten; Kontinuitäten in der österreichischen Literatur von den dreissiger zu den fünfziger Jahren," in Aspetsberger et al., *Literatur der Nachkriegszeit*, 46–47.

24. See Elfriede Jelinek, "*Totenauberg* (Death/Valley/Summit)," trans. Gitta Honegger, in *DramaContemporary: Germany,* ed. Carl Weber (Baltimore: Johns Hopkins University Press, 1996).

25. See Gerhard Rühm, *Die Wiener Gruppe* (Reinbeck bei Hamburg: Rowohlt, 1967); Maria Fialik, *Der Charismatiker: Thomas Bernhard und die Freunde von einst* (Vienna: Löcker, 1992).

26. Ulrich Greiner, *Der Tod des Nachsommers* (Munich: Carl Hanser, 1979), 44.

27. Krista Fleischmann, *Thomas Bernhard: Eine Begegnung* (Vienna: Österreichische Staatsdruckerei, 1991), 195–96.

28. Conversation with Wieland Schmied, Vorchdorf, Dec. 27, 1996.

29. Thomas Bernhard, *Wittgenstein's Nephew,* trans. David McLintock (New York: Knopf, 1989), 18–19.

30. Conversation with Jeannie Ebner, Vienna, Aug. 3, 1996.

31. Conversation with Alfred Pfabigan, Minneapolis, November 1996.

32. Fleischmann, *Thomas Bernhard,* 53–54.

33. See Allan Janik and Stephen Toulmin, *Wittgenstein's Vienna* (New York: Simon & Schuster, 1973), chap. 3.

CHAPTER 4

The Staging of Kinship

1. Conversation with Wieland Schmied, Vorchdorf, December 1996.

2. Conversation with Klaus Gmeiner, Salzburg, December 1996.

3. Quoted in Maria Fialik, *Der Charismatiker: Thomas Bernhard und die Freunde von einst* (Vienna: Löcker, 1992), 54.

4. Wieland Schmied and Erika Schmied, *Thomas Bernhards Häuser* (Salzburg: Residenz, 1995).

5. Conversation with Ingrid Bülau, Hamburg, June 19, 1997.

6. None of these works has been published in English.

7. Conversation with Kiki Kogelnik, New York, Jan. 20, 1996. Kogelnik, a visual artist born in Carinthia, was an early participant in the Wiener Gruppe's presentations. She lived and worked in New York City until her death of breast cancer in February 1997.

8. Conversation with Christa Altenburg, Breitenschützing, June 10, 1997. Ingeborg Bachmann appeared as Maria in *Extinction.*

9. Conversation with Ingrid Bülau, Hamburg, June 19, 1997.

10. Ingeborg Bachmann, "Thomas Bernhard: Ein Versuch," in her *Gesammelte Werke* (Zürich: Piper, 1978), 4: 361–64.

11. Louis Huguet, *Chronologie: Johannes Freumbichler, Thomas Bernhard* (Weitra: Bibliothek der Provinz, 1995), 398, 416.

12. Ibid., 405.

13. See Sepp Dreissinger, ed., *Thomas Bernhard: Portraits. Bilder und Texte* (Weitra: Bibliothek der Provinz, 1992), 190; André Müller, *Andre Müller im Gespräch mit Thomas Bernhard* (Weitra: Bibliothek der Provinz, 1992), 55.

14. Jens Dittmar, ed., *Thomas Bernhard: Werkgeschichte,* 2nd ed. (Frankfurt am Main: Suhrkamp, 1990), 64.

15. Conversation with Thomas Bernhard, Obernathal, Feb. 27, 1981.

16. See Schmied and Schmied, *Thomas Bernhards Häuser,* 17.

17. Ibid., 18.

18. Bernhard to Gitta Honegger, Mar. 26, 1979.

19. Conversation with Karl Ignaz Hennetmair, Ohlsdorf, Dec. 12, 1996.

20. Thomas Bernhard, *Yes,* trans. Ewald Osers (London: Quartet Books, 1991), 31.

21. Hennetmair to Bernhard, Sept. 29, 1965, in *Thomas Bernhard–Karl Ignaz Hennetmair; Ein Briefwechsel,* ed. Hennetmair (Weitra: Bibliothek der Provinz, 1994), 37. Quotations from the following letters are from this source.

22. Bernhard to Hennetmair, Oct. 12, 1965, 45.

23. Hennetmair to Bernhard, Sept. 29, 1965, 37.

24. Bernhard to Hennetmair, Oct. 12, 1965, 45.

25. Bernhard to Hennetmair, June 27, 1967, 71.

26. Bernhard to Hennetmair, July 9, 1967, 87.

27. Conversation with Erika Schmied, Vorchdorf, Dec. 27, 1996.

28. Conversation with Karl Ignaz Hennetmair, Jan. 2, 1996.

29. Thomas Bernhard, *"The President" and "Eve of Retirement,"* trans. Gitta Honegger (New York: Performing Arts Journal Publications, 1982), 196-97.

30. Bernhard, *Yes,* 59-60. Subsequent page references are supplied in parentheses in the text.

31. Rudolf Brändle, who met Bernhard at the sanitarium in Grafenhof, in an interview with Krista Fleischmann. See Krista Fleischmann, *Thomas Bernhard: Eine Erinnerung* (Vienna: Österreichische Staatsdruckerei, 1992), 42.

32. Annemarie Siller-Hammerstein, quoted ibid., 28.

33. In Fialik, *Der Charismatiker,* 107.

34. Conversation with Victor Hufnagl, Vienna, September 1998.

35. Gerda Maleta, *Seteais* (Weitra: Bibliothek der Provinz, 1992), 20.

36. Ibid., 34.

37. Thomas Bernhard, *In the Cold,* in his *Gathering Evidence,* trans. David McLintock (New York: Knopf, 1985), 321-24.

38. Thomas Bernhard, *Gargoyles,* trans. Richard and Clara Winston (New York: Knopf, 1970), 74, 75.

CHAPTER 5
Fatherland/Mother's Body

1. Thomas Bernhard, *A Child,* in his *Gathering Evidence,* trans. David McLintock (New York: Knopf, 1985), 31.

2. *Amras* has not yet been published in English. It is unique among Bernhard's works. Although it anticipates many of his later themes, such as incest, madness, suicide, and extinction, it is more intimate, erotic, and transgressive than anything else he wrote.

3. These galleries, opened in 1976, display portraits formerly in Vienna's Kunsthistorisches Museum.

4. From the directives of Joseph II, quoted in Bernhard Grois, *Das Allgemeine Krankenhaus* (Vienna: Maudrich, 1965).

5. Thomas Bernhard, *Gargoyles,* trans. Richard and Clara Winston (New York: Knopf, 1970), 54-55. Subsequent page references are supplied in parentheses in the text.

6. Note that in German, the prison's location in Garsten (which does exist) evokes the milieu the name suggests, *garstig,* nasty.

7. Conversation with Susanne Kuhn, Grossgmain, June 11, 1997.

8. *Entweiblicht.*

9. Thomas Bernhard, *Amras* (Frankfurt am Main: Suhrkamp, 1964), 35–36. Subsequent page references are supplied in parentheses in the text.

10. Luce Irigaray "Plato's Hystera," in her *Speculum of the Other Woman,* trans. Gillian C. Gill (Ithaca: Cornell University Press, 1985), 243–364; see also Michelle Boulouse Walker's reading of Irigaray in her *Philosophy and the Maternal Body: Reading Silence* (New York: Routledge, 1998), chap. 1.

11. Thomas Bernhard, *The Lime Works,* trans. Sophie Wilkins (New York: Knopf, 1973), 6–7. Subsequent page references are supplied in parentheses in the text.

12. Thomas Bernhard, "Der Wahrheit und dem Tod auf der Spur," *Neues Forum* 15, no. 173 (May 1968): 349.

13. Conversation with Hilde Spiel, Vienna, June 1989.

14. From the program of the Burgtheater production of Thomas Bernhard's *The President,* 1975, as quoted in *Thomas Bernhard: Werkgeschichte,* ed. Jens Dittmar, 2nd ed. (Frankfurt am Main: Suhrkamp, 1990), 99.

CHAPTER 6
Native Son

1. Conversation with Karl Ignaz Hennetmaier, Ohlsdorf, Dec. 16, 1996.

2. Peter Handke: *Kaspar* and *Offending the Audience,* in his *"Kaspar" and Other Plays,* trans. Michael Roloff (New York: Farrar, Straus & Giroux, 1975), and *My Foot, My Tutor,* in his *"The Ride Across Lake Constance" and Other Plays,* trans. Michael Roloff in collaboration with Carl Weber (New York: Farrar, Straus & Giroux, 1976).

3. Conversation with Günther Bauer, Salzburg, Aug. 16, 1996.

4. Conversations with Klaus Gmeiner, Salzburg, Dec. 16, 1996; Sybille Dahms, Salzburg, Aug. 16, 1996; and Hedda Parson, Aug. 12, 1999.

5. See Hans Höller, *Thomas Bernhard,* 2nd ed. (Reinbek bei Hamburg, 1993), 99–100.

6. Thomas Bernhard to Deutsche Akademie für Sprache und Dichtung, open letter, *Frankfurter Allgemeine Zeitung,* Dec. 8, 1979, in *Thomas Bernhard: Werkgeschichte,* ed. Jens Dittmar, 2nd ed. (Frankfurt am Main: Suhrkamp, 1990), 126.

7. Thomas Bernhard, *Wittgenstein's Nephew,* trans. David McLintock (New York: Knopf, 1989), 66–67.

8. Dittmar, *Thomas Bernhard: Werkgeschichte,* 126.

9. Ibid., 117.

10. Hilde Spiel, "Das Dunkel ist Licht genug," *Theater Heute,* September 1972, 11.

11. Josef Kaut, *Die Salzburger Festspiele* (Salzburg: Residenz, 1982), 106–8.

12. Spiel, "Das Dunkel ist Licht genug," 9.

13. Ibid., 9–10.

14. Herbert Gamper, *Thomas Bernhard* (Munich: Deutscher Taschenbuch Verlag, 1977), 190.

15. Peymann's production was transferred to the Hamburg Schauspielhaus, where it opened in 1973.

16. Gamper, *Thomas Bernhard,* 201.

17. Conversation with Bernhard, Ohlsdorf, Feb. 27, 1981.

18. Ibid.

19. Telephone conversation with Robert Jungbluth, former general secretary of the Austrian State Theaters, Mar. 9, 1999

20. See Gitta Honegger, "Bernhard Minetti as Bernhard's *Minetti,*" *Theater* 30, no. 1 (2000): 49-55.

21. Henning Rischbieter, "Die Festspielkrise und das neue Kunstbetriebsstück Thomas Bernhards," *Theater Heute,* September 1974, 36.

22. Siegfried Melchinger, "Das Material ist die Wahrheit der Welt," *Theater Heute,* June 1974, 9.

23. *Die Zeit,* May 10, 1974, quoted in Dittmar, *Thomas Bernhard: Werkgeschichte,* 154.

24. *Die Zeit,* Aug. 2, 1974, quoted in Rolf Michaelis, "Verstörung und Totentänze: Thomas Bernhard's Stücke—Anfang und Schluss der Saison," *Theater Heute,* yearbook, 1975, 75.

25. *Theater Heute,* September 1974, 31.

26. *Frankfurter Rundschau,* July 31, 1974, quoted in Michaelis, "Verstörung und Totentänze," 75.

27. *Frankfurter Allgemeine Zeitung,* Aug. 10, 1974, quoted in Dittmar, *Thomas Bernhard: Werkgeschichte,* 158.

28. Michaelis, "Verstörung und Totentänze," 75.

29. Telephone conversation with Robert Jungbluth, Sept. 3, 1999.

30. Quoted by Peter von Becker in his "Eine Geschichte in 15 Episoden," *Theater Heute,* yearbook, 1978, 84.

31. *Frankfurter Rundschau,* May 23, 1975, quoted in Michaelis, "Verstörung und Totentänze," 75.

32. Michaelis, "Verstörung und Totentänze," 75-76.

33. Karl Kraus, *Die letzten Tage der Menschheit* (Munich: Deutscher Taschenbuch Verlag, 1964), 1: 5.

34. See Dittmar, *Thomas Bernhard: Werkgeschichte,* 172-75.

35. Louis Althusser, "Ideology and Ideological State Apparatuses," in his *"Lenin and Philosophy" and Other Essays,* trans. Ben Brewster (London: NLB, 1971), 163.

36. Dittmar, *Thomas Bernhard: Werkgeschichte,* 174.

CHAPTER 7
Playing Against

1. *Theater Heute,* yearbook, 1978, 159-61.

2. Jörg W. Gronius and Wend Kässens, *Theatermacher* (Frankfurt am Main, 1987), 114.

3. Ibid., 115.

4. Ibid. 116–17.

5. Henning Rischbieter, ed., *Theater im Geteilten Deutschland, 1945–1990* (Berlin: Propyläen, 1990), 200.

6. Manfred Görtemaker, *Geschichte der Bundesrepublik Deutschland: Von der Gründung bis zur Gegenwart* (Munich: C. H. Beck, 1999), 484.

7. Thomas Bernhard, *"The President" and "Eve of Retirement,"* trans. Gitta Honegger (New York: Performing Arts Journal Publications, 1982), 161.

8. Wolf-Rüdiger Baumann et al., *Die Fischer Chronik: Deutschland, '49–'99* (Frankfurt am Main: Fischer, 1999), 606–7.

9. Ernst Jäger, "Gerechtigkeit und Terror," *Theater Heute*, June 1976, 9–12.

10. Gronius and Kässens, *Theatermacher*, 125.

11. *Theater Heute*, October 1977, 1–3.

12. Stefan Aust, *Der Baader Meinhof Komplex*, 2nd ed. (Hamburg: Hoffmann & Campe, 1997), 646.

13. The funeral is the starting point for the German documentary *An Autumn in Germany*.

14. Gordon A. Craig, *The Germans*, 2nd ed. (New York: Penguin, 1991), 229; Rolf Hochhuth, *Juristen* (Reinbek bei Hamburg: Rowohlt, 1979).

15. *Der Spiegel*, May 22, 1978. All quotes from magazines and newspapers referring to the Filbinger case were taken from an exhibition: *50 Jahre geteiltes Deutschland*, Gropius Haus, Berlin, summer 1999.

16. Görtemaker, *Geschichte der Bundesrepublik Deutschland*, 588.

17. Rolf Hochhuth, *A German Love Story*, trans. John Brownjohn (London: Weidenfeld & Nicolson, 1980), 51.

18. Quoted in *Frankfurter Allgemeine Zeitung*, May 16, 1978.

19. *Die Welt*, Aug. 10, 1998; see also Hans Filbinger, *Die geschmähte Generation* (Munich: Universitas, 1987).

20. Thomas Bernhard, *The German Lunch Table*, trans. Gitta Honegger, *Performing Arts Journal* 6, no.1 (1981): 26–29.

21. Görtemaker, *Geschichte der Bundesrepublik Deutschland*, 484.

22. Karl Carstens, *Erinnerungen und Erfahrungen* (Boppard am Rhein: Harald Boldt, 1993), 91.

23. Görtemaker, *Geschichte der Bundesrepublik Deutschland*, 444.

24. Ibid., quoting Willy Brandt, *Begegnungen und Einsichten: Die Jahre 1960–1975* (Hamburg: Hoffmann & Campe, 1976).

25. Peter von Becker, "Die Unvernünftigen sterben nicht aus: Über Thomas Bernhards 'Vor dem Ruhestand,'" *Theater Heute*, August 1979, 4–6.

26. Baumann et al., *Die Fischer Chronik*, 633.

27. Bernhard, *"The President" and "Eve of Retirement,"* 204. Subsequent page references are supplied in parentheses in the text.

28. Von Becker, "Die Unvernünftigen sterben nicht aus," 4–6.

29. Benjamin Henrichs, "Herr Bernhard und die Deutschen," *Die Zeit*, July 13, 1979, 17.

30. Quoted by Peter von Becker in his "Die Unvernünftigen sterben nicht aus," 6.

31. Quoted in Gronius and Kässens, *Theatermacher*, 124.

32. Quoted in Peter Iden, *Theater des Widerspruchs* (Munich: Kindler, 1984), 230.

33. Thomas Bernhard in a letter to Henning Rischbieter, *Theater Heute*, yearbook, 1975, 29.

34. Thomas Bernhard, *Minetti*, trans. Gitta Honegger, *Theater* 30, no.1 (2000): 80.

35. See Gitta Honegger, "Bernhard Minetti as Bernhard's *Minetti*," *Theater* 30, no. 1 (2000): 48-55.

36. Quoted in *Theater Heute*, October 1980; reprinted ibid., November 1998, 17.

37. Ibid., 10.

38. Jonathan Kalb to Gitta Honegger; conversation with Klaus Völker, Berlin, summer 1999.

39. *Theater Heute*, November 1998, 28.

40. Quoted ibid., 27.

41. Conversation with Hermann Beil, Vienna, June 1997.

42. See Louis Althusser, "Ideology and Ideological State Apparatuses," in his *"Lenin and Philosophy" and Other Essays*, trans. Ben Brewster (London: NLB, 1971); and Judith Butler, "Althusser's Subjection," in her *The Psychic Life of Power* (Stanford: Stanford University Press, 1997).

43. Thomas Bernhard, *Amras* (Frankfurt am Main: Suhrkamp, 1964), 66-67.

44. *Eve of Retirement* was the only Bernhard play produced in East Germany during his lifetime. *Der Theatermacher* opened a few weeks after his death, also at the Deutsches Theater.

45. Reviews and dramaturgical material were generously made available to me by the archives of Deutsches Theater.

CHAPTER 8
Writing Wittgenstein

1. The letter was part of an exhibition in Ohlsdorf, June 1997.

2. Thomas Bernhard, *Prosa* (Frankfurt am Main: Suhrkamp, 1967), 39-40.

3. Thomas Bernhard, "Watten," in his *Die Erzählungen* (Frankfurt am Main: Suhrkamp, 1979), 252-320.

4. Thomas Bernhard, "Ungenach," in his *Die Erzählungen*, 185-251. Subsequent page references are supplied in parentheses in the text.

5. Jens Dittmar, ed., *Thomas Bernhard: Werkgeschichte*, 2nd ed. (Frankfurt am Main: Suhrkamp, 1990), 131-132.

6. Thomas Bernhard, "Walking," trans. Kenneth Northcott, *Conjunctions* 32 (1999): 14.

7. See Ludwig Wittgenstein, *Tractatus Logico-Philosophicus*, trans. C. K. Ogden (New York: Routledge, 1990), 66.

8. Norman Malcolm, "Memory and the Past," in *Knowledge and Certainty*, ed. Malcolm (Englewood Cliffs, N.J.: Prentice-Hall, 1963), 187.

9. Norman Malcolm, "Wittgenstein's *Philosophical Investigations*," ibid., 96.
10. David G. Stern, "The availability of Wittgenstein's philosophy," in *The Cambridge Companion to Wittgenstein*, ed. Hans Sluga and David G. Stern (Cambridge University Press, 1996), 452.
11. Thomas Bernhard, *Correction*, trans. Sophie Wilkins (New York: Knopf, 1979), 25. Subsequent page references are supplied in parentheses in the text.
12. "Der hier Eingetretene ist gezwungen, alles, was er vorher, bis zu dem Augenblick seines Eintretens in die höllersche Dachkammer gedacht hat, aufzugeben, abzubrechen, um von diesem Augenblick an nur mehr das in der höllerschen Dachkammer zulässige Denken zu denken, denn denken allein genügt nicht, um in der höllerschen Dachkammer auch nur die geringste Zeit überleben zu können, es mußte das Denken in der höllerschen Dachkammer sein, das Denken, welches sich ausschliesslich auf alles mit der höllerschen Dachkammer und mit Roithamer und mit dem Kegel Zusammenhängende bezieht" (Thomas Bernhard, *Korrektur: Roman*, 3rd ed. [Frankfurt am Main: Suhrkamp, 1988], 24).
13. Bernhard, *Correction*, 24.
14. Rucksacks make an anecdotal appearance in the Wittgenstein lore. After Wittgenstein's death, a friend, Mrs. David Ennals, reportedly took three rucksacks filled with his papers and, "alone, burnt them in Wales, Austria and Norway, as he had wished." The scene could have been staged by Bernhard. (Interview with Mrs. David Ennals, *Daily Telegraph*, quoted in "Availability of Wittgenstein's philosophy," 473.) It is quite likely that the story circulated in Austria and reached Bernhard through Paul or other rural neighbors and friends in the orbit of the Wittgenstein clan, who were visited frequently by the trustees of Wittgenstein's estate.
15. Thomas Bernhard, *Wittgenstein's Nephew*, trans. David McLintock (New York: Knopf, 1989), 21–22.
16. Interview with Theodor "Teddy" Podgorsky, one of Vienna's most popular actors and operetta stars, a friend of Paul who also knew Bernhard; Vienna, June 1997.
17. ORF Hörbilder, radio program, *Gott ist gleich 13*, Oct. 24, 1992. Author's archive.
18. Podgorsky interview.
19. Bernhard, *Wittgenstein's Nephew*, 63.
20. Christian Sapper, "Die Familie O'Donnell in Österreich," dissertation, Universität Wien, 1977.
21. Translation in Philip B. Miller, *An Abyss Deep Enough: The Letters of Heinrich von Kleist* (New York: Dutton, 1982).
22. Stern points out that "the source texts span a twenty-two-year period and are, in large part, still unpublished" ("Availability of Wittgenstein's philosophy," 449). Scholars translate the casually vernacular remark into the magisterial proposition "The special thing about progress is that it always looks greater than it really is" (Newton Garver, "Philosophy as grammar," in Sluga and Stern, *Cambridge Companion to Wittgenstein*, 167).

CHAPTER 9
Self-Projections/Self-Reflections

1. See Joseph Roach, *Cities of the Dead: Circum-Atlantic Performance* (New York: Columbia University Press, 1996).
2. Thomas Bernhard, *Der Italiener* (Salzburg: Residenz, 1971), 24.
3. Roach, *Cities of the Dead*, 14.
4. Louis Huguet, *Chronologie: Johannes Freumbichler, Thomas Bernhard* (Weitra: Bibliothek der Provinz, 1995), 376-77.
5. Bernhard, *Der Italiener*, 74.
6. Ibid., 75-76.
7. See Gitta Honegger, "Thomas Bernhard," *Partisan Review* 63, no. 3 (1996): 528-31.
8. Thomas Bernhard, *Der Kulterer* (Salzburg: Residenz, 1974).
9. *Neunzehn Deutsche Erzählungen* (Munich: Nymphenburger, 1963), 65-87; Thomas Bernhard, *An der Baumgrenze: Erzählungen* (Salzburg: Residenz, 1969), 7-53. See Jens Dittmar, ed., *Thomas Bernhard: Werkgeschichte*, 2nd ed. (Frankfurt am Main: Suhrkamp, 1990), 57-58.
10. In characteristic fashion, Bernhard borrowed the name from a writer, Hubert Fabian Kulterer, who edited the literary journal *Eröffnungen* and published some of Bernhard's early short stories. See Dittmar, *Thomas Bernhard: Werkgeschichte*, 57.
11. Bernhard, *Der Kulterer*, 100. Subsequent page references are supplied in parentheses in the text.
12. Ludwig Wittgenstein, *Tractatus Logico-Philosophicus*, trans. C. K. Ogden (New York: Routledge, 1990), 39: 2.1511 Thus the picture is linked to reality; it reaches up to it. 2.1512 It is like a scale applied to reality.
13. The complexity of his self-reflective approach is much more evident in his text than in the film. The story's deliberate pacing and minute observations lent themselves to the fashionable "art movie" aesthetic of the 1970s. In the film, the pondering voice-over seems a clumsy, pseudo-documentary device that overexplains the obvious.
14. Thomas Bernhard, *Der Stimmenimitator* (Frankfurt am Main: Suhrkamp, 1978); published in English as *The Voice Imitator*, trans. Kenneth J. Northcott (Chicago: University of Chicago Press, 1997).
15. Ibid., 101.
16. Bernhard, "Impossible," in *Voice Imitator*, 68.
17. Bernhard, "A Self-Willed Author," in *Voice Imitator*, 70.
18. Bernhard, "A Famous Dancer," in *Voice Imitator*, 45.
19. Bernhard, "The Prince," in *Voice Imitator*, 77.
20. Bernhard, "Prince Potocki," in *Voice Imitator*, 78.
21. Bernhard, "After You," in *Voice Imitator*, 86.

22. See Wendelin Schmidt-Dengler, "Thomas Bernhard und die Kulturschickeria," *Fidibus* 20, no. 1 (1992).
23. Thomas Bernhard, "The Auszügler," in *Voice Imitator,* 53.
24. Bernhard, "Inner Compulsion," in *Voice Imitator,* 9.
25. The voice imitator's predicament may have been inspired by an actual incident. The actor Hans Moser, Austria's Jimmy Durante, was known for his peculiar, instantly recognizable and frequently imitated speech mannerisms. When a contest for Moser imitators was held at a costume ball, Moser himself was among the masked participants, but didn't win. See Wendelin Schmidt-Dengler, *Der Übertreibungskünstler: Studien zu Thomas Bernhard* (Vienna: Sonderzahl, 1989), 55.
26. The play was commissioned by Claus Peymann for his Württembergisches Staatstheater Stuttgart, where it premiered Apr. 15, 1978.
27. Thomas Bernhard, *Immanuel Kant* (Frankfurt am Main: Suhrkamp, 1978), 89.
28. Ibid., 45.
29. Hermann Beil refers to Bernhard's later novels as *Rollenprosa* (conversation, Vienna, June 12, 1997).
30. Thomas Bernhard, *Yes,* trans. Ewald Osers (Chicago: University of Chicago Press, 1992).
31. See Wendelin Schmidt-Dengler, *"Ritter, Dene, Voss; Alte Meister,"* in his *Bruchlinien* (Salzburg: Residenz, 1995), 460-478.

CHAPTER 10
Theatermacher

1. "Monologe auf Mallorca 1981," in Krista Fleischmann, *Thomas Bernhard: Eine Begegnung* (Vienna: Österreichische Staatsdruckerei, 1991), 37. The interview is available on video cassette: *Thomas Bernhard — Eine Herausforderung: Monologe auf Mallorca"* (ORF; Verlag Österreich, 1991). Subsequent page references are supplied in parentheses in the text.
2. André Müller, "Der Wald ist gross, die Finsternis auch: Ein Gespräch mit Thomas Bernhard," *Die Zeit,* July 6, 1979.
3. Thomas Bernhard, *A Child,* in his *Gathering Evidence,* trans. David McLintock (New York: Knopf, 1985), 66.
4. Ibid., 60-61.
5. Rolf Michaelis, "Ohrfeigen vom Theaterschmierfinken," *Die Zeit,* Sept. 4, 1981, 19.
6. A study could be made of the vocabulary and formal twists that Bernhard introduced into the German language. *Naturgemäss* is the most prominent example. Literally "according to nature," it has been translated as "in the nature of things" or "naturally." A rarely used term before it was reenergized by Bernhard, it has become a journalistic cliché. Bernhard's many uses of un- as the prefix of nega-

tion and destruction, as in *Ungeist* (unspirit), encouraged lesser talents to forge new words from old opposites. His terse subtitles are routinely appropriated.

7. Peter von Becker, "Bei Bernhard: Eine Geschichte in 15 Episoden," *Theater Heute,* yearbook, 1978, 80.

8. Ibid., 84.

9. Michaelis, "Ohrfeigen vom Theaterschmierfinken," *Die Zeit,* Sept. 4, 1981, 19.

10. Thomas Bernhard, "Der pensionierte Salonsozialist," *Profil,* Jan. 26, 1981, 53. See also Dittmar, *Thomas Bernhard: Werkgeschichte,* 218–19.

11. Gerhard Roth and Peter Turrini, *Bruno Kreisky* (Berlin: Nicolaische Verlagsbuchhandlung, 1981).

12. Heinz Fischer, *Die Kreisky-Jahre: 1967–1983* (Vienna: Löcker, 1993), 146; Reinhard Sieder, Hans Steinert, and Emmerich Talos, eds., *Österreich 1945–1995* (Vienna: Verlag für Gesellschaftskritik, 1995), 679.

13. Haider's success was also due in large part to his aggressive but nevertheless justified criticism of the snug, if corrupt, ten-year coalition between the Socialist and People's parties. Ironically, his rhetoric against corruption and hypocrisy in government echoed Bernhard's chastening tirades.

14. Bernhard, "Der pensionierte Salonsozialist," 53.

15. Paradoxically, it would be the presidency of Waldheim (1986–92) that forced them finally to take responsibility for their past choices. As an S.A. officer in the Balkans, Kurt Waldheim acquiesced in Nazi assignments. His later denial of any personal responsibility and his claim that he had only done his duty was typical of the majority of Austrians, who duly elected him.

16. Quoted in Jens Dittmar, *Thomas Bernhard: Werkgeschichte,* 2nd ed. (Frankfurt am Main: Suhrkamp, 1990), 219.

17. Published also in Thomas Bernhard, *Der deutsche Mittagstisch* (Frankfurt am Main: Suhrkamp, 1988), 9–19.

18. Helmut Schödel, "Unsere Welt? Unser Theater," *Die Zeit,* Nov. 20, 1981.

19. Heinz Klunker, "Viele Stücke an einem Abend: Das Bochumer Spektakel," *Theater Heute,* January 1982, 10.

20. Günther Rühle, "Unsicherheit und welche Ziele: Ein Rückblick auf die deutsche Theaterspielzeit," *Theater Heute,* yearbook, 1979, 28–37.

21. Quoted in Peter Iden, "Was geht vor: Soziale Sicherung oder Ensemblebildung? Zum Bochumer Konflikt zwischen Peymann und der Bühnengenossenschaft," *Theater Heute,* March 1979, 3; reprinted in Peter Iden, *Theater des Widerspruchs* (Munich: Kindler, 1984), 230.

22. Quoted in Iden, *Theater des Widerspruchs,* 230.

23. Quoted in Peter von Becker and Michael Merschmeier, "Ich fürchte mich nicht vor Wien," *Theater Heute,* June 1984, 4.

24. Henning Rischbieter, ed., *Theater im geteilten Deutschland 1945–1990* (Berlin: Propyläen, 1990), 208.

25. Ibid.

26. Heiner Müller, "The Task," trans. Carl Weber, in *"Hamlet-Machine" and Other*

Texts for the Stage, ed. Carl Weber (New York: Performing Arts Journal Publications, 1984).

27. Uwe-K. Ketelsen, *Ein Theater und seine Stadt: Die Geschichte des Bochumer Schauspielhauses* (Cologne: SH Verlag, 1999), 301–3.

28. Thomas Bernhard, *Am Ziel* (Frankfurt am Main: Suhrkamp, 1981), 43.

29. Michaelis, "Ohrfeigen vom Theaterschmierfinken," 19.

30. Urs Jenny, "Rette sich, wer kann," *Der Spiegel,* Aug. 24, 1981.

31. Ralf Schnell, *Geschichte der deutschen Literatur seit 1945* (Stuttgart: J. B. Metzler, 1993), 521.

CHAPTER 11
Stand-Up Writer

1. Conversation with Elfriede Jelinek, Vienna, December 1994.

2. Elfriede Jelinek, "Der Einzige, und wir, sein Eigentum," in *Von einer Katastrophe in die andere: 13 Gespräche mit Thomas Bernhard,* ed. Sepp Dreissinger (Weitra: Bibliothek der Provinz, 1992), 159.

3. Quoted in Ralph-Rainer Wuthenow, *Paul Valéry* (Hamburg: Junius, 1997), 162.

4. Thomas Bernhard, "Drei Tage," in his *Der Italiener* (Salzburg: Residenz, 1971), 87. Jeannie Ebner talked about Bernhard's early reading of *Monsieur Teste* in a conversation with the author, Vienna, Aug. 3, 1996.

5. Wuthenow, *Paul Valéry,* 104.

6. Paul Valéry, *Monsieur Teste,* trans. Jackson Mathews, Bolingen Series no. 14 (Princeton: Princeton University Press, 1973), 127; my italics.

7. Ibid., 1.

8. Ibid., 78.

9. Wuthenow, *Paul Valéry.*

10. Paul Valéry, *Monsieur Teste,* trans. Achim Russer, Max Rychner, and Bernd Schwibs (Frankfurt am Main: Suhrkamp, 1995), 81.

11. Valéry, *Monsieur Teste,* trans. Mathews, 142. Subsequent page references are supplied in parentheses in the text.

12. E. M. Cioran, *Über das reaktionäre Denken,* trans. François Bondy (Frankfurt am Main: Suhrkamp, 1996), 91.

13. René Wellek, "Paul Valéry's Poetic Theory," in *Paul Valéry,* ed. Harold Bloom (New York: Chelsea, 1988), 119.

14. Quoted by Wuthenow, Paul *Valéry,* 111.

15. In the late 1950s, the original director of *Köpfe,* Hermann Wochinz, a frequent visitor at the Tonhof, also ran a highly regarded experimental theater in Vienna, the Theater am Fleischmarkt. He introduced the plays of the European avant-garde, among them Ghelderode, Ionesco, Beckett, and Genet. Designed by young artists who later gained international recognition as the Fantastic Realists, such as Josef Mikl, Wolfgang Hutter, Ernst Fuchs, and Wolfgang Hollegha, his productions attracted the local avant-garde and also Thomas Bernhard. Wochinz knew

Genet, who came to see his production of *The Maids,* which he translated and directed.

16. Thomas Bernhard, *Frost* (Frankfurt am Main: Suhrkamp, 1972), 7. Subsequent page references are supplied in parentheses in the text.

17. Thomas Bernhard, *Concrete,* trans. David McLintock (New York: Knopf, 1984), 3.

18. Ibid., 13-14.

19. Ibid., 103.

20. Arthur Schopenhauer, *The World as Will and Representation,* trans. E. F. J. Payne, 2 vols. (New York: Dover, 1966), 1: 322.

21. Ibid., 2: 99.

22. Ibid., 1: 331.

23. Peter F. Ostwald, *Glenn Gould: The Ecstasy and Tragedy of Genius* (New York: W.W. Norton, 1997), 331.

24. Ibid., 314.

25. Ibid., 165.

26. Thomas Bernhard, *The Loser,* trans. Jack Dawson (London: Quartet Books, 1992), 83. Subsequent page references are supplied in parentheses in the text.

27. Ostwald, *Glenn Gould,* 39.

28. Ibid., 43.

29. Thomas Bernhard, *Wittgenstein's Nephew,* trans. David McLintock (New York: Knopf, 1989), 63.

30. Ibid., 82.

31. Bernhard, *The Loser,* 81.

32. Arthur Danto, *The Philosophical Disenfranchisement of Art* (New York: Columbia University Press, 1986).

33. Bernhard, *Wittgenstein's Nephew,* 90-91.

34. *As You Like It,* Act II, scene 1.

35. Thomas Bernhard, *Woodcutters,* trans. David McLintock (New York: Knopf, 1987), 95.

36. See Jens Dittmar, "Bernhard gegen Lampersberg," in his *Sehr Gescherte Redaktion: Leserbrief-Schlachten um Thomas Bernhard* (Vienna: Verlag der österreichischen Staatsdruckerei, 1993), 134-43; Alfred Goubran, ed., *Staatspreis: Der Fall Bernhard* (Klagenfurt/Vienna: edition selene, 1997), 38-63.

37. Peter Buchka, "Nörgelei als Widerstand," *Süddeutsche Zeitung,* Oct. 10, 1982, quoted in Jens Dittmar, *Thomas Bernhard: Werkgeschichte,* 2nd ed. (Frankfurt am Main: Suhrkamp, 1990), 247-48.

38. Thomas Bernhard, *Woodcutters,* 173.

39. Martin Heidegger, *Holzwege* (Frankfurt am Main: Vittorio Klostermann, 1980), i.

40. George Steiner, *Martin Heidegger* (Chicago: University of Chicago Press, 1989), xix.

41. Wendelin Schmidt-Dengler, "Thomas Bernhard und die Kulturschickeria," *Fidibus* 20, no. 1 (1992): 73.

42. Conversation with Wolfgang Greisenegger, Vienna, July 1999.
43. Wendelin Schmidt-Dengler, *Bruchlinien* (Salzburg: Residenz, 1995), 468
44. Thomas Bernhard, *Extinction,* trans. David McLintock (New York: Knopf, 1995), 160-61.
45. Ibid., 161-62.
46. Ibid., 165.

CHAPTER 12
Questions of Genius

1. *Der Spiegel,* no. 33, 1983, 145-48.
2. Thomas Bernhard, *Histrionics* (the English title of *Der Theatermacher*), in *Histrionics: Three Plays,* trans. Peter Jansen and Kenneth Northcott (Chicago: University of Chicago Press, 1990), 254; translation modified. Subsequent page references are supplied in parentheses in the text.
3. Conversation with Christa Altenburg, Oct. 29, 1999.
4. Hilde Spiel, "Eine verkrachte Familienaffäre," *Frankfurter Allgemeine Zeitung,* July 31, 1970.
5. Ivan Nagel, "Hamlet oder der lebendige Leichnam: Oskar Werner spielt und inszeniert Hamlet im Salzburger Landestheater," *Süddeutsche Zeitung,* July 31, 1970.
6. Conversation with Christa Altenburg, Oct. 29, 1999.
7. Werner was well aware of the film's shortcomings. In a television interview shortly before his death the ravaged actor touchingly recounted his "conversations" with Mozart in the Salzburg house where the composer was born. He apologized to his idol for taking on the part, which he did only because he knew that Mozart's music would outlast any such travesty and that no film could ever do justice to his genius. See *Ich durfte am Tisch der Götter sitzen,* ORF video, 1984.
8. Thomas Bernhard, *The Loser,* trans. Jack Dawson (London: Quartet Books, 1992), 9.
9. Bernhard, *Histrionics,* 267; translation modified.
10. Hans Jürgen Syberberg, *Oskar Werner: Von letzten Dingen* (Munich, 1995), 34-35. Syberberg is probably best known in the United States for his film *Our Hitler.* His book is a searing indictment of the so-called Sixty-eighters, who in their zeal to purge themselves of their fathers' guilt destroyed even what was the best in German tradition. Syberberg speaks of the theater as taking on the church's function of granting absolution for the guilt of those who grant state support for the arts. In Syberberg's highly controversial view, Oskar Werner, the heir apparent to the great classic tradition, who was unwilling to adjust to the aesthetic and political dictates of the leading directors and critics of the 1960s, became their most tragic victim. In his book he reprints the reviews of some of the most influential critics, whom he accuses of making Werner the scapegoat of their politics.

11. Thomas Bernhard, *Der Theatermacher* (Frankfurt am Main: Suhrkamp, 1984), 83-85. I translate from this edition, because the English translation misses the vulnerability of the moment.

12. Bernhard, *Histrionics*, 246.

13. Conversation with Erika Schmied, November 1999.

14. Bernhard, *Der Theatermacher*, 58-59, 61.

15. Thomas Bernhard, *Ritter, Dene, Voss* (Frankfurt am Main: Suhrkamp, 1984), 61.

16. Thomas Bernhard, *Old Masters: A Comedy*, trans. Ewald Osers (Chicago: University of Chicago Press, 1992), 20. Subsequent page references are supplied in parentheses in the text.

17. See Wendelin Schmidt-Dengler, *"Ritter, Dene, Voss; Alte Meister,"* in his *Bruchlinien* (Salzburg: Residenz, 1995), 460-78.

CHAPTER 13
The Staging of a Nation

1. Hermann Beil, Jutta Ferbers, Claus Peymann, and Rita Thiele, eds., *Weltkomödie Österreich: 13 Jahre Burgtheater, 1986-1999* (Vienna: Szolnay, 1999), 2: 48.

2. Thomas Bernhard, *Elisabeth II* (Frankfurt am Main: Suhrkamp, 1987), 63-64. Subsequent page references are supplied in parentheses in the text.

3. "ORF Kulturjournal" (radio program, Aug. 29, 1984), quoted in Alfred Goubran, *Staatspreis: Der Fall Bernhard* (Klagenfurt: edition selene, 1997), 49.

4. Stefan Zweig, *The World of Yesterday* (Lincoln: University of Nebraska Press, 1964), 14-15.

5. Ernst Haeussermann, *Das Wiener Burgtheater* (Vienna: Fritz Molden, 1975), 15. Ernst Haeussermann headed the Burgtheater from 1959 to 1968.

6. Ibid. See also Verena Keil-Budischovsky, *Die Theater Wiens* (Vienna: Zsolnay, 1983), 106.

7. Keil-Budischovsky, *Die Theater Wiens*, 112-15.

8. Sigrid Löffler, "Der Reformist—Ein Revolutionär? Wie sich das Burgtheater zwischen 1976 und 1986 (nicht) verändert hat," *Theater Heute*, yearbook, 1986.

9. W. W. Yates, *Theatre in Vienna* (Cambridge: Cambridge University Press, 1996), 49-50. Schreyvogel is not to be confused with Friedrich Schreyvogl, the Burg's resident playwright during the Hitler years.

10. Keil-Budischovsky, *Die Theater Wiens*, 312-15; and Löffler, "Der Reformist—Ein Revolutionär?" 110-21.

11. Gertrude Obzyna, ed., *Burgtheater, 1776-1976: Aufführungen und Besetzungen von 200 Jahren* (Vienna: Ueberreuter, n.d.), 628.

12. Anton Pelinka et al., *Zeitgeschichte im Aufriss: Österreich seit 1918* (Vienna: Dachs, 1995), 35-36.

13. Zweig, *World of Yesterday*, 295-96.

14. Peymann must have regretted that he missed Haider 's stunning success in the 1999 elections by a couple of months. He had already moved to Berlin. In his first

year as artistic director of the Berlin Ensemble, he tried to transplant the Austrian drama in Brechtian soil with a series of Bernhard revivals. But by that time they had lost their sting. To everyone's surprise, they fitted comfortably in the classic canon. Peymann's "Austrian season" in Berlin, spearheaded by Bernhard and augmented with new plays by other Austrian writers, felt more like an ethnic festival than a confrontation with Austrian politics.

15. In 1979, Mann's *Mephisto* served as the starting point for a celebrated production by the Théâtre du Soleil, under the direction of Ariane Mnouchkine. At that time the novel was still banned in Germany. Gründgens' adopted son, Peter Gorski, initiated proceedings to prohibit its distribution. Mnouchkine's production and Istvan Sazabo's film adaptation led to the publication of the book in Germany in 1981. Publication is still prohibited de jure, but no longer de facto. See Peter Michalzik, *Gustaf Gründgens: Der Schauspieler und die Macht* (Berlin: Ullstein Buchverlag, 1999), 21-22.

16. Roland Koberg, *Claus Peymann: Aller Tage Abenteuer* (Berlin: Henschel, 1999), 26.

17. Interview reprinted as "Ich habe mir den Arsch nicht vergolden lassen," *Theater Heute*, July 1988, 2-9.

18. Weigel made the statement when he accepted an award by the Ministry of Education for "meritorious Austrians in foreign countries." See *Theater Heute*, July 1988, 3.

19. Conversation with Bernhard in Vienna, June 1988.

20. Conversation with Christa Altenburg, summer 1997.

21. Thomas Bernhard, "Heldenplatz," trans. Gitta Honegger, *Conjunctions* 33 (1999): 343. Subsequent page references are supplied in parentheses in the text.

22. *Kronenzeitung*, Oct. 12, 1988; quoted in Dramaturgie, Burgtheater Wien, ed., *Heldenplatz: Eine Dokumentation* (Vienna: Burgtheater, 1989), 44.

23. *Kurier*, Oct. 12, 1988; reprinted in Dramaturgie, *Heldenplatz*, 35.

24. Quoted in *Kronenzeitung*, Oct. 9, 1988; reprinted in Dramaturgie, *Heldenplatz*, 22.

25. See Pierre Bourdieu and Hans Haacke, *Free Exchange* (Stanford: Stanford University Press, 1994), 78-80.

26. Dramaturgie, *Heldenplatz*, 187.

27. Marcel Reich-Ranicki, *Mein Leben* (Stuttgart: Deutsche Verlags-Anstalt, 1999), 540-41. The debate about Fassbinder's play flared up intermittently over the years, though it was produced outside Germany without objections from Jewish communities. In the spring of 1999 Bubis, then president of the Zentralrat der Juden in Deutschland (Central Council of Jews in Germany), prevented another production in Berlin's Gorki Theater. Ten years after Germany's reunification, when the country was struggling with the economic problems of the former GDR, fear was voiced that amid the rising anticapitalist sentiment of East Germany's young people, with its concomitant anti-Semitic groundswell, a production of the play, aside from its tastelessness, would give the wrong signals. The play finally pre-

miered in Tel Aviv in April 1999 with acting students under the direction of Joshua
Löwenstein. This son of German Jews who had fled to Palestine before World
War II found the play a "manifesto against anti-Semitism" (*Der Tagesspiegel,*
Apr. 20, 1999).

28. See Wendelin Schmidt-Dengler, "Bernhards Scheltreden: Um- und Abwege der
Bernhard-Rezeption," in his *Der Übertreibungskünstler: Studien zu Thomas
Bernhard* (Vienna: Sonderzahl, 1989), 123-39.

29. Dramaturgie, *Heldenplatz,* 187.

30. Ibid., 280, quoting *Frankfurter Rundschau,* Nov. 7, 1988.

31. Ibid., quoting *Die deutsche Bühne,* Dec. 1, 1988.

32. Ibid., 283.

33. Ibid., 264, quoting *Jüdische Rundschau,* Nov. 10, 1988.

34. Ibid., 134, quoting *Die Zeit,* Oct. 21, 1988.

35. Bernhard, *Heldenplatz,* trans. Honegger, 374.

36. Ruth von Ledebur, "Reading Shakespeare's *The Merchant of Venice* with German
Students," in *Reading Plays: Interpretation and Reception,* ed. Hanna Scolnicov
and Peter Holland (Cambridge: Cambridge University Press, 1991), 124.

37. Thomas Bernhard, *Heldenplatz,* trans. Honegger, 323.

38. Bernhard, *Elisabeth II,* 30.

39. Judith Butler, *Excitable Speech: A Politics of the Performative* (New York: Routledge, 1997), 25.

40. Ibid., 28.

EPILOGUE

1. Quoted in Hans Höller, *Thomas Bernhard,* 2nd ed. (Reinbek bei Hamburg:
Rowohlt, 1993), 7.

2. Ibid.

Illustration Credits

Thomas Bernhard with mother. Photo: Thomas Bernhard Nachlassverwaltung.

Thomas Bernhard and stepfather. Photo: Thomas Bernhard Nachlassverwaltung.

Thomas Bernhard and Johannes Freumbichler. Photo: Thomas Bernhard Nachlassverwaltung.

Thomas Bernhard and Anna Bernhard. Photo: Thomas Bernhard Nachlassverwaltung.

Salzburg Cathedral after bombing. Photo: Archiv der Stadt Salzburg.

Thomas Bernhard, 1957. Photo: A Scope.

Mozarteum, *Antigone.* Photo: A Scope.

Mozarteum, *Enchanted Forest.* Photo: A Scope.

Mount Heukareck. Photo: Erika Schmied.

Contemporary view from Mönchsberg. Photo: Erika Schmied.

Bernhard's farmhouse. Photo: Erika Schmied.

A Party for Boris. Photo: Hamburg Theatersammlung; Archiv Rosemarie Clausen.

The Ignoramus and the Madman. Photo: Steinmetz; Archiv der Salzburger Festspiele. Copyright Salzburger Festspiele.

Force of Habit. Photo: Steinmetz; Archiv der Salzburger Festspiele. Copyright Salzburger Festspiele.

The Hunting Party. Photo: Elisabeth Hausmann; Archiv Burgtheater.

Minetti. Photo: Deutsches Theatermuseum Munich; Archiv Abisag Tüllmann.

Immanuel Kant. Photo: Deutsches Theatermuseum Munich; Archiv Abisag Tüllmann.

Eve of Retirement. Photo: Deutsches Theatermuseum Munich; Archiv Abisag Tüllmann.

Der Weltverbesserer. Photo: Deutsches Theatermuseum Munich; Archiv Abisag Tüllmann.

Bernhard in Ohlsdorf, 1981. Photo: Barbara Klemm.

Bernhard and Hedwig Stavianicek. Photo: Thomas Bernhard Nachlassverwaltung.

Bernhard and Hedwig Stavianicek, 1967. Photo: Erika Schmied.

The Court Cripple. Photo: Kunsthistorisches Museum, Vienna.

Gregor Baci. Photo: Kunsthistorisches Museum, Vienna.

Hans Leinberger, *Little Death.* Photo: Kunsthistorisches Museum, Vienna.

Bernhard, 1970. Photo: Erika Schmied.

Bernhard plays Twenty-one, 1974. Photo: Erika Schmied.

Bernhard with Amalia Altenburg. Photo: Thomas Bernhard Nachlassverwaltung. Copyright Amalia Altenburg.

Am Ziel. Photo: Hosch; Archiv der Salzburger Festspiele. Copyright Salzburger Festspiele.

Steinhof. Photo: Georg Riha.

Paul Wittgenstein, ca. 1948. Photo courtesy of Camillo Schäfer.

Paul Wittgenstein, 1977. Photo courtesy of Camillo Schäfer.

Der Theatermacher. Photo: Weber; Archiv der Salzburger Festspiele. Copyright Salzburger Festspiele.

Oskar Werner. Photo: Hildegard Steinmetz; Archiv der Salzburger Festspiele. Copyright Salzburger Festspiele.

Ritter, Dene, Voss. Photo: Weber; Archiv der Salzburger Festspiele. Copyright Salzburger Festspiele.

Glenn Gould, 1955. Photo: Dan Weiner, courtesy Sara Weiner and Sony Classical.

Glenn Gould, 1980. Photo: Don Hunstein, courtesy Sony Classical.

Bernhard and children. Photo: Sepp Dreissinger.

Bernhard at Café Bräunerhof. Photo: Sepp Dreissinger.

Bernhard and Susanne Kuhn. Photo: Thomas Bernhard Nachlassverwaltung.

Burgtheater in flames. Copyright *Kronenzeitung*.

Heldenplatz. Photo: Oliver Herrmann.

Bernhard and Claus Peymann. Votava Foto.

Index

DATE DUE
